Archives of Infamy

Nancy Luxon, Editor

Archives of Infamy

FOUCAULT ON STATE POWER IN THE LIVES OF ORDINARY CITIZENS

University of Minnesota Press
Minneapolis / London

Cet ouvrage a bénéficié du soutien des Programmes d'aide à la publication de l'Institut Français. This work received support from the Institut Français through its publication program.

The publication of this book was supported by an annual award from the University of Minnesota Provost's Office, Imagine Fund for the arts, design, and humanities.

 Chapter 2 is a translation of the radio program *Les Lundis de l'histoire* (History Mondays); copyright 1983 INA. This show was recorded on November 27, 1982, and broadcast on France Culture on January 10, 1983.

Copyright 2019 by the Regents of the University of Minnesota

All rights reserved. No part of this publication may be reproduced, stored in a retrieval system, or transmitted, in any form or by any means, electronic, mechanical, photocopying, recording, or otherwise, without the prior written permission of the publisher.

Published by the University of Minnesota Press
111 Third Avenue South, Suite 290
Minneapolis, MN 55401-2520
http://www.upress.umn.edu

Printed in the United States of America on acid-free paper

The University of Minnesota is an equal-opportunity educator and employer.

Library of Congress Cataloging-in-Publication Data
Names: Luxon, Nancy, editor.
Title: Archives of infamy : Foucault on state power in the lives of ordinary citizens / Nancy Luxon, editor.
Description: Minneapolis : University of Minnesota Press, [2019] | Includes bibliographical references and index. |
Identifiers: LCCN 2018055262 (print) | ISBN 978-1-5179-0110-3 (hc) | ISBN 978-1-5179-0111-0 (pb)
Subjects: LCSH: Families—France—History. | Police—France—History. | France—Social conditions. | State, The—History. | Foucault, Michel, 1926–1984.
Classification: LCC HV8204 .A73 2019 (print) | DDC 364.10944/09033—dc23
LC record available at https://lccn.loc.gov/2018055262

Contents

Preface and Acknowledgments	vii
Introduction	
***Policing and Criminality in* Disorderly Families**	
Nancy Luxon	1

PART I *Archival Materials: Audiences and Contexts*

1 ***Lives of Infamous Men*** (1977)	
Michel Foucault	67
2 ***"All about the* Lettres de Cachet"** (1983)	
André Béjin, Roger Chartier, Arlette Farge,	
Michel Foucault, and Michelle Perrot	85
3 ***Review of* Disorderly Families** (1983)	
Jean-Philippe Guinle	127
4 ***Denunciation, a Slow Poison*** (1983)	
Michel Heurteaux	131

PART II *Letters and Events: From Composition to Contestation*

5 ***The Order of Discourse*** (1970)	
Michel Foucault	141
6 ***The Public Sphere and Public Opinion*** (1990)	
Roger Chartier	175

7 *The Return of the Event* (1972)
Pierre Nora — 195

8 *Thinking and Defining the Event in History* (2002)
Arlette Farge — 215

9 *Home, Street, City: Farge, Foucault, and the Spaces of the* Lettres de Cachet
Stuart Elden — 227

10 *Parisian Homosexuals Create a Lifestyle, 1700–1750: The Police Archives* (1985)
Michel Rey — 247

11 *Sovereign Address* (2012)
Elizabeth Wingrove — 263

12 *Gender, Agency, and the Circulations of Power*
Nancy Luxon — 295

13 *Foucault's Rhythmic Hand*
Lynne Huffer — 341

Contributors — 359
Publication History — 361
Index — 363

Preface and Acknowledgments

This volume, *Archives of Infamy*, serves as a scholarly companion to the English translation of *Disorderly Families*. If that translation sought to lightly encase the original volume and the disorderly letters it contained, then *Archives of Infamy* offers resources for scaffolding a historical and interpretive framework for those same letters. On its own, Arlette Farge and Michel Foucault's *Disorderly Families* is a queer, elliptical text. The letters of arrest it contains are both historically distant and urgently modern. Originating in 1720, the *lettres de cachet de famille* (often mistakenly glossed as "poison-pen letters") were letters addressed to the king, letters that invoked his absolute power to intervene in problems of marital and family life by imprisoning family members on charges of theft, debauchery, drunkenness, infidelity, and other violations of civil order. Although some French notables were arrested on these charges (notably Diderot and the Marquis de Sade), the letters were penned mostly by the poor and illiterate with the help of hired scriveners. The words of the letter writers breathlessly tumble out and are hastily written down by others, and in a way that leaves their phrasing both antiquated and intense. To think about policing, the street, and neighborhoods as the locus of power and justice for ordinary people means that twenty-first-century readers can't help but read these letters through the lens of contemporary racialized policing, a gender subordination that is alternately intimate and violent, or the sexual division of labor that tears through households.

Much as in contemporary policing, these eighteenth-century letters of arrest speak of the lives of the infamous: "the discourse of 'infamy' has the duty of saying what is most resistant to being said—the worst, the most secret, the most insufferable, the shameless." Foucault muses that these lives would be overlooked if not for that brief contact

vii

viii *Preface and Acknowledgments*

with power that left an epistolary trace. Similar to the memoirs of Herculine Barbin or Pierre Rivière, the authors of these letters are those malfeasants—literally, those wrongdoers—whose existences refuse containment or easy categorization. To read these letters is to be confronted with questions of history and philosophy, questions that hover around the exclusions that found political and philosophic order, around the nature of authorship and authority, and around the circulations of power that sinew through society. The letters challenge their readers to identify ordinary, intimate injustices that belie the failures of public order and justice to coincide.

Contained within *Archives of Infamy* are essays organized into two parts. The first part treats the primary materials related to the *Disorderly Families* project and includes Foucault's earlier essay "Lives of Infamous Men" in which he details his encounter with the *lettres de cachet* that have threaded through his work from *History of Madness* (1961) until *Disorderly Families* (1982). In the radio broadcast moderated by Roger Chartier, Foucault describes these letters as offering "a model of writing, or a game, created by the staging of plea and then its guttural cry—a game between the public audience and the eruption of a sort of spontaneity." The public reception of this volume was rather quiet, with reviews in the *Nouvelle Revue Française* and *Le Monde,* both of which sought to place the volume in contemporary context.

The second part of *Archives of Infamy* treats the broader context of the volume: the clash between philosophers and historians on how to interpret historical events, but especially a French Revolution that has become a touchstone for both fields. If the Revolution, and the broader philosophic Enlightenment, instantiated modern political order and subjects, historians and philosophers debated the extent of its rupture with previous traditions and the significance of the Restoration that followed swiftly at its heels. Foucault's academic itinerary sought to take its distance from canonical texts of philosophers as much as the fetish events of historians. Beginning with his inaugural lecture, "The Order of Discourse" (published here with a fresh translation), Foucault instead called attention to the discourses that murmured behind official events and ideology. At the moment of *Disorderly Families'* publication, Foucault was engulfed in a serious dispute with leading French historians including Jacques Léonard, Emmanuel Le Roy Ladurie, Robert Mandrou, and Emmanuel Todd, many of whom doubted his historical chops and questioned his collaboration on this volume with a female unknown, Arlette Farge. Subsequently, however, the thematics of *Disorderly Families* have been taken up by a later generation of historians. Some find in the letters a precursor to the public life that emerges post-Revolution. Others, such as Roger Chartier in "The Public Sphere and Public Opinion," emphasize the collective anonymity of the impersonal "they say" that emerges through the rhetorical staging of ills teetering on the divide between domestic and civil life. Rather than anchoring the Revolution in its ideology, Chartier instead turns to the political mechanisms and collective representations in which ideology and events are inscribed. Annales historian Pierre Nora, known for his immense *Realms of Memory: The Construction of the French Past,* wonders at the more contemporary turn to the event and the challenge it poses to the interpretive authority of cultural and political elites. For her part, Arlette Farge captures this inchoate public discourse so critical to Chartier when she characterizes the letters on the paradoxical terms of the "history of a secret." The letters disclose something designed to be concealed and obscured. Rather than considering "events" as discrete and sharply delimited, Farge argues that events arrive loaded with perceptions formed over time and play out long after their activity appears exhausted. Events, then, demand to be thought within a nested series of time frames and political struggles. Only then can we tell the history of daily life. That daily life has its own perambulations, be they the spatial organization of urban life (treated by Stuart Elden in his "Home, Street, City"), the sexuality defined by the itineraries of sodomites (sketched by Michel Rey in "Parisian Homosexuals Create a Lifestyle, 1700–1750"), or letters posted and thus set in motion by prisoners of the Bastille (analyzed by Elizabeth Wingrove in "Sovereign Address"). Each of these three essays takes up a different dimension of the discourse of infamy, to think through how this discourse circulates through neighborhoods, muffles a variety of queer conducts, and generates the effluence of words by those *sans-aveux* for whom quite literally nobody will attest. The volume concludes by reflecting on the regulating role played by the family as a "switch point" of power in both daily life and at the heart of sovereign order, in the essay "Gender, Agency, and the Circulations of Power." Lynne Huffer's essay "Foucault's Rhythmic Hand" explores the queer poetics possible in this moment of historical unraveling, when modalities of power shift and strange affinities emerge between affect and power, between individual exempla and queer singularity, and even between Foucault and psychoanalysis.

These essays return readers to those political mechanisms and discursive constructions that can be reduced neither to the terms of structure nor to the terms of agency. Each essay in different ways tackles the politics that intervenes in the form of regulatory mechanisms, social formations, or economic logics to make the eighteenth century more than a history of revolutionary consciousness on the one hand, or deep-seated structure on the other. Beyond such methodological questions, the essays (as well as the letters that prompt them) raise searching questions about how power and justice touch on everyday people. Subsequent to the Revolution, political order will be conceived from the top (of those in power) down (to those excluded). The letters, then, offer a unique perspective. They are written from the perspective of ordinary lives in disorder, not by those who sought to universalize a vision of the political subject or sovereign order but by those who sought justice in their most intimate affairs. Faced with lost income, imprisonment, debauchery, adultery, wayward children, and more, these letter writers sought justice for their particular situation and demanded that this justice have a place in public order. In so writing, their letters trace the chasm between public order and justice. In the present moment, when citizens worry about the state acting in a predatory manner toward its citizens, these letters voice the opposite fantasy: of a state that acknowledges, and seeks to remedy, the vulnerabilities and personal misfortunes of its members. Both the eighteenth-century fantasy and the twenty-first-century fears of predation show us how distant public order and justice have grown from everyday lives. These letters thus push us to ask why questions of persistent unemployment, unacknowledged domestic labors, and incarceration appear to be so intractable today.

In researching *Disorderly Families*, Philippe Artières was an invaluable source of information about the context for Farge and Foucault's collaboration, and the histories that reverberate from the infamies of eighteenth-century street life, to the politics of twentieth-century intellectual debates, to the marginalizations that persist into the twenty-first century. His own *Archives de l'infamie*, written by the collective Maurice Florence, is marvelously creative in thinking through and alongside Foucault and was a constant source of inspiration. I also thank Daniel Defert and Arlette Farge for talking to me about their own recollections of the *Disorderly Families* project, and to Arlette Farge for reflecting on the experience in her elegant Afterword to the translation. Both in their work and in their persons, each exudes a remarkable intellectual generosity and astuteness of thought.

Translator Thomas Scott-Railton worked assiduously on the essays and materials available only in French, and his translations retain both the precision and verve of the originals. In particular, we are proud to include a new translation of Foucault's inaugural lecture at the Collège de France, "The Order of Discourse." This underappreciated essay offers a remarkable vista of the research trajectory to unfold at the Collège, as well as searching reflection on the lability of words and desire.

Earlier versions of the essays contained in *Archives of Infamy* were presented at the 2017 annual meeting of the Western Political Science Association (WPSA) in Vancouver, British Columbia, and at the Cornell Political Theory Workshop. The essays benefited from the thoughtful comments of Thomas Dumm, Jason Frank, Jill Frank, Shai Gortler, Renee Heberle, Alexander Livingston, Diane Rubenstein, Jacob Swanson, Edward Quish, and other audience participants. Shai Gortler also provided meticulous research assistance throughout the project's different stages.

Institutionally, *Archives of Infamy* benefited from the support of a 2016 Imagine Fund award from the Provost's Office and a 2017 Talle Family Faculty Research Award, both at the University of Minnesota, Twin Cities. The French Embassy's French-American Cultural Exchange (FACE) Foundation offered support in the form of an Acquisition of Rights Grant toward the costs of the French permission rights.

Finally, both *Disorderly Families* and *Archives of Infamy* owe their Anglophone existence to the unflagging intellectual support and biblical patience of Danielle Kasprzak at the University of Minnesota Press. In her guidance of this project, she has been uniquely attuned to the intersections of family, desire, and politics and to the queer modernity of the eighteenth-century letters at the heart of both volumes.

INTRODUCTION

Policing and Criminality in Disorderly Families

Nancy Luxon

There is more than one family in the tribe of Clio.
— *Jacques Léonard*

My books aren't treatises in philosophy or studies of history;
at most, they are philosophical fragments put to work in the
historical field of problems.
— *Michel Foucault, "Questions of Method"*

From Disorderly Families to Discordant Politics

Vagabonds, libertines, adulteresses—in short, bad subjects. These
are some of the personages that populate the pages of the eighteenth-
century *lettres de cachet* (loosely, letters of arrest), as discovered by
Arlette Farge and Michel Foucault in the archives of the Bastille.[1]
Farge and Foucault's collaborative *Disorderly Families* curates some
ninety-four of the plaints, or *placets,* that provoke these letters from
the king.[2] Each *placet* was chosen for its affective intensity, resistance to sentimentalism, and intransigence to power. These pleas, en-
treaties, attacks, and denunciations of family members are encased in
ornately written letters addressed to the king and sent to the lieutenant
general of police of Paris. Immediately, the letters strike an intimate
note. These are not dry legal documents, but a mixture of written and
oral language that veers between formalized openings, bitter rancor,
and stock phrasing supplied by the public scrivener. Many dossiers

2 Introduction

contain multiple letters, written by the neighbors across the landing, interested relatives, and that all-important figure, the parish priest. These letters are the point of contact with sovereign power. Reading these letters is to be returned to an eighteenth-century France in which the administrations of law and order are slowly pried apart, a new police prerogative fitfully develops in their wake, and police jurisdiction reaches across the threshold of home or workshop and into an emergent public order. The letters would seem to tell this story "from below," as it were—from the perspective of ordinary people whose lives are touched by power.

Given the poignancy of these "poem-lives," it is surprising to note the quiet reception of *Disorderly Families* when it was first published in 1982. Certain explanations could be given for this silence: Arlette Farge was just at the beginning of what was to be an illustrious career; the volume contained many documents but "little Foucault";[3] and the volume arrived as Foucault continued to suffer scorn for his editorials on the Iranian Revolution. More significantly, the book emerged from a period of silence on the part of Foucault, partly as a response to the reception for *Discipline and Punish* and the *Will to Know,* and partly because of his commitment to political activism. In addition to Iran, Foucault remained preoccupied with the prison activism of the GIP (Groupe d'information sur les prisons) and interventions around human rights.[4] Indeed, one interview about *Disorderly Families* was redirected toward comments on the imposition of martial law in Poland. Foucault's death came shortly afterwards. But in general, the volume was met with silence both from the critical public and, informally, among other intellectuals.[5]

Farge and Foucault's collaboration itself unfolded slowly and quietly. Mentions of the eighteenth-century *lettres de cachet* are scattered throughout *History of Madness*—with its detailed descriptions of prison hospitals such as Bicêtre and Charenton. They are also glancingly mentioned in the *Abnormal* lectures (1975), and lyrically described in Foucault's essay "Lives of Infamous Men" (1977). That essay tantalizes with the promise of a book-length project in its opening sentence, a book never published in its original intended form of a brute archive.[6] More curious is the stark contrast between Foucault's lectures for *The Punitive Society* (1973) and the final architecture of *Discipline and Punish* (1975), the text that emerged from those lectures. If the letters figure prominently in *The Punitive Society,* they are utterly absent from *Discipline*. *Discipline* resolutely maintains a focus on the view of prisons and prison society as seen from administrative institutions and as captured in their discourse—very few utterances of any other kind interrupt the grayness of this administrative terrain.[7] Once again, silence. Silence as the letters are excluded from this text. Silence as Foucault deliberately does not publish much. Silence between him and Farge; if Farge's *Le Vol d'aliments* (1974) was one of the few contemporary books cited by Foucault, they do not meet until a 1978 radio broadcast on prisons.[8] And yet this period of philosophical silence is one of an effusion of archival research, in which Foucault discovers and publishes (1975) the dossier on nineteenth-century parricide, Pierre Rivière, then the anguished memoirs of Herculine Barbin (1978), and finally contacts Farge with a proposed collaboration.[9] In the meantime, Farge has likewise embarked on a second project, a "thèse d'État" under Emmanuel Leroy Ladurie, one that also draws the support of Jacques Revel and is published as *Vivre dans la rue à Paris au XVIIIe siècle*.[10] Such an extended but uneven chronology behind Farge and Foucault's collaboration on the volume raises questions about how to situate it.

This volume contends that to situate *Disorderly Families* in its context, and to recover the problematics, themes, and political struggles from which it unfolded, is to recover the place for agency in Foucault's work even as this agency is enmeshed in the contradictory logics of sovereign power, discipline, and governmentality. It is also to consider the place for interpretive authority in politics, both as exercised by eighteenth-century letter writers and through the authorial collaboration and archival research that mark Farge and Foucault's intellectual peregrinations. Several research questions emerge immediately from even a cursory reading of *Disorderly Families*. First, what is the nature of the political agency on hand in the *lettres de cachet,* and what kind of utterances does it provoke? Second, how do the crisscrossing circulations of police and police bulletins, the itineraries of daily lives, and epistolary correspondence slowly give rise to something like "civil order"—and what place do relations of gender and sexuality have in this order? Third, and at some remove from the context of the volume's initial publication, how might Farge and Foucault's project offer a new resource for seizing the event as something to compose rather than control? To address these questions, I will explore these three dimensions present in my own reading of the text.

4 *Introduction*

First, I will situate the *lettres de cachet* as letters that attest to a complicated political agency. Anglophone readers will find this claim surprising, given the well-known critiques of Foucault in the 1980s by philosophers such as Charles Taylor on precisely this point.[11] However, on this point *Disorderly Families* takes French historians and their debates around the French Revolution as its primary interlocutors. Although aristocrats such as Mirabeau—himself imprisoned in Vincennes by his father—loudly denounced the letters as symbolic of an arbitrary, excessive royal power, these letters found their greatest use at the hands of ordinary people who used the letters to wrest some control, rightly or wrongly, over their lives. How should such interventions in relations of power be understood—as popular actions contravening royal power, as middling efforts to uphold convention, or as actions caught between the logics of sovereignty or policing? Answering this question will require revisiting the elliptical place for political agency in Foucault's corpus. After all, the absence of the letters in *Discipline* accords that text a stubborn fixation on the impersonal, inexorable logic of institutions, discourses, and practices. In *The Punitive Society* lectures, the letters serve to illustrate Foucault's claims about a combative civil society, one in which "power is war, the continuation of war by other means";[12] they thus inject agency into Foucault's account of prisons and politics in *Discipline*. More than illustrative of the figure of the criminal as social enemy, the letters serve as an important hinge between two historical developments. On the one hand, they demonstrate the increasing disciplinary effects that the police will have in targeting individual bodies and drawing upon other social domains (education, psychiatry, social work) to reach normative evaluations of "bad subjects." On the other hand, the letters also reveal the capaciousness of social categories and the openness of a variety of relationships—marital, parental, economic, social—to being revised, negotiated, and defined by those people most directly affected (rather than in accordance with impersonal social norms). Either way, the letters suggestively promise to offer a window onto political agency, with all of its constraints and evasions.

A second theme emergent from *Disorderly Families* concerns its resolute attention to *dis*order—to the circulations and contacts that hum through eighteenth-century marital, political, and economic life and that resist a ready stabilization into public order. The letters explore the lived experiences of this disorder, in all its variegation and messiness. Indeed, first in *Fragile Lives* and later in *Subversive Words*, Farge goes to great lengths to argue that nothing like "the public," much less a "public order," existed in the eighteenth century, and that such a representative voice and body emerged haltingly and in part through these letters. For all that the *lettres de cachet*, then, represented a strategic deflection of and intervention into power relations, in doing so they seized the language of civil order and began to legitimate it as a measure for political stability and regulation. Farge's later work reveals an important dimension to this preoccupation with order: the retrospective projection of a gendered patriarchal order onto family relations that restricts women's political and economic participation.

Perhaps most innovative is, third, Farge and Foucault's turn to the "event" as a means to analyze the confluence of relations of hierarchy, social interaction, and historical conjuncture. *Discipline and Punish* had caused a scandal for its unorthodox approach to prisons, its reliance on the pronoun "one" (thus stripping agency of its subjectivity, its gender, perhaps even eliminating the agent in agency). *Disorderly Families* complicates this analysis. The volume draws on archival materials much in the manner of *Herculine Barbin* or *I, Pierre Rivière*; the latter volume was also a collaborative and archival work, one whose organization emphasized the instability of the primary historical documents, the possible perspectives they embolden, and so the activity of authorship. *Disorderly Families* heightens these challenges to agency and authorship. On Farge and Foucault's read, conjunctural moments form part of "the dramaturgy of the real," the "theater of the quotidian," and ultimately result in "a new mise-en-scène" for politics.[13] The language of theater and event captures the tussle between police and ordinary people in their efforts, alternately, to control or to compose events. It is no wonder that this volume, in contrast to *Discipline and Punish*, is composed entirely of different voices—police, parents, children, clergy, husbands, wives, neighbors, apprentices, workshop masters—that jostle with one another and exceed both the social categories and the institutions that would organize them. The language of theater and event also captures the ambivalence around the agency to be accorded this emergent public and to be regulated according to the terms of a not-yet-defined public order. If the seventeenth century had conceived of any public audience primarily as beholders of spectacle—as audience, not agents, and one subject to manipulation—

6 *Introduction*

then the letters capture the moment prior to the emergence of the active (bourgeois) public. Associated with public spectacle, the king was the only agent capable of disposing of spectacle and certifying the resurgence of civic well-being. Paradoxically, secrets were confided to public agents so as to counter efforts at dissemination. The *lettres de cachet* quite literally circumnavigate these changes, as the secrets they circulate are both shared with public servants and contained to a privy few, so as to avoid the shaming associated with legal proceedings announced through public bans.

If *Disorderly Families* initially was met with silence, perhaps that silence reflects the untimeliness of the book itself. The very composition of the book refuses to heed the disciplinary strictures of either history or philosophy and unrepentantly challenges its readers to construct their own terms of evaluation. As such, it demands a lot from its readers. Taken together, these three thematics intimate both a political and an interpretive response to the questions of agency that linger around the edges of many of Foucault's texts and place the accent on a new set of actors—those Foucault will call "exchangers"—and their ability to secure or reverse the terms of political order. In direct riposte to Hegel, Foucault's civil society becomes the matrix in which different elements of power come to function, reconfigure, and reactivate. For, as Foucault says in *The Punitive Society,* these crimes of people who refuse to work, evade taxes, produce children, impose levies, punish, and have a good time also define another group: the aristocrats. "Read in this way, the text takes on an extraordinary violence: what is the rule of peasant self-defense if not a call to insurrection?"[14]

Political Agency, Circulation, and Police

The first problematic opened up by the *lettres de cachet* concerns political agency, and the terms on which to capture the vibrant life that hums on the threshold between household and street. Farge pursues this agency in greater detail over the rest of her career, as she deftly unskeins the relationships and interactions that twine around rumor, riots, and Parisian street life in her subsequent books. Yet, the cries and clamoring heard in the letters stand in sharp contrast to Foucault's institutional account of prisons in *Discipline and Punish,* as well as the vocalizations of criminality contained in nineteenth-century legal proceedings. Considering the place for political agency in the *lettres de cachet,* then, entails analyzing their eighteenth-century historical context and, more specifically, the role played by the police in changing the relationship of social life to political power. In Foucault's own work on power and policing, the letters come at a transitional moment. They attest to Foucault's disaggregation of sovereign power, technologies of discipline, and apparatuses of security by illustrating how these mechanisms work with and against each other to redefine the very exercise of power itself. The result is a "regime of practices" that "have at once prescriptive effects in regards to what is to be done (effects of 'jurisdiction') and codifying effects in regards to what is to be known (effects of 'veridiction')."[15] Caught in this transition, the letters witness two kinds of agency. One is jurisdictional in nature, of those defiantly out of place and out of order who disrupt the organization of urban space. The other is veridictional, and the agency of those who seize an inchoate, as yet unsanctioned language of public order to make their plaints audible. Ultimately, the letters and analysis in *Disorderly Families* indicate how those at the margins of state power came to be invested in such power—and came to serve alternately as relays and diverters in its circulation.

Historical Context of Eighteenth-Century France

Remarkably, the *lettres de cachet* illustrate a context in which the political and interpretive visibility of wrongdoing and truth telling are being profoundly reworked. The letters show everyday people not just exercising agency (by contacting the king) but seeking a venue and a language at the threshold of public and personal, and of criminal and licit. They thereby sought to insert themselves into the circuits of power and to shape and direct the prerogatives of police and king. It's tempting to gesture toward Foucault's earlier involvement with the prison activism group, the GIP, and to conclude that the letters offer a similar instance of including those deemed criminal. On such an account, agency depends on membership and inclusion and is expressed through voice.[16] Although Foucault's work with the GIP was undoubtedly an influence, such speculation neglects the historical particularity of these eighteenth-century plaints, and what would count as "inclusion," let alone "voice." Namely, the letters were equally written by men, women, and a panoply of neighbors; women's letters generated equal responses from the king as men's letters; they were wildly popular at a time when marital separation, let alone divorce, was hard to

8 *Introduction*

obtain; and the letters attested more to persistent *dis*orders than the violation of public order—for the simple reason, as will be examined in the next section of this Introduction, that a homogeneous public order did not exist. The more familiar binaries that divide those inside prison from those outside, public from private, licit from illicit have not yet crystallized. Indeed, the locator that Farge and Foucault use most is that of "threshold." To think of the agency of jurisdiction and veridiction, then, is to go beyond absolutist expressions of membership. Although Foucault casts membership during the Western sixteenth and seventeenth centuries in terms of inclusion and exclusion, along with reason and unreason, such categorical terms don't capture eighteenth-century France. Instead, as power becomes subject to redirection and as the police struggle to adapt their mission to a changing relation to the state and a changing urban landscape, the experience of agency is profoundly disaggregated. Social life is not yet contoured through discipline and normalization, whereby agency entails the self-regulation of individuals in reference to unspoken norms. Instead, the visible circulations of police, neighborhood life, and letters trace the unseen and fitful transition from sovereign to disciplinary political order and the scope for political subjects' agency.

Indeed, the letters are written at the threshold of a shift in how power flows, operates, and is exercised, especially through the medium of policing. In the essays framing *Disorderly Families,* Farge and Foucault emphasize this prerevolutionary period as one perched uneasily between sovereign and disciplinary power. The letters thus complicate the notorious account of disciplinary power found in *Discipline and Punish* (1978). If *Discipline* opens with sovereign power's spectacle around the scaffold, it closes with a disciplinary power dispersed "by and through" a self-managing population. The lectures for *Society Must Be Defended* (1975–76) and *Security, Territory, Population* (1977–78) slow down and disarticulate this account. Foucault acknowledges that if sovereign power reaches its apogee in the late seventeenth century, it continues to coexist alongside the emergence of disciplinary power and its administration through apparatuses of governmentality. By *Security,* Foucault has worked out the nuances of the shift from a sovereign model in which power is centralized over a geographic territory and flows from top down, to a disciplinary model whose technologies target individuals and allow for power to move from bottom up. A third set of apparatuses of security bolsters this transition by making rule in part a question of the management of populations. Foucault crisply distinguishes: "sovereignty is exercised within the borders of a territory, discipline is exercised on the bodies of individuals, and security is exercised over the whole population."[17] Critically, these three mechanisms of power do not perfectly overlay one another; they comprise different agents, follow distinct logics, and unfold over different temporalities. Taken together they compose different dimensions of the same positive reality.[18] These shifts in power and its techniques open the opportunity for new actors to seize power and to use it for different purposes.

The eighteenth-century history of the police bears out this account. Caught between these three mechanisms (of sovereignty, discipline, and security), the mission and organization of the police change radically between the sixteenth and eighteenth centuries. Specifically, the police in France (but also across western Europe) changed their institutional prerogative, their organizational structure, and their interactions with neighborhood communities.[19] Initially, the police vivified what seemed like the kingdom's necessary order. In France, it isn't until 1674, with the formation of separate civil and criminal lieutenancies, that legal justice and policing become institutionally separated. As late as 1720, writes Lieutenant General Nicolas Delamare in his *Traité de la police*, "police" was essentially a synonym for government; certainly, that was common usage well into the seventeenth century.[20] Many matters were resolved by the *police judiciaire*, a body that both rendered and enforced judgments in matters not considered a threat to society at large (such as trash removal). The circuits that made up a well-organized urban space were taken to be homologous to the circuits that make up a good kingdom. Implicit to such a conception of urban space were principles resonant with physiocracy, an economic theory that privileged land development and the tranquil circulation of agricultural products and labor. Namely, both policing and economic theorists believed that good order should be stable and needed a social organization that could direct natural roles and energies.

Agency relied on the ability to circulate without impediment through an already-established order; it entailed knowing and acting within the constraints of that order. If the police functions observed by commissioner Nicolas Delamare (1667–1723) sought such harmonious order, then Lieutenant General Jean Charles Pierre Lenoir (1774–85) was the

10 *Introduction*

first to recognize that urban rhythms had changed and that the police needed to change with them.[21] Beyond citizens' mere survival or "being," by the 1760s the police are entrusted with securing public "well-being" *(bien-être).*[22] Their charge spans everything from maintaining streetlights; to provisioning grain; to regulating the health concerns provoked by waterways, butchers, and slaughterhouses; to walking neighborhood beats. The police must "ensure that everything in their activity that may go beyond this pure and simple subsistence will in fact be produced, distributed, divided up, and put in circulation in such a way that the state really can draw its strength from it."[23] If sovereign power regulates the terms of political membership through mechanisms of inclusion and exclusion, then the police transform this preoccupation with order and coherence into one that regulates through surveillance. The recurrent pattern, across these charges, is one of circulation. The police circulate through public spaces, limn the city perimeter *(les barrières)* punctuated by customs gates *(portes),* secure the circulation of economic goods, and prevent (in theory, at least) miasmas from settling over the Seine. Initially designed to strengthen state power, these circulations permit the police to develop technologies of surveillance beyond the logic of sovereignty.

Penned at this threshold, the *lettres de cachet* reveal the very struggles, tactics, and operations of power that surround exclusions. In *Disorderly Families,* Farge and Foucault suggest that these letters, compiled across two generations, catch the inadvertent shift in the exercise and experience of power that come with the deepening of governmental administration. Different facets of the letters refract different dimensions of power in Foucault's work. The letters alternately illustrate the dynamics of exclusion *(History of Madness)* or manifest counterinvestments in power so as to relay or divert it *(The Punitive Society)*; they trace the connection between grain riots and the fear of vagabonds *(Security, Territory, Population),* but also show everyday people how "to appropriate this [absolutist political] power, channel it, capture it, and bend it in the direction one wanted" ("Lives of Infamous Men"). These indeterminate effects result from the variable use of the letters; they are the vestige of an earlier period in which arrest need not be followed by either police investigation or legal examination and so the letters reflect the stages prior to surveillance or confession. Farge's subsequent work excavates the unevenness of social context pierced by rumor *(Subversive Words),* changing fortunes, the whimsies of family and circumstance *(Fragile Lives),* and not yet regulated by homogenizing social convention or police administration. These political subjects were defined neither by constraint nor poverty. Although the police were called upon to investigate the letter writers' accusations, the frequency and scope of these investigations were uneven; the accused never stood trial; families were responsible for the cost of bed and board in prison; and so sentencing was determined as much by familial request and solvency as it was by judicial prerogative.[24] The letters make one point clear: depending on one's power and position, the nature, scope, and participation in power in eighteenth-century France were volatile and subject to redirection.

Political Agency and Jurisdiction

Disorderly Families tells a story of this transition, and of how agency comes to be pulled across two dimensions: jurisdiction and veridiction. The police abandon their search for harmonious order and concede that they must adapt to the heaving tide of human movements. To analyze the capacity for the reversal of power's direction, and to identify who is empowered, one must return to the insistent circulations of urban space. If Delamare, serving as lieutenant general at the end of the seventeenth century, understood governance to be the security of order, then by the time of Sartine and Lenoir, "the art of governing" moves from stable order to fluid responsiveness. If the restless city and social classes can move, then the police must move alongside them. No longer was Paris a static order connected by roads; no longer was it "just" a reflection of the order and security of the Maison du Roi. Instead, under Lenoir the police placed a renewed emphasis on listening and surveying everyone from the haves to the have-nots, as a way to discern movements in the social order, worker unrest, and political machinations, alongside the more mundane sex work, illegal gambling, and unauthorized drinking holes. For the police to be mobile, these practices of listening and surveying needed a different legitimacy. What had been an emphasis on the King's Order became an emphasis on the circulation of goods, people, and ideas. With these changes to policing came changes to what could be done— that is, changes to the jurisdictional effects of power—by police and policed alike.

In being concerned for circulation, for the professions, and for neighborhoods, the police become newly concerned for a kind of sociality.

12 *Introduction*

In one of the first examinations of the *lettres de cachet,* Frantz Funck-Brentano reprints a police register that details who was surveyed: printers, theaters, markets (with attention to livestock, grain, and butchers), mendicancy, prostitutes and kept women, pederasty, wet nurses, foreign Protestants, charlatans, native Protestants, and others. As policing intervenes into the ambiguous jurisdictions of professions, ways of life, and types of people, it attaches to those who appear out of place and at the wrong time. The letters, then, should be read against this backdrop of police itineraries, registers, and bulletins that fumbled for a vocabulary adequate to social life, especially in the absence of a clear mission. In developing the administration of the state apparatus, then, the police exercise considerable agency in redefining and extending their mission beyond that envisioned by the sovereign. They fuel the relocation of power to social sites—sites "that are exchangers between power from above and power from below"[25]—themselves composed of knotted social, economic, and family relations.

Amid the welter of competing jurisdictions and mandates, the letters open onto a social life defined by confrontation, but one where the boundaries of conflict remain similarly hazy and ill-defined. The definition of what can be done and where is not settled. Foucault comments in passing that notions of illegality and their enforcement varied according to social status and context. The letters reflect such variations and seize upon irregularities in the name of public order so as to right local wrongs. Less the violation of clear ideals of marriage or family, such a staging of conflict exposes "a whole field of confrontations that stemmed more from economic conflicts, physical violence, standing in the household, reputation in the neighborhood, and blows to a person's character."[26] Prominent in this account is the role of social intermediaries who occupy what I call "switch points of power" in an evolving context of law and order. These switch points, or "exchangers"—be they sites or agents of power—extend power in multiple ways.[27] First and most obviously, they mediate between power above and below; they channel and regulate the extension alternately of sovereign and disciplinary power.[28] Second, these exchangers often trespass into shadowy sites: Farge recounts police efforts at entrapment of homosexuals by propositioning potential *dragueurs,* bribing innkeepers, and hiring petty criminals in exchange for early release from prison. Third, these exchangers might knit together disparate parts of the social fabric, by connecting different sites, classes, and social experiences. Across all of these experiences, the exchangers play a polyvalent role in mediating power and social representations. They come to serve as the relays, or switch points, of power. Both exchangers and bad subjects, in their own ways, seek to knit together or reactivate power in an emergent social context.

The social and political status of these exchanges is potent yet precarious. The term "exchanger" comes from Foucault's *The Punitive Society,* his most Marxist of lectures with its attention to the circulations of money and power.[29] The term evokes Marx's *Trägern,* or "bearers," those people and objects that play an important role in transforming economic relations into commodity exchange.[30] By *Discipline and Punish,* Foucault will rework their role using the language of "entourage"—he speaks about a "social entourage" that will later be composed of the "teacher-judge, the doctor-judge, the educator-judge, the 'social-worker'-judge; [on whom] the universal reign of the normative is based."[31] Finally, in the first volume of *The History of Sexuality,* Foucault declares "the family is the interchange *[échangeur]* of sexuality and alliance."[32] If those figures are the nodal points between power and the everyday, in *Disorderly Families* these exchangers are more ambivalent, and perhaps even polyvalent in their ability to meld power and social meaning. They create "circuits of diversion so that, at different points of the State apparatus, certain individuals, who do not necessarily belong to the ruling class or have the same interests, can locally [divert] a fraction of power and use it on their own account."[33] Their power does not wholly derive from or connect to the disciplining power of surveillance. After all, the counteritineraries of bad subjects and those who would indict them blaze with a similar potency; these "poem-lives" flash with the lightning of sovereign power, seized for a moment by the *infîme* and *infâme* (insignificant and infamous). As Foucault writes, "Providing one knew how to play the game, every individual could become for the other a terrible and lawless monarch."[34] Instead, much like Marx's *Trägern,* the exchangers transform the value and force that inhere in political and economic relations. Operating in sites that participate in the formation of moral consensus, they "are exchangers between power from above and power from below."[35] Theirs is a strange jurisdiction possessed of the capacity to reinforce or invert the circuits of power around them. Even as they do not share the political or economic interests of those in power, these exchangers bear and are born by power.

14 *Introduction*

Herein lies the crux of the halting, fitful transition from the logic of sovereignty to the logic of discipline. No longer is public life dominated by "the all too visible radiance of force, grace, heroism, and might" associated with an absolutist sovereign. Instead, a new art of language emerges alongside a new art of governance, one that seeks "to tell the last and most tenuous degrees of the real."[36] That "the real," in all of its positivity, emerges from the tangle of sovereignty, discipline, and security opens up the possibility for any of these logics of power to be seized and legitimated as the locus of political authority. These mechanisms not only generate investments in the apparatus of power on the part of a range of public agents—from sovereign, to police, to *intendants*—but these investments are also met with counterinvestments of lateral social agents. The workshop masters, bourgeois households, and parish priests have their own counterinvestments in using these letters to seek justice for themselves. And so, both letter writer and king became "caught in the trap of their complicity" as this dreadful power transmuted into administrative authority.[37] The circulations of police, and the countercirculations of "bad subjects" pursued by those they impugn, reinforce the investment of *all* persons in the state apparatus. As Foucault describes, "So with police there is a circle that starts from the state as a power of rational and calculated intervention on individuals and comes back to the state as a growing set of forces, or forces to be developed, passing through the life of individuals, which will now be precious to the state simply as life."[38] In being concerned for circulation, for the professions, for neighborhoods, the police are concerned for a kind of sociality. What kind of sociality will survive, however, remains an open question in the letters.

The changing relationship to law and jurisdiction brings with it a changing relationship to knowledge and truth. Alongside this emergent, disciplinary power comes a new discourse, humming with the murmurs of "traps, weapons, cries, gestures, attitudes, ruses, intrigues for which words were the instruments."[39] These letters seize and redirect the existing rules of engagement; in addition to redefining the jurisdiction of power (that is, its relation to law and social space), the letters signal changes to regimes of truth, or veridiction. For all that the ornate openings of the letters invoked a terrible, royal power through a language that was decorative, supplicating, and maledictory, the letters also constitute avowals of a sort. They are not yet the avowals *(aveux)* so central to nineteenth-century criminology, with its investigations and demand for confession. Instead, the letters are claims made about and on behalf of the *sans-aveux,* those individuals for whom, quite literally, no one will attest. The embattled language here recalls their context—the emergence of technologies of discipline (most closely associated with the police) that pinpoints persons and relations to be monitored and controlled—and the apparatuses of security that extend outwards, from police informants, to parish priests, to urban planners, and *parlementaires,* so as to integrate the domains of regulation and the knowledge they produce. Tactically working with and against the usual practices of veridiction, letter writers seize the as yet undefined language of public order and use it to make claims and demands.

For all that the letter writers reach for the language of "bad subject," that category remains remarkably capacious and open to definition. The most common offenses—charges of vagabondage and adultery—amount to claims that a relationship of obligation has been shattered, and so a shared space has become unlivable. Vagabonds, whose restlessness draws them past the frontiers of neighborhood, village, or city, abandon commitments to family and impose new demands—demands of financial support, usually—on the parishes where they settle. Should readers sympathize with the restless independence stifled by relationships of proximity, or with the disruptions to the taxes of *taille* and *corvée* that increase the burden on those left behind? If sovereign conceptions of order—abetted by the physiocrats and their own economic theories of agricultural circulation and harmonious economic order—emphasized equilibrium, the police adapt to these movements by establishing routes of surveillance. They develop their own itineraries: canvassing the line of butchers and abattoirs along the Seine, ranging the city limits with their cheap taverns, tracing the routes of prostitutes through the shadows of the Tuileries. Police, unruly subjects, ordinary people all wrangle over what makes for a "bad subject."

Other charges—of domestic violence, excessive drinking, or gambling—seem written from desperation. Divorce was all but unavailable in the eighteenth century, and drinking or gambling often were a drain on already-precarious household economies. These letters seize for themselves the right to accuse, judge, and punish—to act as sovereign in the site of marriage or household. These emanate from a social context in which the vulnerable were a large, underdefined and overlooked group whose illegalities often went unexplored and unregulated. As the eighteenth century continues, however, two changes

16 *Introduction*

emerge. First, the figure of judge shifts. No longer are the accused judged by their peers—the officious neighbors from the *voisinage*—but instead they are judged "in the name of society by its representatives."[40] Proximity becomes replaced by the abstraction of distance. As a result, and second, a different set of knowledge-effects emerges around the criminal as "'estranged from society,' irreducible to laws and general norms."[41] Differently from the letters of 1728, a language of education and resipiscence creeps into the later letters. Resipiscence "is as much remorse in the moral sense as return to health; a reference, also, to the instrument of a regular life, to a regularity of social life as well as of a monastic rule observed in a community."[42] In his lecture notes, Foucault added, "The other essential element is not arbitrariness, it is correction. With all the possible ambiguities of this word, which designates a pedagogy, a cure, a religious repentance, and a moral conversion."[43] Although not yet the fully interior turn to the soul or the self, this language and the injunction to *rentrer en soi-même* (look within) begins to shed the sense of returning to a grounding set of social relations and to suggest a different turn inwards.[44] The knowledge that will serve as point of reference for veridiction begins to change. The disorderly are not simply those straining the lives of others around them; they now violate a norm—rooted in impersonal social knowledge and demanding obedience—that reflects a putative social consensus. And yet, at the moment of the *lettres de cachet,* neither the letters nor their exchanger-authors have quite that normalizing effect. The letters intermittently seize on claims to "public order" but in a way both vague and instrumental. Reading the letters, and the additional testimonies submitted by neighbors and family members, alongside the notes by investigating police, it becomes impossible to stabilize these claims into something like knowledge *(savoir)* or to identify which party is "criminal." The veridictional agency expressed through the letters, then, is at once potent and capricious. Potent because of the possibility to seize the obscurity of the practice and its distance from other discourses and to twist the practice to fit the situation at hand. And capricious because one could never be certain if the charge would land or be redirected against oneself.

Reading *Disorderly Families* entails recovering agency within a moment of disjuncture. This recovery has multiple layers. At the level of Foucault's published works, it means countering the institutional account of prisons and policing in *Discipline and Punish* with the cacophony of plaints and countercharges found not just in *Disorderly*

Families but also with the testimonies in works such as *I, Pierre Rivière* and *Herculine Barbin*. Each of these works scopes out the topography of different switch points of power, and the claims to knowledge and power at work in them. At the level of history and philosophy, this recovery puts pressure on the conditions under which agency can be said to hold. If Foucault finds that post-Kantian philosophy at least self-reflexively scrutinizes the ground from which it evaluates, he leans heavily on history to carry this process all the way to an autocritique of philosophy's own starting assumptions. With its focus on agency within disjuncture, such a historicizing project further entails an admission that the process of change and its (necessarily retrospective) consolidation through narrative have two different cadences and histories. This frictive work *à deux vitesses* without the expectation of harmony makes disjunctures within individuals and across their lived experiences into something philosophically and politically productive.[45] In holding on to the irreducibility and particularity of these letters, Foucault fixes on agency as something that resists consolidation within the confines of an ideal subject. Here we might follow Michel-Rolph Trouillot in thinking of people as possessing three distinct capacities: "1) as *agents,* or occupants of structural positions; 2) as *actors* in constant interface with a context; and 3) as *subjects,* that is, as voices aware of their vocality."[46] These capacities suggest that people constantly are *in circulation*: not only do they move about through urban space, but they also are constantly moving in and out of different roles, defined in part by the surrounding context, and these roles do not perfectly reflect either "psyche" or "order." Circulation wends between the personal and the collective, and between the particular and the structural. Instead, the challenge may well be to disentangle the practices and histories that capture these movements and their inevitable bottlenecks, so as to compose a context that captures something of the limitations *and* the possibilities inherent in undoing domination.

Public *Disorders*: Circulations of Power, Police, and Interpretive Authority

From these crisscrossing circulations of police, the itineraries of daily lives, and their capture in epistolary correspondence, what can be intimated about the rise of something like "civil order"—and what place do relations of gender and sexuality have in this order? Although it is

18 *Introduction*

a commonplace to characterize the eighteenth century in terms of the back-and-forth exchanges of a masculine "public sphere," these letters attest to a very different set of circulations. In fact, the police struggled to use their presence to patrol public order in part because a clear sense of a "public" did not exist. Despite the standard philosophical account of emergent publics anchored in Kant's 1784 essay "What Is Enlightenment?," the dictionary of the French Academy does not list "public" as the opposite of "private" *(privé)* until 1835.[47] For much of the eighteenth century, there was no clear dividing line between family and public life, and close quarters meant that many familial and social interactions unfolded in the street. Instead, "public" was opposed to the particular *(particulier)* with its connotations of a person or place "apart" (e.g., *un hôtel particulier* walled off from the street).[48] As a result, the very notion of "public opinion" in early eighteenth-century France made little sense—particularity was the very quality of something as idiosyncratic as "opinion." These familial plaints, then, index the crosscurrents of claim-making in a variety of registers (rumor, personal correspondence, judicial memoir, police bulletin) and the process by which these discursive practices became attached to abstract notions of "public order."[49] Rather than presuming an order defined by uniform speech and subjects, the letters chart the disorders whose investigation fashions "public order" from who and what is left.

The plaints demanding *lettres de cachet,* then, adopt the perspective of *disorder.* They describe the people and injuries not yet or obviously criminal, and grope for an image of civic order and public well-being that could be marshaled into support of claims to harm. To be successful, particular experiences needed to be linked to a larger representation of social life. For contemporary readers of these plaints, it is tempting to reach automatically for images of privacy or family as the foil to civic order and public. Life in the eighteenth century proceeded differently, however: the perambulations of men and women were intermingled, references to "family" and "household" included servants and occasionally distant relatives, and one-room living quarters made conceptions of privacy fanciful. As the following section explores, the eighteenth-century street life sketched in these letters counters three standard conceptions of "public": first, as defined against a property-owning individual; second, as characterized by a private sphere defined by family relations; and third, as a literary public anchored by market relations. Absent from the letters, the power of these three ideal types thus can only be retrospective—they emerge in the wake of the French Revolution, codify through the Napoleonic Code first published in 1804, and solidify during a nineteenth century that deliberately institutionalizes the split between masculinist public and feminine domesticity, as well as between state and society.

Forging Social Hierarchies into a Public

One of the most flamboyant claims in support of a *lettre de cachet* comes from the lawyer for the comtesse de Mirabeau as she asked for separation from her husband. Mirabeau—a dissolute aristocrat and later a revolutionary orator—was a "bad son, bad husband, bad father, bad citizen, and dangerous subject." An extravagant claim—what is one to make of the charges of being a "bad subject" in a moment that lacked clear binaries between public and private, between inside (political society) and outside (its margins), or even order and disorder? Such binaries would seem necessary in order for charges of transgression and being a "bad subject" to be possible. Instead, the plaints written by families reveal a power that flows agilely across the threshold of the home and makes its activities central to public well-being. Social life serves as a different kind of threshold in the eighteenth century. Lacking a coherent conception of "society" or "civil society," the eighteenth century instead thinks in terms of milieus or sites that bundle together relations that sprawl between family, neighborhood, workplace, parish, and emergent public order.[50] Proximity, rather than demarcated categories of public and private, organizes social space in a welter of conflicting hierarchies and distinctions that govern when and how others intervened in or judged conflicts. Farge emphasizes: "[T]he impossibility of distinguishing between 'open' and 'closed' in a situation where each space communicated with the next, opened out onto another, or overlooked and was overlooked by everyone else, offering no protection at all."[51] Different relations might be privileged in different sites or at different moments, but these relations are not clearly reducible to social categories such as "class," "gender," "political position," or "sexuality." That is not to say that eighteenth-century French lacked social hierarchy. It *is* to say that these hierarchies were not rooted in or expressed through individualized social identities, and that family politics was not yet a patriarchal politics.

When the police write about "public well-being" or "order," then, their words are more aspirational than material. Searching for a regulatory ideal, Des Essarts writes, "Police is the science of governing men and doing good for them, the art of making them happy as far

20 *Introduction*

as possible and to the extent that they ought to be in the general interest of society."[52] This mission for policing offers the bare schema for a *civic* order with no sense of how that might look differently than the existing king's order rooted in socioeconomic hierarchies of honor and sustained through mercantilism. As the 1747 reforms of Nicolas Berryer enlarge the mandate and scope of police investigation, pressure mounts to define this purview.[53] His successor, Lieutenant General of Police Duchesne, in his own Code of Police (1757), writes: "The object of police is the public general interest, hence the objects that it embraces are in a sense unlimited."[54] The doubling of public and general interest here, and the haunting fear of "unlimited objects" of attention, reveal something of the process of rendering an affair public. The doubling suggests the need to make a particular matter rise to *general* interest so as to be considered a matter for collective, *public* debate. The nature of this public, its mode of evaluation, and its ideal members, however, are defined as police, ordinary people, and political contestants wrangled over the terms, mechanisms of power, and goals of order. As noted in the preceding section, these police reforms unfolded amid contestations of royal power at the hands of both Jansenists and local *parlements*.[55] Both political movements challenged the centralization of royal power and interpretive authority, and entertained the possibility of the king's fallibility and mortality—a serious step toward contemplating political order on other terms.

In this political context, the *lettres de cachet* became associated with the alternating spectacle and secrecy of royal power as compared to a power construed on more general terms. Commenting on his strategies to make domestic melodramas into political causes célèbres, lawyer Pierre Louis de Lacretelle notes, "Any particular affair that leads to general considerations that is suited to becoming a great object for public attention, must be considered a great event."[56] Fashioning these "great events," however, took work. The eighteenth century saw a proliferation of documents—landmark legal decisions *(arrêts notables)*, legal briefs (first called *factums*, then *mémoires*), notable pleadings *(plaidoires)*—all seeking to elevate various scandals to public notice. These different documents circulated and narrated contests with law that were also contests with law's source in royal authority.[57] However, these avenues were available to wealthier families with the means to pay lawyers and other jurists. Most familial *lettres de cachet* proceeded without lawyers such as Lacretelle, sought secrecy rather than celebrity (so as to protect family honor), and yet still needed to generalize their claims to injury. Peculiarly, where the upper and middle classes resisted the letters' secrecy as emblematic of arbitrary royal rule, ordinary people valued that secrecy. The disconnect between socioeconomic position and political standing, however, is precisely the key to their popularity. Secrecy was the only way to avoid the publicity of an arrest and trial so harmful to reputation, and the letters further offered ordinary people a means to enjoy the same status of political subject as the upper classes. This contact with power offered political status and reputational protection, however meager. Raising plaints to "general interest," then, meant something different to both parties. Could it be that two different publics (one royalist, one incipiently civic) with two different regulatory mechanisms (secrecy versus publicity) offered two different responses to disorder? If so, the police remained precariously perched between the two. Absent a social collective recognizable as "the public," the Code of Police strained to discriminate between behaviors that bore on general rather than particular interests. Secrecy hinted at a knowledge of things and persons they should better control.

Concomitant to the eighteenth-century transition from sovereign to disciplinary power (and its administration) came the delineation of public order and the knowledge relevant to it. As police jurisdiction expanded, social interactions relied less on face-to-face contact on the street and more on authoritative accounts "verified" by police and informants.[58] These avowals attached to family plaints were not yet confessions proscribed by social convention and normative injunction. These avowals bore witness to the variegated social and economic spaces that occasionally rose to political significance. Police surveillance and specifically public spaces arose in tandem. Public spaces and roads—from the Tuileries Garden, to the cours de la Reine and the quais along the Seine—become subject to the surveillance of public agencies rather than emblematic of royal power.[59] In the face of these plaints—not to mention the spread of rumor, and the frequency and unpredictability of grain riots—the police sought to know their subjects and the parameters of public space. Already in 1671, Nicolas de la Reynie, the first lieutenant general of police in Paris, had said "It is much easier to preserve [calm] now than it would be to restore it once it is disturbed."[60] Both to bolster their jurisdictional reach and

22 *Introduction*

to know the truth of the population, police commissioners begin to innovate micropractices of surveillance: the keeping of registers, circulation throughout neighborhoods, as well as the use of police spies and informants. In charting the confluence of apparatuses of security and disciplinary techniques, Foucault writes that "order is to be established by taking the point of view of disorder and analyzing it with increasing subtlety, that is to say, order is what remains. Order is what remains when everything that is prohibited has in fact been prevented."[61] Security sought less to prohibit than to nullify. In that sense, the police (and their network of spies, innkeepers, market vendors, etc.) became powerful agents who quite inadvertently shaped the lived experience of power as public order. This is not to say, however, that the police had a vision of this public—quite the opposite. Simply put, police were driven to discover an order they could administer through ever more pointed investigations into "disorderliness," petty violence, and failed social obligations.

In reading the plaints demanding family members' arrest, the reader is initially struck by the helter-skelter nature of the complaints and the capaciousness of categories such as "infamy" and "debauchery," which renders these charges all but incoherent.[62] The profusion of disorderliness initially charts the refusals of those who would wander beyond the usual scope of household activities. A few letters stand out: a wife, Françoise Lesquoy who seizes her dowry and flees an abusive husband to her parents' home only to be accused of theft and waywardness; those spouses whose gambling or drinking pushes them to sell everything "down to the bed"; the couple, Jean Allis and Toinette Valancier, imprisoned by one set of parents for failing to seek parental consent to marry; the son Edme Joseph Eli, already imprisoned once, who is apprenticed out as a mason but refuses to work regularly.[63] Gradually, certain patterns of complaints and the hazy contour of "good subjects" take form. Each disorderly subject violates a different set of reciprocal social obligations and destabilizes an order constituted locally yet impressed with the stamp of absolutist power. However, many of these figures (although not all) also violate some stricture around property, and the relations of authority that legitimate male property owners—personal relationships of authority that will later allow men (and not wives, children, or servants) to move into the public sphere.[64] These personal relationships, anchored in the symbolic order of the family, become the flash points for the transmutation of political order.

Retrospectively it becomes easier to see the role played by gender and sexuality in "engendering" this new civic order as it moved from a ritualistic, "feminized" royal order to the fraternal republic of the revolutionary tribunal. In a world regulated by socioeconomic position and relations of proximity, sex between men was initially perceived on class terms and became transgressive—infamous—when social hierarchies were threatened.[65] In the early eighteenth century, certain sexual behaviors deemed "affected" were permitted to the middle and upper classes and were seen as a sign of status rather than sexuality per se; they were considered alongside other affectations of court society.[66] Still, sexual behaviors did not go unsanctioned.[67] Euphemistic references to *les infâmes* appear frequently in police archives (although *Disorderly Families* includes only one such instance: Nicolas Fieffé).[68] Insofar as sex between men led to encounters between people with different statuses, it could lead to "grave disorders."[69] Historian Michel Rey cites concerns that the "aristocratic vice" might spread to commoners, as well as the efforts by Haimier, officer of the Provost and Mounted Constabulary, who "had made a judgment about impeding the effects of infamy . . . especially because he knew that the young man did not seem to be of the same status as that of His Lordship the Count."[70] Sex between men was tied less to an identity than to the indulgences of high society or the waywardness of errant schoolboys. Less concerned about the affectations of the established, police feared the publicity of those adventures that wandered beyond established social conventions. Rey writes: "In the eighteenth century, sodomy no longer appears to the police as a sin, but as an offense on order, because of its furtive encounters, the social slippages (even if imaginary) it seemed to permit, and also because of a long-term trend toward the revalorization of the family milieu and its enclosure as a private space."[71] To justify their surveillance and interventions, in the second half of the eighteenth century police increasingly reached for the language of moral order and, eventually, family. In 1748, Lieutenant General Berryer designated special departments to concentrate their surveillance on certain activities and persons, including one for "pederasty."[72] The police spoke of "pederasts" (and no longer "sodomites") to designate a type of person and broader range of interaction, rather than a specific act that takes its meaning from context.[73] Pederasty—derived from the ancient Greek word to designate institutionalized educational and erotic relationships—also resituates homosexuality as a violation of the family's educational role. As will be seen in the

24 *Introduction*

next section, the connotations of morality and nature will further be used to consolidate household life on the gendered terms of patriarchy.

In short, the familial *lettres de cachet* (as distinct from those motivated by politics, concern for military or religious discipline, or theatrical representations), fueled police efforts to construe "public" interests and spaces through regulations of social behavior. Inadvertently, as ordinary families sought to participate in the king's order, they empowered the police to redefine social interactions in terms of impersonal norms that extend across social spaces. From the perspective of royal power, police interventions sought to render personal relationships in the service of royal order and authority. From the perspective of police administration, changes to surveillance and policing resulted in the gradual association of politics with a public distinct from either particulars or households. Alongside this public came the entrenchment of the family as a separate, enclosed space. Gradually, the personal relationships of the household became rewritten in terms of property ownership and the family's educational mission—a revision that facilitated the organization of the public through the gendered and sexual norms of masculinity. If this eighteenth century witnesses the emergence of "civil society," "revolutionary people," and "nation" as the entities capable of countering the state, then the separation of public and private excludes women from all three.[74]

Households: From Social to Private Space

"The conjugal bond was also a site," write Farge and Foucault in "Marital Discord," the essay that precedes plaints about husbands and wives in *Disorderly Families.*[75] What might it mean to consider marriage as a social, legal, or economic site? Within the site of the household, what are the jurisdictional and veridictional conditions of agency? Farge and Foucault's spatial language at least suggests that marriage operated on terms other than the psychology of affection, and so was regulated by different expectations and conventions. Not only was the public initially *not* structured around a contrast between civic order and individual (as argued above), it was also not opposed to "family" as part of a putatively "private sphere." If "family" has come to have connotations of race, blood, or kinship relations, its meaning was rather different in the eighteenth century.[76] The *Dictionnaire de Trévoux* defines family as a household with domestic servants (including wives, children, and attendants), while Antoine Furetière's

Dictionnaire universel extends "family" to include relatives beyond the immediate family.[77] In Diderot's *Encyclopedia,* the Chevalier de Jaucourt distinguishes: "we call *families* those ranks of citizens who, rising above the dregs of the populace, participate in the State and pass from father to son honest jobs, proper responsibilities, well-matched marriages, a decent upbringing, and gentle and educated manners."[78] "Family" thus carried with it the sense of household, and was defined against, on the one hand, the Maison du Roi (the royal court, but literally, the King's Household) and, on the other, the undifferentiated "dregs of the populace."[79] Only by the end of the eighteenth century does the family come to play a supporting role to the state.[80] Until then, households had their own regimes of jurisdiction and veridiction that governed what people could do and say.

Jurisdictionally, the sprawling households of *Disorderly Families* shed light onto the powerfully charged process of fashioning families into a civil society oriented to public order. In the eighteenth century, that process is narrated through the language of social contract theory. One of the central claims to social contract theory is that free social relations took the form of a contract between political subjects to delegate powers to a government to rule over them. It explains why the exercise of political right is legitimate. As Carole Pateman has argued, the conventional story says little about the patriarchal or sex right exercised by men over women so as to limit their political rights and standing.[81] It simply presumes a divide and hierarchy between public and private. The eighteenth-century *lettres de cachet,* however, complicate this story. Stuart Elden notes, in his essay for this volume, that the letters stretch between home, street, and city and cannot be contained to any "private" sphere. They hint at how the jurisdictional status of the family became accompanied by a new language that attested to the truth of that relationship. "I offer a foolproof way to elevate the soul of women; it is to join them to all the activities of man," writes Olympe de Gouges, in laying out a new marriage contract.[82] If contemporaries such as Olympe de Gouges seized on the language of contract to highlight the contract between public right and private practices, then the earlier *lettres de cachet* reveal those aspects of social life excised to accommodate this language: honor and reputation. The preceding section argued that the eighteenth century did not yet have a conception of "public" or "civic order"; this section will argue that the family was neither seen as opposite to public nor defined as a putative "private sphere." Instead, the letters suggest that the family was a social and economic space that, over the course of the eighteenth century, came to be politically charged around gendered lines.

The definitions of *famille* reveal, once again, the organizing place for socioeconomic position at the heart of the household. For much of the eighteenth century, "family" referred to all those living together and included servants. Family was defined in the dictionary of the Académie Française (1694) as "all those who live in the same household, under the same head."[83] Family includes the head of household, a range of familial relations, and household servants; women and children were sometimes grouped among these "domestic servants." Families were organized less around abstract respect for property than economic survival, especially if children were involved. Mutual work and trust were necessary to maintain economic stability and reputation; families were most obviously undone when the husband gambled away his wife's dowry, or when she refused to work, or when either neglected to care for the children.[84] This extended, economic sense of family is reinforced by understanding the son as someone who "lives under the authority of the head of household"—a complicated notion when adult sons become apprenticed to another household, and perhaps one of the reasons why those sons who abandoned their jobs were seen as particularly infamous. To be sure, there were variations. Although women were not legally permitted to own property or enter into contracts, there was more variation in economic practice across the popular classes than in bourgeois or aristocratic households.[85] In those households, social status and economic position created a different site that more obviously prepared sons for life as a male laborer, property owner, and head of household. When Foucault calls attention to marriage alliances in the first volume of *The History of Sexuality,* he echoes Louis de Jaucourt's comments about the upper classes: "Families are formed by matrimonial alliances, by polite behavior, by conduct distinguished from that of the lower orders, and by cultivated manners, which are passed on from father and son."[86] The close marriage of kinship, household, and patriarchy won't be fully achieved until the nineteenth century; the eighteenth century records the slow process of naturalizing the family, establishing men at its head, and anchoring it in a fraternal civil society.

One of the remarkable dimensions of the *lettres de cachet* is that they originated from plaints penned equally by women and men, and garnered equal response from the king. Likewise, for all that women lacked legal standing and protections, women were not automatically excluded from this order, although their gender roles conditioned how and when they intervened; their economic and informational roles were often quite powerful. Especially among the lower classes, women and men intermingled in all aspects of life, as there was "a sort of *mixité* between men and women—they work together, they journey *[cheminent]* together, they go to the cabaret together—whereas the nineteenth century, by contrast, will try to make *mixité* more difficult."[87] In practice, gender roles were overwritten by socioeconomic necessities; the familial plaints attest to households that understood themselves as cohesive economic units and suffered when men *and* women failed to contribute economically. So, Marie Lecocq describes that with her husband Henry Petit "there is no excess of harshness that her husband has not used to deprive her of her freedom to earn her bread."[88] Even more surprisingly, duties such as child rearing and education fell to men as well as to women. Many parents take pride in claiming that "they exhausted themselves giving as happy an upbringing as was possible"—a plaint that reflected the necessities of close living quarters and limited economic means.[89] Often one spouse wrote to request that the other be released, so as to have another wage earner or caregiver in the household. Although Marianne Perrin chastises her husband Pierre Blot for failing his parental obligations, she later writes to request that the lieutenant general "release said Pierre Blot her husband, so that he could return home to work as before and earn a living for his children."[90] Although women hardly participated equally in political or economic life, the transition from royal order to republic was also a transition from socioeconomic positioning to patriarchy.

The veridictional agency outlined earlier in this Introduction afforded women a tenuous opportunity to participate in public affairs outside the patriarchal family, to be later established by the Napoleonic Code. This veridictional agency plays out along two dimensions: first, the literary agency of women that initially countered the interpretive role of the police; and second, the role of family members in corroborating these epistolary accounts charts the stabilization of social judgment around civil norms concerning gender, parental roles, and the family.

In the seventeenth and eighteenth centuries, both men and women

28 *Introduction*

wrote or dictated memoirs that detailed their encounters with the law. These memoirs and legal briefs became one way to acquire information about legal contests as well as a rhetorical device for vetting arguments in the court of opinion as in the court of law. All sorts of news circulated in a variety of formats—rumors, maxims, cartoons, doggerel, legal briefs, bulletins, and so on—and women used this variety to inflect popular opinion. In *Subversive Words,* Farge notes that their constrained economic and legal position made them especially skillful at manipulating rumor and opinion. As historian Sarah Hanley has documented, women wrote in a variety of voices and about a variety of topics, ranging from philosophic tracts on marriage to judicial indictments of property, contract, and their role in trapping women in unbreakable marriage contracts. These writings shuttled between streets and law courts, and so created a curious form of legal knowledge, as Elizabeth Wingrove finds in her essay in this volume that treats the profusion of letters penned by Bastille prisoner Geneviève Gravelle. In addition to well-known figures such as Olympe de Gouges, other women used their ability to petition for marital separation *(séparation de biens)* and divorce *(séparation de corps)* to dramatize the injustice of their position. Marriage was often likened to tyranny, despotism, arbitrary royal rule, or enslavement so as to vitiate the claims that its "contract" obliged both parties. Most of these petitions failed.[91] The analogy of family to political rule itself was politically fraught. Even as it allowed women to elevate claims of abuse and to argue for a more limited scope of power, this same analogy camouflaged the ideological reworking of the family on closer-knit terms of kinship and shared residence. The *lettres de cachet* offered an appealing alternative solution for circumventing a legal system disinclined to grant requests for divorce. They were but one way that women intervened in a range of literary activities characterized by efforts to unsettle the public spaces charted alternately by police patrols and legal right; nonetheless, the risks of these interventions fell unevenly on women and men.

Similarly, in both the plaints requesting police intervention and other forms of speech and writing, women appealed to social knowledge. The letters reflect nascent social norms—about child rearing, physical violence, economic activity—and injunctions, and seek to make them binding in their particular case. Voluminous dossiers, such as that of Jean Baptiste Boissier, are efforts to contextualize and to draw on the social knowledge of the neighborhood, rather than to appeal to impersonal norms. Later in the eighteenth century, however, judgment of these cases moved away from "common knowledge" to the "judgment of peers." If the first model of judgment sought to render decisions adequate to the particularities of each case, then the second asked peers to judge the similarity and severity of alleged transgressions. The second model also changes the statute of the family unit, and suggests an ideal against which deviations could be measured. With the waxing of police power and the waning of these letters, "the family" became a unit to be reconstructed on terms of kinship and paternal power.

From Personal Correspondence to Public Exchange

In their very form and medium, family plaints and the resulting *lettres de cachet* attest to the point of contact between power and ordinary lives. If these letters challenged the notion that public order was to be contrasted to privacy or to home and family, then these letters also complicate the history of any literary public sphere. These letters are unusual in the ways that they trouble usual divides between public debate (in the sense of the public affairs of governance) and personal communications (to which letters, memoirs, and other texts are usually consigned).[92] Indeed, much of the writing and circulations of the eighteenth century reveals the ideology that will divide public and private after the French Revolution; the *lettres de cachet,* as well as the autobiographical memoirs of public figures, the court commentaries or legal briefs *(mémoires),* the tracts, police bulletins *(gazetins),* all were forms of writing that sought to elevate the merely anecdotal to a subject of collective interest. Absent a clear referent such as "the public," some other conduit was necessary in order to bring particular events to public attention.

The *lettres de cachet* reveal this work. In reading familial plaints and *lettres de cachet* alongside police records, pamphlets, and news sheets from the eighteenth century, the letters illustrate the processes of cultivating a new interpretive authority. This public bore little resemblance to literary salons and philosophic clubs; its vocabulary of rupture came less from philosophic debates than from the street. Written by police spies, these reports recorded a marked change in popular talk. They recorded "[the spies'] surprise and anxiety at the thoughts everyone was expressing, and the entirely novel way in which these thoughts were being put."[93] Not only were ordinary people expressing strong convictions, they were doing so with a new level of detail and conviction. Arlette Farge claims, "The new talk was so invasive and so variegated that the observers tried to show its new countenance to the lieutenant of police; they were the first to realize that public opinion . . . was turning into a perceptibly political discourse."[94] Although the letters collected by Farge and Foucault focus on family disputes, they emerge from a similar unsettled discursive context: that of contests over religious interpretation and practice (associated with Jansenism), the increasing ire of local *parlements* against the abuses of royal power, and a continuous stream of rumor associated with everything from foreign affairs to the price of bread. Awash in the tide of pamphlets, broadsides, police reports, and rumor, ordinary people experienced a veritable tide of paper. Placards, notices, hastily scribbled notes were posted on public walls and outside the local police office. If each of these were to be considered and conserved, Paris would have succumbed to the weight of *"papier mâché,"* as one observer notes.[95] The accumulation of multiple and conflicting opinions makes the cultivation of interpretive authority—the ability to weigh, conclude, and justify—all but inevitable. What if the letters were understood as another component of this papier-mâché—as one way among many that ordinary people—along with cultural and political exchangers, such as police, informants, priests, local officials, and the like—came to participate in the construction of publics and public spaces?

To be sure, this claim about the construction of "public opinion" immediately needs to be qualified and made precise. Too easily it collapses into a story of the rising bourgeoisie or the coming to awareness of the plucky popular classes. In her exhaustive work on rumor, subversive words, and popular opinion, Arlette Farge carefully notes that this process is uneven and fitful. She traces the popular rumors (circulated and dominated by women, and tied to the fickle intensities of street crowds); the subversive words that circulated in the clandestine Jansenist press (that pounced quickly on the emergence of a Jansenist reading public, but reported the spectacle of the regicide Damien's death some three months after the act); and the intersection of these with official power that often exceeded its terms (as in the kidnapping of street children in the early 1700s, and their deportation to overseas French colonies). Farge notes drily, "It may be true that subversion has a memory, but this does not mean that popular emotions succeeded one another in a linear progression of consciousness."[96] Instead, the specificity of these different mechanisms by which rumor circulated, or new speech acquires meaning, must be queried. For their part, familial *lettres de cachet* offered a chance to rectify or exploit disconnects between political standing and socioeconomic status, and to regulate economies of social obligation. Yet they are not naive representations of a world in miniature. As will be explored in the next section, conjunctural moments of change demand that discursive and social practices be kept separate to avoid the overly simplistic claim that thought translated immediately into action.

From Disorder to the Ordering of the Napoleonic Code

By 1760, a few years after the last letter collected in *Disorderly Families,* these family disputes had become burdensome for a police already taxed to work in so many areas. "As [the statesman] Malesherbes was quick to point out, no one could fail to be struck by the fact that low-ranking police officials had become the real masters of royal orders," writes Farge. If, for the king, such a substitution violated existing caste hierarchies, the Paris police saw something else when they gazed upon the city and its bad subjects. Lieutenant General Lenoir writes, in October 1774: "It is dangerous to use, in regard to children not subject to penal servitude, a punishment [prison] that throws them together with older individuals who cannot but serve as bad examples . . . Prison, which is inflicted upon them as punishment, does not cure them of vice but teaches them new ways of being vicious . . . Except in cases of grave offense, they should be returned to their parents rather than sent to the school of vice."[97] With this letter, Lenoir signals a broader transformation of prison from a space of imprisonment to one of rehabilitation; the emergence of the figure of the innocent subject; and the educational and corrective role of parents and police. Not only have the police come to eclipse the sovereign power of the king, but the role of Foucault's "exchanger" figures has also broadened to include more people. Slowly, the line between private and public orders is being drawn. These exchangers, as those who can traverse this line, come either to weave together the capillary relations of power that knit public and private, or to trespass against that order altogether.

With the rise of capitalist economic relations and its pressures on late-eighteenth-century social and political order comes the activation of different political units—as well as Foucault's riposte to the tyranny

32 *Introduction*

of Hegel in French thought.[98] Where previously families, households, and neighborhoods were unexplored parts of a king's order—left to their own practices, so long as disruptions were kept to a minimum—these come to be politically charged as supporting components of a new civic order. If Hegel offers an account of political history rooted in the subsumption and supersession of the family by civil society and sustained by the state, then Foucault reverses this causal flow. However, it should be stressed that the familial plaints do not recount a classic Hegelian contest between state and society; the letters paradoxically support state power. *Disorderly Families* gives us an account of state and society in which the state already penetrates and is foundational to political society. The wane of absolutism leads not toward the further incorporation of society but to the dispersion of social forces and their consolidation in the nineteenth century around social sites such as families, asylums, prisons, factories, and militaries. In this sense, their society should not be seen "as external to power or as interrupted by power, but as a matrix within which elements of power come to function, are reactivated, break up, but in the sense of parts breaking away from each other without thereby losing their activity, in which power is re-elaborated, taken up again in a mythical form of ancient forms."[99] The letters do not attest to some irreducible social reality that expressed itself through coherent discourse that could beget political ideology. Far from it. To the contrary, the plaints index a series of disjunctures: between social and discursive practices; between discursive practices and ideology; between the entanglements of the demise of one order and the halting construction of another.

With the consolidation of the public comes the consolidation of the family, and new attention to its own regulatory capacities. Although the revolutionaries initially proposed to abolish the *lettres de cachet*—and even, perhaps, the prison—as symbols of the worst excesses of absolutist power, these proposals foundered on hesitations that perhaps those imprisoned were truly guilty. The debates of the constitutional convention circled around questions at once political and interpretive: What about those already imprisoned? Should their trials and investigations go forward, and on whose investigation and authority? Were they indeed a threat to public order and well-being? In the course of constitutional debates, Guillotin and Robespierre argued for the creation of family tribunals to settle issues at the threshold of family and public life. Initially enthusiastic, the revolutionaries shied away from embracing wholesale these demands; as the Revolution exhausted itself, and the Napoleonic Restoration gathered steam, parental power was rewritten as paternal power. Families could continue to denounce errant members but needed to supply six witnesses in support—and those witnesses should be men. The tendency for the law and social conventions to usually—although not always—favor men became legally codified. Retrospectively, it can be seen that elements of political society participated in the re-elaboration of relations of power in terms of a surveillance state.

These questions of civil order are more than just managerial questions of regulation and administration. Alongside these procedural changes unfold ruminations on what counts as part of "civil order," its very rules and codes—and who gets to decide. Even as police, parents, priests, and others come to reinforce the presence of power in private lives, the eighteenth century also sees the emergence of the antiheroic hero who seeks to unsettle the mores that fix political order. As Farge and Foucault note, the letters pick up on themes found elsewhere in literature—the heroic story of vagabondage in *Gil Blas,* the exile to the colonies of young lovers in *Manon Lescaut,* and the letters of arrest prominently figured in *The Three Musketeers.* Such works of literature, for Foucault, belong

> to the great system of constraint by which the West obliged the quotidian to enter into discourse. But literature occupies a special place within that system: determined to seek out the quotidian beneath the quotidian itself, to cross boundaries, to ruthlessly or insidiously bring our secrets out in the open, to displace rules and codes, to compel the unmentionable to be told, it will thus tend to place itself outside the law, or at least to take on the burden of scandal, transgression, or revolt.[100]

The family plaints, then, serve as an intermediary between what is recognizable as literature and the flotsam of ordinary life not considered deserving of record. They write their way from a social frontier barely cognizable to elites to its codification of the center as political order—"the discourse of 'infamy' . . . has the duty of saying what is most resistant to being said—the worst, the most secret, the most insufferable, the shameless."[101] These "poem-lives" are flash existences not because of the lightning strike of absolutist power but because of the brief glimpse they offer readers of the circulations and mechanisms

34 *Introduction*

of power as they grind into motion. These insurgent tales emerge from a fragile space in between resistance to discursive production and surrender to its terms. Representational mechanisms transform the calumnies of being a bad husband, bad citizen, and dangerous subject into the more stable figure of the criminal.[102]

Even as the circulation of letters, of police bulletins, and of official announcements compels the quotidian to reorganize and present itself to be intelligible to an outside world, these letters and the figures that populate them are a special sort of transgressive "exchanger." They connect *and* trespass different domains, all the while revolting against those plot lines already developed. Their truth effect differs from that of public agents such as police, officials, and priests. Such infamous texts draw their reader into unfamiliar, uncharted territory and then flamboyantly turn around and confront the reader. Did this just happen? Is what happened true? What do *you* make of this person and these events that are out of place and out of time? How will *you* decide to restitute order in the face of scandal? The texts challenge their readers—be they neighborhood beat police, the lieutenant general and his inquisitive *commissaires,* or local neighbors—to decide where the truth lies and to supply the criteria for its evaluation. If literature "promis[es] to produce effects of truth that were recognizable as such,"[103] then the short tales of these letters, these "poem-lives," demand much from their audiences. As the next section will argue, they demand not only the distinction of social and discursive practices, but also a more searching analysis of interpretive conventions. Readers must ferret out the infamous *(l'infâme)* from the insignificant *(l'infime)*—or challenge that task altogether.

Composing the Event

Behind the ornate salutations for the *lettres de cachet* lie signs of the social and economic status of the letter writers. Letter writers drew on *secrétaires*—a term that indicates both the popular letter-writing manuals and private secretaries—to fashion their claims.[104] Some of the most ornately inscribed letters came from the impoverished and illiterate; these letters were penned by public scriveners. Others, written in a neat, compact hand, came from middle-class authors more confident in their prose. In all cases, the stilted, baroque language fell away toward the middle of the letter, as the writer struggled to stay abreast of a torrent of spoken words, emotional anguish, and the conflicting desires to tell all to the king so as to hide a dishonorable family secret. The letters thus trace the presence and limits of social convention, as epistolary graces, social mores, and the desire for personal justice jostle each other on the page. These letters were composed in every sense. Most important, they are compositions of scenes of injustice and disorder at a time when conceptions of order and moral expectations were in flux. They trace that back-and-forth negotiation between the frontiers of positive experience and critique. As "philosophical fragments put to work in the historical field,"[105] they are snapshots of conjunctural moments: conjunctures between overlapping political mechanisms, conjunctures between variant interpretive positions, and way stations between transmuting political orders. "From above," the letters demonstrate the tension between the governmental management of events and the invocation of sovereign power to serve as an alibi for continued police intervention. Yet, "from below," they hint at limited and ultimately ephemeral seizures of power and speech by those most vulnerable to power. Juxtaposed against one another, the two perspectives—from above and from below—capture the fleeting experience of insurgency as a struggle over the conditions of possibility. These insurgent lives are more than aesthetic moments of intensity; they illustrate the dynamics behind popular efforts to compose events rather than ceding to their governmental control.

The compositional elements of these letters return to Foucault's concept of the event and "eventialization" that are scattered across disparate texts, essays, and lectures.[106] In *Disorderly Families*, Farge and Foucault describe these letters and lives as "heavy with events," woven as they are from clashes and dissatisfactions, and punctuated with births, illnesses, and infidelities. Here, as in "Lives of Infamous Men," the language of staging, mise-en-scène, and tableau is used to characterize this "theater of the quotidian."[107] The letter writers themselves are "characters from Céline, trying to make themselves heard at Versailles."[108] These writings all grapple with events as interruptions of historical continuity and the certainties of discourse. Foucault reaches this language of staging and theatrical representation through the evolution of his own thought on the event. Events figure frequently in his early writings as the irreducible that escapes beyond the patterns, conventions, and intelligibility of language.[109] Between 1968 and 1970, Foucault's reflections on critique and history

36 *Introduction*

reach a turning point, as his thought on events, discontinuities, and mechanisms of power and representation sharpens. In contrast to the continuity of historical epoch or its collective mechanisms, Foucault urges an emphasis of the discontinuities that push beyond the text to unfold in the space "between institutions, laws, political victories and defeats, demands, behaviors, revolts, and reactions."[110] Such discontinuities should oblige investigation of the mechanisms of power and representation that suture over these ruptures and assimilate them into the terms of the new order. The familial plaints and *lettres de cachet* offer insight into these discontinuities. They offer shards of one order—shards of failed representations, expired practices, exhausted symbolic forms—as well as fragments that were never quite absorbed into the order that replaced it.

Farge and Foucault's recourse to the event immediately raises questions, especially given the term's associations with the traditional history of monumental events, the evential level of history *(histoire événementielle)* of the Annales school, or the symbolic associations that organize events of cultural history.[111] Events would seem to offer the opportunity either to focus on singular moments—the great acts of great men—or to determine that some events stabilize into patterns or symbolic associations *(mentalités)* that characterize a time or place. As literary theorist Franco Moretti notes, "What is at issue . . . is the orientation of the historian's gaze: whether one should look only at what is behind the masterpiece, unilaterally emphasizing a break, a rupture of the historical tissue—or whether, by showing the consequences of every great work, one should accentuate its function as a genuine producer of historical stability."[112] In both cases, events are supposed to have privileged access to the real, and to display something of its palpability. Farge and Foucault, however, contrast their attention to the event with historians' tendencies to focus either on long-standing, epochal trends (as with historians of the Annales school, such as Marc Bloch and Fernand Braudel) or on the history of collective mentalities (as with historians such as Robert Mandrou and Jacques Le Goff).[113] Their approach resonates more closely with Carlo Ginzburg's *microstoria*—an association that Ginzburg rejected— although they sought to use the everyday to query impersonal patterns and conventions rather than to personify them through biographical narrative.[114] Consistently, Farge and Foucault emphasize that events are never self-evident; instead, they arise from the friction between social practices and discourse, and the reactions provoked by events invoke a range of interpretive conventions and constraints.[115] In interviews, Farge reflects that "it is important to remember that, on the one hand, the anecdote or raw fact are never the reflection of the real [réel], they are already a mise-en-scène, a production of the text—a well-defined text in a similarly well-defined situation, a socially and culturally constructed testimony; on the other hand, one must ask if this fact is exogenous in relation to what happens habitually, or homogeneous, and so representative."[116] Events demand that one look beyond the surface of experience to the relations of domination that organize thought and action. To the extent that they organize or contest collective experience, they further demand the disaggregation of the political and interpretive conventions that govern their intelligibility.

Immediately such a goal gives a more political cast to the composition of events, and raises the question of who, exactly, authors such compositions. On these questions of interpretation and authority, Farge and Foucault would seem to differ from Pierre Nora, the historian and cultural pessimist whose writing on the event is in this volume. As in *Disorderly Families,* Nora celebrates the materialism of daily life insofar as it weaves together a social fabric. Originally to be the editor of a book-length *Lives of Infamous Men* proposed by Foucault, Nora's work as a historian and editor for Gallimard has sustained a generation of innovative cultural historians.[117] For Nora, the "realms of memory" *(lieux de mémoire)* are sites of mediation: mediation between private and collective experience, between popular democracy and conservatism, and between plural perspectives and singular nation-state. The event interrupts and transforms this mediation. On Nora's account, the event is defined by a play between immediacy and distance, but one too easily corrupted into the voyeurism of celebrity gossip or the *fait divers.*[118] However, to read the *lettres de cachet* as a direct window onto the eighteenth-century everyday would be to succumb to this conservative voyeurism. Such a reading narrows and constrains the story that they tell, by promising to tell events as they "really" happened while leaving unchanged central, organizing concepts and categories: family, household, the policing that traces the *infâme* and *infime,* and circulatory power. Likewise, to read these plaints as the voices of the voiceless is to succumb to a sentimentalist reading that obscures the machinery of hierarchy and gives to ordinary people an "alienated and exigent participation" curiously

38 *Introduction*

stripped of power.[119] The connection between interpretive and political authority becomes strained. If Nora celebrates the perspective "from below," he mourns the eclipse of historians and other interpretive authorities who shape collective meaning and suggests that such meaning cannot be forged in their absence. For all of his attention to plurality, Nora ultimately privileges the coherence of history and its categories of interpretation, if not the continuity of order.

What would it mean to read the event instead as a kind of *découpage*—that is, to resist the temptation to submerge it in a series, or to elevate its exceptionalism? After all, the curating of events through decoupage deliberately disrupts the original mise-en-scène of representation. It also puts pressure on questions of creation and production: who chooses and juxtaposes these representations? What relationships (of power, social interaction, moral principle, concepts, and categories) vivify these images and cause some to land and others to miss their target? What different set of "exchangers" mediate this relationship, if not reporter spectators, cultural figures, political leaders, or others? What public audience will they conjure, if any? In the context of the eighteenth century, such an approach makes it possible to back away from two presuppositions behind many readings of the *lettres de cachet*. First, this approach refuses to operate through the categories of the French Revolution, and to insist that revolutionaries envisioned and enacted a clean break with the old regime. It thus resists the determinism of the Revolution, and the straight line drawn from philosophic thought to revolutionary action. And second, it resists presuming that Foucault's analysis of disciplined society means that society could only ever be disciplined, and that the *lettres de cachet* are the secret origins of disciplining technologies. Thinking in terms of the event recovers the *politics* of disjunctive moments.

Foucault's turn to "eventfulness" speaks to the questions just posed. By 1978, Foucault's writing on events has matured into a critical theory. In "What Is Critique?" Foucault situates this work within the double political and philosophical project of theorizing within moments of conjuncture. For Foucault, the unpredictability of the event results not from historical accident or individual thought and action, but from changes to relations of power. From its singular emergence, the event both is present and recedes as these changes entrench through repetition. Its power lies in making something new appear, even as that "something new" loses the power of intimacy and proximity—

the power of its secret—through the very mechanism of power that discloses it. By eventialization *(événementialisation)* Foucault means "to take ensembles of elements where one can detect . . . connections between mechanisms of coercion and contents of knowledge."[120] If Kant's *Aufklärung* encounters a slippage between an ideal end and the process of achieving it, then "eventialization" concentrates attention squarely on this disjuncture.[121] Events are noteworthy not in and of themselves, but for the machinery of power and hierarchy, as well as opacity and illumination, that animates them. For all that Foucault's earlier essay "Lives of Infamous Men" celebrates the aesthetics of the *lettres de cachet,* their real power lies in discerning from them the circulations of police entwined with those of the itinerant, as well as the swirl of claims, counterclaims, rumors, and investigation.

Politics here is not the politics of representation. Politics emerges from ordinary demands for justice and thus discloses the jagged, imperfectly sutured edges of an official order that seeks integration, and a lived experience of stubbornly kaleidoscopic disintegration. In such moments, any politics rooted in positionality becomes untenable and undesirable; politics is the very effort to step outside of the recursivity and repetition of official order, and to undo the hierarchies that structure it. Interpretively, it demands constant attention to the multiple frames, contexts, histories, and archives in play. Politically, these demands seek to dissolve old relationships and limits—to law, tradition, and knowledge—into new insurgent affinities and solidarities that would distend and transmute hierarchy.

Analysis of the event thus grasps the politics and possibilities of the interstitial. It seeks to apprehend "a perpetual mobility, an essential fragility, or rather an intermingling, between that which accompanies the same process and that which transforms it. In short, it would be a matter here of deriving a whole mode of analyses that could be called *strategic.*"[122] A strategic mode of analysis approaches political problems not as questions of knowledge and legitimation—questions that revert to an analysis of cause and effect that leaves unexplored and intact the structures that legitimate the status quo—but with an eye toward the dislocations that would torque the very framing of these problems. Thinking in terms of the event is not just to scrutinize the political and normative claims in play, but also to query why these claims present themselves in one frame of interpretation and not another. In subsequent interviews, Foucault associates the event with Nietzsche's

40 *Introduction*

understanding of philosophy as an activity: "We are traversed by processes, movements, forces," says Foucault in a 1978 interview in Japan. "The role of the philosopher, without a doubt, is to be the diagnostician of these forces, to diagnose the present *[l'actualité].*"[123] Events, then, are composed by, and irreducible to, people acting amid unstable conjunctural relations of power whose cries and deeds will always be in excess of these relations. These events, whose claims and meanings are never quite grasped retrospectively, adhere to and exceed the interpretive conventions at play. The coercive force of an event becomes dissipated not by questioning and then returning to the legitimacy of an idea, principle, or norm; it requires that those within a given strategic field or site refuse to see their conditions as fixed and simply *act.*

One way to understand *Disorderly Families,* then, is as the critical complement to Foucault's genealogical project in *Discipline and Punish.* It foregrounds the emergence of regulatory structures that channel the circulation of people, goods, and words while allowing the discursive regularities (of an inchoate "public opinion" or public well-being; the tussle between parental education as sentimental or corrective; the supersession of the family's economic prerogatives with masculinist morality) to hover in the background. Through the uneven claims vocalized through the letters, emphasis falls on the *contest* between competing models (of public, family, political order) rather than the inevitability of their discursive consolidation. In reconstructing a context for these lives, the reader must "resist deducing practices from thoughts, thoughts from readings, and readings from texts."[124] To facilitate such interpretive resistance, *Disorderly Families* needs a method to capture the work of being a "historian of the present."

In looking at the "herbarium of lives" collected in *Disorderly Families,* one can see a familiar strategy of constructing a thought-space through "acts of selection, decoupage, and restitution."[125] This strategy is pursued at times quite literally: sifting through Foucault's archives for *Disorderly Families* reveals sheaves and sheaves of familial plaints. Some of them are painstakingly copied (in the handwriting of Christiane Martin, Arlette Farge, and Foucault).[126] Others are glossed with an effort to systematize key elements of the letters (name, occupation, age, transgression). Still other folders contain photocopies of entries from Lieutenant General René d'Argenson's journal that have been cut and pasted onto quadrille note paper.[127] These entries report breathlessly, sometimes hour by hour, on events as heard from his window and are reported devoid of any context save a chronological one. The resulting impression—of both Foucault's archives but also of the eighteenth-century artifacts—is of "the construction of an edifice in the form of a collage."[128] It is something more than pastiche or anecdote: these collections are the trace of diagnostic work that records its own process; as Lynne Huffer will argue in this volume, the result is to disturb historicizing by defamiliarizing "our" archive. These decoupages scaffold together a different perspective, rooted in social practices not yet consolidated into coherent discourse.

Foucault's turn to the event and his method of decoupage thus ask how political actors put power in motion. What techniques, both political and interpretive, did eighteenth-century actors use to create the consensus for power's new constitution, what interpretive conventions organize its shared meaning, and how did *both* interpretive and political techniques combine to facilitate its reproduction? To prevent the interpretive uncertainty of claims not yet discourse from collapsing into political practices, the specificity of the mechanisms of power and interpretation must be preserved. For historian Roger Chartier, Foucault's event returns to the space of the writer and how she produces meaning. As events, the plaints and *lettres de cachet* operate with the space of three constraints. First, letter writers were constrained in the range of meaning effects sought by the words, images, and symbolic associations used; these meanings needed to be sufficiently collective to resonate. Second, the very *form* of the plaint allowed them to draw on the conventions of the epistolary genre to move their request from particular to general interest. At once intimate and public, secret and shared, the duality of this epistolary form opened up a struggle for control over mechanisms of power through disclosure. Finally, the interpretive conventions of the time came to work *against* the ends of the letter writers, as they came to support a different set of meanings (parental education as rehabilitative, not corrective; families as moral, not economic units) as administered by police. How did political agents manipulate that same logic so as to install new relations of domination not authorized by either king or letter writers? The *lettres de cachet* take on unusual importance, then, for their siting at the intersection of interpretive mechanisms of representation *(représentance),* and policing mechanisms of security *(lieutenance).* Their authors seek access to the political scene, and so must represent events on terms sensible to royal power; yet, these representations must muffle any potential contradictions with the information revealed through the lieutenant general's own investigations. For their part, circulations of police seek to stabilize the site in which events are represented, and to mute the singularity of any plaints by submerging it within a "series of events," one "that will have to be regulated within a multivalent and transformable framework."[129] The letters thus become a "contact surface" between "the conduct of individuals and the state bodies of control and punishment."[130] They offer more than simply "the view from below" or the inverse of power's perspective—they seek to rewrite the terms of power's contact with social life itself.

Events, then, return to us to the already-explored dynamics that organize relations between the particular and the general. Their critical imperative is to identify the conditions that made possible a different order with a different horizon of intelligibility. Farge writes: "On this question of the singular and the collective, . . . I am convinced that the importance of an anecdote or a singular archival fact has sense only if it can be linked back to a collective phenomenon or to some kind of representativity."[131] In the nineteenth century, this link will be the case history and the resolution of collective anger and individual misfits into pathologies of different kinds. These letters, however, pursue a different tact. The letter writers write their way from a social frontier barely cognizable to elites to its codification of the center as political order—"the discourse of 'infamy' . . . has the duty of saying what is most resistant to being said—the worst, the most secret, the most insufferable, the shameless."[132] Again, the politics here is more than one of aesthetic shock and inversion—again, if the letters were read solely at the level of affect, the effect would quickly become sentimental and the politics conservative. Instead, the circulation of letters seizes and redirects the instabilities provoked by disclosure. It vocalizes the competing perspectives from cops shuffling along their beats, apprentices rebelling against their guild master, parents agonizing over the waywardness of their kids. But the *act* of writing—of narrating to a scrivener, writing the account down, delivering the letter to the king, orally presenting the case, dispatching inspectors to investigate—the act of writing changes things. Each of these steps furthers a process of abstraction; that is, each of these steps transforms a personal plaint into something socially cognizable, something politically binding for a population (maybe), and a violation of shared normative expectations. Already, the letters establish a playful interchange between authors and authority—might they suggestively hint that the disjunctive moment of events might be opened up and radicalized?

Differently from theatrical representation, the *lettres de cachet* seize the potentiality of such disjunctive moments to involve others and generalize the claims and hierarchies at hand. If a simple chiasmus enables, if briefly, the lowly letter writer to seize the power of the monarch, the epistolary form of the letters and their circulation pulls in bystanders and compels them to action. For all that the letters are framed around the promise of secrecy, they announce themselves in a remarkably visible manner: with a red, royal wax seal, the witness testimony of neighbors, and a police investigation. The letters promise less to get to the bottom of an affair—a response that presumes a legitimate plaint to be confirmed or denied—than to announce the potential re-siting of power on the terms of disclosure. From the public declamation of the scrivener and resulting reformulation of the plaint, to the multiple authorities (police, sovereign, court) reading the letters and writing their own, to the intervention of families and neighbors, more people become interpellated into the process. The *process* of establishing the general authority of singular incidents involves many authors; after all, acts of reading and paraphrase are acts of writing and rewriting. This process also changes the field of power to that of disclosure: power lies in determining which authors decide what can be seen and through which interpretive framework.

Authority thus becomes the central node in play between two different orders and two different forms of power. Authority should be understood as a metonymic act that traces and retraces the lines between the act (as the trace left by the written) and authority. Writing on authority, Émile Benveniste states: "One designates as *auctor* the one who, in every domain, promotes, takes initiative, is the first to produce some activity; the one who founds, who guarantees, and who is finally the 'author.' In that way, the abstract *auctoritas* regains its full value through the act of production."[133] Although Foucault does not cite Benveniste, he finds that the *lettres de cachet* are a conduit by which individuals enter into a social system of signs; they give us "socially accepted and recognized signs of individuality irregularity."[134] They are "marks" of the contact between power and individual that, once extended, will elaborate relationships that will bind political and

44 *Introduction*

household spheres. These letters are particularly potent yet susceptible to inversion, alternating the current of power between author (letter writer) and authority (king). And yet, these letters are more than a mechanism of power. Their ability to redirect the circuits of absolute power comes from their participation in more far-reaching changes to the mediation of voice and act. In "Lives of Infamous Men," Foucault suspects that "they manifest . . . an important event, in which political mechanisms and discursive effects intersected."[135] In telling this story, Foucault compares the personal intimate nature of Christianity to that new language bubbling up in the street and overheard by police spies. The partiality and immediacy of the voice has been replaced by "social mapping and control." This voice is no longer heaven-bound: "it accumulates on earth in the form of written traces. An entirely different type of relations is established between power, discourse, and the quotidian, an altogether different way of governing the latter and of formulating it. For ordinary life, a new mise-en-scène is born."[136] When a family member sends a plaint to the king, "An entire chain of political authority became entangled with the threads of daily life."[137] Political sovereignty reaches into relations between husbands, wives, children, and laborers that upends other relations of authority and obedience. Families, administration, and sovereign discover a site of overlapping tactics and interests, one that enmeshes political power more firmly into the family and turns individuals into "semi-spontaneous agents of public order."[138] The practice of the *lettres de cachet* opens up relations of authority to be reworked on different terms and in different spaces. These practices rely on the constraints of norms and policing, as well as the inventive capacities of individuals (family members, police, neighbors, priests), to create a new set of political strategies. Beyond the composition of their "flash existences," letter writers are also creating an authority—a new political form—that will come to supersede their particular circumstances.

We can now better understand the profusion of words that tumble over one another. These letters do not yet participate in the nineteenth-century literary forms (such as the case history), in which the particular becomes elevated and understood as symptomatic of something broader. That strategy is not yet available to either authors or readers, or at least is not useful to them. Instead, writers use these extraordinary acts to create a rostrum and enter onto the public scene. For there is so much to tell. Pierre Rivière, notably, devotes only a single sentence in his confession to his confession of the actual crime.[139] As historian Philippe Artières notes, "the authors speak little of [their] crime because the essential of their lives is likely elsewhere. The extraordinary act which inspires them to write is the crime, but what they write next are the ordinary acts of their lives."[140] Those accused of criminal acts, along with their families, write to achieve epistemological stability for their lived experiences rather than to confess the truth of themselves.

It may seem romantic to see the germs of power's reversal in these letters. After all, few of the letter writers go on to hold institutional positions of power, and the letter writers never articulate a coherent principle to argue for or against, nor do they organize something as powerful as a collective movement. However, Foucault locates the power of these letters beyond the personalities of the letter writers or the content of their claims. Using the same language of eventialization in his seeming unrelated essay "What Is Critique?" Foucault writes: "it is not a matter of making power understood as domination or mastery by way of a fundamental given . . . ; on the contrary, it is always a matter of considering [power] as a relation in a field of interaction, it is a matter of thinking it an inseparable relation with forms of knowledge, and it is always a matter of thinking it in such a way that one sees it associated with a domain of possibility and consequently . . . of possible reversal."[141] As diagnostic traces of acts committed beyond the pen strokes on paper, the letters redirect attention to their framing context. Moving beyond the text, Foucault claims that power needs to be confronted at the site of its contact with knowledge, with interactions, and so with the horizon of possibility it presumes. Challenging and claiming power are part of the same process.

Perhaps it should come as no surprise, then, that the notes and lectures surrounding Foucault's work on *Disorderly Families* touch on civil war and insurrection. Although some of these preparatory materials touch on prison revolts in which prisoners sought escape, most often the revolts that surround policing and incarceration speak to the fragmentation of political, rather than carceral, power. All aspects of these events—from the political sites and agents who make up different "switch points of power," to the "forms, processes, and rites of power," to the creation of social institutions from prison to revolutionary tribunal, to the reinvigoration of exhausted symbolic forms— constitute a searching political challenge.[142] Most forcefully, Foucault

46 *Introduction*

challenges Hegel by revealing the irreducibility of events or ideas to philosophical subjects, the fragmentation of civil society, the historically particular construction of the family, and the interpenetration of state into society and dispersion of power. The project around *Disorderly Families* both performatively and substantively rejects the coherence and universality of history as it moves through subject, family, civil society, and state. Instead, Foucault returns to and radicalizes Kant's *Aufklärung* project. Politics in moments of conjuncture results from the productive friction between new claims to political *and* interpretive authority. Foucault's language about the reactivation of power resonates with Kant's motto that events challenge their audiences to at once "rememorate, commemorate, and prognosticate"—to incarnate the permanence of a new power, and to render violent struggle on new symbolic terms.[143]

Perhaps inadvertently, however, Foucault's work with the family plaints, a transmuting political society, and resistance at once political and interpretive has two other effects. First, and least surprisingly, *Disorderly Families* meditates on the conditions and mechanisms that structure political agency. Not only do the cries, plaints, and condemnations of the letters contrast with the gray institutions of *Discipline and Punish* where quite literally nobody speaks, but the letters also raise the question of action under conditions of constraint and contingency. The letters, their broader political context, and the book's rhetorical approach place the agency of interpretation and action at the heart of any reading. From the perspective of power, the potential to act and disrupt is always a threat with sober political possibilities: "For after all, these characters who refuse to work, who evade taxes and thus place the whole of the fiscal burden on an increasingly restricted mass of people, who produce natural children, impose their subsistence levies, punish, and have a good time, are also all those who are least itinerant, the nobles, the tax agents."[144] If itinerancy receded and instead all individuals were considered as "persons of qualities," it might be noticed that the qualities of the disorderly and the qualities of aristocrats were not so dissimilar. Hovering around the edges of this text lies the possibility for insurrection and insurgency. No wonder, then, that the revolutionaries so quickly abandoned their proposed abolition of prisons and settled for reforms; that the Restoration sought to divide the power of households by separating private from public and thus restricting the economic and political power of women; that the furtive language of property came to re-structure relations between husbands and wives, parents and children, masters and servants. The second effect created by *Disorderly Families* is to insinuate a set of questions about property and personal relationships into the heart of modern conceptions of political order. How uncanny that these three personal relationships regulated by these letters should also be those central to Locke's account of political society in the *Second Treatise*. Beyond the scope of Foucault's own research agenda, then, *Disorderly Families* invites its readers to return to personal relationships to authority—and specifically those within the family—to query their role in symbolically, materially, and politically investing Western subjects in a politics that rewrites those relationships on terms of contract and property. *Disorderly Families* would seem to suggest that any political resistance, let alone collective insurgency, would need to target these relationships as nodes of power susceptible to inversion and reactivation on other terms.

Disorderly Families has a remarkably modern feel to it. Readers do not have to reach too far to find resonances between its letters and more recent events. Even now, the police continue to be the first contact that most people have with public power, and how that contact unfolds has implications for their view onto power and justice.[145] The dilemmas about whether or not to appeal to public agents and to invite them into private life continue to affect how and whether many people contact the police. Sociologist Beth Richie has written at length in *Arrested Justice* about the intersectional demands of race, gender, and economics that lead African American women to hesitate over asking the police to intervene in domestic violence incidents.[146] Such invitations pit the gendered logic of security (against abusive partners) against the economic need for a second income, and the recognition that personal security cuts against the racialized logic of American incarceration. When the police arrive, women face the same dilemma as the letters of how to compose themselves according to legal standards as suffering abuse. Much like the letter writers, these plaints must make the complexities of intimate life intelligible as a threat to personal and public order, and women are exhorted to find corroborating witnesses or evidence. They must make these assertions even as they themselves often are in disbelief that things could have gotten so bad, and even as their partners dispute their credibility. As with the *lettres*

48 *Introduction*

de cachet, these invitations also risk empowering public agents who may go on to abuse that power in other contexts.

The interventions and petitions of neighbors are just as fraught. In France, the publication of *Disorderly Families* recalled the poison-pen letters of Vichy, when people reported their neighbors as resisting the regime governing occupied France. Although the analogy is inapt— the Vichy letters were anonymous, the *lettres de cachet* relied on named witnesses—both incidents call to mind moments when what would count as popular justice is uncertain. Perhaps a more immediate analogy for American readers would be the public response to the shooting of Trayvon Martin in 2012. Director Nonny de la Peña has curated public court records and 911 calls to structure the story of the confrontation that ended in the shooting death of unarmed Trayvon Martin by George Zimmerman. The virtual-reality film *One Dark Night* captures the mix of written and oral testimonies that come together in giving an account of others, as well as the ambiguities of aesthetics and truthfulness that come with such compositions. Reading the requests for *lettres de cachet* is to confront similar dynamics absent the familiarity of social and political context. Their historical distance pushes us to disaggregate the political, social, and perhaps psychological mechanisms that govern the internalization of norms and expectations for power and justice. After all, the letter writers did not immediately protest the sociopolitical inequities that organized their lives; they simply asked that the person most obviously connected to perceived disruption be removed. For the letters' later readers, however, to read these letters is instead to read symptomatically—to read across the curated collection of letters looking for patterns that might point to broader underlying structures (an antiquated tax system, the impossibility of divorce, changing legal norms around testimony) whose failure cathects disorder onto some bodies and not others.

For a period in the United States, a similar process not of arrest but of epistolary curation was implemented by President Barack Obama.[147] From the voluminous correspondence sent to the White House, ten letters were selected each day for him to read. As for Louis XV and XVI, the goal was similar: to give him stories that reflected the people he served, stories that he couldn't collect himself by walking out onto the street. As with the *placets,* these letters offered a narrative of American life at once shambling and urgent: stories of vets returning with PTSD who lashed out at their families, of farmers hurt by drought, of the inmate who sells crack but insists he can be reformed, of escalating health-care costs with bills enclosed. Struck by their intensity, staffers could nominate ten for inclusion with the day's portfolio for the president, and agonized over which to select and in what order they should be compiled. Many of the letters offered stories of how policies were lived rather than reasoned argument. Some made their way into public policy, and one onto a White House wall as a framed testament to the need for the Affordable Care Act. After the presidential election of 2016, the letter handlers faced the wrenching task of communicating the tumultuous views of a stunned country—some jubilant, some heartbroken—to the president. It's not clear if the process of curation has continued under the Trump administration.

For their part, the usage of *lettres de cachet* was greatly reduced in 1784 by the Baron de Breteuil, minister in the King's Household.[148] Quite simply, the police had become overwhelmed with requests, and Breteuil's reforms sought to rationalize their use and to reduce the prison terms associated with them. The later decree of March 16, 1790, mostly abolished the practice and freed those imprisoned, but with important exceptions: it did not apply to those with legal judgments against them; those whose families submitted additional evidence against them; beggars and vagabonds arrested by police; or those committing capital crimes. From fear that some of these plaints might be justified, the legislature called for a family arbitration court involving no less than eight relatives and neighbors to serve as witnesses to decide future plaints. "We are caught between two major concerns," said the abbé Maury, "that of liberty, which should extend to everyone in society, and that of society, which should never be disturbed."[149] From these twin concerns emerges a society organized around guilt and punishment, a punitive society in which the distinction between guilty and innocent becomes paramount.

Telling this history from the perspective of disorder means refusing to stabilize it or contain its effusions and torments. Indeed, the theme of circulation that threads through *Disorderly Families* and these essays of *Archives of Infamy* suggests that these poem-lives find their articulation at the shifting frontiers of multiple domains and discourses. Interpretive authority here is not fixed and certain, or if it is, it is paradoxically grounded on the shifting terrain of conflicting desires and powers that irrupt into violence. In the face of such overwhelming particularity, the challenge is not to choose, once and for all, structure

50 *Introduction*

or event. It is to recognize that each choice offers different perspectives onto the lived experience of violence. As Lynne Huffer suggests in her essay that closes this volume, our relationship to the violence of these letters can only be oblique and mediated by the history told of the past, with all of its complicities and perverse investments. Collectively, the essays presented here argue that the events recounted can never be stabilized, and their wounds never healed. The histories told here are thieved—they are for us as contemporary readers, who reflect on the interminglings of desire and power that have wrought discourses and counterdiscourses, and as authors who thieve, rather than inherit (and legitimate), so as to force ourselves to confront our entanglements, interrogate them, and sometimes refuse them.

NOTES

1. Foucault writes about the *lettres de cachet* in a variety of texts. In *History of Madness* (1961), the letters appear in his discussion of hospitals, prisons, and asylums; in "Truth and Juridical Forms" (1973), they are "a way of regulating the everyday morality of social life" (66) and deeply connected to the capitalist expansion beyond landed property (68–69). Discussed at length in *The Punitive Society* (1973) and briefly referenced in *Psychiatric Power* (1974), the letters are situated as an element to the development of the police and mechanisms of governmentality. By the time of "Lives of Infamous Men" (1977), the letters are treated in their own right as individual encounters with power. See *History of Madness*, ed. Jean Khalfa, trans. Jonathan Murphy and Jean Khalfa (New York: Routledge, 2006); "Truth and Juridical Forms," in *Power: Essential Works of Michel Foucault, 1954–84*, vol. 3, ed. James D. Faubion, trans. Robert Hurley (New York: New Press, 2000); *The Punitive Society: Lectures at the Collège de France, 1972–1973*, ed. Bernard Harcourt, trans. Graham Burchell (New York: Palgrave Macmillan, 2015); *Psychiatric Power: Lectures at the Collège de France, 1973–1974*, ed. Jacques Lagrange, trans. Graham Burchell (New York: Palgrave Macmillan, 2006); "Lives of Infamous Men," in *Power*.

2. The phrase *"lettres de cachet"* designates the letters of arrest written by the king that order the arrest and imprisonment of disorderly persons without trial. The *cachet,* or seal, on the letter distinguished that correspondence from everyday mail; most letters were simply folded over and delivered without seals or envelopes. These letters were used to remedy four kinds of disorder: political opposition to the king; transgression of religious or military codes; misrepresentations of the king by actors, directors, and others associated with the theater; or ordinary complaints between husbands and wives, parents and children, or workshop masters and apprentices. The originator of the complaint would write, or hire a public scrivener to compose, a complaint letter *(placet)* addressed to the king or the lieutenant general of police. Ideally, the king would review the letter, decide if it merited attention, and then ask the police to investigate its claims and arrest the named party if the claims had merit. In practice, often the police investigated before receiving orders from the king and some complaints went unheard.

Although *lettre de cachet* refers narrowly to the arrest letter written by the king, many historians often use the phrase to refer to the body of correspondence between families, police, and royal household. For a longer description of the process and its history, see Arlette Farge and Michel Foucault, *Disorderly Families: Infamous Letters from the Bastille Archive,* ed. Nancy Luxon, trans. Thomas Scott-Railton (Minneapolis: University of Minnesota Press, 2016).

3. See interview with Laurent Vidal, "Arlette Farge, le parcours d'une historienne," *Genèses,* no. 48 (2002–3): 115–35, 120–21.

4. Indeed, one of the dossiers of recopied *placets* from 1728 is encased by a letter dated December 10, 1973, from Daniel Prement. The letter invites Foucault to work with the 17th arrondissement's section of the Ligue Française pour la Défense des Droits de l'Homme et du Citoyen (BNF-Richelieu, Fonds Michel Foucault, NAF 28730, Boîte 68, poche 0).

5. Two reviews are reprinted in this volume, one from *Le Monde* and the other from *La Nouvelle Revue Française.* Additionally, in 1982 the weekly magazine *L'Express* published an exchange with Farge and Foucault that touched on the main themes of *Disorderly Families.* See "L'âge d'or de la lettre de cachet," in *Dits et Écrits,* vol. 2, ed. Daniel Defert, François Ewald, and Jacques Lagrange (Paris: Gallimard, 2001), 1170–71. Michael Ignatieff reviewed the book in "At the Feet of the Father," *Times Literary Supplement,* no. 4177, April 22, 1983, 409. More recently, see Lynne Huffer, "Foucault's Ethical Ars Erotica," *SubStance* 38.3 (2009): 125–47; *Foucault, the Family, and Politics,* ed. Robbie Duschinsky and Leon Antonio Rocha (New York: Palgrave Macmillan, 2012).

6. Foucault initially intended for an anthology of *lettres de cachet* to be published in the series *Parallel Lives,* and entirely without an interpretive apparatus save the opening essay known now as "Lives of Infamous Men." The contrast of this essay to the Introduction that opens *Disorderly Families* is striking for the contrast in tone. "Lives" is lyrical where the introductory essay is more prosaic, perhaps even more social-scientific, in presenting its facts and figures about the whole of the *lettres de cachet* archived in the Bastille. Perhaps these editorial choices reflect Foucault's intervening debates with historians in the wake of their reception of *Discipline and Punish.* See Foucault, "Lives of Infamous Men."

7. The closest points of contact come in the discussion of generalized punishment, when Foucault charts the distillation of one model of criminality and punishment from a profusion of illegalities that variously define different parts of the social order. However, despite Foucault's discussion of vagabondage (a common complaint in the families' *placets*) and the reform of penal justice following the Revolution (which denounced the arbitrary nature of the letters), Foucault makes no mention of the letters.

8. See Arlette Farge, *Délinquance et criminalité: Le Vol d'aliments à Paris au XVIIIe siècle* (Paris: Plon, 1974).

9. See Michel Foucault, *I, Pierre Rivière,* trans. Frank Jellinek (Omaha: University of Nebraska Press, 1982); Michel Foucault, *Herculine Barbin: Being the Recently Discovered Memoirs of a Nineteenth-Century French Hermaphrodite,* trans. Richard McDougall (New York: Vintage, 1980).

10. See Arlette Farge, *Vivre dans la rue à Paris au XVIIIe siècle* (Paris: Gallimard-Julliard, collection Archives, 1979).

11. Famously, Taylor argues that Foucault's "monolithic relativism" leaves him unable to orient agency toward progressive truths or freedoms (and so unable to

52 Introduction

distinguish better from worse political regimes), in "Foucault on Freedom and Truth," *Political Theory* 12.2 (May 1984): 152–83. For an insightful overview and critique of these debates, see Paul Patton, "Taylor and Foucault on Power and Freedom," *Political Studies* 37.2 (June 1989): 260–76. Although Foucault occasionally acknowledges these critiques, he never directly responds to them. Elsewhere I have argued that Foucault does indirectly return to freedom, trust, and agency in his later work on *parrhesia*, although on terms quite different from the usual ones of liberalism or ideal theory. See Nancy Luxon, "Foucault on Freedom and Trust," symposium essay in *Review of Politics* 77.4 (fall 2015): 653–59.

12. See Michel Foucault, *Society Must Be Defended: Lectures at the Collège de France, 1975–1976,* English series ed. Arnold Davidson, trans. David Macey (New York: Picador, 2003), 15.

13. Foucault, "Lives of Infamous Men," 70, 75, 76.

14. Foucault, *The Punitive Society,* 51.

15. Michel Foucault, "Table ronde du 20 mai 1978," in *L'Impossible Prison,* ed. Michelle Perrot (Paris: Éditions du Seuil, 1980), 42. Translation is mine.

16. And even speech in the GIP is more than giving voice to the voiceless.

17. Michel Foucault, *Security, Territory, Population: Lectures at the Collège de France, 1977–1978* (New York: Palgrave Macmillan, 2007), 11.

18. In "What Is Critique?" Foucault argues that "archaeology, strategy, and genealogy" are three different dimensions or approaches to positive reality; they outline the conditions that render singularities intelligible (Michel Foucault, "What Is Critique?" in James Schmidt, ed., *What Is Enlightenment? Eighteenth-Century Questions and Twentieth-Century Answers* [Berkeley: University of California Press, 1996], 397).

19. Many histories of policing and incarceration have been written, with different emphases of geographic scope and time period. Some landmark works include Abram de Swaan, *In the Care of the State* (Oxford: Oxford University Press, 1988); Alan Williams, *The Police of Paris, 1718–1789* (Baton Rouge: Louisiana State University Press, 1979); Vincent Milliot, *Un policier des Lumières* (Seyssel: Éditions Champ Vallon, 2011).

20. Lieutenant General Nicolas Delamare, in his *Traité de la police,* writes: "The first legislators of the famous [Greek] republics, considering life to be the basis of every other good that is the object of police, and considering life itself, if not accompanied by a good and wise conduct, and by all the external aids necessary for it, to be only a very imperfect good, divided all of police into these three parts, the preservation, the goodness, and the pleasures of life." See "Idée générale de la police," in *Traité de la police,* vol. 1, 2d rev. ed. (Paris: Michel Brunet, 1722), 3.

21. Delamare was the commissioner at Châtelet entrusted with carrying out a series of administrative reforms to the police beginning in 1667; he was involved in responding to grain riots as late as 1709. The names and dates of the fourteen lieutenants general of police for Paris are Gabriel Nicolas de La Reynie (1667–97); Marc René de Voyer d'Argenson (1697–1718); Louis Charles de Machault d'Arnouville (1718–20); Marc Pierre de Voyer d'Argenson (1720; 1722–24); Gabriel Taschereau de Baudry (1720–22); Nicolas Baptiste Ravot d'Ombreval (1724–25); René Hérault (1725–40); Claude Henri Feydeau de Marville (1740–47); Nicolas René Berryer (1747–57); Henri Baptiste Bertin de Bellisle (1757–59); Antoine Gabriel de Sartine (1759–74); Jean Charles Pierre Lenoir (1774–75; 1776–85); Joseph

François Raymond d'Albert (1775–76); Louis Thiroux de Crosne (1785–89). For a longer discussion of the historical evolution of the police and its different divisions, see *Disorderly Families,* 5–8, 19–23.

22. For an overview of police functions and prerogatives, see the "Introduction" and "Editor's Introduction" to *Disorderly Families.* A more detailed presentation can be found in Alan Williams, *The Police of Paris, 1718–1789;* Marc Chassaigne, *La Lieutenance générale de police de Paris* ([1906] Geneva: Slatkine reprints, 1975), 146–60; Claude Quétel, *Les Lettres de cachet: Une légende noire* (Paris: Perrin, 2011); Milliot, *Un policier des Lumières.*

23. Foucault, *Security, Territory, Population,* 326.

24. Foucault, *The Punitive Society;* Quétel, *Les Lettres de cachet;* Milliot, *Un policier des Lumières.*

25. Foucault, *The Punitive Society,* 131.

26. Farge and Foucault, "Parents and Children," in *Disorderly Families,* 126.

27. In *The Punitive Society,* Foucault uses "exchangers" sometimes to designate people and sometimes to designate their context and conditions of possibility. In his most extensive discussion of the term, exchangers serve as a hinge between different levels of analysis (36–37n). In the context of the letters, he writes that they come from "socially important places in that they become relays and diversions *[échangeurs]* of power" (131). The letters come at once from the level of communities and also the "site of the formation of a sort of consensus that asks power to respect its morality, order and regularity." And so "these sites are exchangers *[échangeurs]* between power from above and power from below" (131). I use the term "switch points of power" to refer to these sites, and "exchangers" or "exchanger figures" to refer to those who act within those sites.

28. Foucault has an extended discussion of these switch points of power, or the "exchanger element," in the January 10, 1973, lecture of *The Punitive Society,* 33–38.

29. Foucault responds more specifically to Marxism, and the context of the transition from *lettres de cachet* to disciplinary society, in "Truth and Juridical Forms," in which he argues that "capitalism penetrates much more deeply into our existence" (86) than Marxists allow. See "Truth and Juridical Forms," in Faubion, *Power.*

30. "As we proceed to develop our investigation, we shall find, in general, that the characters who appear on the economic stage are merely personifications of economic relations; it is as the bearers of these economic relations that they come into contact with each other." The translator notes, "The concept of an object (or person) as the receptacle, repository, bearer *[Träger]* of some thing or tendency quite different from it appears repeatedly in *Capital.*" See Karl Marx, *Capital,* vol. 1, trans. Ben Fowkes (New York: Vintage Books, 1977), 179.

31. Foucault, *Discipline and Punish,* 304.

32. Michel Foucault, *History of Sexuality,* vol. 1, *An Introduction,* trans. Robert Hurley (New York: Vintage Books, 1990), 108.

33. Foucault, *The Punitive Society,* 126.

34. Foucault, "Lives of Infamous Men," 78.

35. Foucault, *The Punitive Society,* 131.

36. Foucault, "Lives of Infamous Men," 83.

37. Ibid., 78.

38. Foucault, *Security, Territory, Population,* 327.

54 *Introduction*

39. Foucault, "Lives of Infamous Men," 70.

40. Foucault, *The Punitive Society,* 35.

41. Ibid.

42. Ibid., 130.

43. Ibid., 130n. The additional language can be found in Foucault's original lecture notes at the Bibliothèque Nationale de France, NAF 28730, Boîte III, folio 11–12.

44. Longer discussion of the connotations for *rentrer en soi-même* can be found in Luxon, "Editor's Introduction," in *Disorderly Families,* 15–16.

45. Lynne Huffer differently emphasizes the ethical, rather than the political, dimension of this truth telling and its effects on contemporary actors and the archival historians who follow much later. She finds in the letters the basis for a speech and listening between people not yet reducible to subject–object relations, and so the conditions for a relation to oneself not yet defined by an ideal and potentially normalizing subjectivity. I am persuaded by her claim that these archives disrupt habitual relations to knowledge and history. As Huffer acknowledges, the relation between the ethics and politics of critique is more complicated; it will be discussed more fully in the later section on the "event." See Huffer, "Foucault's Ethical Ars Erotica," 125–47.

46. Michel-Rolph Trouillot, *Silencing the Past* (Boston: Beacon Press, 1995), 23.

47. Mona Ozouf notes that, in the dictionaries, *publique* doesn't become the opposite of *privé* until the 1835 edition of the dictionary of the French Academy ("L'Opinion publique" in *The French Revolution and the Creation of Modern Political Culture,* vol. 1, *The Political Culture of the Old Régime,* ed. Keith M. Baker [New York: Pergamon Press, 1987], 419–34).

48. On the juxtaposition of *publique* and *particulier,* see *Histoire de la vie privée: de la Renaissance aux Lumières,* vol. 3, ed. Roger Chartier (Paris: Éditions du Seuil, 1986), 15–18, 23, 413–53; Sarah Maza, "Domestic Melodrama," *American Historical Review* 94.5 (December 1989): 1249–64, 1251. Keith Michael Baker argues that public opinion appeared in the second half of the 1700s, and as a political (rather than a philosophical) concept and one divorced from sociological representations of any "public" (Keith M. Baker, *Inventing the French Revolution: Essays on French Political Culture in the Eighteenth Century* [Cambridge: Cambridge University Press, 1990], 168).

49. Arlette Farge, *Fragile Lives,* trans. Carol Shelton (Cambridge: Harvard University Press, 1995); *Subversive Words: Public Opinion in Eighteenth-Century France,* trans. Rosemary Morris (University Park: Pennsylvania State University Press, 1995).

50. Farge, *Fragile Lives.*

51. Ibid., 20.

52. Nicolas Toussaint Le Moyne Des Essarts, *Dictionnaire universel de police,* vol. 8 (Paris: Moutard, 1790), 343.

53. An overview of these reforms is offered in the preceding section and in the Editor's Introduction for *Disorderly Families,* 1–16.

54. Quoted in Arlette Farge, "The Honor and Secrecy of Families," in *A History of Private Life,* vol. 3, ed. Roger Chartier, series eds. Philippe Ariès and Georges Duby, trans. Arthur Goldhammer (Cambridge: Harvard University Press, 1993), 594.

55. Jansenism was a heretical sect within Catholicism and located primarily in

France. Among other convictions, the Jansenists believed in predestination; this challenge to Catholic doctrine and religious hierarchy was understood equally as a challenge to political absolutism and as the kernel of a protodemocratic political discourse. Damiens, who attempts to kill the king and whose story opens *Discipline and Punish,* was a domestic for several prominent Jansenists in the *parlement* of Paris. See Dale K. Van Kley, *The Jansenists and the Expulsion of the Jesuits from France, 1757–1765* (New Haven: Yale University Press, 1975); Dale K. Van Kley, *The Damiens Affair and the Unraveling of the Ancien Régime, 1750–1770* (Princeton, N.J.: Princeton University Press, 1984). Interestingly, the Jansenists were open to female participation, in the context of minimizing ecclesiastical hierarchy and making religious interpretive authority more broadly accessible. To the extent that the Jansenists also divided and subordinated church to state, this participation was compatible with female subordination to men. Although it opened interpretive authority to women, its moral language directed against a degenerate monarchy was later used to divide fraternal public from womanly domestic spheres. See Daniel Bell, "The 'Public Sphere,' the State, and the World of Law in Eighteenth-Century France," *French Historical Studies* 17.4 (autumn 1992): 912–34, 930.

56. Pierre Louis de Lacretelle, *Mémoire pour le Comte de Sanois,* 15. Cited in Maza, "Domestic Melodrama," 1253.

57. For a lengthier discussion of the creation of legal-cum-social courts of public opinion, and the gendered relations therein, see Sarah Hanley, "Social Sites of Political Practice in France: Lawsuits, Civil Rights, and the Separation of Powers in Domestic and State Government, 1500–1800," *American Historical Review* 102.1 (February 1997): 27–52, 33.

58. The testimonies of witnesses were not always investigated thoroughly. As the use of familial *lettres de cachet* exploded, police investigation into these charges became cursory. Likewise, those who served as police spies—frequently recruited from petty offenders—were not the most reliable sources. See Milliot, *Un policier des Lumières.*

59. Jeffrey Merrick, "Patterns and Concepts in the Sodomitical Subculture of Eighteenth-Century Paris," *Journal of Social History* 50.2 (2016): 273–306; Turmeau de la Morandière, *Plan de Police contre les Mendians, les Vagabonds, les Escrocs, les Filles de débauche et les Gens sans aveu* (Paris: Dessaint Junior, 1764); cited in Milliot, *Un policier des Lumières,* 183.

60. Quoted in Michel Rey, "Police and Sodomy in Eighteenth-Century Paris: From Sin to Disorder," *Journal of Homosexuality* 16.1–2 (1988): 129–46, 130. It is worth biographically noting that historians Michel Rey (1953–93) and his teacher Jean-Louis Flandrin (1931–2001) were among the first to research homosexuality and gay culture in France. Flandrin and Foucault traveled in the same circles of historians, and Foucault cites his work on numerous occasions; notably, they both contributed essays to *Western Sexuality,* ed. Philippe Ariès and André Béjin, trans. Anthony Forster (Oxford: Basil Blackwell, 1985).

61. Foucault, *Security, Territory, Population,* 46.

62. Both infamy and debauchery cover a range of acts and behaviors. Infamy includes sex between men, but it also can be used to describe a range of actions said to be shameful, undignified, or sordid (such as: being fined, selling off household possessions, engaging in shady business deals) that injure honor and reputation, or to indicate a room that has been badly cleaned. Speaking to the broad sense

56   *Introduction*

of "infamy," Foucault writes "Lives of Infamous Men," included in this volume. For a more specific attention to homosexuality, see Michel Rey, "Parisian Homosexuals Create a Lifestyle, 1700–1750: The Police Archives," trans. Robert A. Day and Robert Welsh, in this volume and originally published in *'Tis Nature's Fault: Unauthorized Sexuality during the Enlightenment,* ed. Robert Purks Maccubbin (Cambridge: Cambridge University Press, 1988), 179–91.

Debauchery had an extensive meaning in eighteenth-century French, with nearly a whole page of definitions and usage in the *Dictionnaire universel.* Although it could be used in a playful sense, to indicate merrymaking among "honest people," it also indexed moral and social disorder. "To debauch" meant to live with corrupted mores, to throw oneself toward vice, to leave the path of virtue. According to the *Dictionnaire universel,* "good-for-nothings debauched lots of people, and drew them toward gambling, carousing with women, and frequenting the cabarets." The dictionary of the Académie Française for 1762 defines debauchery as disorderliness, or excess in drink and food, or incontinence. Starting in 1713, "public debauchery" falls under the jurisdiction of the lieutenant general, or occasionally the criminal court at Châtelet. Under Lieutenant General of Police Lenoir, sentences of exile for debauchery almost entirely disappear, and instead prostitutes are imprisoned for three to six months; these sentences harden in the second half of the century. Foucault discusses debauchery in *History of Madness* (84–90), and then again in the context of unreason (106, 109). See Antoine Furetière, *Dictionnaire universel,* 1727 edition, revised and expanded by Henri Basnage de Beauval and Jean-Baptiste Brutel de La Rivière. See also the online Dictionnaires d'autrefois project at https://artflproject.uchicago.edu/; David Garrioch, *Neighbourhood and Community in Paris, 1740–1790* (Cambridge: Cambridge University Press, 1986), 76; Erica-Maria Benabou, *La Prostitution et la police des mœurs au XVIIIe siècle* (Paris: Éditions Perrin, 1987).

63. Farge and Foucault, *Disorderly Families,* 109–20 (Jean Baptiste Boissier and Françoise Lesquoy), 139–44 (Jean Allis), 178–79 (Edme Joseph Eli).

64. These relationships to authority—relations between husbands and wives, parents and children, masters and apprentices—are powerful for their role in composing households as social and economic units. They also are troublesome for the challenges they pose to thinking these relationships on contractual terms. The three relationships directly recall Locke's *Second Treatise,* along with philosophical critiques of contract (by Carole Pateman, among others) and historical explorations of their limits (by Julie Hardwick and Suzanne Desan, among others). See Carole Pateman, *The Sexual Contract* (Stanford, Calif.: Stanford University Press, 1988); Julie Hardwick, *Family Business* (Oxford: Oxford University Press, 2009); and Suzanne Desan, *The Family on Trial in Revolutionary France* (Berkeley: University of California Press, 2004).

65. The dossiers for those stopped for "infamous" behaviors are in the series Archives of the Bastille (AB) 10254–67. Other dossiers compiled by police commissioners, as well as other dossiers around the *lettres de cachet,* also contain such records; identifying the relevant files requires going through each bundle of letters one by one. Jeffrey Merrick outlines these archival dilemmas and seeks a more comprehensive perspective on police investigation of the *infâmes* in "Patterns and Concepts in the Sodomitical Subculture of Eighteenth-Century Paris." Didier Eribon writes about Foucault's interest in *les infâmes,* and reads forward the social

creation of homosexual identity in *Insult and the Making of the Gay Self,* trans. Michael Lucey (Durham, N.C.: Duke University Press, 2004).

66. Of course, this association reflects the perspective of the police and upper-crust society; historian Michel Rey has argued that the *infâmes* had their own subculture.

67. Notoriously, Bruno Lenoir and Jean Diot were arrested for *"l'infamie,"* tried and publicly burned for committing sodomy. The two men—one a cobbler, the other a domestic servant—were arrested in January 1750 on rue Montorgeuil near the covered market of Les Halles in Paris. They were imprisoned at Châtelet, tried in April 1750, and sentenced to being burned alive at the place de Grève in front of what is now the town hall; the judge ordered that they be secretly strangled before being burned. They were the last two people executed in France for the sole crime of sodomy, although surveillance, imprisonment, and other punishments continued. Punishment for sodomy ended in 1791, although "crimes against nature" *(attentats infâmes contre la nature)* remained part of the penal code until August 4, 1982. The Lenoir/Diot affair was unusual. Police generally sought to prohibit homosexual acts in public places and to limit any ensuing publicity. The more usual punishment was arrest. See Jeffrey Merrick, "Brutal Passion" and "Depraved Taste," *Journal of Homosexuality* 41.3–4 (2002): 85–103.

68. Farge and Foucault, *Disorderly Families,* 212–14. The Nicolas Fieffé dossier includes letters that attest to the consistent interventions into homosexual practices on the part of police investigator Simmonet, public official Haimier, and the abbé Théru.

69. See Rey, "Parisian Homosexuals Create a Lifestyle"; Jeffrey Merrick, "Sexual Politics and Public Order in Late Eighteenth-Century France: The *Mémoires secrets* and the *Correspondance secrète," Journal of the History of Sexuality* 1.1 (July 1990): 68–84; Jeffrey Merrick, "Sodomitical Inclinations in Early Eighteenth-Century Paris," *Eighteenth-Century Studies,* special issue *Only Connect: Family Values in the Age of Sentiment* 30.3 (spring 1997): 289–95.

70. Rey, "Police and Sodomy in Eighteenth-Century Paris," 134. Translation is mine.

71. Ibid., 145. Translation is mine.

72. Berryer created specialized departments headed by one or more inspectors, and these were either maintained or expanded by his successor, Sartine, to twenty-five such departments. These departments specifically surveilled and policed certain activities (e.g., printing and distribution of written material, grain provisionment, theatrical spectacles) and certain categories of person (e.g., mendicancy, prostitutes and kept women, pederasty, wet nurses, foreign Protestants, charlatans, native Protestants). Each of these departments regulates circulations of goods and persons, but as a whole their scope lacks coherency. See Alan Williams, *The Police of Paris, 1718–89* (Baton Rouge: Louisiana State University Press), 100–104.

73. Foucault writes: "As defined by the ancient civil or canonical codes, sodomy was a category of forbidden acts; their perpetrator was nothing more than the juridical subject of them. The nineteenth-century homosexual became a personage, a past, a case history, and a childhood, in addition to being a type of life, a life form, and a morphology, with an indiscreet anatomy and possibly a mysterious physiology" (*The History of Sexuality,* vol. 1, *An Introduction,* trans. Robert Hurley [New York: Vintage Books, 1990], 43).

58 *Introduction*

74. Sarah Hanley, "Engendering the State: Family Formation and State Building in Early Modern France," *French Historical Studies* 16.1 (spring 1989): 4–27. The literature of women and the public sphere is quite rich. Landmark texts include Joan Landes, *Women and the Public Sphere in the Age of the French Revolution* (Ithaca, N.Y.: Cornell University Press, 1988); Lynn Hunt, *The Family Romance of the French Revolution* (Berkeley: University of California Press, 1993); Desan, *The Family on Trial in Revolutionary France*; Sarah Maza, *Private Lives and Public Affairs: The Causes Célèbres of Prerevolutionary France* (Berkeley: University of California Press, 1993). The emphasis on women in the public sphere among French historians is slightly different. See Farge, *Subversive Words*; Arlette Farge, "Protesters Plain to See," in *A History of Women in the West: Renaissance and Enlightenment Paradoxes,* ed. Arlette Farge and Natalie Zemon Davis, trans. Arthur Goldhammer, series eds. Georges Duby and Michelle Perrot (Cambridge: Harvard University Press, 1993), 489–507; Natalie Zemon Davis, "Women on Top," in *Society and Culture in Early Modern France* (Stanford, Calif.: Stanford University Press, 1975), 124–51; Jean-Louis Flandrin, *Families in Former Times: Kinship, Household, and Sexuality,* trans. Richard Southern (Cambridge: Cambridge University Press, 1979).

75. Farge and Foucault, *Disorderly Families,* 34. Farge and Foucault use the word *lieu* here. Their usage recalls Foucault's discussion of *milieu* in *Security, Territory, Population* (1978): "[S]overeignty capitalizes a territory, raising the major problem of the seat of government, whereas discipline structures a space and addresses the essential problem of a hierarchical and functional distribution of elements, and security will try to plan a milieu in terms of events or series of events or possible elements, of series that will have to be regulated with a multivalent and transformable framework. The specific space of security refers then to a series of possible events; it refers to the temporal and the uncertain, which have to be inserted within a given space. The space in which a series of uncertain elements unfold is, I think, roughly what one can call the milieu" (20). Foucault goes on to say that the milieu "is therefore the medium of an action and the element in which it circulates. It is therefore the problem of circulation and causality that is at stake in this notion of milieu" (21). The same notions of circulation, uncertain elements, and the event can be found in *Disorderly Families*; they will be treated at greater length in the next section of this Introduction. In the context of the family, *milieu* is also taken up in *Psychiatric Power* as Foucault argues that the nineteenth century saw both the disciplinarization of the family and the familialization of the asylum; the two milieus are part of the same historical process that defines family and asylum in terms of older notions of "custody."

76. For an overview of debates among eighteenth-century historians around the family, and then a series of essays that interrogate the production and ideological definition of the family, see *Family, Gender, and Law in Early Modern France,* ed. Suzanne Desan and Jeffrey Merrick (University Park: Pennsylvania State University Press, 2009).

77. *Dictionnaire universel françois et latin,* vol. 3 (Nancy, 1738–42), 666. Accessed March, 28, 2017, at http://www.cnrtl.fr/dictionnaires/anciens/trevoux/. Locke employs a similar definition of "family" in the *Second Treatise*: "The first society was between man and wife, which gave beginning to that between parents and children; to which, in time, that between master and servant came to be added: And . . . all these might, and commonly did meet together and make up but

one Family" (John Locke, *Two Treatises of Government,* ed. Peter Laslett [Cambridge: Cambridge University Press, 1988], §77).

78. Chevalier Louis de Jaucourt, "Family, House," In *The Encyclopedia of Diderot & d'Alembert Collaborative Translation Project,* trans. J. E. Blanton (Ann Arbor: Michigan Publishing, University of Michigan Library, 2005). http://hdl .handle.net/2027/spo.did2222.0000.442 (accessed July 3, 2016). Originally published as "Famille, Maison," *Encyclopédie ou Dictionnaire raisonné des sciences, des arts et des métiers* (Paris, 1756) 6:392.

79. Jean-Louis Flandrin, *Families in Former Times: Kinship, Household, and Sexuality,* trans. Richard Southern (Cambridge: Cambridge University Press, 1979).

80. Differently from Foucault, Jacques Donzelot argues that by the eighteenth century the state went from being the rule of families to rule *through* the family and specifically fathers; by the late nineteenth century, psychoanalysis and social workers become implicated in such governance. For more on the historical development of the family and its connection to rule in the context of the *lettres de cachet,* see Jacques Donzelot, "Government through the Family," in *The Policing of Families,* trans. Robert Hurley (Baltimore: Johns Hopkins University Press, 1997). Foucault participates in a round table on social work with Donzelot and others originally published as the special edition "Normalisation et Contrôle social (Pourquoi le travail social?)," for *Esprit,* no. 413 (April–May 1972) and reprinted in Michel Foucault, *Dits et Écrits I, 1954–1975,* ed. Daniel Defert, François Ewald, and Jacques Lagrange (Paris: Gallimard, 2001), 1184–1207.

81. Pateman, *The Sexual Contract*; *The Disorder of Women: Democracy, Feminism, and Political Theory* (Stanford, Calif.: Stanford University Press, 1989).

82. Olympe de Gouges, *Declaration of the Rights of Woman and the Female Citizen,* in *Women in Revolutionary Paris 1789–1795: Selected Documents Translated with Notes and Commentary,* ed. Daline Gay Levy, Harriet Branson Applewhite, and Mary Durham Johnson (Urbana-Champaign: University of Illinois Press, 1979), 87–96, 95.

83. The definition for *famille* is retrieved from the ARTFL database, cooperatively produced by the Centre National de la Recherche Scientifique (CNRS) and the University Chicago. The entry can be retrieved at http://artflsrv02.uchicago .edu.ezp1.lib.umn.edu/cgi-bin/dicos/quickdict.pl?strippedhw=famille.

84. For a longer discussion of the economic risks of marriage, see Farge, *Fragile Lives.*

85. Families were their own sites of circulation; indeed, Julie Hardwick structures her research on eighteenth-century French families around economies of: marriage, justice, family politics, markets, and violence *(Family Business).*

86. Jaucourt writes these lines for the entry on "family" in Diderot's Encyclopedia. See Flandrin, *Families in Former Times,* 7.

87. *Mixité* is the term often used in contemporary French politics to discuss gender parity and, more recently, multicultural diversity. It is less a commitment to what North Americans might call "gender equality" or "affirmative action" than the copresence of men and women in a given context. The French Revolution interpreted *mixité* on the terms of gender complementarity. Girls and boys shared the same primary-school classrooms, but parted ways so as to prepare for the demands of domesticity (girls) and public life (boys). See Sylvain Parent, "Entretien avec Arlette Farge," *Tracés: Revue des Sciences humaines* 5 (spring 2004): 143–48, 145.

88. Farge and Foucault, *Disorderly Families,* 85.

60 *Introduction*

89. Ibid., 224.

90. Ibid., 94.

91. On the difficulties of obtaining divorce, see Giacomo Francini, "Divorce and Separations in Eighteenth-Century France: An Outline for a Social History of Law," *History of the Family* 2.1 (1997): 99–113; and Julie Hardwick, "Seeking Separations: Gender, Marriages, and the Household Economies in Early Modern France," *French Historical Studies* 21 (1998): 157–80.

92. Philippe Artières and Dominique Kalifa extend the analysis of personal correspondence and public attention in "L'Historien et les archives peronnelles: pas à pas," *Sociétés et Représentations* 1.13 (2002): 7–15.

93. Farge, *Subversive Words,* 23.

94. Ibid., 23–24.

95. Louis-Sébastien Mercier, *Tableau de Paris,* vol. 4 (Paris: Virchaux & Compagnie, 1781–89), 28.

96. Farge, *Subversive Words,* 110.

97. Quoted in Farge, "The Honor and Secrecy of Families," 598.

98. Foucault's preparatory dossiers for *Disorderly Families* contain several fiches with notes on Hegel's *Philosophy of Right* and German historians concerned with civil society, state, and ideology. In his inaugural lecture at the Collège de France (which appears in this volume), Foucault describes his era as "attempting to escape from Hegel," 170.

99. Foucault, *The Punitive Society,* 31. This quotation speaks directly to Foucault's preoccupation with Hegel in preparing the *Disorderly Families* manuscript.

100. Foucault, "Lives of Infamous Men," 83–84.

101. Ibid., 84.

102. As in *The Punitive Society,* the accent of *Disorderly Families* falls on the social and political struggles around "dangerous subjects" rather than those persons themselves. Foucault reprises that term in his lectures for *Psychiatric Power* and *Abnormal,* and at greater length in "About the Concept of the 'Dangerous Individual' in 19th Century Legal Psychiatry" (1078), republished in *Power.*

103. Foucault, "Lives of Infamous Men," 83.

104. For a longer discussion of the *secrétaires,* see *Disorderly Families,* 8–9.

105. Michel Foucault, "Questions of Method," in *The Foucault Effect: Studies in Governmentality: Studies in Governmentality,* ed. Graham Burchell, Colin Gordon, and Peter Miller (Chicago: University of Chicago Press, 1991), 74.

106. Foucault discusses events and history in *The Archaeology of Knowledge* (1969); discursive events in *Lectures on the Will to Know* (1971); events, history, and daily life in the interview "Le retour de Pierre Rivière" (1976); events, structures, and critique in an interview originally published in *Microfisica del potere: interventi politici* (1977); and finally eventialization in "What Is Critique?" (1978), as well as in the 1978 interview with Moriaki Watanabe, specialist in theater and French literature, in "La scène de la philosophie." And, of course, the language of events figures in Foucault's essays on Kant. See Michel Foucault, *The Archaeology of Knowledge,* trans. A. M. Sheridan Smith (New York: Pantheon Books, 1972); Michel Foucault, *Lectures on the Will to Know: Lectures at the Collège de France, 1970–1971,* trans. Graham Burchell (New York: Palgrave Macmillan, 2013); "Le retour de Pierre Rivière," reprinted in *Dits et Écrits II, 1976–1988,* ed. Daniel Defert, François Ewald, and Jacques Lagrange (Paris: Gallimard, 2001), 114–23; "Entretien avec Michel Foucault," in *Dits et Écrits II,* 140–60; "La scène de la philosophie," in *Dits et Écrits II,* 571–95.

Introduction 61

107. For examples of these phrases and other similar ones, see *Disorderly Families*, 41, 257, 260, 288; and "Lives of Infamous Men," 75.

108. Foucault uses this phrase in "Lives of Infamous Men," 81; in *Disorderly Families* he writes "characters out of Callot or Le Nain arriving in Versailles, desperate to make themselves heard" (257).

109. See, for example, Foucault's essay "Dire et voir chez Raymond Roussel," in *Dits et Écrits I, 1954–1975,* ed. Daniel Defert, François Ewald, and Jacques Lagrange (Paris: Gallimard, 2001), 233–43. Foucault writes: "The intimate secret of the secret is to be able to 'make appear,' thus hiding itself in a fundamental movement that is linked to the visible and is in harmony, with neither conflict nor misrepresentation, with the order of things . . . The event is buried—simultaneously present and beyond reach—in repetition, just as process is buried in narrative *[récit]* (at once structuring and eluding it)."

110. Foucault, *Lectures on the Will to Knowledge,* 194.

111. The Annales school emphasized continuity along three, imperfectly aligned, levels of history: geographic or epochal time *(histoire de la longue durée),* history of political and economic cycles *(l'histoire des conjonctures),* and the history of events *(l'histoire événementielle).* Foucault situates himself against the primary three ways of conceiving historical continuity in "On the Archaeology of the Sciences: Response to the Epistemology Circle," in *Aesthetics, Method, and Epistemology: Essential Works of Michel Foucault, 1954–84,* vol. 2, ed. James Faubion, trans. Robert Hurley et al. (New York: New Press, 1998).

112. Franco Moretti, *Signs Taken for Wonders: On the Sociology of Literary Forms* (New York: Verso, 2005), 13.

113. Already in 1970 Foucault had written about the Annales school in "Revenir à l'histoire," reprinted in *Dits et Écrits I, 1954–1975,* 1136–49. Farge and Foucault discuss their relation to French historians, and the influence of Robert Mandrou and Philippe Ariès on their work, in the interview with journalists F. Dumont and J.-P. Iommi-Amunategui, "Le style de l'histoire," *Le Matin,* no. 2168 (February 21, 1984), reprinted in *Dits et Écrits II, 1976–1988,* 1468–74.

114. *Microstoria,* or microhistory, "took a particular situation (normal because exceptional) and attempted to reconstruct the way individuals use alliances and confrontations to produce the social world through the ties of dependency that link them or set them apart. Hence the object of history was not—or was no longer—the structures and mechanisms, lying beyond all subjective grasp, that govern social relations but rather the multiple rationalities and strategies put into operation by communities, kinship groups, families, and individuals" (Roger Chartier, *On the Edge of the Cliff,* trans. Lydia G. Cochrane [Baltimore: Johns Hopkins University Press, 1997], 15).

115. In an early draft of "Lives of Infamous Men," Foucault writes: "One cannot draw from these reliable accounts of the living conditions of the popular classes. But if these living conditions are a part of reality, the manner of living them out is no less real, nor the way to react, to inflame one's passions, and to manifest these in relations with others" (BNF-Richelieu, Fonds Michel Foucault au département des manuscrits, NAF 28730, Boîte 68, poche 7, 8).

116. Sylvain Parent, "Entretien avec Arlette Farge," *Tracés: Revue de Sciences humaines* [online], vol. 5 (2004): 147. Translation is mine.

117. The essay "Lives of Infamous Men" draws on research conducted in part by Foucault's research assistant, Christiane Martin, who had a precarious economic background and passed away before the publication of *Disorderly Families.* Farge

62 *Introduction*

and Foucault dedicated the book to her and donated the royalties to her daughter. In an early draft of "Lives of Infamous Men," Foucault wrote: "A few years ago, my student Christiane Martin undertook to systematically survey this under-used material and produce an analysis in due form. Her work should have merited a choice better than this one. For if she had a thousand reasons to feel the intensity of [these letters], she floundered before the tasking of deciphering them. Death has since carried her away.

"I have not wished to take up and continue her work; others will do it, perhaps. But if I have decided to publish this short volume, rather than to continue on my own this collection of infamous lives that had really no reason to see the light of day, it's because she would have liked—she told me so herself—that one could read certain of these brief, anonymous, earth-bound *[terranées]* lives that can be found here" (BNF-Richelieu, Fonds Michel Foucault au département des manuscrits, NAF 28730, Boîte 68, poche 2).

118. Pierre Nora, "The Return of the Event," 201–2. A similar essay can be found in "L'événement monstre," *Communications* 18 (1972): 162–72.

119. Nora, "The Return of the Event," 203.

120. Michel Foucault, "What Is Critique?" 393. A few months earlier, he stated: "To eventialize singular ensembles of practices, to make them appear as different regimes of jurisdiction and veridiction—this is, on extremely barbaric terms, what I would like to do" ("Table ronde du mai 1978," 47).

121. Foucault takes Kant as a major pivot in modern philosophy for Kant's historicization of philosophic critique in "What Is Enlightenment?" and the effects of this historicization on philosophic reflection and political action. For a longer discussion, see Nancy Luxon, *Crisis of Authority: Politics, Trust and Truth-telling in Freud and Foucault* (Cambridge: Cambridge University Press, 2013); David Owen, *Maturity and Modernity* (New York: Routledge, 1994); Amy Allen, "Foucault and Enlightenment: A Critical Appraisal," *Constellations* 10.2 (June 2003): 180–98; Colin Gordon, "Question, Ethos, Event: Foucault on Kant and Enlightenment," *Economy and Society* 15.1 (February 1986): 71–87; Lynne Huffer, *Mad for Foucault: Rethinking the Foundations of Queer Theory* (New York: Columbia University Press, 2010).

122. Foucault, "What Is Critique?" 397.

123. Michel Foucault, "La scène de la philosophie," interview with Moriaki Watanabe, in *Dits et Écrits II,* 573. Watanabe is a specialist in French theater and literature, and opens the interview by asking why Foucault's writings are organized through motifs of the gaze and theatrical representation. The interview was conducted on April 22, 1978, and published in *Sekai* in July 1978.

124. Chartier, *On the Edge of the Cliff,* 74.

125. Philippe Artières, Jean-François Bert, Pascal Michon, Mathieu Potte-Bonneville, and Judith Revel, "Dans l'atelier de Michel Foucault," in *Lieux de savoir: Les mains de l'intellect,* vol. 2 (Paris: Éditions Albin Michel, 2011), 953.

126. BNF-Richelieu, Fonds Michel Foucault au département des manuscrits, NAF 28730, Boîte 67, poche 6.

127. Ibid., Boîte 68, poche 1.

128. Artières et al, "Dans l'atelier de Michel Foucault," 960.

129. Foucault, *Security, Territory, Population,* 20.

130. Farge and Foucault, *Disorderly Families,* 252.

131. Parent, "Entretien avec Arlette Farge," 147. Translation is mine.

132. Ibid., 84.

133. Émile Benveniste, *Le vocabulaire des institutions indo-européennes*, vol. 2 (Paris: Minuit, 1969), 150.

134. Foucault, *The Punitive Society*, 131.

135. Foucault, "Lives of Infamous Men," 74.

136. Ibid., 76.

137. Farge and Foucault, *Disorderly Families*, 252.

138. Ibid., 253.

139. I owe this insight to Garrett Johnson. See Foucault, *I, Pierre Rivière*, 112.

140. Philippe Artières, Arlette Farge, and Pierre Laborie, "Témoignage et Récit Historique," *Sociétés et Représentations* 13 (April 2002): 201–6, 203. This debate initially occurred during the broadcast "L'Histoire autrement" on radio station France Culture.

141. Foucault, "What Is Critique?" 397.

142. Foucault, *The Punitive Society*, 29ff.

143. Foucault refers to Kant's *Conflict of the Faculties* in *The Government of Self and Others: Lectures at the Collège de France, 1982–1983*, ed. Frédéric Gros, trans. Graham Burchell (New York: Palgrave Macmillan, 2010), 16.

144. Foucault, *The Punitive Society*, 51.

145. In 1972, Foucault speaks about the growing role of the police in dividing social groups, marginalizing "dangerous subjects," and impeding any popular justice, in "Popular Justice: A Conversation with Maoists," in *Power/Knowledge: Selected Interviews and Other Writings, 1972–1977*, ed. and trans. Colin Gordon, trans. Leo Marshall, John Mepham, and Kate Soper (New York: Pantheon Books, 1980). The idea that the *lettres de cachet* are ordinary people's first contact with power resonates with Shatema Threadcraft's notion of "intimate justice" (*Intimate Justice* [Oxford: Oxford University Press, 2016]).

146. Beth Richie, *Arrested Justice: Black Women, Violence, and America's Prison Nation* (New York: New York University Press, 2012). In this context, Richie's other work on the need for wraparound services to help those released from prison underscores that policy attention should be directed at the political and social regimes that bear on inequalities rather than at the "disorderly."

147. Jeanne Marie Laskas, "To Obama with Love, and Hate, and Desperation," *New York Times*, January 27, 2017, https://www.nytimes.com/2017/01/17/magazine/what-americans-wrote-to-obama.html.

148. For Farge and Foucault's analysis of the 1784 circular written by Breteuil, see *Disorderly Families*, 261–66.

149. Abbé Maury, *Archives parlementaires*, séance of March 13, 1790, vol. XII, 160.

PART I

Archival Materials
Audiences and Contexts

CHAPTER 1

Lives of Infamous Men (1977)

Michel Foucault

Michel Foucault began working in the archives of the Bastille and drew on the lettres de cachet *as early as* History of Madness *(1961), returning to them extensively in his lectures on* The Punitive Society *(1973). Aside from* Disorderly Families *(1982), the letters received their fullest attention in "Lives of Infamous Men," which was first published in 1977 in* Les Cahiers du chemin. *In this essay, Foucault writes about the singular lives contained in the familial* lettres de cachet *found in the archives of the Bastille. This short essay was written as an introduction for an "anthology of lives" to be published in the collection* Parallel Lives *(Gallimard), a version that was scrapped as Foucault fell out with editor Pierre Nora. More lyrical than the essay that precedes the published letters, it reflects on the interpretive movement that begins with aesthetic startlement. These poem-lives have neither history nor future. They oblige the reader to work through their emotional intensities and factual uncertainties to construct a framework of interpretation.* ◆

This is not a book of history. The selection found here was guided by nothing more substantial than my taste, my pleasure, an emotion, laughter, surprise, a certain dread, or some other feeling whose intensity I might have trouble justifying, now that the first moment of discovery has passed.

It's an anthology of existences. Lives of a few lines or a few pages, nameless misfortunes and adventures gathered into a handful of words. Brief lives, encountered by chance in books and documents. *Exempla,*

68 *Michel Foucault*

but unlike those collected by the sages in the course of their reading, they are examples that convey not so much lessons to ponder as brief effects whose force fades almost at once. The term "news" would fit them rather well, I think, because of the double reference it suggests: to the rapid pace of the narrative and to the reality of the events that are related. For the things said in these texts are so compressed that one isn't sure whether the intensity that sparks through them is due more to the vividness of the words or to the jostling violence of the facts they tell. Singular lives, transformed into strange poems through who knows what twists of fate—that is what I decided to gather into a kind of herbarium.

As I recall, the idea came to me one day when I was reading, at the Bibliothèque Nationale, a record of internment written at the very beginning of the eighteenth century. If I'm not mistaken, it occurred to me as I read these two notices:

> Mathurin Milan, placed in the hospital of Charenton, 31 August 1707: "His madness was always to hide from his family, to lead an obscure life in the country, to have actions at law, to lend usuriously and without security, to lead his feeble mind down unknown paths, and to believe himself capable of the greatest employments."

> Jean Antoine Touzard, placed in the castle of Bicêtre, 21 April 1701: "Seditious apostate friar, capable of the greatest crimes, sodomite, atheist if that were possible; this individual is a veritable monster of abomination whom it would be better to stifle than to leave at large."

It would be hard to say exactly what I felt when I read these fragments and many others that were similar. No doubt, one of these impressions that are called "physical," as if there could be any other kind. I admit that these "short stories," suddenly emerging from two and a half centuries of silence, stirred more fibers within me than what is ordinarily called "literature," without my being able to say even now if I was more moved by the beauty of that Classical style, draped in a few sentences around characters that were plainly wretched, or by the excesses, the blend of dark stubbornness and rascality, of these lives whose disarray and relentless energy one senses beneath the stone-smooth words.

A long time ago I made use of documents like these for a book. If I did so back then, it was doubtless because of the resonance I still experience today when I happen to encounter these lowly lives reduced to ashes in the few sentences that struck them down. The dream would have been to restore their intensity in an analysis. Lacking the necessary talent, I brooded over the analysis alone. I considered the texts in their dryness, trying to determine their reason for being, what institutions or what political practice they referred to, seeking to understand why it had suddenly been so important in a society like ours to "stifle" (as one stifles a cry, smothers a fire, or strangles an animal) a scandalous monk or a peculiar and inconsequential usurer. I looked for the reason why people were so zealous to prevent the feebleminded from walking down unknown paths. But the first intensities that had motivated me remained excluded. And since there was a good chance that they wouldn't enter into the order of reasons at all, seeing that my discourse was incapable of conveying them in the necessary way, wouldn't it be better to leave them in the very form that had caused me to first feel them?

Whence the idea of this collection, done more or less as the occasion arose. A collection compiled without haste and without a clear purpose. For a long time I thought of presenting it in a systematic order, with a few rudiments of explanation, and in such a way that it would exhibit a minimum of historical significance. I decided against this, for reasons that I will come back to later. I resolved simply to assemble a certain number of texts, for the intensity they seem to me to have. I have appended a few preliminary remarks to them, and I have distributed them so as to preserve, as best I could, the effect of each.

So, this book will not answer the purpose of historians, even less than it will others'. A mood-based and purely subjective book? I would say rather—but it may come to the same thing—that it's a rule- and game-based book, the book of a little obsession that found its system. I think that the poem of the oddball usurer or that of the sodomite monk served as a model throughout. It was in order to recapture something like those flash existences, those poem-lives, that I laid down a certain number of simple rules for myself:

- The persons included must have actually existed.
- These existences must have been both obscure and ill-fated.
- They must have been recounted in a few pages or, better, a few sentences, as brief as possible.

70   *Michel Foucault*

- These tales must not just constitute strange or pathetic anecdotes; but, in one way or another (because they were complaints, denunciations, orders, or reports), they must have truly formed part of the minuscule history of these existences, of their misfortune, their wildness, or their dubious madness.
- And for us still, the shock of these words must give rise to a certain effect of beauty mixed with dread.

But I should say a little more about these rules that may appear arbitrary.

I wanted it always to be a matter of real existences: that one might be able to give them a place and a date; that behind these names that no longer say anything, behind these quick words which may well have been false, mendacious, unjust, exaggerated, there were men who lived and died, with sufferings, meannesses, jealousies, vociferations. So, I excluded everything in the way of imagination or literature: none of the dark heroes that the latter have invented appeared as intense to me as these cobblers, these army deserters, these garment sellers, these scriveners, these vagabond monks, all of them rabid, scandalous, or pitiful. And this was owing, no doubt, to the mere fact that they are known to have lived. I likewise ruled out all the texts that might be memoirs, recollections, tableaus, all those recounting a slice of reality but keeping the distance of observation, of memory, of curiosity, or of amusement. I was determined that these texts always be in a relation or, rather, in the greatest possible number of relations with reality: not only that they refer to it, but they be operative within it; that they form part of the dramaturgy of the real; that they constitute the instrument of a retaliation, the weapon of a hatred, an episode in a battle, the gesticulation of a despair or a jealousy, an entreaty or an order. I didn't try to bring together texts that would be more faithful to reality than others, that would merit inclusion for their representative value, but, rather, texts that played a part in the reality they speak of—and that, in return, whatever their inaccuracy, their exaggeration, or their hypocrisy, are traversed by it: fragments of discourse trailing the fragments of a reality they are part of. One won't see a collection of verbal portraits here, but traps, weapons, cries, gestures, attitudes, ruses, intrigues for which words were the instruments. Real lives were "enacted" *["jouées"]* in these few sentences: by this I don't mean that they were represented but that their liberty, their misfortune, often their death, in any case their fate, were actually decided therein, at least in part. These discourses really crossed lives; existences were actually risked and lost in these words.

Another requirement of mine was that these personages themselves be obscure; that nothing would have prepared them for any notoriety; that they would not have been endowed with any of the established and recognized nobilities—those of birth, fortune, saintliness, heroism, or genius; that they would have belonged to those billions of existences destined to pass away without a trace; that in their misfortunes, their passions, in those loves and hatreds there would be something gray and ordinary in comparison with what is usually deemed worthy of being recounted; that, nevertheless, they be propelled by a violence, an energy, an excess expressed in the malice, vileness, baseness, obstinacy, or ill-fortune this gave them in the eyes of their fellows—and in proportion to its very mediocrity, a sort of appalling or pitiful grandeur. I had gone in search of these sorts of particles endowed with an energy all the greater for their being small and difficult to discern.

But in order for some part of them to reach us, a beam of light had to illuminate them, for a moment at least. A light coming from elsewhere. What snatched them from the darkness in which they could, perhaps should, have remained was the encounter with power; without that collision, it's very unlikely that any word would be there to recall their fleeting trajectory. The power that watched these lives, that pursued them, that lent its attention, if only for a moment, to their complaints and their little racket, and marked them with its claw was what gave rise to the few words about them that remain for us— either because someone decided to appeal to it in order to denounce, complain, solicit, entreat, or because he chose to intervene and in a few words to judge and decide. All those lives destined to pass beneath any discourse and disappear without ever having been told were able to leave traces—brief, incisive, often enigmatic—only at the point of their instantaneous contact with power. So that it is doubtless impossible to ever grasp them again in themselves, as they might have been "in a free state"; they can no longer be separated out from the declamations, the tactical biases, the obligatory lies that power games and power relations presuppose.

I will be told: "That's so like you, always with the same inability to cross the line, to pass to the other side, to listen and convey the language

72 *Michel Foucault*

that comes from elsewhere or from below; always the same choice, on the side of power, of what it says or causes to be said. Why not go listen to these lives where they speak in their own voice?" But, first of all, would anything at all remain of what they were in their violence or in their singular misfortune had they not, at a given moment, met up with power and provoked its forces? Is it not one of the fundamental traits of our society, after all, that destiny takes the form of a relation with power, of a struggle with or against it? Indeed, the most intense point of a life, the point where its energy is concentrated, is where it comes up against power, struggles with it, attempts to use its forces and to evade its traps. The brief and strident words that went back and forth between power and the most inessential existences doubtless constitute, for the latter, the only monument they have ever been granted: it is what gives them, for the passage through time, the bit of brilliance, the brief flash that carries them to us.

In short, I wanted to assemble a few rudiments for a legend of obscure men, out of the discourses that, in sorrow or in rage, they exchanged with power.

A "legend" because, as in all legends, there is a certain ambiguity between the fictional and the real—but it occurs for opposite reasons. Whatever its kernel of reality, the legendary is nothing else, finally, but the sum of what is said about it. It is indifferent to the existence or nonexistence of the persons whose glory it transmits. If they existed, the legend covers them with so many wonders, embellishing them with so many impossibilities, that it's almost as if they had never lived. And if they are purely imaginary, the legend reports so many insistent tales about them that they take on the historical thickness of someone who existed. In the texts that follow, the existence of these men and women comes down to exactly what was said about them: nothing subsists of what they were or what they did, other than what is found in a few sentences. Here it is rarity and not prolixity that makes reality equivalent to fiction. Having been nothing in history, having played no appreciable role in events or among important people, having left no identifiable trace around them, they don't have and never will have any existence outside the precarious domicile of these words. And through those texts which tell about them, they come down to us bearing no more of the markings of reality than if they had come from *La Légende dorée* or from an adventure novel.[1] This purely verbal existence, which makes these forlorn or villainous individuals into quasi-fictional beings, is due to their nearly complete disappearance, and to that luck or mischance which resulted in the survival, through the peradventure of rediscovered documents, of a scarce few words that speak of them or that are pronounced by them. A dark but, above all, a dry legend, reduced to what was said one day and preserved down to our day by improbable encounters.

That is another trait of this dark legend. It has not been transmitted like one that was gilded by some deep necessity, following continuous paths. By nature, it is bereft of any tradition; discontinuities, effacement, oblivion, convergences, reappearances: this is the only way it can reach us. Chance carries it from the beginning. It first required a combination of circumstances that, contrary to all expectations, focused the attention of power and the outburst of its anger on the most obscure individual, on his mediocre life, on his (after all, rather ordinary) faults: a stroke of misfortune that caused the vigilance of officials or of institutions, aimed no doubt at suppressing all disorder, to pick on this person rather than that, this scandalous monk, this beaten woman, this inveterate and furious drunkard, this quarrelsome merchant, and not so many others who were making just as much of a ruckus. And then it had to be just this document, among so many others scattered and lost, which came down to us and be rediscovered and read. So that between these people of no importance and us who have no more importance than they, there is no necessary connection. Nothing made it likely for them to emerge from the shadows, they instead of others, with their lives and their sorrows. We may amuse ourselves, if we wish, by seeing a revenge in this: the chance that enabled these absolutely undistinguished people to emerge from their place amid the dead multitudes, to gesticulate again, to manifest their rage, their affliction, or their invincible determination to err—perhaps it makes up for the bad luck that brought power's lightning bolt down upon them, in spite of their modesty and anonymity.

Lives that are as though they hadn't been, that survive only from the clash with a power that wished only to annihilate them or at least to obliterate them, lives that come back to us only through the effect of multiple accidents—these are the infamies that I wanted to assemble here in the form of a few remains. There exists a false infamy, the kind with which those men of terror or scandal, Gilles de Rais, Guillery or Cartouche, Sade and Lacenaire, are blessed.[2] Apparently infamous, because of the abominable memories they have left, the misdeeds

74   *Michel Foucault*

attributed to them, the respectful horror they have inspired, they are actually men of glorious legend, even if the reasons for that renown are the opposite of those that constitute or ought to constitute the greatness of men. Their infamy is only a modality of the universal *fama*. But the apostate friar, the feeble minds lost on unknown paths, those are infamous in the strict sense: they no longer exist except through the terrible words that were destined to render them forever unworthy of the memory of men. And chance determined that these words, these words alone, would subsist. The return of these lives to reality occurs in the very form in which they were driven out of the world. Useless to look for another face for them, or to suspect a different greatness in them; they are no longer anything but that which was meant to crush them—neither more nor less. Such is infamy in the strict sense, the infamy that, being unmixed with ambiguous scandal or unspoken admiration, has nothing to do with any sort of glory.

In comparison with infamy's great collection, which would gather its traces from everywhere and all times, I'm well aware that the selection here is paltry, narrow, a bit monotonous. It comprises documents that all date approximately from the same hundred years, 1660–1760, and come from the same source: archives of confinement, of the police, of petitions to the king, and of *lettres de cachet*. Let us suppose that this may be a first volume and that *Lives of Infamous Men* will be extended to other times and other places.

I chose this period and this type of texts because of an old familiarity. But if the taste I've had for them for years has not diminished, and if I come back to them now, it's because I suspect they manifest a beginning, or at any rate an important event, in which political mechanisms and discursive effects intersected.

These texts from the seventeenth and eighteenth centuries (especially when compared with the flatness of later administrative and police documents) display a brilliance, reveal a splendor of phrasing, a vehemence that belies, in our judgment at least, the pettiness of the affair or the rather shameful meanness of intent. The most pitiful lives are described with the imprecations or emphasis that would seem to suit the most tragic. A comical effect, no doubt: there is something ludicrous in summoning all the power of words, and through them the supreme power of heaven and earth, around insignificant disorders or such ordinary woes. "Unable to bear the weight of the most excessive sorrow, the clerk Duschene ventures, with a humble and respectful confidence, to throw himself at the feet of Your Majesty to implore his justice against the cruelest of all women . . . What hope must not rise in the breast of this unfortunate one who, reduced to the last extremity, today appeals to Your Majesty after having exhausted all the ways of gentleness, remonstrance, and consideration to bring back to her duty a wife who lacks all sentiment of religion, honor, probity, and even humanity? Such is, Sire, the state of this poor wretch who dares to voice his plaintive appeal to the ears of Your Majesty." Or that abandoned wet nurse who asks for the arrest of her husband on behalf of her four children "who may have nothing to expect from their father but a terrible example of the effects of disorder. Your justice, my Lord, will surely spare them such a degrading lesson, will prevent opprobrium and infamy for me and my family, by rendering incapable of doing any injury to society a bad citizen who will not fail to bring it harm." We may laugh at this, but it should be kept in mind that to this rhetoric, grandiloquent only because of the smallness of the things to which it is applied, power responds in terms that appear no less excessive—with the difference that its words convey the fulguration of its decisions—and their solemnity may be warranted, if not by the importance of what they punish, then by the harshness of the penalty they impose. If some caster of horoscopes is locked up, this is because "there are few crimes she has not committed, and none of which she is not capable. So there is as much charity as justice in immediately ridding the public of so dangerous a woman, who has robbed it, duped it, and scandalized it with impunity for so many years." And about a young addlebrain, a bad son and a ne'er-do-well: "He is a monster of libertinage and impiety . . . Practices all the vices: knavish, disobedient, impetuous, violent, capable of deliberate attacks on the life of his own father . . . always in the company of the worst prostitutes. Nothing that is said about his knaveries and profligacies makes any impression on his heart; he responds only with a scoundrel's smile that communicates his callousness and gives no reason to think he is anything short of incurable." With the least peccadillo, one is always in the abominable, or at least in the discourse of invective and execration. These loose women and these unruly children do not pale next to Nero or Rodogune. The discourse of power in the Classical age, like the discourses addressed to it, produces monsters. Why this emphatic theater of the quotidian?

Christianity had in large part organized power's hold on the ordinary preoccupations of life: an obligation to run the minuscule everyday world regularly through the mill of language, revealing the common faults, the imperceptible failings even, and down to the murky interplay of thoughts, intentions, and desires; a ritual of confession in which the one speaking is at the same time the one spoken about; an effacement of the thing said by its very utterance, but also with an augmentation of the confession itself, which must remain secret, and not leave any other trace behind it but repentance and acts of contrition. The Christian West invented that astonishing constraint, which it imposed on everyone, to tell everything in order to efface everything, to express even the most minor faults in an unbroken, relentless, exhaustive murmur which nothing must elude, but which must not outlive itself even for a moment. For hundreds of millions of men and over a period of centuries, evil had to be confessed in the first person, in an obligatory and ephemeral whisper.

But, from the end of the seventeenth century, this mechanism was encircled and outreached by another one whose operation was very different. An administrative and no longer a religious apparatus; a recording mechanism instead of a pardoning mechanism. The objective was the same, however, at least in part: to bring the quotidian into discourse, to survey the tiny universe of irregularities and unimportant disorders. In this system, though, confession does not play the eminent role that Christianity had reserved for it. For this social mapping and control, long-standing procedures are used, but ones that had been localized up to then: the denunciation, the complaint, the inquiry, the report, spying, the interrogation. And everything that is said in this way is noted down in writing, is accumulated, is gathered into dossiers and archives. The single, instantaneous, and traceless voice of the penitential confession that effaced evil as it effaced itself would now be supplanted by multiple voices, which were to be deposited in an enormous documentary mass and thus constitute, through time, a sort of constantly growing record of all the world's woes. The minuscule trouble of misery and transgression is no longer sent to heaven through the scarcely audible confidence of the confession: it accumulates on earth in the form of written traces. An entirely different type of relations is established between power, discourse, and the quotidian, an altogether different way governing the latter and of formulating it. For ordinary life, a new mise-en-scène is born.

We are familiar with its first instruments, archaic but already complex: they are the petitions, the *lettres de cachet* or king's orders, the various internments, the police reports and decisions. I won't go back over these things, which are already well known; I'll just recall certain aspects that may account for the strange intensity, and for a kind of beauty that sometimes emanates from these hastily drawn images in which unfortunate men assume, for us who perceive them from such a great distance, the guise of infamy. The *lettre de cachet,* internment, the generalized presence of the police—all that usually evokes only the despotism of an absolute monarchy. But one cannot help but see that this "arbitrariness" was a kind of public service. Except in the rarest of cases, the "king's orders" did not strike without warning, crashing down from above as signs of the monarch's anger. More often than not, they were requested against someone by his entourage—his father and mother, one of his relatives, his family, his sons or daughters, his neighbors, the local priest on occasion, or some notable. They were solicited for some obscure family trouble, as if it involved a great crime meriting the sovereign's wrath: rejected or abused spouses, a squandered fortune, conflicts of interest, disobedient young people, knavery or carousing, and all the little disorders of conduct. The *lettre de cachet* that was presented as the express and particular will of the king to have one of his subjects confined, outside the channels of regular justice, was nothing more than the response to such petitions coming from below. But it was not freely granted to anyone requesting it: an inquiry must precede it, for the purpose of substantiating the claims made in the petition. It needed to establish whether the debauchery or drunken spree, the violence or the libertinage, called for an internment, and under what conditions and for how long—a job for the police, who would collect statements by witnesses, information from spies, and all the haze of doubtful rumor that forms around each individual.

The system of *lettre de cachet* and internment was only a rather brief episode, lasting for little more than a century and limited to France. But it is nonetheless important in the history of power mechanisms. It did not bring about the uninvited intrusion of royal arbitrariness in the most everyday dimension of life. It ensured, rather, the distribution of that power through complex circuits and a whole interplay of petitions and responses. An absolutist abuse? Maybe so, yet not in the sense that the absolute monarch purely and simply abused his own power; rather, in the sense that each individual could avail himself, for his own ends and against others, of absolute power in its enormity—a sort of placing of the mechanisms of sovereignty at one's disposal, an

78 *Michel Foucault*

opportunity to divert its effects to one's own benefit, for anyone clever enough to capture them. A certain number of consequences followed from this: political sovereignty penetrated into the most elementary dimension of the social body; the resources of an absolutist political power, beyond the traditional weapons of authority and submission, could be brought into play between subject and subject, sometimes the most humble of them, between family members and between neighbors, and in relations of interests, of profession, of rivalry, of love and hate. Providing one knew how to play the game, every individual could become for the other a terrible and lawless monarch: *homo homini rex.* A whole political network became interwoven with the fabric of everyday life. But it was still necessary, at least for a moment, to appropriate this power, channel it, capture it, and bend it in the direction one wanted; if one meant to take advantage of it, it was necessary to "seduce" it. It became both an object of covetousness and an object of seduction; it was desirable, then, precisely insofar as it was dreadful. The intervention of a limitless political power in everyday relations thus became not only acceptable and familiar but deeply condoned—not without becoming, from that very fact, the theme of a generalized fear. We should not be surprised at this inclination which, little by little, opened up the relations of appurtenance or dependence that traditionally connect the family to administrative and political controls. Nor should we be surprised that the king's boundless power, thus operating in the midst of passions, rages, miseries, and mischiefs, was able to become—despite or perhaps even because of its utility—an object of execration. Those who resorted to the *lettres de cachet* and the king who granted them were caught in the trap of their complicity: the first lost more and more of their traditional prerogatives to an administrative authority. As for the king, he became detestable from having meddled on a daily basis in so many hatreds and intrigues. As I recall, it was the Duke de Chaulieu who said, in the *Mémoires de deux jeunes mariées,* that by cutting off the king's head, the French Revolution decapitated all family men.[3]

For the moment, I would like to single out one element from all the foregoing: with this apparatus comprising petitions, *lettres de cachet,* internment, and police, there would issue an endless number of discourses that would pervade daily life and take charge of the minuscule ills of insignificant lives, but in a completely different manner from the confession. Neighborhood disputes, the quarrels of parents and children, misunderstandings between couples, the excesses of wine and sex, public altercations, and many secret passions would all be caught in the nets of power that stretched through rather complex circuits. There was a kind of immense and omnipresent call for the processing of these disturbances and these petty sufferings into discourse. An unending hum began to be heard, the sound of the discourse that delivered individual variations of behavior, shames, and secrets into the grip of power. The commonplace ceased to belong to silence, to the passing rumor or the fleeting confession. All those ingredients of the ordinary, the unimportant detail, obscurity, unexceptional days, community life, could and must be told—better still, written down. They became describable and transcribable, precisely insofar as they were traversed by the mechanisms of a political power. For a long time, only the actions of great men had merited being told without mockery: only blood, birth, and exploit gave a right to history. And if it sometimes happened that the lowliest men acceded to a kind of glory, this was by virtue of some extraordinary fact—the distinction of a saintliness or the enormity of a crime. There was never a thought that there might be, in the everyday run of things, something like a secret to raise, that the inessential might be, in a certain way, important, until the blank gaze of power came to rest on these minuscule commotions.

The birth, consequently, of an immense possibility for discourse. A certain knowledge of the quotidian had a part at least in its origin, together with a grid of intelligibility that the West undertook to extend over our actions, our ways of being and of behaving. But the birth in question depended also on the real and virtual omnipresence of the monarch; one had to imagine him sufficiently near to all those miseries, sufficiently attentive to the least of those disorders, before one could attempt to invoke him: he had to seem endowed with a kind of physical ubiquity himself. In its first form, this discourse concerning the quotidian was turned entirely toward the king; it was addressed to him; it had to slip into the great ceremonious rituals of power; it had to adopt their form and take on their signs. The commonplace could be told, described, observed, categorized, and indexed only within a power relation that was haunted by the figure of the king—by his real power or by the specter of his might. Hence the peculiar form of that discourse: it required a decorative, imprecatory, or supplicating language. All those little everyday squabbles had to be told with the emphasis of rare events worthy of royal attention; these inconsequential affairs had to be dressed up in grand rhetoric. In subsequent periods, neither the dreary reports of police administration nor the case histories of medicine or psychiatry would ever recapture such effects of language. At times, a sumptuous verbal edifice for relating an obscure piece of meanness or a minor intrigue; at others, a few brief sentences that strike down a poor wretch and plunge him back into his darkness; or the long tale of sorrows recounted in the form of supplication and humility. The political discourse of banality could not be anything but solemn.

But these texts also manifested another effect of incongruity. It often happened that the petitions for internment were lodged by illiterate or semiliterate persons of humble circumstance; they themselves, with their meager skills, or an underqualified scribe in their place, would compose as best they could the formulas or turns of phrase they believed to be required when one addressed the king or high officials, and they would stir in words that were awkward and violent, loutish expressions by which they hoped no doubt to give their petitions more force and truthfulness. In this way, crude, clumsy, and jarring expressions would suddenly appear in the midst of solemn and disjointed sentences, alongside nonsensical words; the obligatory and ritualistic language would be interspersed with outbursts of impatience, anger, rage, passion, rancor, and rebellion. The rules of this stilted discourse were thus upset by a vibration, by wild intensities muscling in with their own ways of saying things. This is how the wife of Nicolas Bienfait speaks: she "takes the liberty of representing very humbly to your Lordship that said Nicolas Bienfait, coachman, is a highly debauched man who is killing her with blows, and who is selling everything having already caused the deaths of his two wives, the first of whom he killed her child in the body, the second of whom after having sold and eaten what was hers, by his bad treatment caused her to die from languishment, even trying to strangle her on the eve of her death. . . . The third, he wishes to eat her heart on the grill, not to mention many other murders he did. My Lord, I throw myself at the feet of Your Highness to beseech Your Mercy. I hope that from your goodness you will render me justice, because my life being risked at every moment, I shall not cease praying to God for the preservation of your health."

The texts that I've brought together here are homogeneous, and they may well appear monotonous. Yet they function in the element of disparity. A disparity between the things recounted and the manner of telling them; a disparity between those who complain and those who have every power over them; a disparity between the minuscule order of the problems raised and the enormity of the power brought into play; a disparity between the language of ceremony and power and that of rage or helplessness. These are texts that nod in the direction of Racine, or Bossuet, or Crébillon; but they convey a whole stock of popular turbulence, of misery, and violence, of "baseness" as it was called, that no literature in that period could have accommodated. They bring tramps, poor wretches, or simply mediocre individuals onto a strange stage where they strike poses, speechify, and declaim, where they drape themselves in the bits of cloth they need if they wish to draw attention in the theater of power. At times they remind one of a poor troupe of jugglers and clowns who deck themselves out in makeshift scraps of old finery to play before an audience of aristocrats who will make fun of them. Except that they are staking their whole life on the performance: they are playing before powerful men who can decide their fate. Characters out of Céline, trying to make themselves heard at Versailles.

One day, all this incongruity would be swept away. Power exercised at the level of everyday life would no longer be that of a near and distant, omnipotent, and capricious monarch, the source of all justice and an object of every sort of enticement, both a political principle and a magical authority; it would be made up of a fine, differentiated, continuous network, in which the various institutions of the judiciary, the police, medicine, and psychiatry would operate hand in hand. And the discourse that would then take form would no longer have that old artificial and clumsy theatricality: it would develop in a language that would claim to be that of observation and neutrality. The commonplace would be analyzed through the efficient but colorless categories of administration, journalism, and science—unless one goes a little further to seek out its splendors in the domain of literature. In the seventeenth and eighteenth centuries, we are still in the rough and barbarous age when all these mediations don't exist: the body of the *misérables* is brought into almost direct contact with that of the king, their agitation with his ceremonies. There, not even a shared language but, rather, a clash between the cries and the rituals, between the disorders to be told and the rigor of the forms that must be followed. Whence, for us who look from afar at that first upsurge of the everyday into the code of the political, the strange fulgurations that appear, something gaudy and intense that will later be lost, when these things and these men will be made into "matters," into incidents or cases.

An important moment, this one, when a society lent words, turns of phrase, and sentences, language rituals to the anonymous mass of people so that they might speak of themselves—speak publicly and on the triple condition that their discourse be uttered and put in circulation within a well-defined apparatus of power; that it reveal the hitherto barely perceptible lower depths of social existence, and through the access provided by that diminutive war of passions and interests, it offer power the possibility of a sovereign intervention. Dionysius's ear was a small, rudimentary machine by comparison. How light power would be, and easy to dismantle no doubt, if all it did was to observe, spy, detect, prohibit, and punish; but it incites, provokes, produces. It is not simply eye and ear: it makes people act and speak.

This machinery was doubtless important for the constitution of new knowledges *[savoirs]*. It was not unconnected, moreover, with a whole new regime of literature. I don't mean to say that the *lettre de cachet* was at the point of origin of new literary forms; rather, that at the turn of the seventeenth and eighteenth centuries relations of discourse, power, everyday life, and truth were knotted together in a new way, one in which literature was also entangled.

The fable, in the proper sense of the word, is that which deserves to be told. For a long time in Western society, everyday life could accede to discourse only if it was traversed and transfigured by the legendary: it had to be drawn out of itself by heroism, the exploit, adventures, Providence and grace, or occasionally the heinous crime. It needed to be marked with a touch of impossibility—only then did it become expressible. What made it inaccessible enabled it to function as lesson and example. The more extraordinary the tale, the more capable it was of casting a spell or of persuading. In this game of the "exemplary fabulous," indifference to truth and untruth was therefore fundamental. If someone happened to describe the shabby side of reality, this was mainly to produce a comical effect: the mere fact of talking about it made people laugh.

Starting in the seventeenth century, the West saw the emergence of a whole "fable" of obscure life, from which the fabulous was banished. The impossible or the ridiculous ceased to be the condition under which the ordinary could be recounted. An art of language was born whose task was no longer to tell of the improbable but to bring into view that which doesn't, which can't and mustn't, appear—to tell the last and most tenuous degrees of the real. Just as an apparatus was being installed for forcing people to tell the "insignificant" ["l'infime"]—that which isn't told, which doesn't merit any glory, therefore, the "infamous"—a new imperative was forming that would constitute what could be called the "immanent ethic" of Western literary discourse. Its ceremonial functions would gradually fade; it would no longer have the task of manifesting in a tangible way the all too visible radiance of force, grace, heroism, and might but, rather, of searching for the things hardest to perceive—the most hidden, hardest to tell and to show, and lastly most forbidden and scandalous. A kind of injunction to ferret out the most nocturnal and most quotidian elements of existence (even if this sometimes meant discovering the solemn figures of fate) would mark out the course that literature would follow from the seventeenth century onward, from the time it began to be literature in the modern sense of the word. More than a specific form, more than an essential connection with form, it was this constraint—I was about to say "principle"—that characterized literature and carried its immense movement all the way to us: an obligation to tell the most common of secrets. Literature does not epitomize this great policy, this great discursive ethic by itself; and, certainly, there is more to literature than that; but that is where it has its locus and its conditions of existence.

Whence its dual relation to truth and to power. Whereas the fabulous could function only in a suspension between true and false, literature based itself, rather, on a decision of nontruth: it explicitly presented itself as artifice while promising to produce effects of truth that were recognizable as such. The importance that was given, in the Classical period, to naturalness and imitation was doubtless one of the first ways of formulating this functioning of literature "in truth." Fiction thus replaced fable, the novel broke free of the fantastical and was able to develop only by freeing itself from it ever more completely. Hence, literature belongs to the great system of constraint by which the West obliged the quotidian to enter into discourse. But literature occupies a special place within that system: determined to seek out the quotidian beneath the quotidian itself, to cross boundaries, to ruthlessly or insidiously bring our secrets out in the open, to displace rules

84 *Michel Foucault*

and codes, to compel the unmentionable to be told, it will thus tend to place itself outside the law, or at least to take on the burden of scandal, transgression, or revolt. More than any other form of language, it remains the discourse of "infamy": it has the duty of saying what is most resistant to being said—the worst, the most secret, the most insufferable, the shameless. The fascination that psychoanalysis and literature have exerted on each other for years is significant in this connection. But it should not be forgotten that this singular position of literature is only the effect of a certain system *[dispositif]* of power that traverses the economy of discourses and strategies of truth in the West.

I began by saying that these texts might be read as so many "short stories." That was saying too much, no doubt; none of them will ever measure up to the least tale by Chekhov, Maupassant, or James. Neither "quasi" nor "subliterature," they are not even the first sketch of a genre; they are the action, in disorder, noise, and pain, of power on lives, and the discourse that comes of it. *Manon Lescaut* tells one of the stories that are presented here.[4]

NOTES

1. This is the name given to the collection of lives of saints that was compiled in the eighteenth century by the Dominican Jacques de Vorágine, *La Légende dorée* (Paris: Garnier-Flammarion nos. 132–35, 1967), 2 vols.

2. Gilles de Rais was the original Bluebeard (he killed six of his wives, and was discovered by his seventh); Cartouche was a famous highwayman; Sade is the Marquis de Sade, after whom "sadism" is named; Lacenaire was a serial murderer condemned to death during Louis-Bonaparte's tenure (1840s), and also the author of a notorious memoir of his exploits.

3. This is an allusion to remarks by the Duke de Chaulieu, reported in the *Lettre de Mademoiselle de Chaulieu à Madame de L'Estorade,* in Honoré de Balzac, *Mémoires de deux jeunes mariées* (Paris: Librairie nouvelle, 1856), 59: "En coupant la tête à Louis XVI, la Révolution a coupé la tête à tous les pères de famille."

4. A. F. Prévost, *Les Aventures du chevalier Des Grieux et de Manon Lescaut* (Amsterdam, 1733).

CHAPTER 2

"All about the Lettres de Cachet*"*   (1983)

André Béjin, Roger Chartier, Arlette Farge, Michel Foucault, and Michelle Perrot

One of the few roundtables or reviews on Disorderly Families, *this broadcast of the radio show* Les Lundis de l'histoire *(History Mondays) brought together Michel Foucault, Arlette Farge, historian Michelle Perrot, sociologist André Béjin, and historian Roger Chartier as moderator. During the broadcast, Farge and Foucault explain their writing process, their selection of the volume's letters, the historical context of eighteenth-century Paris, and general patterns that emerge. Participants discuss the mise-en-scène created by the letters when juxtaposing stylized language with ideologies of family and state. Dispute erupts around Farge and Foucault's claims that the paternal and political orders did not obviously overlap; that these letters do not demonstrate the abuse of royal power but instead their popular appeal; and over the political potentials in "speaking so as not to be spoken about." The radio address illuminates Foucault's efforts to cast the eighteenth century as caught between two different logics of politics: the sovereign and the governmental.*   ➴

MODERATOR: To begin today's show, we will listen to two petitions. Both date back to the year 1728 and come from the archives of the Bastille, which are now stored in the Bibliothèque de l'Arsenal. Both were addressed to "My Lord the Lieutenant General of Police of Paris." The first tells of the worries and fears of a mother and father.

86 *"All about the* Lettres de Cachet*"*

Arlette Farge reads the letter written by Jean-Jacques Cailly

To My Lord
the Lieutenent General of Police

Jean Jacques Cailly lawyer in the Parliament and Marie Madeleine du Poys his wife most humbly beseech, stating that Marc René Cailly their son age twenty-one, forgetting the good education that they gave him frequents only prostituted women and persons of ill repute with whom he has delivered himself to such an outrageous debauch, that it is to be feared that the consequences for him will be dire, it is in order to forestall this that the suppliants, after having vainly remonstrated with their son to recall him to his duty, and that he live a more orderly life, appeal unto the authority of Monsieur.

In consideration of this, Monsieur, may it please you, to order that Marc René Cailly, the supplicants' son be taken to the house of the H. Fathers [R. *Pères*] of Saint-Lazare to be detained and corrected until he has shown signs of repentance; with the offer that the supplicants will pay his pension, they hope for this grace from the Justice of Monsieur, which could not be granted on a more just and necessary occasion.

MODERATOR: The second request, coming from the wife of a cobbler, weary of her husband's behavior.

Arlette Farge reads the letter of Margueritte Le Maire, wife of Vincent Croyseau

ARLETTE FARGE:

To My Lord
the Lieutenant General of Police

My Lord,

Margueritte Le Maire wife of Vincent Croyseau cobbler residing rue des Canettes, Madeleine en la Cité parish, most humbly remonstrates unto Your Highness that around seventeen years or so ago she married said Croyseau, and he after having spent time during his marriage living calmly was unable to stop himself from making known his debauches, his oaths, and his blasphemies, which led to the supplicant appealing to all of her relatives both on his side as on hers to testify to the truth and to request of My Lord that after having been informed of the acts committed by said Croyseau which the supplicant gives proof of through the undersigned to give the order that he judges fit. This would be the means to put her in a state to see to her salvation and to purge the public of a man

"All about the Lettres de Cachet*"* 87

who seeks only to make an affront to his family by coming to a shameful end, the supplicant will continue her wishes and prayers for the health and prosperity of Your Highness.

Margueritte Le Maire (wife of said man).

ROGER CHARTIER: The undersigned, on behalf of Margueritte Le Maire, are three in number: le curé of Sainte-Madeleine, the parish where she lives, and two brothers of Vincent Croyseau. They state:

I certify the truth of the facts declared in the above petition and that said Croyseau is a very bad subject *[mauvais sujet]* who deserves to be locked up, so that he no longer has occasion to continue his libertinage.

MODERATOR: Two petitions, and thus two family conflicts, two requests for imprisonment, each with its own unique story. And yet these texts belong to a collection where they can be found by the hundreds. This collection is the basis of the book that Arlette Farge and Michel Foucault have just cowritten, *Disorderly Families.* This book is the ninety-first installment in the Archives series published by Gallimard-Juilliard, and it adheres to the format of the collection by offering readers the chance to engage with the same archival documents that the authors studied and interpreted.

This morning, with the help of Arlette Farge and Michel Foucault, we will seek to gain a better understanding of the motivations, mechanisms, and meanings of these requests for imprisonment that emerged from within the very heart of families themselves. We will have an open discussion over the different themes in this book, the first of which is just how unique this procedure, which fell outside the scope of the ordinary justice system, was. Then we will turn to the conflicts themselves, between husbands and wives, between children and parents, which were often quite drawn out. Finally, we will look at the importance of imprisonment by order of the king within the long history of judicial punishment.

We have two other guests here with us this morning to discuss these questions with Arlette Farge and Michel Foucault, and to help us understand this book in a broader historical context. One is a historian of the nineteenth century, Michelle Perrot, who assembled a collection of materials—including several contributions by Michel Foucault—about the penitentiary system in an edited volume that appeared with Seuil two years ago under the title *The Impossible Prison*. And our second guest is the sociologist André Béjin, who just coedited, along with Philippe Ariès, a collection of studies on marriage, eroticism, and homosexuality for a special issue of the journal *Communication*. This was issue 35, published in 1982 under the title *Sexualités occidentales: Contributions à l'histoire et à la sociologie de la sexualité*. I believe, Arlette Farge and Michel Foucault, that this book began, as I have just mentioned, with a collection of archival documents. Could you tell me about your joint encounters with these materials, with the former archives of the Bastille that are now stored and can be consulted at the Arsenal?

ARLETTE FARGE: I think that our encounter with these materials was somewhat extraordinary, since according to the popular conception, or at least to received wisdom, *lettres de cachet* were first and foremost a way to imprison royalty. And I believe that at the beginning most people thought that they were in fact a way for the king to get rid of people around him, meaning princes. And what was in fact so striking about this collection of materials, which is vast and stored at the Bibliothèque de l'Arsenal, was just how tiny the number of nobility in the Bastille was. And that, in fact, there were police cases of all kinds here. Not only that, but it was not limited to the family requests for imprisonment that we worked on either. There is in fact a massive body of texts here dealing with all manner of cases, some of which involve the poorest of the population, those who belong to the lowest social classes. One is just as likely to come across a labor strike, for example, for which the leader would be taken off to prison through the means of a *lettre de cachet*, or utterly minor police business, such as swindling on the Pont Neuf. This is something that we had not known at the outset and that is in fact quite interesting.

MODERATOR: Here you have selected two specific series from this body of material, those involving two types of family conflicts.

MICHEL FOUCAULT: Yes, we picked these two series out of this enormous body of material for a number of reasons. The first was that this selection was the intersection between Arlette Farge's work and the work on these materials that I had been engaged in for around two decades. What struck me, in the late fifties, early sixties, when I was working on this material for the *History of Madness*, what struck me was what Arlette Farge has just described: namely, that the *lettre de cachet* was popular practice. It was popular practice in two senses. First, because it is especially among the common people that we see this mechanism at work. And second, because the requests for *lettres de cachet* came from below. It was a process that worked from the bottom up: one *requested* a *lettre de cachet* from the king to resolve certain kinds of problems—family problems, problems with neighbors, problems with relatives, and work problems as well. And then, a second thing struck me: the extraordinary beauty of these texts. I say extraordinary beauty in part because, of course, here we find conflicts, problems, anxieties, angers, and emotions. And, in truth, it is really quite rare for the emotional dimension to translate itself directly into texts. We can observe family hatreds, grudges, fears, anguish. And moreover there is a curious feature about these documents, there is a, how can I say this, a quite disparate linguistic juxtaposition: to the extent that people made these requests for *lettres de cachet* using their own language, they spoke their emotions in *their* language, but behind them, there was always a public scribe or just someone else who was helping them to draft this request, or who drafted it, in the official, grandiloquent, superb, and flowery style of the time.

ANDRÉ BÉJIN: I believe that the contrast between this letter from the lawyer, or the lawyer's wife, which was visibly well written and which proceeds in a less reverential style, and then this letter from this cobbler's wife who perhaps hired a public scribe, which was much more chaotic and is more closely related to the spoken word . . .

MICHELLE PERROT: And a diversity in how things were framed, as well.

ARLETTE FARGE: Especially since in the letter itself . . . when someone was addressing a public scribe, there would be a complete shift between the formulations at the beginning and end, which are superbly archetypal formulations, and the middle, which would be this kind of chaos of the spoken and the written, of insults, and of emotions. It is the mixture of the two that is so interesting.

MICHELLE PERROT: Yes. There are a few questions that I would like to ask you about this. In your opinion, why is it that up until now we had been overlooking, as we are now saying, this fundamental feature of the *lettres de cachet,* and had only been looking at them inside of the relationship of the king to his subjects. What might this tell us about our historiography?

MICHEL FOUCAULT: That would indeed be an interesting study. I think that the starting point was the fact that opposition to this practice of the *lettres de cachet,* the critiques in the eighteenth century and especially on the eve of the Revolution, came especially from nobles, as well as parliamentarians, who, as legal professionals, frowned up this practice, which circumvented their own authority. So we had criticism from on high . . . there were in fact a few nobles who were imprisoned by *lettres de cachet* and who complained loudly, and then there were these legal professionals. So, we should examine the French historiography of the nineteenth century regarding the monarchy, the monarchy's abuses. How and why was there always this desire to link the *lettre de cachet* with the arbitrariness of the king? As well as, in a certain sense, with authoritarian intervention into the heart of society. With the result that the fact that the *lettre de cachet* was the product of a societal demand was completely lost. A product that was . . . at least motivated, at least sustained, and lived such a such long life, because there was a strong societal demand for it.

MICHELLE PERROT: Do when know when this societal demand, this recourse, began on a large scale? Do we know whether the eighteenth century represented a period of growth, a special moment, and what might the implication of this be over the long term?

MICHEL FOUCAULT: Here I will just give the beginning of an answer, as I believe that Arlette Farge will have much more to say about this. First, the practice of the *lettres de cachet* began on a large scale with the creation of the position of the lieutenant general of police. Second, at the end of the seventeenth century, and still at the beginning of the eighteenth, the documents in this area that have been passed down to us are particularly focused on political and religious cases. There are also many cases of spying. The affairs of Port-Royal, the affairs of Saint-Médard, things like that, take up the majority of the files that we have for the end of Louis XIV's reign.[1] And beginning then . . . here I will hand the answer over to . . .

ARLETTE FARGE: With regard to family requests for imprisonment, it might seem as if it was in the mid-eighteenth century that there were the greatest number, specifically from 1730 to 1760. But this is a product of archiving. By which I mean that the reason we don't find any after 1760 was not because there weren't any but because none were preserved in the Arsenal Library after 1760. On the other hand, we do have quite a good idea, thanks to the memoirs of Lieutenant General of Police Lenoir, which are preserved in the Bibliothèque d'Orléans, we have a quite, quite good idea that Lenoir made extensive use of this practice, since of the lieutenant generals he was one of the most convinced that the family was in fact a privileged space where private tranquility created a certain kind of public order. And here in fact I believe that this—yes, he does indeed say so, in the memoirs he wrote after the Revolution, he says so in 1804, 1808, when he's drafting his memoirs, which were never published. And in fact, since Lenoir was there during the last quarter of the eighteenth century, we know that all of these family requests for imprisonment must be missing; they are not in the Arsenal, even though there was a great profusion of them at this time, which only began tapering off in the 1780s. And then we can see, through another system of archives, the archives of the police superintendents, we can see the police superintendents getting fed up with this absolutely maddening task—but surely we will return to this and discuss how this happened in greater detail—and the nobles, and the parliamentarians, and public opinion were all getting fed up on a large scale. So, then there was this very powerful movement near the end of the eighteenth century that heralded the collapse of this practice.

MODERATOR: In terms of chronology, you chose to study systematically, exhaustively, as a corpus, the year 1728, for which there were 168 requests, and then the year 1758, for which there were seventy-four, as well as looking at the years before and after. And one thing that I think will be interesting for our listeners and future readers is that in the book you publish ninety-four dossiers in their entirety. I was saying earlier that the book adhered to the rules of the collection in which it was published, but, in truth, it goes much further than that, because the texts are presented as is, as unabridged dossiers, without framing, without real analysis, and such that anyone can come up with their own readings alongside yours, and can invent the histories of these lives whose few traces you offer up here.

One point about the fact that this was popular practice: did this reflect the Parisian milieu? Because I remember an article in *La Revue historique* written by a colleague who works on the provinces, [François-Xavier] Emmanuelli, in which he showed that in the provinces, this practice did not descend quite so low on the social ladder.[2] The mechanisms were fundamentally similar; people did not address their requests to the lieutenant general of police, but rather to the governor or the royal intendant. But its use in society was less widespread. Was this perhaps a reflection of the big-city milieu with its greater reserves of knowledge or its higher levels of literacy or its relationship to written culture, which made it party to a greater political culture? Was that part of it, or do you think that the Parisian situation is typical and it was the provinces that were the exception?

ARLETTE FARGE: This also makes me think of Nicole Castan's work on Languedoc.[3] I think that the procedure was quite significant because, for example, in Languedoc, requests for family imprisonment were directed to the military authorities, and she specifies this. In Paris, from 1767 on, from the moment the position of lieutenant general of police was created, he was someone who was, in the same way that superintendents were, very close to the common milieus, but also quite feared. In a twofold and ambiguous way, he was a protector, both a reassuring and a feared figure. I think that the fact that it was to the lieutenant general that people went, that this is what gave it this popular dimension. I am perhaps mistaken in this interpretation, but I think that the police's role among the people was much more complex than it might appear at first glance.

MICHEL FOUCAULT: And then the police was itself an essentially urban institution, with an urban role. It is possible that family conflicts in rural milieus would have been handled differently. With pitchforks!

MODERATOR: Can we actually talk a little about this procedure? Because it was the procedure itself that left behind this archival sedimentation that we find in the dossiers, which are not always complete, since some dossiers are quite thin, consisting solely of the initial request, while others are much ampler, having been filled out by a steady stream of new documents. Could you tell us what happened when someone, a father or a wife, wanted to register a complaint about their daughter or their son or their husband?

ARLETTE FARGE: Yes, the procedure was relatively simple, which is to say that at the outset there was a petition *[placet]*, of the kind we read earlier, which was a supplication to the lieutenant general of police. After that had been received, the lieutenant general would order an investigation—what this actually meant was quite fuzzy, but that was simply a reflection of how the eighteenth-century police operated. This investigation would be carried out either by the superintendent of police or the inspector, and we don't really know why it would be one or the other.

MICHEL FOUCAULT: There was one for each neighborhood and one of each—roughly speaking.

ARLETTE FARGE: There were forty-eight superintendents in Paris; there were twenty inspectors (there were fewer of them). So, the police inspectors carry out what were called clarifications *[éclaircissements]*, but that were in fact rather opaque [laughs]. Especially since there were no rules for these clarifications. Which is to say that maybe a neighbor or a brother would be summoned and questioned, and then the investigation would be handed over to the lieutenant general of police, who would give his ruling. Let's say that he determined that the person in question did indeed deserve to be sent to prison or something equivalent. The order, the *lettre de cachet,* would follow, signed by the king. After that, if someone did in fact get imprisoned, then it meant that the story was going to be a long one, it was not going to end there. By this I mean, and the dossiers we included bear this out quite clearly, imprisonment was the beginning of a whole new story. There would be, on the one hand, correspondence between the members of the family, those who were not in prison and those who were and were asking to be let free. And then further investigations would also be carried out, either in the form of additional testimony from the curé or testimony from neighbors. So, there would be a whole story that would drag out over a relatively long period of time, often lasting one or two years. So, it was a fairly lengthy procedure.

MICHEL FOUCAULT: But sometimes there would be quite spectacular twists. There are cases—there are several in fact in this book—in which the tables were turned, which is to say that the accused became the accuser, the unworthy son became the accuser of his parents.

94   *"All about the* Lettres de Cachet*"*

ARLETTE FARGE: Here is where I would like to specify that when reading these texts, well, obviously, you recognize that you can't always take it as the truth, of course, you must approach the material differently, because, of course, when the tables turn like this we can see that in fact what was being requested at the outset did not always reflect the truth.

MODERATOR: Do we often hear the voice of the accused?

MICHEL FOUCAULT: Not all that often in these dossiers. These investigations were really carried out at the request of a person's family and they themselves only spoke out in a few cases or when they were trying to turn the situation by explaining that the accusations against them—for example, their parents' request for their imprisonment—actually stemmed from a dispute over inheritance, that their parents were trying to cheat them. This would often happen when one of their two parents had died and the surviving one, who would often have remarried, requested the imprisonment of a child from the first marriage *[enfant du premier lit]*. At this point, the child of the first bed would declare that the parent was accusing him for reasons of personal interest, or sometimes from the depths of his imprisonment he would dispatch a letter to the king or to the King's Household *[Maison du Roi]* requesting that he be freed and claiming that he had been unjustly accused. But outside of that there was not a strict right to confront one's accuser as in the legal system . . .

MICHELLE PERROT: For me, the thing that struck me about the texts that you read earlier was first of all that people are presenting this as a kind of last resort. They did everything they could to resolve their problems and were unable to do so. This seems interesting to me, because perhaps this already reflects the idea that, despite everything, one did not discuss one's private business right away, one did not immediately bring it before an audience. And then it seems to me that there was this interplay with the neighbors, and I was very struck by the presence of the family in the neighborhood. After all, this was certainly not self-evident; one can imagine that these individuals could have been migrants, as was the case, as we well know, for a large portion of the population in the eighteenth century. There were very often brothers and cousins around, and this shows up quite often in these texts. This reminds me a little of those endogamous neighborhoods where people came together . . . which is to say that at the same time these texts open a window for us into city life in the eighteenth century, that they in fact tell us about much more than simply what they were trying to say. And then we can also see the characters that made up the neighborhood: the neighbors (this is always fascinating), the curé, and cultural intermediaries such as public scribes. And this can lead us to think about the models of writing that might have governed the *lettres de cachet,* and about this game, this tension, that might have existed between the well-practiced framing of this situation and then the howl that we can still perhaps make out through all of this. And therefore I think that this game between the audience, and the style, the style above all—and despite this, the irruption of a certain spontaneity—both poses a problem and is at the same time illuminating.

MODERATOR: But as to the procedure itself, given what Arlette Farge has said, I think that a question, a central question, is understanding the relationship that could exist between a type of ideology of the family and a type of ideology of the state. Because here we are at the intersection of the two. These were family affairs, but once it seemed that they could not be resolved through private efforts, they were brought before the king or his representative, the lieutenant general of police. Do you think we could say there is some kind of equivalency between the paternalist ideology of the monarchy that remained dominant, at least late into the eighteenth century, and a monarchical ideology of the family, such that the head of the family on one side, the head of state on the other, would occupy comparable positions, or ones that were tightly intertwined?

MICHEL FOUCAULT: I would not see this as an equivalency, exactly. One thing that struck us was that the father did not in fact seem to play an especially important role. It was always the father and the mother, or the father, the mother, the brothers, the cousins, etc. It was therefore truly a group, or even a small collectivity, much more than some kind of monarchical family, that was at play here. That being said, it is absolutely true that there was a relationship between family and the royal power it addressed, a relationship, I would say, of strategic interdependence, in the sense that the family considered that it was normal, it was natural, it was perhaps even

96 *"All about the* Lettres de Cachet*"*

a duty, for the king to intervene in these family affairs, in these private affairs. So, I think that between family and royal power you have whole series of tangled interconnections. But I do not think that we must see this as a type of society in which the paternal image was echoed both high and low, with the king being the general father of all families, and each head of a household a little king within the family. Interconnection, yes; equivalency, no.

MODERATOR: Indeed. I believe, André Béjin, talking about the nineteenth century, there was an interesting point that was emphasized off-air earlier, which is the fact that the supreme authority of the father appeared at the very moment when the ideology and reality of the King-Father collapsed.

ANDRÉ BÉJIN: Yes, this is, I believe, a movement that is rather conspicuous when reading your book, and I even wonder if you did not—since the latest documents in your study are from 1758—if you did not have a tendency, perhaps, to slightly exaggerate the importance of this rupture and of this concentration of authority in the father figure, as it might have happened—at least, this is what you somewhat imply—at the beginning of the nineteenth century and as it was codified by the Napoleonic Code, by the Civil Code. In the book it is only an aside, it only takes up two or three pages, but I nonetheless had the feeling that this shift must have been both less sudden and much more heterogeneous. You were just mentioning that authority within a family was very, very divided: between parents, children, etc. I believe that if we study the long-term evolution of relationships, of relationships between powers and counterpowers within the family, the neighborhood, etc., the evolution will not proceed unilaterally in the direction of a reconcentration of authority around the father figure.

MODERATOR: I would like to know why you had a tendency to view this rupture as both sudden and . . .

MICHEL FOUCAULT: This procedure disappeared, the Civil Code gave authority back to the male head of the household within the private sphere without any regulatory oversight, neither legal oversight, nor this unique form of oversight that was the relationship to the king through these *lettres de cachet.*

ARLETTE FARGE: For me this is a hypothesis . . . which is to say that there's more to the situation, and the thing that seemed quite interesting to me was that wives and husbands were equally able—or nearly so—to request the imprisonment of their spouses. As Michel Foucault underlined earlier, in the case of children it would be the father and the mother acting together . . . there was nothing like a dominant figure as represented by the man. In the book it's presented as a hypothesis; we put forward as a hypothesis the idea that ultimately the disappearance of the *lettres de cachet* might have favored the emergence of a much more powerful head of the family, and that in any event it caused women to disappear. I think that this is the sense in which our reasoning should be understood. It has less to do with the father than with the sudden disappearance of the possibility for women to intervene on an equal footing with male authority. And it is in this sense that perhaps . . . though it is not perhaps precise enough, and it gives rise to—

ANDRÉ BÉJIN: If this is in fact only a hypothesis that you are suggesting— I am thinking, for example, of this passage on page 49: "It was men who would assure the link between the two and who would, for this reason, relegate women to the confined space of private life. The Civil Code would represent the culmination of this movement." And on page 266: "The old practice of family imprisonment would be forced to retreat to the confines of the rights of parents over minors." But this is absolutely not a criticism. I perceived a slight, perhaps a slight exaggeration of the abruptness of this rupture.

MICHEL FOUCAULT: We must draw a distinction between two things. On the one hand, there is the, let us call it the social process, which will necessarily be long and complex, passing through a thousand channels, and then there is the fact, which is really quite clear-cut, that under the Revolution, once the *lettres de cachet* had disappeared, once all these policing institutions had been pushed to the side, the question that arose was: how are we going to handle these questions, these family problems? And the answer came quite quickly: the responsibility will fall to paternal authority. So, you had the legal-institutional response in the form of a principle, which did not necessarily presume the way in which the social evolution of fatherly privilege would take place. So, you have abruptness on one side, a certain suddenness, and then below it, alongside it, you have a slow process. There you have it.

MICHELLE PERROT: As to this relationship between men and women, before we return to the problem of the king, I would like to say a few more things. To me, it seems, there are some Dutch historians, Pieter Spierenburg, to name one, whose research is very similar to yours.[4] He studied family imprisonment in Holland in the eighteenth and nineteenth centuries, because over there it continued for a very, very long time. And he noted the same thing: that not only was there some equality in the frequency with which men and women solicited imprisonment, but that women actually did so with greater frequency.

Some have tended to see this as a sign of equality. But I wonder whether it might not be the other way around. In the end, if women appealed more frequently to the king, to power, to settle their family conflicts, was this not perhaps because men found it easier to handle their problems directly? They did not shy away from physical violence. And because women found themselves at a disadvantage, as a result, they turned to the fatherly authority of the king. Could we not imagine that on the contrary—

ARLETTE FARGE: I am of course not saying that women were not dominated, that is not the question.

MICHELLE PERROT: —we could see this as an expression, a sign, of the position of women in paternalistic relationships? And then there is another thing, which is that we should not forget that in the nineteenth century, there was something that was a little bit indicative of what you have shown, which is the problem of the separation of body and board. The question of the separation of body and board was studied by the historian Bernard Schnapper.[5] He showed that the majority of cases of separations of body and board, 74 percent, came at the behest of women. He also shows that in 80 percent of cases the cause was domestic violence. It was not, he says, women whose husbands had been unfaithful, but abused women who requested these separations. There is an analogy here with what you have shown. So, therefore, perhaps we should not make too much of this equality of men and women in these cases; perhaps we should even see them as a sign of the weakness of women who were not able to manage their problems directly. What do you think?

ARLETTE FARGE: I think that I would like to answer this question somewhat differently. I do not believe that, when it says that . . . it was ultimately as a last resort that women requested the imprisonment of their husbands, while husbands were better at taking care of their problems. I think that we could perhaps think about and draw a connection with . . . well, there must have been a reason for this. Ultimately, it was nonetheless upon women that responsibility for the children fell and, in effect, women had often been putting it off as long as possible, and they will often say this in the documents, they will say, "I come to you, beaten, after so many years"—we calculated an average, and found that it was usually after fifteen years, twenty years of blows and beatings . . . well, of course the documents and the requests contain some exaggerations. But was this because she couldn't find her way out of this or was it simply that, being responsible for the children, it would have been impossible to request that her husband be imprisoned? I do not know if we should interpret this as if, by seeking justification and respite from the king, she entered into a paternalistic framework because this would be seeing them as very, very weak, and I do not know if we should go that far. But, in truth, I cannot really answer this question.

MICHEL FOUCAULT: Could we not say that this was nonetheless somewhat linked to the specific problems of wives? The problems that wives faced were being beaten and having unfaithful husbands. Which is to say that the husband found himself in a doubly powerful situation: he could beat his wife (much more easily than she could him), and secondly, he could leave and go off with the neighborhood tramp, or simply just pick up and leave. And thus, against these two dangers, which were serious, what could the woman do, what recourse did she have? I rather agree, from this perspective, there is indeed a lack of power, yes, and above all problems that were altogether specific and that only imprisonment could resolve.

ANDRÉ BÉJIN: But don't the texts that you cite reveal that the wife was not, that she did not confront these marital dangers alone, isn't that right, that when her husband was violent, the reaction of the neighborhood, of the neighbors, was generally swift and energetic, was it not?

MODERATOR: One thing that is quite present in the first collection of texts in the book, which deal specifically with the tensions between husbands and wives, and that seems altogether interesting, is that in these documents expectations were shared and were specific to both sexes, and reflected a model of what a normal or orderly family life should look like. And there are two things that seem rather striking in what you have put forward. One was this wife's expectation that the husband would be present; this goes back a little to Arlette Farge's answer, because there was a role that he was expected to play in the upbringing of the children that was undoubtedly a much larger role than before. And then when it came to men's expectations, there was still—with regard to what Michel Foucault was saying, of course, so many were women—there was still the fact that these husbands would request imprisonment to defend their honor, because female infidelity had put it at risk. Perhaps we could take the two—the texts are very rich and your commentary is as well, so we cannot talk about everything—but perhaps we could pick up on these two threads. For the first, the expectation of the husband's participation in the children's upbringing, was this indicative of a greater valorization, which was also manifested in a new religious family morality in the eighteenth century, as well as in acculturation effort, which passed through the schools—well, not only through the schools—since the Catholic reforms? In your opinion, do you think it might be possible to connect this new role that women gave their husbands to something bigger: the increased valorization of the educational charge throughout the social body in the eighteenth century?

ARLETTE FARGE: Well, what I wonder is whether this really was a *new* role for the husband, because the thing that actually *is* new is this argument; up until now, the family has always been presented as a place where the father had no obligation, or almost none, to have anything to do with his children. In any case, with regard to the common people, this is what you heard. And from there to discover—and for me as well this was a discovery—that in fact wives could expect the husband to be present in caring of the children—this was always the expression that was employed, "caring for the children"—this is significant in many ways. It seems to me that I'm unsure whether we can say if this role was new or not without doing a lot more research on the subject. I also wonder if the realization that this has been continually overlooked might not also lead us to rethink some of the work that has been done on the family or children's upbringings or on the maternal instinct. This idea is so prevalent in these texts that it doesn't seem likely that it was a novelty, but rather something that might have fit into a tradition that had gone unnoticed until now.

ANDRÉ BÉJIN: This insistence on the father's role, doesn't it stem from the rhetoric of honor, to which you alluded? Which is to say, this was a model and there was reason to adhere to this model in order for the complaint to be considered acceptable.

ARLETTE FARGE: As I see it, this was not so much a reference to the rhetoric of honor as to the image of a couple as an economic partnership, where each partner's work was of equal importance, the husband's as much as the wife's, where idleness was condemned on both sides, on the part of either the husband or the wife. So therefore, within this economic relationship between the two of them, the children were another additional responsibility to share. And all of this created a unit, and perhaps honor came in later.

ANDRÉ BÉJIN: As to this new role, I am reminded of what I was being shown yesterday—and, I believe, in a rather clear way—by [Jean-Louis] Flandrin, which was a displacement of the familial morality communicated by religious texts in the eighteenth century that listed the duties of parents toward much older children.[6] This might have been a husband's duty toward his wife such that pregnancy would not put her life in danger, or it might have been have been this greater attention to the children, participating in children's upbringing until they had established themselves, something that was shared by the couple, but in which the husband also had a role. Might this have, in a somewhat paradoxical way, perhaps spread the idea of resorting to antithetical practices? After all, one way of providing better care for one's children was perhaps to have fewer of them. Thus, in a way that was not anticipated by these religious teachings, this practice might have been contrary to the church's discourse. But, well, what do you think? This is perhaps not a new role in the context of the family experience, but it is nonetheless a new imposition of norms that these texts seem to indicate had been interiorized.

MICHEL FOUCAULT: This is something quite striking about these texts. On the one hand, of course, they reveal a whole series of conflicts that perhaps offer a quite dark portrayal of family life; these stories are quite awful, yes, that's true. But out of all this emerged a certain positive image, or at least a system of values to which people referred, relating to the upbringing of the children, the good sentiments that the spouses should show one another, a certain image of the family that was obviously in contradiction with what we're seeing here, but that appeared as a system of norms on the basis of which the bad behavior of the father, of the children, of the mother could be defined. And this positive image, in truth these positive values, they do not seem so far removed, so foreign, from what we find in the theoretical, philosophical texts, whether religious or not, that are often purported to have invented these new family values. I'm not saying that the image of the family that emerges from the texts is Rousseau's, it's not exactly *Émile,* but nevertheless there's not all that much distance between these values, which were solemnly formulated as new ideas by philosophers, and then the sensibility we can make out with regard to family values in these texts. Well, perhaps I am pushing this a little far, but . . .

ARLETTE FARGE: No, I completely agree. Completely agree.

MICHEL FOUCAULT: It's rather impressive.

MICHELLE PERROT: It's quite interesting because these social practices might have, in certain ways, trickled up into these theories, which is the opposite picture to the one that we usually imagine.

MICHEL FOUCAULT: Yes! Absolutely, absolutely.

ANDRÉ BÉJIN: This reminds me of our discussion earlier, about the sediments, the successive layers. There was this eighteenth-century atmosphere . . . There was still, in my opinion, nevertheless the success, or at least the partial success, of the inculcation of the values of the Catholic reforms, and perhaps then, at an even deeper level of sedimentation, where we encounter problems of marital fidelity, of honor, I have the impression that in the letters husbands wrote against their wives, there was this ancient value system that is somewhat surprising in this Parisian world of the nuclear family, where we wouldn't have expected to find it. There was this homogeneity of the social group, which bore and defended a collectively shared honor, within which, when a woman was behaving badly, the testimony of her own parents was of capital importance when it came to having her locked up. There was this identification, somewhat like in the Spanish Comedia in the sixteenth century, between honor and reputation, and then all honor came to rest in these cases on feminine virtue. You get the impression of a bedrock of values that is among the most traditional within the ensemble that you've described.

MICHELLE PERROT: Well, I would like to say one or two more things about that. It also seems to me that the family, within this migrant milieu that was Paris, was probably the basic line of defense against all that was the nation. This is something we see with later stories of immigration, so it is therefore perhaps not so surprising that people leaned even more heavily upon the family, because they needed it so badly, not only on the economic level, as Arlette was saying, but also at the level of human warmth, so it was very important. But, on the other hand, these documents involve the family by definition. So, there was a world, and perhaps even a quite vast one, that was not caught here, and therefore we should be a little hesitant to go too far. There were probably also individuals in Paris without families, people who lived different lives. Therefore, we shouldn't be surprised to find the family in documents that placed everything onto the family.

ARLETTE FARGE: I think that it's also interesting to see that in this process of imprisonment, at the end of the day, it was women who were more likely to seek the release of their husbands than the other way around. This is also interesting, and we should think about all that it might mean. Was this in fact a reflection of economic powerlessness, given how much they needed them, or was it that from this moment on certain things were established of the kind that Lenoir has described elsewhere? Was this not also a rather simple way for a man to get rid of his wife, and then to live in libertinage, which for that matter might also turn into delinquency and became quite troublesome? Whereas a wife who was responsible for a child or children could not behave in this way while the husband was in prison. These contrasts are far too simplistic, but in any event it's interesting that we see such differences.

MICHEL FOUCAULT: Systems of values also brought with them somewhat semantic systems of translation. And in the cases that we've evoked, there was the idea that prostitution or debauch were the necessary translation of what could only have been marital unfaithfulness. And all of this rhetoric of honor was also a process of translation, of expression, so as to be understood.

MICHELLE PERROT: For me, this is also very interesting, because this was the only way of speaking of a woman's behaviors. If she was living outside of the family, because she took . . . she had a liaison, or she was living in concubinage with someone, then it couldn't simply be described as such. One needed to use words that were the most . . . the language of prostitution, even of whoring, even insults, which is to say that one was obliged to employ a completely different language from the reality that existed and constituted the offense. Whereas with men things were completely different. I think that here as well, that this intersects with all of these popular texts about women, that women can only be treated as saints or whores. I think that here we are coming up against a whole tradition, which we should investigate further, but a whole semantic tradition as well.

ANDRÉ BÉJIN: If this was possible it was because the system of values that placed the foundations of honor on female virtue was no longer fully accepted by the authorities as being enough in and of itself to motivate these proceedings. And so, translating the matter into this different language had the aim of pushing them a little bit. I was saying that this was a system that was perhaps in relationship with an archaic system of the values of honor, but that at the same time . . . One gets the impression that these petitioners did not think that the authorities would intervene solely on that basis and they believed they had to, as you say, go much further in their accusations, even to the point of straining the truth.

MICHEL FOUCAULT: I believe that in these texts, the category of debauchery, which was a complete tangle, was at the same time quite interesting. Debauch also meant . . . the conduct that constituted debauch could be leaving your job, your work, your obligations, your place. It can refer to womanizing, it can refer to sexual debauch. It is thus remarkable that there were no complaints based upon homosexuality. The parents never complained of it. Wives never complained of the homosexuality of their husband or vice versa. Even with all this discussion of debauch.

MICHELLE PERROT: Do you have any hypotheses about this?

MICHEL FOUCAULT: We would have to study—and I think this is actually being done right now—the dossiers that are dedicated specifically to homosexuality. But these were police dossiers in the proper sense of the term. Which is to say, they dealt with people who had been picked up in the traditional, centuries-old locations for cruising—Saint-Germain-des-Prés, Luxembourg, the Palais Royal—for provoking the attention of the police. But there was no family request that was explicitly based, explicitly motivated by, an individual's homosexuality.

MICHELLE PERROT: Now, that is very interesting.

MICHEL FOUCAULT: We can guess at it in one or two cases, we can have our suspicions, but beyond that, nothing, nothing. But back to the category of debauch. It would seem that because this was the fundamental category employed, people must have believed, and must have been given to believe as well, that it was a category of interest for the state as much as the family. This was the intersection where the interest of the state, the concerns of the state, and the needs of the family crossed paths. Neither a well-ordered family, nor an orderly state, could countenance debauched persons.

Musical interlude for listeners just tuning in:

MODERATOR [sotto voce]: The second collection of dossiers that were published in this book, *Disorderly Families,* from the Archives series from Gallimard, which has just been published by Arlette Farge and Michel Foucault, onto the second collection of documents, about sixty or so dossiers, dealing with conflicts between parents and children.

MODERATOR: In the book you've offered a category that helps explain the connection between these various individual conflicts, which is the idea of "the threshold." What do you mean by this term?

MICHEL FOUCAULT: I think that there was, obviously, a large spatial problem that confronted people in the eighteenth century. I was struck by the fact that in nineteenth-century texts—and if I'm mistaken, Michelle Perrot will correct me—it seemed to me that the moralizing enterprise was especially focused on themes that were in a certain sense temporal. People were not supposed to lead dissipated lives—"leading a dissipated life" meaning not planning today for tomorrow. Not leading a dissipated life meant having a savings account, having a stable job, etc. It seems to me that in the texts we have here from the eighteenth century, the problems were more spatial than temporal. The people whose imprisonment was requested were those who, it was felt, needed to be corrected, those who were restless, those who went out, who left, who came back, who left again, etc. And, of course, when children grew up, this was the basic problem. There were two basic cases. There was the case of the girl who left, and who left with a man or perhaps with several, but there again the word *prostitution* simply designated the general fact that they were living outside of marriage with someone; therefore we should not exaggerate the lack of virtue of these women [laughs], but she had left. Then there was the case of the boy, the boy who was apprenticed off, who could not endure his apprenticeship, and who returned home, having stolen a little money or having obtained it with threats . . . and then, left, came back, etc. And it was these back-and-forths, it seems to me, that were the fundamental problem, and the spatial threshold of family and lodging seems to me to be the point at which a crisis was triggered and an imprisonment request followed.

MODERATOR: Going back to the threshold of independence and the majority—

ANDRÉ BÉJIN: Are we talking about boys or girls?

MICHEL FOUCAULT: It lasts until . . . almost age thirty. Then it seems that—and some calculations were necessary, and it's very difficult to make any exact calculations for this—in most cases, and I think I include this on a page in the book, it was between twenty and twenty-five that the crisis . . .

ANDRÉ BÉJIN: So, right before what demographics normally show as the average age of marriage?

MICHEL FOUCAULT: That's right. It was the premarriage stage that provoked these crises.

MICHELLE PERROT: I'm quite struck just how old these people are who are being referred to as children. What's more, the word *child* has much more to do with a situation of dependency than biological age. And I completely agree with what you just said about this difference between space and time. Having said that, I think that the history of the incorporation of time into the planning of actors and families in the nineteenth century was also a very long one. And, as a result, there was a whole period where you could find the same types of behavior. Whereas for children in the nineteenth century . . . it becomes, perhaps, fatherly correction, which was a little like the pursuit of this system but solely for children, with fairly clear boundaries in time. The father's reproaches often had to do with space, meaning vagrancy, or running away; this was the big criticism of children, that they didn't know how to stay put. So, we find this criticism, which had been directed at much older individuals, now aimed at children, and actual children at that. It's true that this is very striking.

ANDRÉ BÉJIN: And the notion of the public scandal at play in these "threshold" conflicts, because in addition to those who left, there were also those who were present in the neighborhood: the girl who prostituted herself nearby, or the boy who came and went . . .

MICHEL FOUCAULT: That's it, that's it. Once they had totally disappeared, people stopped looking for them, and technically it wasn't possible to find them again. It was those who came and went, who reappeared.

MICHELLE PERROT: But I find that your documents actually somewhat upend the received wisdom about the independence of youth. And in the end, isn't what was called "majority," from the moment that it was legally defined, which would happen in the nineteenth century . . . Was it that in the eighteenth century the family unit was longer lived? What do you think? I don't know . . . I was very struck by how old these children were. In the nineteenth century, I don't think they would say "a thirty-year-old boy."

ARLETTE FARGE: I completely agree with Michelle and I also think that this is something that we found quite astonishing as well, because we've always said that in the eighteenth century, people were very much nomadic, especially when it came to the common people. So why criticize twenty- to twenty-five-year-olds for vagrancy, when traditionally they were, indeed, migrants or the like, etc.? What kinds of questions does this raise?

MICHEL FOUCAULT: This is undoubtedly one of the core elements of the book, and it has little in common with the image constructed by the historical demography of the family in the urban environment, completely severed from their roots, a large family that existed solely as a nuclear cell with a great deal of autonomy across generations. That whole portrait is practically completely upside-down:

this nuclear family emerged in a fabric that was communitarian not only with respect to the neighbors, but also to the immediate family, a dependency that was perpetuated up until a quite late age. And in this sense we have two images that do not fit together very well.

MICHELLE PERROT: It's true.

ARLETTE FARGE: These family disorders paradoxically give us an idea of the strength of the family.

MICHEL FOUCAULT: And in the replies of the lieutenant general of police—because it was quite common for the lieutenant general of police to give an opinion that was not favorable to imprisonment—never that I know of did he make a comment along the lines of "Well, now he is too old for you to have him locked up." They might say, "No, he's not such a vagabond as all that," or "No, the parents have ulterior motives for getting rid of him." But never at age twenty-five or thirty did you hear, "He has the right to come and go as he pleases, or the right to go where he pleases." Never.

MICHELLE PERROT: In the nineteenth century, the age of the majority was continually being lowered, for example.

ANDRÉ BÉJIN: Was the criterion for maturity simply the fact of being married or not? Might it be that taking biological age into account would not be perfectly appropriate for this period?

ARLETTE FARGE: Not always, because some of these documents involved married children. The daughter who married someone and had a life elsewhere, or the husband who led a completely libertine life.

ANDRÉ BÉJIN: And the vocabulary that is used is the same as with unmarried children of the same age?

ARLETTE FARGE AND MICHEL FOUCAULT: Yes, yes.

MICHELLE PERROT: It seems to me that there is a notable absence of what we might call the rights of adolescents, for example.

ARLETTE FARGE AND MICHEL FOUCAULT: Yes, definitely. Absolutely.

MODERATOR: This brings us to another important theme, which is the corrective role played by the *lettre de cachet* and especially what followed it, imprisonment, when it had been granted, which raises questions about the position and meaning of this "repressive" form of justice. This is a story of Ancien Régime penalization. Because at the beginning this was nonetheless quite unique with regard

"All about the Lettres de Cachet*"* 109

to . . . the way that the justice system operated. And the idiosyncrasy of how this worked, I think you show this several times, by showing that here, with the idea of secrecy or the idea of reclusion that necessarily entailed a certain secretiveness, we have elements and values that were totally antinomical to how the judicial system functioned. You have placed a great deal of importance to this idea of the secret.

ARLETTE FARGE: Yes, of the secret, and first of all—

MICHEL FOUCAULT: And then at the level of the procedure—

ARLETTE FARGE: Yes, and of a practice that is totally different from that of ordinary justice, and not enough attention has been paid to this up until now. Which is to say, in effect, that families thought that public justice was shameful, and it was precisely because of this perception that they personally appealed to the king. But these personal appeals to the king came with certain economic conditions attached. Which is to say that you would ask the king to imprison a member of your family, but at the same time you would have to pay for this imprisonment. And furthermore, I think the haggling in some of these dossiers highlights this particular feature. And I believe that in fact there was something quite interesting about this undertaking, which was altogether parallel to the justice system, by which you presented yourself to the king in all your insignificance, and perhaps underneath this with the idea that by confessing and being the first to do so, doing so without having been ordered to by anyone . . . when you were the first to confess this secret to the king, your secret could be buried away forever through the intermediary of the supreme person, the supreme authority of the king, and you would be completely washed clean of any stain. Whereas with the justice system, which was justice that was declaimed from the public squares and involved trials that were written about, as well as punishments that took place in front of everyone. While here we are outside of the spectacle, returning once again to the shadows of the family, the dark underbelly of the family.

MICHELLE PERROT: The king was the grandfather of the confessor. But I would like to know what you think, Michel Foucault, about this figure of the king. I myself found this very, very, impressive about these texts and this relationship of the people to the king through justice. And then when the king disappeared from the public scene,

110 *"All about the* Lettres de Cachet"

the great distress that might perhaps have been felt among the common people. I'm not sure, what do you think of this political mechanism?

MICHEL FOUCAULT: Yes, yes, this was indeed something that was quite important. Well, first of all we should say that people were wary of ordinary justice, as it was called at the time. Everyone was wary of it, of course. And this was a great crisis for the functioning of ordinary justice all throughout the eighteenth century, culminating with the dawn of the Revolution. So there was that. There was the fact that many of these offenses, of these wrongs, that were punished by imprisonment, many of these wrongs would clearly not have been brought to trial. Earlier, Arlette Farge highlighted a very important feature of this: the economic problem. Because ordinary justice was terribly expensive. And you never knew where it would lead. While you still paid for imprisonment, you were paying a pension, you were paying a hospitality fee, and you knew what you were getting into, there was a contract of sorts; the king imprisoned, the king requested a pension, and you would discuss this with the king or his representatives, you would settle on a price, and then you would pay it year by year, up until you claimed that you couldn't afford to pay it anymore. So there was something in that, an economic advantage, even if imprisonment was no less expensive than . . . There was indeed, behind all of this appealing the king and the problem of this confession of sorts that was made to the king to avoid a public scandal. The king then became the bearer of the secret. And this was a role that was quite curious and quite interesting. I know that quite recently, there has been a great deal of emphasis on the fact that the king was only the representation of the king, the body of the king as the visible, ritual element, etc. But we should also see the other side of this, which is to say the king as an internal person, in a certain sense, to whom secrets were confided. There is a whole field of invisibility in the relationship each person had to the king. And these things, which you didn't want to be said or to be known publicly, they would be whispered to him through a petition. So, there was the king's protective wing, under which an individual would be placed in the secrecy of imprisonment, in one of the houses that we will certainly have to talk about a little later. Where he would remain, out of sight and out of mind, up until the moment when it was time for him to appear again. So, the body of the king as the site of a secret might have represented this as well . . . [laughing]. It's the complete opposite of a ceremony.

ANDRÉ BÉJIN: You have emphasized the economic factor. But was there perhaps not also another factor? Because it seemed to me that these police clarifications did not look very deeply into the lives of the families involved. And from the moment that the problem was sufficiently well established according to the model that you have emphasized, from that moment on, these clarifications did not shed much light on family discord. Whereas the subject, did he not, produced his own truth. While in the other hypothesis, of course, the judicial hypothesis, this would have been more expensive, and furthermore the subject would probably have been in a position of far less control over the truth that he wished to present to the outside world. Wasn't that also quite important? I think you found a way to sum it up in a sentence: "speaking so as not to be spoken about" [dire pour ne pas être dit]. To me, that seems fundamental. This was simultaneously a preventative undertaking—you highlight this elsewhere—preventative in the sense of avoiding the need to resort to judicial procedures. But at the same time, it was also equally a question of the families involved getting a head start on defining the terms of the debate.

MICHEL FOUCAULT: That is the paradox, if you will, of this. The more petitioners addressed themselves to the king, the more they remained masters of the situation [maîtres de la situation]. From the moment when the law was handed over to the machinery of the judicial system, they no longer had a good idea of where things would end up. Whereas here they had a relatively good sense of how things would proceed and, what you said was exactly right, they were more or less masters of the truth [maîtres de la vérité]. Having said that, police investigations were in fact carried out. So, you're right that up to a certain point, often all they did was repeat . . . the police would say "yes, that's true" instead of truly investigating. Did the policemen actually check, or were they simply repeating . . . I think that Arlette Farge has things she could say about . . .

MODERATOR: Were there analogous possibilities that survived into the nineteenth century?

ANDRÉ BÉJIN: Possibilities . . .

112 *"All about the* Lettres de Cachet*"*

MICHEL FOUCAULT: . . . to be the master of the truth in a proceeding . . . ?

MODERATOR: Or was this something that disappeared with the Ancien Régime?

MICHELLE PERROT: Paternal correction, I find that a little—perhaps internment in psychiatric asylums. I often get the impression that the asylum picked up where the *lettre de cachet* left off. This would then be something else to develop, to interrogate.

ARLETTE FARGE: I would like to underline something that you just said, about this idea of "speaking so as not to be spoken about." I think that there is something completely paradoxical about secrecy, and at the same time in the whole secrecy process, because in fact the neighbors and the whole neighborhood would often know all about it, from the very beginning. So, when the subject produced the truth, he produced his own truth, but in light of what was being said about him. And the only means by which to erase—and I think this was one of the other features of this procedure—the only efficient way of erasing gossip, the reputation that was being spread around, which was so important for the people, was precisely to go to the king; because here again, ordinary justice could not douse the flames. I think that the secret told to the king was also a way to defuse all of the rumors that circulated about certain behavior. And so this was also an absolutely paradoxical feature of it.

ANDRÉ BÉJIN: Did not the king act as the guarantor of the version put forward by the petitioner?

ARLETTE FARGE: I think that it was really from the personal request that everything came, I think that it was the personal request that caused the king to act, and the king allowed himself—as Michel Foucault was saying earlier—in the end he allowed himself to be controlled in this way.

MICHEL FOUCAULT: And far more easily than a magistrate would. Thus, it was altogether natural for someone to address themselves to the good person of the king. In the *lettres de cachet* he was a positive figure, a favorable figure. And that is what has been completely turned upside down in the historiography.

ARLETTE FARGE: Something else that was also important was the pleasure the king took in this. The pleasure that came when the lieutenant general of police arrived every week to explain all this to the king, and the king, as we know, was quite amused by all this, quite interested in all this. And so there was also the pleasure of the king, and his good pleasure was not nothing . . .

MICHELLE PERROT: Were the magistrates jealous of this power of the king's?

MICHEL FOUCAULT: Yes, yes, horribly so.

MICHELLE PERROT: Horribly?

ARLETTE FARGE: They fought against . . .

MICHEL FOUCAULT: The policing institution, well, police in the sense that the term was used in the eighteenth century, was not the same as ours. It was they, the magistrates, who were constantly calling for this system to be abolished. And then we encounter the problem that was discussed in *The Impossible Prison,* which is the paradox that all the people who criticized the eighteenth-century administrative-judicial-etc. system, focused on prison and imprisonment, saying that this practice had to be absolutely abolished. And that is why all of the reform projects were antiprison, up until the real reform that followed immediately afterwards and that led to prisons . . . but that is another story.

ANDRÉ BÉJIN: Yes, but was it the case that, at the level of popular practice, the procedure of the *lettre de cachet* for family reasons might have neutralized certain effects of the negative image of prison? For example, the fact that, in the eyes of parliamentarians, it was tied to the notion of arbitrariness, of Oriental despotism, of secret imprisonment, without the oversight of the justice system. So, everything that was considered negative in this milieu, in the "lettered" or "political" milieu, could not perhaps be superimposed onto the level of the common people and the ordinary practice of using imprisonment for family conflicts might have . . . I remember a page in Sieur Olivier Pinault where you could see all of the obstacles in the imagination to the generalization of prison, everything that was attached to it. But here that doesn't play a role.

MICHEL FOUCAULT: Here that doesn't play a role, and so then we face the problem of this quite curious idea, belied by history, according to which prison corrected people. And here we find it constantly . . . and so again we see how practices, institutions, things that had appeared to be innovations rooted in intellectual milieus

114 *"All about the* Lettres de Cachet*"*

or innovative forms of thinking, we can actually already find all of them taking shape in people's reactions. This way of thinking did not come from thinkers, but rather from the transformation, not only of sensibility and the sentiments, but also of a whole system of thought. We have to take into account the extraordinary reach that it might have had in people's behavior. People did not act *[se conduisent]* unthinkingly.

MICHELLE PERROT: Detention by *lettre de cachet* would therefore have been somewhat of an antecedent of a certain kind of imprisonment.

MICHEL FOUCAULT: Because the words we find in the letters often state as their goal: looking within, penitence, repentance, correction.

ARLETTE FARGE: And then that beautiful expression: "Looking within oneself" *[rentrer en soi-même]*.

ANDRÉ BÉJIN: Which was obtained by a withdrawal from the world. Did this not have to do with these various places of imprisonment that you mentioned, but that perhaps had to be described with one word, to give them unity? Because, in the end, these places varied enormously, if only for the reasons that Michel Foucault mentioned. Imprisonment cost money, and not everyone had the same capacity to pay. Therefore, there were first-class incarcerations, incarcerations that—

MICHEL FOUCAULT: There were the four-star ones, the famous four-star prisons that we're always hearing about did indeed exist. They were the convents. And then you have a steep drop, Saint-Lazare already wasn't exactly a laugh and then there was the lowest rung, of course . . . Salpêtrière, Bicêtre, the Maison de l'Hôpital Général . . .

ARLETTE FARGE: . . . Sainte-Pélagie . . .

ANDRÉ BÉJIN: And in certain of the provinces, the royal fortresses. But despite this, what is it that unified this grouping? This category of withdrawing from the world and reform through solitude and looking within oneself?

MICHEL FOUCAULT: I think that the path from the Christian idea of the practice of monastic imprisonment in a cell in order to withdraw into oneself to the secular idea of imprisonment as correction, that this path passed through this practice, which was an institutional practice, and was at the same time a practice that was not only quite widely accepted but that people also employed voluntarily.

"All about the Lettres de Cachet" 115

ANDRÉ BÉJIN: Because the stated objective was to obtain the prisoner's repentance, isn't it nonetheless the case that these places of imprisonment showed a certain effectiveness? Because you cite very few examples of requests for reimprisonment after release. I only saw a few . . . it seems to me that repentance and improvement must therefore in fact have taken place.

ARLETTE FARGE: It was perhaps not a question of whether someone had repented. First off, there were economic reasons. People were still paying 150 pounds per year, and these were common people, so 150 pounds a year was not nothing. In order to receive very good treatment, one had to pay 400 pounds a year, so at 150 you were really doing quite poorly. There were also people who died there. What is more, we see letters from people who were crippled, or sickly, saying that they can't take it anymore. And then there was also the famous departure for the Islands, those who were sent off, the boys who were sent off to [Île de] la Désirade. And that wasn't nothing either.

MICHEL FOUCAULT: Those were very rare, very . . .

ARLETTE FARGE: They were rare, but . . .

MICHEL FOUCAULT: At last we come to the stories of the infamous "departure for the Islands." And here again we are victims of the great literary texts. Thanks to *Manon Lescaut* people imagine that . . . In fact, there were *a few* boats that left for the Islands in the entire eighteenth century.[7] I think there were some who stayed their whole lives. There were those who really had to get out of town and then they were never seen again. There were also those boys who left for the army, that was the big solution. The army was a place of, it was a pressure valve for society in the eighteenth century. And in the nineteenth century it was the colonies, this was a very important phenomenon as well. As to the effectiveness of correction, when we don't see someone being reimprisoned . . . there were cases of reimprisonment . . . but if we don't see them being reimprisoned that didn't necessarily mean that they had become well-behaved children, or faithful wives, or sober husbands.

MICHELLE PERROT: Sometimes we get the impression that people regretted the procedure that they had put in motion. That they were a little frightened by what happened to those they had had imprisoned.

ANDRÉ BÉJIN: Here I think we pick up again on the discussion of the educational horizon, because there was a kind of continuity between the educational task of the family . . . You showed that it was nevertheless stronger and that, well, when it was thwarted, then it was handed over to another power, which was the power of the state. But, as with school itself, the family continued to pay. Which is to say that in the eighteenth century the state never bore the costs of education, whether it was in the Petites écoles [de Port-Royal]— except when in the case of the former Protestant schools—or the costs that came with reeducation or imprisonment. But finally, there was the transfer from one educational sphere to another, but there was also in a certain sense a continuity of project.

MICHELLE PERROT: And if you didn't have money at all, what happened?

MICHEL FOUCAULT: Sometimes imprisonment could be free.

MICHELLE PERROT: Because with paternal correction in the nineteenth century, around 1836, it was ruled that if parents were too poor, the children could be taken in for free.

MICHEL FOUCAULT: We would have to look more closely at this. But it is plausible that in order for the imprisonment to be free, the disorder needed to be very public, with the threat of troublesome consequences for the public. The more people were willing to pay, the more easily private conflicts could be punished by imprisonment. This deserves a closer look.

MICHELLE PERROT: Do we know much about what happened inside these places of imprisonment?

ARLETTE FARGE: We don't know much, I believe. We looked at some bundles of documents at the Arsenal that deal especially with Sainte-Pélagie, where they kept track of prisoners and some indications as to their conduct was recorded, and we looked at these, but we can't say, these are only a clue. Often—well, at least at levels that were not trivial—women would ask to stay. This might have been something like seeking some kind protection relative to the risks of the city, but I don't know if we should take a leap here, there's not enough evidence.

MICHEL FOUCAULT: But inspections were carried out in these houses of detention and there we have . . . but this was very select . . . it's "good conduct," "remains disturbed," or "the state of his spirit worsens from one year to the next," things like that. So, we can't know exactly what the experience was like, what happened. But it's true that there are cases where people asked to stay.

ARLETTE FARGE: Well, well.

MICHELLE PERROT: Nicole Castan once said that prison in the eighteenth century and these forms of it did not have a connotation of dishonor. That they could be places of protection, in certain cases.

ARLETTE FARGE: I don't know, we would have to take a closer look . . .

MICHEL FOUCAULT: This makes me think of something I heard on the radio earlier, an interview with Gypsies (because they were doing a series on Gypsies). I was quite struck and moved by a woman who said, "You know, I'm eighty-four years old, and I've never been to prison." And she was saying this both to show that she was a good person and to show that she was very lucky to the extent that this had been entirely within the realm of possibility. The connotations of the word *prison* here, of never having been to prison, were quite ambiguous and quite interesting.

ANDRÉ BÉJIN: But there was one request in which someone, I don't remember if it was the husband or the wife, was quite angry that their spouse was in Châtelet and I think this brings me to Michel's opinion. Did they want . . . did the petitioner want the spouse to be transferred into one of these institutions, the Hôpital Général or the convents, because there would not be the same connotations if things remained in the atmosphere of secrecy and of something that could be tolerated? Whereas Châtelet would connote prison?

ARLETTE FARGE: Moreover, in the text, he emphasizes that "a husband would never have thought to have his wife put in Châtelet." That is very, very . . .

ANDRÉ BÉJIN: And there was, here, another text that was quite fascinating, which was the one where someone thought that if things improved a little, their son could be placed in the pension of the Christian schools, the brothers of the Christian schools of Saint-Yon.

ARLETTE FARGE: Which would mean . . . no longer insane.

MICHEL FOUCAULT: Here we find the pedagogical and educative horizon, which can span from family upbringing to this education . . .

ANDRÉ BÉJIN: But how were parents and relatives kept abreast of the development of the prisoners? Were they allowed to visit? It wasn't only through intermediaries . . .

MICHELLE PERROT: But perhaps they wanted to be rid of them, perhaps they did not visit that often.

MICHEL FOUCAULT: But I can remember dossiers where people complained, the prisoner complained that he never received any visits or news of his family. While imprisonment did have some negative connotations, we should also note that the person who requested imprisonment put forward a positive image of themselves (and a very negative image of the person who was imprisoned). But what they were doing was a good thing, it showed that someone was a good person, someone morally concerned with the good conduct of those close to them. This can be seen in the fact that for someone to request imprisonment, there was nothing shameful about requesting imprisonment, even if it was the shameful conduct of someone else that provoked and motivated the imprisonment.

ARLETTE FARGE: Yes, and especially at a time where this completely overlapped with police procedure, which always considered that the harmony of families and public order were equivalent, that *from* family harmony came public order. So, there was this intersection of sorts between a personal request and an eternally unrealized aspiration of the police.

ANDRÉ BÉJIN: But, to return to an idea or a theme that we touched on in passing earlier, would the early-nineteenth-century debates finally establish imprisonment as the central form of legal punishment? And was there either explicitly or implicitly a reference to the positive aspects of imprisonment and internment at the family's orders?

MICHEL FOUCAULT: Absolutely. In the justification for prisons, which had rather negative connotations for enlightened opinion in the eighteenth century, this very sudden reversal took place, in the name of the value of correction. In prisons, at least, people could be trained. This continued to have repercussions throughout the entire nineteenth century . . .

ARLETTE FARGE: . . . Up until Tocqueville's great skepticism, who for his part did not believe in this at all, and this led to the introduction of a whole other kind of prison once again. All of these philanthropists talked endlessly about reform.

ANDRÉ BÉJIN: The characteristics of imprisonment were somewhat similar. Was there a possibility of adjusting the length of the sentence? As you have described it in the case of prison here, we can see that it was possible to request someone's release, so this could vary and obviously there was the possibility of isolation . . .

MICHEL FOUCAULT: The work itself was a little different, because here it was a case, I'm not very sure, but they didn't require work . . . In the Maisons de l'Hôpital Général . . . in the regulations of the Hôpital Général in the middle, in the second half of the seventeenth century, the obligation to work was mandated, but all of the texts show that in practice this had been abandoned. Work in prison was almost always, in practice, fictional.

MODERATOR: But the moral horizon was the same.

MICHEL FOUCAULT: The principle was always the same: if they worked, they would be reformed.

MICHELLE PERROT: You speak of isolation. Would a prisoner really be all that isolated in these places? Given the conditions of the era, people must have all been tossed in together. And then why was there no fear of contagion—that these people, all of these bad people, would end up contaminating each other? This is what you would later hear quite frequently when people were arguing for putting cells into prison so that people would not contaminate one another anymore. That idea is not very present here.

MICHEL FOUCAULT: But isolation was requested and obtained in these four-star places that cost a lot of money and where people effectively had rooms. While among the common people, the idea of imprisoning people who in any event lived in a total lack of privacy—a poor man wasn't made to live alone.

ANDRÉ BÉJIN: It was in the state fortresses, for example, in the provinces, on the Île d'Oléron, or in state prisons, as Mirabeau pointed out, where you did in fact have isolation that was certainly closer to the isolation of nineteenth-century penitentiaries, but in the convents or in the more general-purpose houses of detention, there was something closer to the traditional model of living in community, I believe.

MICHEL FOUCAULT: The principle of imprisonment with isolation for all came relatively late as an idea, as it had appeared so chimerical beforehand. We have the Benthamite principle and then we find it again in the 1830s, 1840s, when there was this feeling that prison

120 *"All about the* Lettres de Cachet*"*

had failed and people were saying that the solution was to isolate everybody. But otherwise, a poor person did not live alone.

ANDRÉ BÉJIN: One chronological question: do you think that the system was falling apart at the dawn of the Revolution? Because here we have two diagnoses that are a little contradictory. There is the provincial diagnosis, I think, which also applies both to Caen, which Jean-Claude Perrot studied, and the broader provinces with the work of [François-Xavier] Emmanuelli and then . . .[8]

MICHEL FOUCAULT: It appears that it persists until 1789, demand doesn't drop off, whereas here and there after the 1760s . . . so perhaps it is not a contradiction at all, but rather that in the popular milieus where information and contestations circulated more intensely, might there not have been an erosion of the image of the king? Earlier, Michelle was talking about the figure of the king as the keystone of the whole system. Was this not largely rooted in these beneficial aspects, even at the level of the common people in the last three decades of the Ancien Régime, in the big cities? Because . . . I'm thinking, for example, of all that Robert Darnton has shown us about the quite lively circulation of pamphlets and lampoons . . .[9] Which had one axis, which was desacralizing, devalorizing, showing that the king belonged in the domain of the arbitrary or even the domain of impurity. Might not there have been some effect of this literature, even on a relatively popular level, that would have somewhat eroded the initial consensus? That could easily explain the disconnect between Paris and the provinces. I don't know, this is a hypothesis, but it seems to me that the image of the king could easily not have been seen the same way in the 1770s and in the 1780s, especially in an environment like Paris. Moreover, while there was a demand for these desacralizing texts, it was still within the literate milieu of access to information, to news, to rumors . . .

ARLETTE FARGE: We can also ask ourselves if this tarnished image of the king—and here I quite agree with what was just said—this tarnished image of the king in the late eighteenth century might have reached the police superintendents themselves. Even before it had reached families. Because in the texts or in the correspondence of theirs that we can find, the police in fact express a desire to withdraw from these affairs; they didn't see them as their responsibility—because they did indeed have quite a bit of work—

"All about the Lettres de Cachet*"* 121

but instead as the expression of an excessive power of the king . . . so here already we have a somewhat divergent vision of the duties of the state. And I wonder if before this made its way to the families—well, "before" or at the same time—if there was an intermediary . . . because in the end there was such a back-and-forth between the police superintendents and the population, that I ask myself whether this wasn't one of the ways . . .

MICHELLE PERROT: Did the system that you studied continue to operate just as intensively in the 1780s?

ARLETTE FARGE: Yes, in the 80s, under Lenoir. This didn't stop in the 60s. It was still going strong in the 1780s. Going strong while, at the same time, cracks were developing, by which I mean the superintendent would be saying, we don't want to do this anymore, and then obviously there was Breteuil's circular, etc.; it was all in the atmosphere.

MODERATOR: Well, I thought we might finish this discussion by evoking something that is in the background of this book that is never explicitly mentioned but that seems to me to have a solid basis. This is a way of putting forward an analysis of historical materials that to me seems quite powerful and that helps to show that the traditional oppositions make hardly any sense. One of oppositions is quite immediate and we find it throughout a whole body of historical literature. This is the division between, on the one hand, the history of everyday life, of daily life, of anonymity. A social-historical tradition comprising several different modalities, both French and Anglo-Saxon.

And then, on the other hand, there is the trend that operates at the level of the history of representations, of mechanisms *[dispositifs],* of norms. And I think that here the book does complete justice, does justice completely, to stick with the vocabulary of this morning, to how utterly flimsy and absurd this opposition is. The true problem is perhaps how to illustrate the encounter between the two.

MICHEL FOUCAULT: Yes, and I think that in the end, what we observed, and then what we wanted to do, was to bridge all these divisions to a certain extent. The division you mentioned just now and that must, I believe, be abolished, in addition to questioning the validity of this historical and political framework that creates an opposition between civil society and the state. Since here we don't see a state growing in a sense for itself and imposing itself on civil society; we see a back-and-forth between different bodies of power and different strategies that are interconnected or tangled up with one another. From this perspective, these documents are quite an interesting way of revisiting these categories and the manner in which they were put into play. And then, if you will—and this is something I am personally quite proud of—there was the possibility of collaboration between a historian and a philosopher beyond the dichotomies and oppositions that would reserve the archives for the historian and ideas for the philosopher. If I'm saying these things it's because I've read them and the sentence with which we begin our preface was an actual sentence written by someone in what is called a top journal.

ARLETTE FARGE: Yes, I think that the encounter that took place here occurred almost completely naturally, precisely because behind it there was the idea that the traditional delineations of history did not correspond well with the work we wanted to do. Something that Michel Foucault said earlier really struck a chord with me, that "people did not act unthinkingly." I think that being able to say that reflection was taking place everywhere seems extremely interesting to me, and this was the way in which an encounter like this could take place, on the basis of this shared perspective.

MICHELLE PERROT: Yes, I think that with Michel Foucault we continue to push against the boundaries that, alas, persist. And we should be proud of this. I think that this book pushes us to think about the popular usages of penalization and to see that the justice system and the state were not external to the population; there was what people did in practice, what they expected, what they concealed, from the justice system, what they turned over to it, and I think that in the nineteenth century, for example, there is an immense amount of work of this kind to be done that could completely renew the history of criminality. And so I find that this book has made a substantial contribution to the body of thought on the difficult boundaries between public and private, and I think that Michel Foucault will really help us think about these problems . . . that will now confront historians, that confront us and that we don't always know how to approach.

ANDRÉ BÉJIN: The problem goes beyond the way in which we qualify things. The real problem is this idea of . . . I think that this is a book about the imposition, the inculcation, of systems of values, because we see them penetrating in from every direction. And this is also a book about gaps, because no matter how ideally defined and well ordered a mechanism is, it is never applied as such. And it is, as Michel was saying, a book about the appropriations and the uses that were still, even when they conformed—of course, when they rejected the mechanism there would be a gap in and of itself—but even when they conformed to it, there was always a small distance or something that created a kind of specificity, of singularity. And I think that this is in fact a question that has been asked, but that is not solely historical, and is instead directed to the whole group of people who are interested in the functioning of society in this relationship between the devalorizations that accompany declines in use and those appropriations that are always, to a certain extent, out of step with their governing norms. This is why this book, even beyond the topics that we have covered this morning, also pushes us toward a new way of thinking.

Musical interlude

Final letters read by Arlette Farge

To My Lord Hérault,
Lieutenant General of the Police

My Lord,

Jeanne Catry represents most humbly unto Your Grandeur, that having married one Antoine Chevalier journeyman mason around forty-six years ago, he had always given some signs of madness, which have gotten worse year by year and which we attributed only to his debauch and bad conduct, because he never behaved like an orderly man, having always spent everything that he earned at the tavern without any concern for his family, and having always sold his belongings and those of his wife to go drinking at the tavern; but My Lord, since for the last few years this madness, accompanied by this bad conduct has increased to such a point that said Antoine Chevalier often returns home at all hours of the night, completely naked, without hat, without clothes, even without shoes, which he leaves at the tavern to pay for what he spends with the first passerby, even perfect strangers, and as he commits a thousand extravagances at home even though he is seventy-four years old the supplicant who is a

124   *"All about the* Lettres de Cachet*"*

poor woman reduced to mendicancy by the behavior of her husband, was counseled by all the undersigned neighbors to most respectfully beseech that Your Grandeur might wish to have the charity to have said Antoine Chevalier her husband locked up, she dares to hope for this grace from Your goodness, My Lord, and she will be obliged to pray the Lord for your health and prosperity.

Charles Cousin, Pierre Roussette, J.-P. Catry.

[Ars. Arch. Bastille 11004, fol. 12 (1728)]

To My Lord
the Lieutenant General of Police

My Lord,

Very humbly represents unto Your Grandeur, Antoine Chevalier, journeyman mason age seventy-eight, who in the month of August 1728 was seized and taken to the house of detention of Bicêtre where he is held in the dungeons, on these orders, he dares to say with certainty that ill-intentioned individuals misled Your Highness's Religion, because he has the advantage of having always behaved irreproachably and at all times provided for the subsistence of his wife and family through his labor; these facts are certified by all of his family, friends and the principal inhabitants of the neighborhood of rue des Vieilles-Tuileries where he resided; the ignominy of being seized in the neighborhood where he was born and has lived his whole life, the solitude and horror of the dungeons, the supplicant's old age, and his good conduct have brought him the compassion of all, especially his family.

The infirmities inseparable from old age no longer permit him to work, his family is in no state to provide him with all of the necessary support, he can hope only for the few comforts that their means permit them to furnish him, but they are not at liberty to do so because he is secreted away in the dungeon; in this situation, he throws himself at the feet of Your Highness alongside all of his family, friends, and the principal inhabitants of neighborhood, and beseeches that it might please you to order that he be placed in the yard and to grant his family the freedom to see him, they will continue their hopes and prayers for the prosperity and good health of Your Highness.

Louis Deschamps, Raphaël Long,
Jacques Sigie, André Sibire, Coussin,
L. Léonard (friend), Delavoix, F. Jeandarme,
Cresseau, Charles Bassille (friend),
Delauney, master of the journeyman employee.

[Ars. Arch. Bastille 11004, fol. 15 (1728)]

To My Lord Hérault,
Lieutenant General of Police

My Lord,

Jeanne Catry represents unto Your Highness that one Antoine Chevalier her husband who has been in Bicêtre since the month of August 1728, at the supplicant's request, recognizing his errors and being most repentant assures the supplicant that he will live with her until the end of his days with all the orderliness required of an honest man, if Your Highness would wish to show him the grace of granting his release and as she is touched with compassion for her husband and as she has reason to expect that said Chevalier being over the age of seventy-five, will keep all of these promises, she beseeches You most humbly, My Lord, that it might please you to have the goodness to order the release of said Chevalier her husband so that he might finish the few days he has left to live at her side.

Both she and he will redouble their hopes and prayers for the preservation of Your Highness.

[Ars. Arch. Bastille 11004, fol. 21 (1728)]

Translation by Thomas Scott-Railton

NOTES

1. [Both the Port-Royal affair and that of Saint-Médard derived from the resistance of Jansenist religious supporters to the French monarchy. Port-Royal distinguished itself for its rigorous application of the rule and its strict adhesion to certain Catholic teachings. Housing the tomb of François de Pâris, the cemetery of Saint-Médard often was visited by the *convulsionnaires de Saint-Médard,* or those religious pilgrims who would fall into religious ecstasy before the tomb of the Jansenist leader, François de Pâris. *Lettres de cachet* were heavily used by Louis XIV to quash this Jansenist movement. The Jansenists believed in predestination; this challenge to Catholic doctrine and religious hierarchy was understood both as a challenge to political absolutism and as the kernel of a protodemocratic political discourse. As lieutenant general, d'Argenson distinguished himself by destroying the Jansenist monastery of Port-Royal in 1704.—Ed.]

2. [François-Xavier Emmanuelli, "Ordres du Roi et lettres de cachet en Provence à la fin de l'Ancien Régime: Contribution à l'histoire du climat social et politique," *Revue historique* 252.512 (October–December 1974): 357–92.—Ed.]

3. [Nicole Castan and Yves Castan, *Vivre ensemble: Ordre et désordre en Languedoc au XVIIIᵉ siècle* (Paris: Gallimard, 1981).—Ed.]

4. [Michelle Perrot may have in mind Spierenburg's dissertation, "Judicial Violence in the Dutch Republic: Corporal Punishment, Executions and Torture in Amsterdam, 1650–1750" (Amsterdam, 1978).—Ed.]

5. [Historian Bernard Schnapper wrote extensively on law and family, and the form of legal separation (here, "separation of body and board") that served as

an alternative to divorce in the eighteenth century. Perrot may be referencing "Le coût des procès civils au milieu du XIX° siècle," *Revue historique de droit français et étranger* 59.4 (October–December 1981): 621–33; or "La séparation de corps de 1837 à 1914: Essai de sociologie juridique," *Revue historique* 259.2 (April–June 1978): 453–66.—Ed.]

6. [André Béjin is likely thinking of Jean-Louis Flandrin, *Familles: Parenté, maison, sexualité dans l'ancienne société* (Paris: Hachette, 1976); or *Le Sexe et l'Occident: Évolution des attitudes et des comportements* (Paris: Éditions du Seuil, 1981). In English: *Families in Former Times: Kinship, Household, and Sexuality*, trans. Richard Southern (Cambridge: Cambridge University Press, 1979); and *Sex in the Western World: The Development of Attitudes and Behaviour*, trans. Sue Collins (Philadelphia: Harwood Academic Publishers, 1991).—Ed.]

7. [*Manon Lescaut*, a short novel by Antoine François Prévost, recounts the adventures of Des Grieux and Manon Lescaut as they run away first to Paris and then to New Orleans, to which Manon has been deported as a prostitute. It offers a romanticized version of some of the social relations associated with the *lettres de cachet*; indeed, Prévost flees to London to avoid being imprisoned under a *lettre de cachet* issued by a prior.—Ed.]

8. [Jean-Claude Perrot, *Genèse d'une ville moderne: Caen au XVIII° siècle*, 2 vols. (Paris: Mouton, 1975).—Ed.]

9. [Likely Robert Darnton, *The Literary Underground of the Old Regime* (Cambridge: Harvard University Press, 1982).—Ed.]

CHAPTER 3

Review of
Disorderly Families

(1983)

Jean-Philippe Guinle

Jean-Philippe Guinle quickly gets to the heart of the Disorderly
Families *project—namely, that the letters are more than a symbol of an arbitrary royal power. Instead, this review calls attention to the lack of continuity between public and private orders.
Consequently (and perversely), the family becomes the site where
a certain public order is fabricated, rather than the other way
around.* ↝

We no longer consider *lettres de cachet* to be nothing more than the
symbol itself of royal arbitrariness. This is especially true in light of
the important distinction between the *lettres* that were purely political or purely police-related and those curious family *lettres,* whereby
the king could grant a private request for imprisonment, so long as the
petitioner agreed to cover (except in cases of exile to the Islands) the
costs of detention. And indeed, the book in question contains only
documents related to this third kind of *lettre,* which seem to be the
most significant, drawn from the Archives de la Bastille in the years
1728 and 1758. More often than not, these cases involved families
of modest means, who would write to the lieutenant general of police (and not directly to the king). The interest of these dossiers—
composed of requests by one spouse for the imprisonment of the
other, which account for one-third of the documents, and, for the remaining two-thirds, requests by parents for the imprisonment of their

children—lies perhaps less in the slices of life and mores of the era that their often formulaic language reveals than for what they can tell us, beyond these family dramas, about the relationship of individuals to a political power that would normally not have been very concerned with them.

Moreover, in these many requests for imprisonment—in which one sometimes gets the impression that the petitioner was hardly the least guilty party—as well as in the stirring requests for release by offenders who claim to have sincerely reformed, the most striking thing is the lack of a division between public order and private order. Indeed, as the presenters note: "Out of a need for order, private and public life melted into one another: the family was a privileged space where private tranquillity yielded a certain kind of public order."[1] For the Ancien Régime monarchy, "peace in the home," the preconditions of which can at least be defined by their opposite in certain of the documents presented, fell under the higher necessity of public order, from which nothing could escape—although, on the other hand, family life did not cease to be private, even when, through these petitions, it was laid bare before the king, whose thaumaturgical power was thought to be as effective for the imprisoned as his goodness.

It is therefore all the more surprising that, under the pretext of family honor, whose defense had imprudently been placed in its hands, or even of these families' need to have their misfortune recognized so that it might be exorcised, royal power did not attempt to extend the reach of its arbitrary rule even further. But the authors are absolutely correct when they note that "it would be utterly imprecise to conceive of the practice of the *lettres de cachet* as simply the functioning of a mechanism of authority that developed according to an autonomous principle of growth."[2] The truth is that, above all, this practice was a mechanism for regulating conflicts as insoluble as youthful rebelliousness or marital strife that had been exacerbated by unfaithfulness. And its mechanism was for that matter so complex, ambiguous, and insufficient, owing to its purely repressive character, that it was destined to disappear once it no longer suited the interests of the parties involved. From which came, over time, a lassitude on the part of authority, which found itself confronted with a proliferation of police investigations, and a concomitant feeling that the "fatherly beneficence" of the sovereign who imprisoned so as not to punish was sometimes, in fact, playing into the hand of arbitrary paternal authority. And yet, if one reads these files without preparing oneself, it is undeniable that, despite the passions and the arbitrariness that rise to the surface here, the concern of both families and authorities to reach a just and humane decision is often conspicuous—if only perhaps because a good number of these cases end with a release from prison, sometimes at the behest of the individuals who, with the same insistence, had originally petitioned for imprisonment. This is not to say that all of the requests for release were clear or disinterested; imprisonment might have frozen a needed inheritance, to give just one example. But this was a society in which, although penal law was unconcerned with it, repentance remained a moral value that the "Most Christian King" was obliged, if not always to respect himself, at least to encourage by releasing those who had shown it most sincerely.

If there is a lesson to be drawn from this odd practice of the family *lettres de cachet,* it lies perhaps paradoxically in the reminder, which the authors do not fail to make, of the system that would follow, seemingly restricted to unemancipated children or minors, but which in fact granted the husband all authority over the family, including his wife, as well as the famous "right of correction" over children, which specifically gave him the right to compel the imprisonment, without needing to offer any reasons, of a recalcitrant child under the age of sixteen for at least a month (Art. 376 of the Civil Code). This brings us to our final question: although it was indeed tainted by the arbitrariness that accompanies all policing power, was royal intervention "upon request" for family reasons more dangerous than the powers that would be conferred upon the head of the household in the name of a law that was, in truth, just as inexorable as the "cold monster" that the Napoleonic state was in the process of becoming?

Translation by Thomas Scott-Railton

NOTES

1. [Arlette Farge and Michel Foucault, *Disorderly Families* (Minneapolis: University of Minnesota Press, 2016), 24.—Ed.]

2. [Ibid., 251–52.—Ed.]

CHAPTER 4

Denunciation, a Slow Poison (1983)

Michel Heurteaux

Writing for Le Monde *on May 15, 1983, Michel Heurteaux extends the context for the* lettres de cachet *in this book review to the twentieth-century letters of denunciation that flourished under the Vichy régime; reemerged during the Baader–Meinhof conspiracy of the 1970s; and flourish even today with hotlines for illegal immigration and terrorism. Similar to the original* lettres, *these forms of denunciation engage in a play between the secrecy of scandal and the illumination of public power. Unlike the earlier letters, these denunciations were anonymous and so sought to reinforce (and secretly participate in) the authority of public order.*

"*Monsieur the Superintendent of police,* one C . . . lives on the fourth floor. He has a long history of stealing things around the neighborhood. Perhaps you could, for example, show up unannounced and ask him about where the four car tires that have recently showed up in his cellar came from . . ."

"*Messieurs,* I wish to bring to your attention that at 14 rue C . . . , there is a group of Brazilians, and, even worse still, transvestites. They prostitute themselves, engage in exhibitionism, and urinate in the courtyard, even in broad daylight . . ."

"The antiques dealer in the market at *place* B . . . is a degenerate individual. What is more, he's said to be an Israelite. I and three of my female friends have been bothered by him on several occasions. I ask that you put an end to his filthy behavior . . ."

Here we have three letters picked at random from the files of a Parisian police superintendent, all written in the same underhanded voice of anonymity. "We read this kind of literature every day," a young inspector assures me, already blasé.

Stuck behind his tiny desk, he describes himself as torn between disgust and bursting out laughing. The fact is that these diligent "tips" are not always of great value. "Of the three to four hundred letters we receive each year, barely 10 percent lead to any kind of investigation. The rest are rubbish, sometimes the result of paranoia, sometimes just pure meanness." Some accusers, moreover, do not hesitate, and pile it on in order to add more weight to their accusations, even if this means at times throwing plausibility to the wind: "They try to lure us in with absolute fairy tales."

Whether the facts reported are precise, grossly exaggerated, or invented out of whole cloth, in the end it matters little. The informant's goal is not so much for the truth to shine through as it is to profit from the denunciation itself. Out of a spirit of revenge, a desire to do harm, or even to see justice to be done, their hope is that the result will be charges being pressed against the "guilty party," and, if possible, his or her punishment. Informants do not address themselves to just anyone; authority is always the recipient, as it wields the power to punish, whether it be the local police, state police, the courts, tax auditors, customs officials, labor and welfare investigators—not to mention the mayor's office and the forest service.

Informants and power, a pair that has often made good bedfellows—and sometimes still does. But the history of this relationship remains to be written. In ancient Athens, someone who denounced a fellow citizen would be rewarded if the accused were found guilty.[1] Seventeenth-century Venice established "informant boxes." The Bastille archives of the prerevolutionary period, as examined by Michel Foucault and Arlette Farge,[2] tell us that the use of petitions *(placets)*—secret requests addressed to the king through the intermediary of the lieutenant general of police—was a convenient means by which families could achieve the imprisonment of a husband, wife, or child accused of debauch, madness, or violence. Closer to our own time, totalitarian regimes, under Hitler and Stalin alike, not only exuded informing, but encouraged it, making it into a civic virtue. In France, during the dark period of the occupation, this practice reached considerable levels.

Lapses in Payments, Lapses in Morals

In an upcoming work, presented as a veritable "laundry list of repulsion," André Halimi, drawing notably from the German archives, examines three to five million letters, both anonymous and signed, sent by French men and women to the authorities.[3] Thousands of Jews could be sent to their deaths simply on the basis of information provided by neighbors, who often began their letters with formulations like: "As a good Frenchman, a good Catholic, and a patriot, certain that I am aiding my country . . ."

Snitching and informing still exist today, albeit at lower levels. Squealing, or, if you prefer, "cooperating," is part of everyday life: playground "tattletales" who go running to the teacher, subordinates who believe it their duty to inform their bosses of so-and-so's activities, people who report their neighbors' bad behavior, village *corbeaux*—literally, crows, a term for writers of poison-pen letters—who gratify ancient grudges. The only differences are in style and in degree of shamefulness or mischief.

And what is it that gets denounced? According to the aforementioned officer, more often than not, "the infractions are more civil than criminal. Letters get written over squabbles." For example: quarrels between neighbors, which have become increasingly frequent. In an elegant Parisian neighborhood police precinct, a police officer tells us that three-quarters of the anonymous letters received refer to disagreements of this nature. "By writing to us, they hope to attract problems for their neighbor. If we go check out their story and they see us show up in our cruiser, they will be rubbing their hands together behind the door . . ."

Perhaps a landlord wishes to get rid of a tenant who is too leisurely with her rent payments? He will not only lecture her through registered letters, he will try to discredit her in the building and the neighborhood through letters listing his every grievance in detail. Take the young woman who was brought to the attention of the public authorities by a vindictive document bearing the signatures of all the collective co-owners of the building: "Miss D . . . is three months late in her rent . . ." and, what's more, "this young woman receives male visitors late at night. Her behavior is a permanent insult to the good reputation of our building . . ."

But when it comes to spreading dirt, malevolent insinuations, and slander pure and simple, the countryside far outdoes the city. The substance of these rural denunciations varies little, but the interlocutors change. In the deep countryside, in the hamlets where everyone shuts themselves in at night, "dirt" almost always makes its way to the police, to Monsieur the mayor or his assistants, and sometimes still to the priests, who in former times were kept up to date on the turpitude of their parishioners by a few good souls.

"Here," observes the assistant to the mayor of a community of a thousand inhabitants in Sologne, "we also get phone calls. We see people fly off the handle over stories about ditches that need cleaning, illegal property line marking, fences moved in the middle of the night, woodpiles blocking people's views!" Recently, a villager was denounced . . . for having surreptitiously built a rabbit hutch in his backyard. Every year, dozens of these affairs add to the chronicles of life in this sleepy country village.

The forest ranger *[garde champêtre],* owing to his bucolic peregrinations, is also on the receiving end of these tangled stories. In the opinion of an "expert" retired policeman, "the forest ranger is the quintessential intelligence officer," to whom a few perfidious tidbits of information will be whispered over glasses of white wine. In uniform in the morning, in civilian clothes in the afternoon, he gets wind of all the little stories, every misdemeanor. This is how he was able to uncover, thanks to "idle chats," the person who, presumably out of vengeance, sawed off the branch of a cherry tree in the butcher's orchard.

In addition to disagreements over property, there are cases of morality, affairs of the heart that ripen into hatred. Wronged wives and jealous husbands will sometimes address their pleas to any authority, trying to make their spouse pay indirectly for their betrayal. In a company in the west of France with two thousand employees, 40 percent of whom are women, a human resources manager admits that every year without fail he receives more than a dozen anonymous messages, as well as phone calls, regarding adultery, the workplace being the most frequent location of extramarital affairs.

Only a direct stake in the matter could break the prohibition on squealing to the boss: "These appeals, sometimes quite poignant, come from individuals denouncing the extramarital relations of their spouse. They come to their bosses saying that the company cannot allow such a situation to persist! There have been cases in which some individuals took this opportunity to demand that the lover or mistress in question be reassigned or even fired."

"A Secret Safe"

Wronged spouses are not the only ones who demand justice. Do not all of the people who alert tax inspectors to the tax fraud, either real or alleged, of their fellow citizens also consider themselves to have been wronged in a certain sense?

In this area, informing seems harder to measure: sometimes these letters are addressed directly to the minister, to the board of directors of the tax service, to the National Tax Investigation Agency (Direction nationale des enquêtes fiscales, or D.N.E.F.), but in general these "tips" end up with the lower-level bureaucracy. "At certain times of the year, we might receive several dozen appeals each week, all anonymous, of course, calling for the audit of such and such a taxpayer," reveals the manager of a branch of the tax auditing service in Paris. "Behind these letters, you sometimes find stories of jealousy: for example, during divorce proceedings, you will see wives denouncing their husbands, accusing them of not paying enough taxes! By doing this, they might be hoping to get more in alimony payments."

But here again, it is vengeance first and foremost that makes someone a casual informant. Take, for example, the recently fired accountant who "gave up" his old boss: "In such and such a place, you will find a secret safe filled with gold ingots and a shadow set of accounts." "We also have taxpayers who alert us to frauds against them," adds a revenue service agent. Still others report malfeasance in the hopes of receiving the famous "informant reward," generally paid in cash, the amount varying depending on the fraud and the sum of money recuperated; the revenue service is not above making formal use of denunciation. "Efficiency in the battle against fraud comes at such a price," a head manager of the revenue service comments laconically.

Another form of fraud, clandestine work, which has become relatively prevalent in certain trades—notably construction and automobile repair—is now increasingly being reported. The first to be told are professional organizations, trade federations, and unions, which are spurred in the battle against this scourge by the tips they receive, either under the table or through the grapevine, from angry craftsmen.

These tips are sufficiently precise that "nine times out of ten, we

136 *Michel Heurteaux*

can fall right upon the clandestine work site," indicates a small construction business owner in Yvelines, who from time to time organizes crackdowns with the police to ferret out cheaters. In hairstyling, where a black market has also emerged, certain tips have allowed professionals to uncover people conducting unlicensed hairdressing or even, in one exceptional case, to catch an amateur barber at dawn . . . shaving a corpse; five hundred francs in his pocket, taken right out of the hands of the neighborhood barber.

"Stealing Work"

Those who "steal work"—to use the expression of an official from the permanent assembly of tradesmen—salaried or unemployed construction workers who do a job for their neighbors, are also anonymously "reported" to the National Agency of Labor, to the Association for Employment in Industry and Trade (ASSEDIC), to the Union for the Collection of Social Security and Family Benefit Contributions (URSSAF), or to labor inspectors. "Denunciations are most common in urban areas, where employment problems are the most pronounced," notes an official from a branch of the National Employment Agency (A.N.P.E.) in the Paris region. These can lead to "requests for information," which can then lead to a summons and even actual legal proceedings if the charges are verified. Immigrants are the most common targets. Letters concerning immigrants are often accompanied by insulting comments in the line of "I'm sick of *bougnoles!*[4] It's no surprise that they're stealing our jobs." Along with immigrants, young people, unmarried women, and, as a general matter, all of those who are perceived as marginal, are the most frequent targets of denunciation, as judges and police officers have observed with little surprise. Perhaps we can add to the above categories the most modern faction of the Catholic church, some of whom have, in the recent past, had to suffer the wrath of the *intégristes,* who do not wish to see a separation between church and state. According to one Dominican: "During the debate over abortion, priests were informed upon by anxious parents, or by members of the faithful who were still very attached to the traditional liturgy. Letters still find their way to the bishop's desk or even the Vatican."

The police themselves say that they are not immune. Small-time criminals have, over the last four or five years, made informing—this time, in no way anonymous—a defense strategy, which, according to the Autonomous National Union of Plainclothes Police Officers (S.N.A.P.C.), "has become a veritable scourge for the police." Once in front of the judge, they accuse the inspectors of police brutality or of stealing from them during searches. "These days, three or four affairs of this kind per month" are sent along to Internal Affairs for investigation. A permanent but marginal phenomenon, informing remains nonetheless potentially dangerous. As history shows us, during tumultuous periods it can spread throughout society, permeating it entirely.

"It is a latent poison," remarks a police superintendent in a large city in the provinces. "We can see it at the present moment with problems of delinquency and debates on public safety. People are anxious, and they'll call us at the drop of a hat, to report the theft of a moped, a theft in a store; people want to be useful, to defend law and order by cooperating."

Sometimes necessary, this cooperation with the authorities can, in certain crisis situations, lead to informing on a mass level. Take, for example, the hunt in West Germany for the Baader–Meinhof terrorist group in 1977. When the antiterrorist section of the B.K.A. (office of the federal police) asked for anonymous information, the popular response was beyond all expectation. And it has left a mark: for several years, a television show that allows spectators to participate by helping police to search for criminals has broken all the records for viewing audience in Germany.

Five Thousand Calls

In France, some policemen might dream of this level of cooperation. Doesn't the criminal code make reporting criminal activity a duty? Last March, after the assassination of a barber in Ajaccio, police and judicial authorities circulated the voices of the criminals on the radio and television. In addition, by calling a certain telephone number, you could listen to a recording of the evildoers. In the space of a few hours, this number received five thousand calls. The tips provided by anonymous witnesses eventually allowed for the arrest of the criminals responsible.

Today, this success might seem to encourage us to continue down this path, one that has been opened by the publication of police sketches of criminals and alleged terrorists. In these cases as well, the public is

138 *Michel Heurteaux*

invited to come forward with information. For one inspector from the criminal division of the Paris police headquarters Quai des Orfèvres who admits that he "does not have many qualms," the dissemination of these police sketches has its drawbacks. "When we do this, we get informants of all kinds showing up. Each one claiming to have seen the guilty party, who turns out the be the next-door neighbor who they never liked. After the Rue de Rosiers bombing, we received about three hundred tips that we had to verify.[5] Eighty-five percent were absolutely fantastical. Some of them were just plain malicious, like this one letter from Marseille; after we went to investigate, we found out that the person denounced to us was an Arab grocer from the neighborhood who looked nothing like the image of the killer published in the press!"

Taking advantage of events like these, some individuals think they can settle their scores in good conscience. "We might find it deplorable," adds this inspector, "but good policing can't forgo intelligence gathering, and therefore a certain form of informing." Sometimes of use to power, a true instrument of social regulation in moments of crisis, informing never quite manages to shake its abject character.

Translation by Thomas Scott-Railton

NOTES

1. A portion of the accused's fortune would go to the accuser. However, if the latter did not obtain one-fifth of the judges' votes, he would have to pay a fine and would lose part of his civil rights. For this reason, some individuals would blackmail the wealthy by threatening to bring them to court.

2. [Arlette Farge and Michel Foucault, *Disorderly Families*, ed. Nancy Luxon, trans. Thomas Scott-Railton (Minneapolis: University of Minnesota Press, 2016). —Ed.]

3. [André Halimi, *Les Délateurs sous l'occupation* (Paris: Alain Moreau, 1983). —Ed.]

4. [Slur for people of African descent that has its roots in the French colonization of Algeria.—Trans.]

5. [This phrase refers to a 1982 terrorist attack on the Jewish restaurant Chez Jo Goldenberg.—Trans.]

PART II

Letters and Events
From Composition to Contestation

CHAPTER 5

The Order of Discourse (1970)

Michel Foucault

This essay served as Foucault's inaugural address to the Collège de France, given on December 2, 1970. Ritualistically, Foucault's address pays homage to Jean Hyppolite, whose death made this position available and who was Foucault's teacher at Lycée Henri IV and later his thesis supervisor. In recalling Hyppolite, Foucault addresses his own departure from Hegel and the paradox at the heart of this lecture and the entirety of his work: that the inaugural potential of power is deeply at odds with the knowledges that precede it. "The Order of Discourse" acknowledges and traces the complicated interplay between speech and text; the rules that variously organize each; and the uneven circulations of brief utterances, the cadences of ritualized speech, and the rarefaction of the speaking subject as discourse settles. Foucault's address ends by reflecting on the "philosophy of the event" as a way to frame this interplay. This essay proves seminal for later work by Roger Chartier, Arlette Farge, and eventually Jacques Rancière on the various circulations of words and publics. ◂

Inaugural Lecture at the Collège de France, December 2, 1970

I wish that I could have slipped myself surreptitiously into the talk *[discours]* that I will deliver today, and into those that I will, perhaps, come to deliver here in years to come. Instead of beginning to speak *[prendre la parole]*, I would have preferred that speech itself surround me and whisk me off far beyond any possible beginning. As I began to speak, I would have liked to have noticed that a nameless voice had

141

long preceded me; then all I would have needed to do was attach myself to it, continue the sentence, slide myself into its interstices unnoticed, as if it had beckoned to me by holding itself, for just an instant, in suspense. Then there would be no beginning; and instead of being the person from whom the discourse *[discours]* came, I would instead be at the whim *[au hasard]* of its march, a slender lacuna, its potential vanishing point.

I would have liked it if behind me (having begun to speak long ago, having already echoed what I am going to say) a voice was saying: "I must go on, I cannot go on, I must go on, words must be spoken as long as there are any left, I must speak them until they find me, until they speak me *[qu'ils me disent]*—a strange punishment, a strange offense, I must continue, perhaps it has already taken place, perhaps they have already spoken me, perhaps they have transported me to the threshold of my own story, before the door that will open onto my story, I would be surprised if it would open."

There are many, I believe, who share my desire to avoid a beginning, a similar desire to find oneself, from the moment one enters the game *[d'entrée de jeu]*, on the other side of the discourse, without having had to consider from the outside everything about it that might be singular, daunting, perhaps even malevolent. To this all-too-common wish, the institution responds in ironic fashion, because it renders beginnings solemn, because it surrounds them with a circle of attention and silence, and because it imposes certain ritualistic forms on them, as if to make them recognizable from a distance.

This desire says: "I wish I did not need to enter into the risky *[hasardeux]* order of the discourse; I don't want to have to deal with its sharp and decisive edge; I want it to surround me, like a calm, deep, indefinitely open, transparent sheen, from which truths would rise, one by one; I would only have to let myself be carried, within it and by it, like a happy shipwreck."[1] And the institution replies: "You need not worry about beginning; we are all here to show you that discourse is in the order of laws *[ordre des lois]*; that we have long kept vigil over its appearance; that a space has been prepared for it, one that will honor it but defuse it; and if, by chance, it wields any power, it is from us, and only us, that this power has come."

But perhaps this institution and this desire are nothing more than two contrasting replies to the same anxiety: anxiety over the discourse in its material reality as something spoken or written; anxiety over

The Order of Discourse 143

a transitory existence that is undoubtedly destined to disappear, but that will do so according to a time frame *[durée]* over which we have no hold; anxiety from the sense that underneath this activity, as gray and everyday as it might be, lurk powers and dangers that are difficult for us to imagine; anxiety from a suspicion that there are struggles, victories, wounds, domination, and servitude, in these many words whose roughness has long been smoothed by use.

But what, then, is so perilous about the fact that people speak, and that their discourses proliferate indefinitely? Where, then, is the danger?

Here is the hypothesis that I would like to advance this evening, so as to pin down the field—or perhaps just the exceedingly provisional theater—of my work: I posit that in every society the production of discourse is simultaneously regulated, selected, organized, and redistributed by a certain number of procedures, whose role is to conjure away its power and its dangers, to master its chance events, to evade its heavy, formidable, materiality.

In a society like ours, we are all well aware, of course, of the procedures for *exclusion*. The most obvious of these, as well as the most familiar, is *prohibition [l'interdit],* We all know, of course, that not everything can be said, that you cannot bring up every subject in every context, and finally, that not just anyone can talk about absolutely anything. The taboo of the object, the ritual of circumstance, the privileged or exclusive rights of the speaking subject: here we have the play of three types of prohibition, which intersect, reinforce, and compensate for one another, forming a complex grid *[grille]* that endlessly changes itself. I will only note that, in our present day, the narrowest sections of this grid, where blacked-out cells proliferate the most, are the areas of sexuality and politics; as if the discourse, far from being that transparent or neutral element inside of which sexuality would be disarmed and the political pacified, was instead one of the places where they exercised, in a privileged manner, some of their most daunting powers. Although, in its appearance, discourse might not seem all that important, the prohibitions that have marked it quickly reveal its ties with desire and with power. And why should this be a surprise? Because discourse—as psychoanalysis has shown us—is not simply that which manifests (or conceals) desire; it is also the object of desire; and because—and this is a lesson that history continually teaches us—discourse is not simply that which translates struggles or systems

144 *Michel Foucault*

of domination, but the Why and the How of the struggle, the power being fought over.

There is another principle of exclusion that exists in our society: not a prohibition this time, but a division and a rejection. I have in mind the opposition between reason and madness. Since the depths of the Middle Ages, the madman has been the person whose discourse cannot circulate like that of others: his word was considered null and void, bearer of neither truth nor importance, unable to bear witness in court, unable to authenticate an act or a contract, and it could not even, during the sacrifice of the Mass, allow for transubstantiation to occur, for bread to become body. Yet, on the other hand, it was sometimes endowed, in contrast to all others, with strange powers: that of being able to speak a hidden truth, of prophesying the future, of seeing in all naïveté what the wisdom of others could not discern. It is curious to realize that throughout centuries in Europe the word of the madman either went unheeded or, if not, was attended to as the bearer of true speech *[parole de vérité]*. Either it tumbled into the void—rejected as soon as it was proffered—or it was believed to contain some naive or sly reason, a reason that would be more reasonable than that of reasonable people. In any event, whether excluded or secretly invested with reason, it did not, in a strict sense, exist. It was through his words that a madman's madness was recognized; they were the site where the division occurred; but they were neither recorded nor heeded. Never, before the late eighteenth century, did it occur to a doctor to find out what was said (how it was said, why it was said) in these words that nonetheless made all the difference. The vast discourse of the madman was returned to noise, and he was only allowed to speak *[donnait la parole]* symbolically, onstage, where he came forth, disarmed and reconciled, playing the role of masked truth.

You will tell me that all of this is now over and done with, or at least is in the process of coming to an end: that the madman's speech no longer rests on the other side of the divide; that it is null and void no longer; that, on the contrary, we are now on the lookout for it; that we search for a meaning within it, or the outline or ruins of something greater; and that we have managed to come across them, these madman's words *[parole du fou]*, in what we ourselves say, in that tiny gap through which what we are trying to say escapes us. But all this attention does not prove that the old divide is no longer at play; just think of the grand armature of knowledge-*savoir* through which we decipher these words; just think of the whole network of institutions that allow someone—doctor, psychoanalyst—to listen to this speech, and that at the same time allow the patient to bring forward, or desperately cling to, his poor words. Contemplating this should be enough to trigger our suspicions that this division, far from having been erased, is at play elsewhere, along different lines, through new institutions and with altogether different effects. And even when the doctor's role is only to lend an ear to words that have at last been liberated, it is always within the maintenance of the caesura that the doctor will listen; listening to a discourse invested with desire, and that believes itself—for its greatest exaltation or its greatest anxiety—to be the bearer of terrible powers. If the silence of reason is what is needed to cure these monsters, it is enough for this silence to be on the alert, and thus the division survives.

It is perhaps risky *[hasardeux]* to posit the opposition between the true and the false as a third system of exclusion, in addition to the two that I have just discussed. How could one reasonably compare the constraints of truth with divisions of this kind, divisions that were arbitrary from their entrance into the game, or that at the very least organized themselves around historical contingencies, that are not only modifiable but in perpetual displacement, that are supported by a whole system of institutions that impose and renew them, whose exercise is not free of constraint, or, for that matter, of a certain element of violence?

Of course, if we position ourselves at the level of a proposition, within a discourse, the divide between true and false is neither arbitrary nor modifiable, neither institutional nor violent. But if we adopt a wider scope, if we ask the question of what has been, and what continues to be, through our discourses, this will to truth *[volonté de vérité]* that has spanned so many centuries of our history, and what kind, in its most general form, of division it is that governs our will to know *[volonté de savoir]*, then it is perhaps something like a system of exclusion (a historical system, modifiable, institutionally constraining) that will begin to appear.

There is no doubt that this divide was historically constituted. For the Greek poets of the seventh century, it was still the case that the true discourse *[discours vrai]*—in the strong and powerful sense of the word—the true discourse that engendered respect and terror, which reigned and thus required submission, was the discourse pronounced

146 *Michel Foucault*

by those with right and according to the requisite rituals; it was the discourse that spoke justice and assigned each person their role; it was the discourse that, in prophesying the future, not only announced the future to come, but contributed to its realization, that brought with it the adherence of men and thus brought itself into destiny. And yet, within a century, the highest truth would no longer reside in what the discourse *was* or in what it *did,* it would come to reside in what it *said*: a day came when the truth was displaced from the ritualized, efficient, and just act of enunciation *[énonciation]* to the statement *[énoncé]* itself: toward its meaning, its form, its object, its relationship to its referent. A specific division was established between Hesiod and Plato, with the true discourse on one side and the false discourse on the other; and this division was novel, because from then on the true discourse was no longer the precious and desirable discourse, since it was no longer the discourse tied to the exercise of power. The sophist was chased off.

This historical divide undoubtedly endowed our will to know with its general form. Yet this did not mean that it stayed put. In fact, it continually displaced itself: the great historical scientific shifts can at times be read as the result of a discovery, but they can also be read as the appearance of new forms of a will to truth. There was undoubtedly a nineteenth-century will to truth that did not intersect, either through the forms that it brought into play, or the domains of objects that it addressed, or the techniques that it employed, with the will to know that characterized classical culture. Let us jump forward a little: at the turn of the seventeenth century (and especially in England), a will to know arose that, prefiguring its actual contents, formulated models of possible, observable, measurable, classifiable objects; a will to know that imposed on the knowing subject (and in a certain sense did so prior to any experience) a certain position, a certain gaze and a certain function (observing rather than reading, verifying rather than commentating); a will to know that prescribed (and in a more general mode than any specific instrument) the technical level at which knowledge-*connaissance* would have to position itself in order be verifiable and useful. This all took place as if, beginning with the great Platonic divide, the will to truth had its own history, which is not that of the constraints of truth: a history of models of objects of knowledge-*connaissance,* a history of the functions and positions of the knowing subject *[sujet connaissant]*, a history of the material, technical, and instrumental investments of knowledge-*connaissance*.

Furthermore, this will to truth, like other systems of exclusion, shored itself up with institutional support: it is both reinforced and renewed by a thick scaffolding of practices, such as pedagogy, of course, as well as the system of books, of publishing, and of libraries; like the learned societies of yesteryear, the laboratories of today. And it is renewed as well, no doubt most deeply by the manner in which knowledge-*savoir* is established by a society, by which it is valorized, distributed, shared, and in a certain sense attributed. Let us recall, purely for symbolic purposes, the old Greek principle: arithmetic might be appropriate for democratic cities, because it teaches relationships of equality, but only geometry should be taught in the oligarchies, because it teaches proportions through inequality.

Finally, I believe that this will to truth, propped up in this manner by institutional support and distribution, tends to exercise on other discourses—I am still talking about our society—a certain kind of pressure and something like the power to constrain. I am thinking of the way in which, for centuries, Western literature had to search for support from the natural, the appearance of truthfulness *[le vraisemblable]*, sincerity, and science as well—in short, from true discourse. I am also thinking of the way in which economic practices, codified as precepts or advice, and potentially as morality, have from the sixteenth century on sought to support, to rationalize, and to justify themselves through a theory of wealth and production; and I am also thinking of the way in which a body as prescriptive as the penal system sought to place its foundations and its justification in, first, of course, a theory of laws, and then, from the nineteenth century on, in sociological, psychological, medical, and psychiatric knowledge-*savoir*; as if even the word of the law could only be authorized, in our society, by a discourse of truth.

Of the three great systems of exclusion stamped upon discourse—prohibitions on speech, the division between madness and reason, and the will to truth—it is to the third that I have devoted the most time. This is because the first two have, for centuries, never halted their long slide in the direction of the third; because it increasingly tries to bring the other two under its own account, both to modify them and to serve as their foundation; because while the first two continually become more fragile, more uncertain to the extent that they have become inflected by the will the truth, the latter, in contrast, never ceases to reinforce itself, becoming deeper and more inescapable.

And yet, it is undoubtedly this third one that is the least discussed; as if the will to truth and its pitfalls were masked by truth itself through the course of its necessary progression. The reason for this is perhaps the following: if the true discourse has not been, since the time of the Greeks, the one that answered to desire or the person who exercised power, then what is at stake in the will to truth, in the will to speak, in this true discourse, if not desire and power? The true discourse, which its own formal necessity emancipated from desire and liberated from power, cannot recognize the will to truth that inflects it; and this will to truth, which has imposed itself upon us for quite a long time now, is such that the truth it desires cannot but mask it.

Thus, all that appears before our eyes is a truth that would seem to be wealth, fecundity, a soft and insidiously universal force. As a result, we miss the will to truth, that prodigious machinery destined to exclude. All of those who, at various points in history, attempted to circumvent this will to truth and to hold it up against the truth and question it, at precisely the places where the truth endeavors to justify prohibitions and define madness, they must all, from Nietzsche, to Artaud, to Bataille, serve us as signposts—though grandiose ones, no doubt—for our daily work.

There are, of course, quite a few other procedures for the regulation and delimitation of the discourse. The ones I have spoken of up until this point are, in a certain sense, exercised from the outside; they function as systems of exclusion; they deal with the element of discourse that brings power and desire into play.

We can, I think, isolate a different group: internal procedures, which are internal in the sense that they are discourses regulating themselves. These procedures come into play through principles of classification, of ordering, of distribution, as if this time their aim was to master another dimension of the discourse: that of the event and of chance [hasard].

And at the forefront, we find commentary. I would imagine, although I am not sure, that there are no societies without major narratives that are told, retold, and varied upon; sayings, texts, ritualized bodies of discourse, recited according to set conditions; things that were once spoken and have since been preserved, because they are thought likely to contain some secret or wealth. In short, we might suspect that in societies there is a quite regular differentiation in the stature of different discourses: the discourses that "speak themselves" over the course of days and interactions, which pass along with the very act of their speaking; and the discourses that are at the origins of a certain number of new speech acts that elevate them, transform them or speak of them, in short, discourses that, imperceptibly, beyond their formulation, *are spoken,* remain spoken, and are still to be spoken. We are familiar with the examples of these in our cultural system: religious and juridical texts, as well as the texts—which are quite curious when we consider their status—that we call "literary," and, to a certain extent, scientific texts.

Certainly, this difference in levels is neither stable, nor constant, nor absolute. There is not, on one side, a category of fundamental or creative discourses established once and for all, and then, on the other, a mass repetition, annotation, and commentary. Many major texts become jumbled or disappear, and commentaries sometimes move to the forefront. But even as the specific points of application change, the function remains the same. And this principle of a differentiation of levels never ceases coming into play. The idea of radically erasing it could only ever be a game, a utopia, or an anxiety: a game like Borges's idea of a commentary that would be nothing more than the rewriting (but this time solemn and expected) of the original text word for word, or the game of a critique that would go on endlessly about a text that didn't exist; the lyrical dream of a discourse that would be reborn in each of its points absolutely new and innocent, and that would reappear continually, completely fresh, on the basis of things, or sentiments, or thoughts; the anxiety of Janet's patient for whom the least utterance was like "the word of the Gospel," harboring inexhaustible treasures of meaning, worthy of being eternally repeated, begun anew, commentated upon: "When I think," he would say after having heard or read something, "when I think about this phrase that it too will also go off into eternity and that I perhaps have not yet fully understood it."

But how could we not see that in each of these cases it is only one of the terms of the relationship that has been struck down, that the relationship itself was never abolished? This relationship that never ceases to modify itself over time; this relationship that in a given era will

150   *Michel Foucault*

take on multiple and divergent forms; juridical exegesis is deeply different (and has been for quite some time) from religious commentary; a single literary work can give rise, simultaneously, to very distinct types of discourses: *The Odyssey* as primary text was repeated, in the same period, by Bérard's translation, by countless textual commentaries, and by Joyce's *Ulysses*.

For the moment I would like to limit myself to indicating that, in what we generally call commentary, the gap between the primary text and the secondary text plays two roles that work in tandem. On the one hand, it allows for the (indefinite) construction of new discourses: the long shadow *[surplomb]* of the primary text, its permanence, its status as an endlessly adaptable discourse, the multiple or hidden meanings it is believed to contain, the reticence and the essential richness bestowed upon it, all of these establish the open possibility of speech. But, on the other hand, commentary's only role, whatever the techniques employed might be, is to *finally* say what was silently articulated *in there*. It must always, in accordance with a paradox that it forever displaces but from which it never escapes, say for the first time that which nonetheless had already been said and tirelessly repeat that which nonetheless had never been said. The endless burbling of commentary is agitated from within by a dream of masked repetition; its horizons are perhaps nothing more than its point of departure: simple recitation. Commentary conjures away the chance element *[hasard]* of discourse by giving it its due; it makes it possible to say something else from the text itself, but on the condition that it be the text itself that is spoken and in a certain sense fulfilled. The gaping multiplicity of meaning and chance *[aléa]* are transferred, by the principle of commentary, from that which could have been said, onto the number, the form, the mask, the circumstances, of repetition. The novelty is not in what is said, but in the event of its return.

I think that there exists another principle for rarifying discourse. This one is, up to a certain point, the complement of the first one. I am referring to the author. By the author I do not mean, of course, the speaking individual who uttered or wrote a text, but the author as the unifying principle of the discourse, as the unity and origin of its significations, as the location of its coherency. This principle is not at play everywhere, nor does it function in a uniform manner; there are quite a few discourses circulating all around us whose meaning or effectiveness was not drawn from an author to whom they could be attributed:

everyday words, erased immediately; decrees or contracts that require signatories, but not an author; technical manuals that are transmitted anonymously. But in the domains where attribution to an author is de rigueur—literature, philosophy, science—we can indeed see that it does not always play the same role. In the order of scientific discourse, attribution to an author was, in the Middle Ages, indispensable, because it was an index of truth. A proposition was considered to draw even its scientific value from its author. Since the seventeenth century, this function has been continually eroded in scientific discourse, and it now serves merely to endow a theorem, an effect, or a syndrome with a name. In contrast, in the order of literary discourse, and beginning in the same period, the function of the author has never ceased to reinforce itself: all of the stories, all of the poems, all of the dramas and comedies that had been allowed to circulate during the Middle Ages in, at the very least, a relative anonymity were now beginning to be questioned (and were ordered to tell) about where they had come from, who had written them; the author was asked to account for the unity of the texts placed under his name; he was asked to reveal, or at the very least to provide through his person, the hidden meaning that ran through them; he was asked to tie them together, through his personal life and his experiences, through the real history that saw them born. The author is what gives the disquieting language of fiction its unities, its knots of coherency, its insertion into the real [réel].

I know what people will say: "But you are talking about the author as he is created by the critic after the fact, once death has come and all that remains of him is a dusty pile of notebooks. A little order must be introduced into all of that, you'll admit. And imagining a project, a coherency, a theme, behind an author's mind or life, can indeed be somewhat fictional, but that does not take away from the fact that he did indeed exist, this real author, this individual who emerged through all the words employed, which carry the genius or disorder of his mind."

It would be absurd, of course, to deny the existence of the individual who writes and invents. But I think that—at least from a certain era onwards—the individual who began to write a text on the horizon of which prowled a possible oeuvre, took on the responsibility of the author's role: what he writes and what he does not; when he sketches out, even if only as a rough draft, an outline of the work, and what he lets fall to the wayside as everyday words, this whole game

152 *Michel Foucault*

of differences is prescribed by the authorial role, either as he receives it from his time period, or as he modifies it in turn—because he can upend the traditional image that we have of the author. From a new authorial position, he can carve out, from everything that he might have said, from everything that he says every day, at every moment, the still-trembling profile of his work.

Commentary limited the chance *[hasard]* of the discourse through the play of an *identity* that takes the form of *repetition* and of *sameness*. The authorial principle limits this same chance through the play of an *identity* that takes the form of an *individuality* and a *me [moi]*.

We must also recognize that another limiting principle exists in what we call, not the sciences, but rather the "disciplines." A principle that is just as relative and mobile. A principle that makes construction possible, but only through a narrowly defined game.

The organization of disciplines is as opposed to the principle of commentary as it is to that of the author. The latter because a discipline defines itself by a domain of objects, a body of methods, a corpus of propositions that are considered true, an interplay of rules and definitions, of techniques and instruments: these all constitute a certain kind of anonymous system available to anyone who can or wants to use it, without its meaning or its validity being tied to the person who happened to invent them. But the principle of the discipline is also opposed to that of commentary: in a discipline, unlike a commentary, the starting assumptions are neither a meaning to be rediscovered nor an identity to be repeated, but are rather the requirements for the construction of new statements. For a discipline to exist, there must therefore be the possibility of formulating new propositions, and of doing so indefinitely.

But there is more; and there is more, undoubtedly, so that there will be less: a discipline is not the sum of all the true things that can be said about something; it is not even the body of everything that could be, with regard to a given subject, accepted according to a principle of consistency or systematicity. Medicine is not constituted by the sum total of true things that could be said about illness; botany is not defined as the sum of all truths concerning plants. There are two reasons for this: first, both botany and medicine, as with all disciplines, are made up as much of errors as truths; errors that are neither vestigial nor foreign bodies, but that have a valid history and serve a positive

The Order of Discourse 153

function, a role that often cannot be disassociated from that of truth. But, in addition, for a proposition to belong to botany or pathology, it must answer to certain conditions—in one sense these are stricter and more complex conditions than those of pure and simple truth and, in any event, they are different ones. It must address itself to a set field of objects. Ever since the end of the seventeenth century, for example, for a proposition to be "botanical" it had to relate to the visible structure of the plant, the system of its similarities both far and near, or the mechanics of its fluids (and it could no longer hold on to—as was still the case in the sixteenth century—its symbolic values, or to the ensemble of virtues and properties attributed to it in antiquity). But, if it does not belong to a discipline, a proposition must utilize a well-defined type of conceptual instruments or techniques; from the nineteenth century on, a proposition was no longer medical, it fell "outside of medicine" and took on the character of individual fantasy or popular imagination if it brought into play concepts that were at once metaphorical, qualitative, and substantial (such as those of engorgement, or of warm liquids and dry solids). On the other hand, it could, and indeed it had to, draw upon concepts that were just as metaphorical, but that were built upon a different model, one that was functional and physiological (tissues could be irritated, inflamed, even degenerative). And there is more: in order to belong to a discipline, a proposition must be able to inscribe itself into a certain kind of theoretical horizon: it is sufficient to recall that the search for the original language, a theme that was perfectly acceptable until the eighteenth century, was enough, in the second half of the nineteenth century, to plunge any discourse not just into error, but into chimera, into fantasy, into nothing less than linguistic monstrosity.

Within its limits, each discipline recognizes true and false propositions, but it also rejects, beyond its margins, a whole teratology of knowledge-*savoir*. The exterior of a science is both more and less populated than we might think: there is, of course, immediate experience, the imaginary themes that endlessly carry and renew beliefs that have no memory; but perhaps there are also no errors in the strict sense, because error can only emerge and be identified within a definite system of practice; on the other hand, there are prowling monsters whose shapes shift along with the history of knowledge-*savoir*. In short, a proposition must fulfill complex and weighty requirements to be able

154 *Michel Foucault*

to belong to the ensemble of a discipline; before being called true or false, it must be, as Monsieur Canguilhem would say, "in the truth" [*"dans le vrai"*].

We have often wondered how it was that the botanists and biologists of the nineteenth century were unable to see the truth of Mendel's claims. The reason for this was that Mendel spoke of objects, employed methods, and placed himself on a theoretical horizon that were foreign to the biology of his time. No doubt Naudin before him had posited the thesis that heritable traits were discrete; however, as new and strange as this principle might have been, it could still participate—at least in the form of an enigma—in the biological discourse. Mendel, for his part, conceptualized the hereditary trait as an absolutely new biological object, thanks to a novel system of distinctions: he uncoupled it from the species, he uncoupled it from the sex that had transmitted it; and the field in which he observed it was the indefinitely open series of generations, where it appeared and disappeared according to statistical regularities. A new object called for new conceptual instruments, and new theoretical foundations. Mendel spoke the truth [*disait vrai*], but he was not "in the truth" of the biological discourse of his era: his rules were certainly not the kind by which biological objects and concepts were formed. It would take a change in scale, the deployment of a whole new model of biological objects for Mendel to enter into the truth and for his propositions to come to appear (for the most part) accurate. Mendel was a true monster, which meant that science could not speak of him; whereas Schleiden, for example, who, thirty years earlier, in the midst of the nineteenth century, denied plant sexuality, but did so within the rules of the biological discourse, was only formulating a disciplinary error.

It is always possible for the truth to be told in the wilderness beyond the discipline; but you can only enter within the truth by obeying the rules of a discursive "police" that you must reactivate in each of your discourses.

The discipline is a principle that regulates the production of discourse. It imposes limits on discourse through the play of an identity that takes the form of an endless updating and readaptation of the rules.

We have habitually seen the productivity of an author, the multiplicity of commentaries, the development of a discipline, as so many infinite resources for the creation of discourses. Perhaps. But they

The Order of Discourse 155

are nonetheless also principles of constraint; and in all likelihood we would be unable to offer an account of their positive roles or their role in proliferation without taking into consideration their function as restrictions and constraints.

There is, I believe, a third set of procedures that allows for the regulation of discourses. Here it is no longer a question of mastering the powers that discourses bring with them, or of conjuring away the chance nature *[hasard]* of their emergence. Instead, the focus is on determining the conditions for bringing discourses into play, imposing a certain number of rules upon the individuals that hold them, and therefore denying others access. This is another form of rarefaction, this time of speaking subjects; none shall enter into the order of the discourse without satisfying certain exigencies or if he is not, from the outset, qualified to do so. More precisely: not all of the areas of the discourse are equally open and accessible; some are highly forbidden (differentiated and differentiating) while others seem open to the winds, as if they were placed, without any preexisting restriction, at the disposal of every speaking subject.

While I am on this theme, I would like to relate an anecdote that is so beautiful that one shudders to think it is true. It brings together in a single figure all of the constraints on discourse: those that limit its powers, those that seek to master its chance emergences, those that differentiate among speaking subjects. At the beginning of the seventeenth century, the Shogun had heard tell that the Europeans owed their superiority—in navigation, commerce, politics, the art of war—to their knowledge-*connaissance* of mathematics, and he wished to accrue this precious knowledge-*savoir* to himself. As he had been told of an English sailor who possessed the secret of this marvelous discourse, he had him brought to his palace and retained him there. He took lessons from him, one on one. He learned mathematics. He was, in fact, able to hold on to power, and lived to be quite old. It was only in the nineteenth century that Japanese mathematicians would appear. But the anecdote doesn't end there: there is also the European side. According to the story, Will Adams, the English sailor, had been self-taught: a carpenter who had learned geometry from working in a naval yard. Should we regard this story as an expression of one of the great myths of European culture? That in contrast to the monopolized and secret knowledge-*savoir* of the Oriental despots, in Europe

156 *Michel Foucault*

there was a universal communication of knowledge-*connaissance,* an indefinite and free exchange of discourses?

This theme, of course, does not hold up under examination. Exchange and communication are positive figures at play within complex systems of restrictions; and they undoubtedly wouldn't know how to function independently of these. The most superficial and the most visible of these systems of restriction is constituted by what we might group together under the name "ritual." Ritual defines the requisite qualifications of speaking individuals (who, in the game of a dialogue, of interrogation, of recitation, must occupy such and such a position and formulate such and such statements). It defines the gestures, behaviors, circumstances, and the whole body of signs that must accompany the discourse; and finally, it sets the supposed or imposed efficacy of words, their effect on those to whom they are addressed, the limits of their value as constraints. Religious, judicial, therapeutic, and even to a certain extent political discourses can hardly be disassociated from this establishment of a ritual that determines both singular properties and appointed roles for speaking subjects.

A somewhat different functioning can be seen in the case of "societies of discourse," whose function was to preserve or produce discourses, but did so in order to circulate them within a closed space, distributing them only according to strict rules and such that their bearers were not dispossessed through this very distribution. An archaic model of this were the groups of rhapsodes who possessed the knowledge-*connaissance* of the poems to recite, and possibly to vary and transform; but this knowledge-*connaissance,* even though its aim was basically ritual recitation, was protected, guarded, and preserved within a set group, through the memory exercises themselves often incredibly complex; apprenticeship brought you admission into a group and a secret that recitation manifested but did not divulge; the roles of speaking and listening were not interchangeable.

Of course, there are no longer any such "societies of discourse" with this ambiguous game of secrecy and divulgation. But let there be no mistake: even in the order of true discourse, even in the order of published discourse that is free of all ritual, forms of appropriating the secret and of noninterchangeability are still exercised. It could very well be that the act of writing as it is institutionalized today in the book, the publishing industry, and the figure of the writer, takes place within a "society of discourse" that, while perhaps diffuse, is undoubtedly constraining. The difference of the writer, ceaselessly opposed through himself to the activity of all other writing or speaking subjects, the intransitive character that he lends his discourse, the fundamental singularity that he long ago granted to "writing," the dissymmetry affirmed between "creation" and every other play of the linguistic system. All of this manifests in its formulation (and, moreover, tends to lead back to the play of practices) the existence of a certain "society of discourse." But there are indeed many others that function in a completely different mode, according to different regimes of exclusivity and divulgation: think of the technological or scientific secret; think of the forms of the diffusion and circulation of medical discourse; think of those who have come to appropriate the economic or political discourses.

At first glance, these "doctrines" (religious, political, philosophical) are the inverse of "societies of discourse," in which the number of speaking individuals, even if it was not fixed, tended to be limited, and it was only among them that the discourse could circulate and be transmitted. Doctrine, in contrast, tends toward diffusion; and it is by having one single body of discourses in common that individuals, as many as we would like to imagine, define their reciprocal belonging. It would appear that the only requisite condition is recognizing the same truths and accepting a certain rule—which can be more or less flexible—of conformity with the validated discourses. If this were all, doctrines would hardly be that different from the scientific disciplines, and discursive regulation would only bear upon the form and content of statements, not on the speaking subject. Yet doctrinal belonging simultaneously implicates both the statement and the speaking subject, and each one through the other. It implicates the speaking subject by and through the statement, as is shown by the exclusionary procedures and the mechanisms of rejection that come into play once a speaking subject has formulated one or several inassimilable utterances; heresy and orthodoxy do not reflect a fanatical exaggeration of doctrinal mechanisms; they belong fundamentally to these disciplines. But, conversely, doctrine implicates statements on the basis of the speaking subject, to the extent that doctrine always functions as the sign, the manifestation, and the instrument of a preexisting belonging—belonging to a class, a social status or a race, a nationality or a shared interest, a struggle, a revolt, a resistance, or an acceptance. Doctrine binds individuals to certain types of enunciations and

158   *Michel Foucault*

in consequence prohibits all others: but, in return, it employs certain types of utterances to bind individuals to one another, and to differentiate them from all others. Doctrine carries out a dual subjectification *[assujettissement]*: of speaking subjects to discourses, and of discourses to the group, at least the virtual one, of speaking subjects.

Finally, on a much larger scale, we must indeed recognize that there are great cleavages in what we might call the social appropriation of discourses. While education may well be, by right, the instrument through which any individual in a society like our own can gain access to any type of discourse, we all know that in its distribution—in that which it permits and that which it prevents—it follows lines marked by social distance, opposition, and struggle. Any system of education is a political means of maintaining or modifying the appropriation of discourses, along with the knowledge-*savoirs* and powers that they bring with them.

I am well aware that it is quite abstract to separate, as I have just done, rituals of speech, societies of discourse, doctrinal groups, and social appropriations. The majority of the time they are bound together constituting grand edifices that distribute speaking subjects among the different types of discourse and that appropriate these discourses to certain categories of subjects. In a word, these are the great procedures for discursive subjectification. What is, after all, a system of teaching, if not a ritualization of speech *[la parole]*; if not that which qualifies and sets the roles of the speaking subjects; if not the constitution of a doctrinal group, or at least a diffuse one; if not a distribution and an appropriation of the discourse along with its accompanying powers and knowledge-*savoirs*? What is "writing" (that of "writers") if not a similar system of subjectification that might in some cases take somewhat different forms but whose major scansions are analogous? Do not the judicial system and the institutional system of medicine, at least in certain aspects, constitute similar systems for subjectifying discourse?

I wonder if a certain number of themes in philosophy have not also emerged both in response to this play of limitations and exclusions as well as, perhaps, in order to reinforce it.

In response to them, initially, by positing an ideal truth as the law of discourse and an immanent rationality as the principle of their development, as well as by renewing an ethos of knowledge-*connaissance*

The Order of Discourse 159

that promises truth only to the desire for truth itself and to the power of thought alone.

And subsequently as a way to reinforce these limitations and exclusions through a denial that this time works broadly upon the specific reality of discourse.

Ever since the Sophists' trade and games were excluded, ever since their paradoxes were more or less securely muzzled, it would seem that Western thought took care to ensure that in discourse there would be as little space as possible between thought and speech; it would seem that it took care to ensure that discourse would appear only as a kind of interjection between thought and speech; it would be thought draped in its signs and rendered visible through words, or conversely, it would be the very structures of language brought into play, producing the effect of meaning.

This ancient elision of the reality of discourse in philosophical thought has taken many forms over the course of history. We have come across it again recently in the guise of several themes that are familiar to us.

It might be that the theme of the founding subject *[sujet fondateur]* makes it possible to elide the reality of the discourse. Effectively, the founding subject is responsible for directly animating the empty forms of language with his designs; passing over the thickness and the inertia of empty things, he grasps intuitively, the meaning deposited there. He is also the one who, beyond time, founds horizons of meaning that history will then only need to explicate, and where propositions, the sciences, and deductive ensembles will, ultimately, find their foundation. In his relationship to meaning, the founding subject has at his disposal signs, marks, traces, letters. But he does not need to pass through the singular instance of discourse to make them manifest.

The theme opposed to this one, the theme of the original experience *[l'expérience originaire]*, plays an analogous role. It assumes that at the bare level of experience, before it had even been able to grasp itself in the form of a *cogito*, preexisting significations, which were in a certain sense already spoken, roamed the world, preparing it all around us and opening it from the outset to a kind of a primitive recognition. Thus, a primeval complicity with the world would have founded the possibility of speaking of it, speaking in it, of designating it and naming it, of judging it, and finally of knowing it in the form of truth. If discourse there is, what could it be, in its legitimacy, if not a

160 *Michel Foucault*

discrete reading? Things were already murmuring a meaning that our language needed only to raise up; and this language, beginning with its most rudimentary project, already spoke to us of a being, and it was like its nervous system.

The theme of universal mediation is, I think, another manner of eliding the reality of the discourse, even though it might appear otherwise. It might seem, at first glance, that by discovering at every turn the movement of a logos that elevates singularities into concepts and that permits immediate consciousness to deploy at long last all the rationality of the world, it is indeed the discourse itself that is placed at the center of speculation. But this logos, truth be told, is nothing more than a discourse already held, or rather it was things and events themselves that imperceptibly made themselves discourse by deploying the secret of their own essence. Discourse is nothing more than the shimmering of a truth in the process of being born in its own eyes; and once everything can at last take the form of discourse, once everything can be said *[tout peut se dire]* and discourse can be pronounced about anything *[se dire à propos de tout]*, it is because all things, having manifested and exchanged their meaning, can recede into the silent interiority of the consciousness of self.

Therefore, whether in a philosophy of the founding subject, a philosophy of original experience, or a philosophy of universal mediation, discourse is nothing more than a game, a game of writing in the first case, of reading in the second, of exchange in the third, and this exchange, reading, writing never bring into play anything but signs. Thus, the discourse cancels itself out, in its reality, by placing itself on the order of the signifier.

What civilization, at least in appearance, has been more respectful of discourse than ours? Where has it been more and better honored? What has it been, or so it would seem, more radically freed of its constraints and universalized? Yet I believe that underneath this apparent veneration of discourse, beneath this appearance of logophilia, a fear is lurking. Everything functions as if prohibitions, barriers, thresholds, and limits were put in place in such a way that the great proliferation of the discourse would be, in part, mastered; such that its richness would be discharged of its most dangerous element and its disorder would become organized according to figures that eschew its most uncontrollable aspects; everything unfolds as if we wished to erase the very marks of its irruption into the game of thought and of language. In our society—and in every other as well, I imagine, but according to different profiles and scansions—there is undoubtedly a profound logophobia, a kind of deaf fear of these events, of this mass of things said, of the outpouring of all these statements, of everything that could be violent, discontinuous, aggressive, disorderly, as well as perilous, and of the great incessant and disorderly buzzing of discourse.

And if we wish to, I won't say do away with this fear but analyze it through its preconditions, its play, and its effects, we must, I believe, resolve to three decisions that present-day thought somewhat resists and that correspond to the three groups of functions that I just mentioned: questioning our will to truth; restituting discourse's character as an event; and finally lifting the sovereignty of the signifier.

These are the tasks, or rather a few of the themes, that will govern the work I wish to carry out here in the years to come. It is easy to see some of the methodological requirements that this will entail.

First, a principle of *reversal*: the sites where the source of discourse was believed to reside, according to tradition, alongside the principle of their proliferation and their continuity, through these figures that seemingly played a positive role, such as the author, the discipline, the will to truth, we must instead understand as a negative game serving to amputate and rarify discourse.

But, once these rarifying principles have been identified, once we have ceased considering them as fundamental and creative bodies, what will we uncover beneath them? Will we be forced to recognize the virtual plenitude of a world of uninterrupted discourses? Here is where other methodological principles must be brought into play.

A principle of *discontinuity*: that rarifying systems exist does not mean that beneath or beyond them, a great unlimited, continuous, and silent discourse reigns, having been repressed or restrained by them, and that our goal would be to raise it back up by restoring it to speech *[en lui restituant enfin la parole]*. We should not imagine that there is something unspoken or unthought *[un non dit ou un impensé]* that crisscrosses the world, intertwining with all of its forms and all of its events, and that it would be a matter of uttering or thinking it at long last. Discourses must be treated like discontinuous practices that sometimes intersect, sometimes converge, but that are just as likely to exclude or remain unaware of one another.

A principle of *specificity*: we must not dissolve discourse into a game of preexisting significations; we must not imagine that the world presents us with a legible face that we would need only to decipher; it is not complicit in our knowledge-*connaissance*; there is no prediscursive providence that inclines it in our favor. We must think of discourse as a violence that we do to things—in any case, like a practice that we impose upon them; and it is in this practice that the events of discourse[2] find the principle of their regularity.

The fourth rule is that of *exteriority*: the path is not from discourse toward its hidden internal kernel, toward the heart of a thought or a meaning that manifests itself within it, but rather it begins with discourse itself, its apparition and its regularity, and travels in the direction of its external conditions of possibility, toward that which gives rise to the chance *[aléatoire]* series of these events and that fixes its boundaries.

Four concepts should therefore serve as principles regulating this analysis: the concepts of the event, of the series, of regularity, and of conditions of possibility. They each have their clear opposite, term for term: event and creation; series and unity; regularity and originality; conditions of possibility and meanings. The latter four concepts (meaning, originality, unity, creation) have, in a rather general manner, dominated the traditional history of ideas that, by common agreement, sought out a point of creation, the unity of a work, of an era, or of a thematic, the mark of individual originality, and the endless treasure of hidden meanings.

There are only two remarks I wish to add to this. The first relates to history. We often credit contemporary history with having stripped the privileges heretofore accorded to the singular event and with having drawn out the structures of the long term *[longue durée]*. Doubtless. But I am not so sure that this was precisely the direction in which the work of historians was pointing. Or rather, I do not think that there is something like an inverse rationale between identifying the event and analyzing the long term. It would seem, on the contrary, that it was by accentuating the granularity of the event to the extreme, by shifting the resolution of historical analysis down to the official price lists *[mercuriales]*, notarized acts, parish registers, port archives, tracking them year by year, week by week, that we were able to see beyond battles, decrees, dynasties, or assemblies, all the way to massive phenomena that spanned a century or centuries. History as it is

The Order of Discourse   163

practiced today does not shy away from events. Instead, it continually broadens their scope, continually unearthing new layers, both shallower and deeper, continually isolating novel ensembles, at times numerous, dense, and interchangeable, at times rare and decisive: from quasi-quotidian price fluctuations to meteoric inflation. But what's crucial is that historians do not examine an event without placing it in a defined series, without specifying the mode of analysis applied to this series, without seeking to understand the regularity of phenomena and the limits on the probability of their emergence, without interrogating variations, inflections, and the shape of the graph, without trying to determine the conditions on which these depended. Of course, history has long given up viewing events through an interplay of cause and effect within the formless unity of a grand destiny, either vaguely homogeneous or rigidly hierarchical. But this rejection did not imply a search for anterior, foreign, structures hostile to the event; it meant establishing diverse, intersecting, divergent series that would make it possible to circumscribe the "site" of the event, the margins of its haphazardness [aléa], the preconditions of its emergence.

The fundamental concepts that become necessary at this juncture are no longer those of consciousness and continuity (along with their correlative problems of liberty and causality), nor those of the sign and the structure. The concepts we need now are those of the event and the series, along with the interplay of related concepts; regularity, hazard [aléa], discontinuity, dependency, transformation. It's through such an ensemble that the discourse analysis I have in mind unfolds, not (of course) along the traditional thematics that philosophers of the past took for "living" history, but rather through the effective work of historians.

But it is also through this shift that my analysis poses philosophical, or theoretical, problems, ones that are in all likelihood rather daunting. If discourses must be treated first as ensembles of discursive events, what status should we give this concept of the event that philosophers only rarely took into consideration? The event is, of course, neither substance nor accident, neither quality nor process; the event is not on the order of bodies. Yet it is in no way immaterial; it is always at the level of materiality that the event takes effect, that it is an effect; it resides and consists in the relationship, the coexistence, the dispersion, the cross-referencing, the accumulation, the triage of material elements; it is neither an act nor a property of a body; it is produced as

164 *Michel Foucault*

an effect of and by material dispersion. Let us say that the philosophy of the event should move in the direction, which may seem paradoxical at first glance, of a materialism of the insubstantial.

Furthermore, if discursive events should be approached according to series that are homogeneous, yet discontinuous with one another, what status should we give this discontinuity? This is not a matter, of course, either of the succession of instants over time or of the plurality of various thinking subjects. This is a question of the caesuras that shatter the moment and scatter the subject into a plurality of possible positions and functions. A discontinuity of this kind strikes against and invalidates the smallest units that are traditionally recognized and the hardest to contest: the moment and the subject. And, below them, independent of them, we must conceive of relationships between these discontinuous series, relationships that are not on the order of succession (or simultaneity) within a single (or several) consciousnesses; we must elaborate—outside of philosophies of the subject and of time—a theory of discontinuous systematicities. Finally, if it is true that, within certain limits, these discursive and discontinuous series have their own regularity, then no doubt it will be impossible to establish between their constitutive elements connections of mechanical causality or ideal necessity. We must allow happenstance *[aléa]* to be introduced as a category in the production of events. Here again we can feel the absence of a theory that would allow us to think about the relationships between chance *[hasard]* and thought.

Thus, in the slight discrepancy that I propose to establish in the history of ideas, which consists in dealing with, not the representations that might lie behind discourses, but discourses as regular and distinct series of events, in this slight discrepancy, I fear that I recognize something along the lines of a tiny (and perhaps odious) machine that could introduce into the very root itself of thought, *chance, discontinuity,* and *materiality*. A triple threat that a certain form of history tries to conjure away by telling the story of a continuous progression of ideal necessity. Three concepts that should make it possible for us to connect the practice of historians and the history of systems of thought. Three paths for our project of theoretical development to pursue.

By following these principles and setting my bearings against this horizon, the analyses that I propose can be arranged into two groups. On one side there is the "critical" group, which will implement the principle of reversal: attempting to pin down the forms of exclusion, limitation, and appropriation that I discussed earlier, showing how they came to be formed, what needs they answered, how they were modified and displaced, what constraint they actually exercised, to what extent they were inflected. On the other there is the "genealogical" group, which will implement the three other principles: how series of discourses were formed, through, despite, or with the assistance of these systems of constraint, what norms were specific to each of them, and what were the conditions of their emergence, their growth, their variation.

Let us first look at the critical group. An initial set of analyses might examine what I have designated as exclusionary functions. In the past I have studied one of these functions over a specific period—such as the division between reason and madness in the Classical era. The next step might be to try to analyze a system of a prohibition on language, such as the one that surrounded sexuality from the sixteenth until the nineteenth century. This would not, of course, be a matter of watching its welcome disappearance over time, but rather of observing how it has been displaced and rearticulated on the basis of a practice of confession in which forbidden behaviors were named, classified, placed in a hierarchy, and all of this in the most explicit manner, up until the rather timid appearance, quite late, of the topic of sex in nineteenth-century medicine and psychiatry. These are, of course, only reference points, and somewhat symbolic ones at that, but I am already prepared to wager that the scansions will not be those we expect and that the prohibitions will not always take place where we might imagine.

For the time being, it is the third system of exclusion to which I would like to turn. And I will conceptualize it in two ways. First, I would like to try to identify how the choice of truth *[choix de la vérité]*—within which we are caught but which we also endlessly renew—was made, as well as repeated; I will first look to the era of sophistry and the beginning of this choice with Socrates, or at the very least with Platonic philosophy, in order to observe the manner in which the effective discourse, ritual discourse, the discourse full of powers and perils, had order brought to it little by little by a division between the true and the false discourse. I will then look to the turn of the seventeenth century, at the time of the emergence, especially in England, of a science of looking, observing, recording, a specific natural philosophy that was no doubt inseparable from the establishment of new political structures—or from religious ideology as well, for that matter. This was undoubtedly a new form of the will to know. Finally, the third reference point will be the beginning of the nineteenth century, with the great foundational acts of modern science, the formation of an industrial society, and the positivist ideology that accompanied it. Three cross sections into the morphology of our will to know; three stages in our philistinism.

I would also like to pick up on the same question from an entirely different angle: tracking the effects of a discourse with scientific aspirations—a medical, psychiatric, and sociological discourse—on the whole body of prescriptive discourses and practices that constitute the penal system. The study of psychiatric expertise and its role in penalization will serve as the starting point and source material of this analysis.

It is with this same critical perspective, but at a different level, that we should analyze procedures for limiting discourses, from among those that I designated earlier as the principles of the author, of commentary, and of the discipline. We can, from this perspective, envisage a number of courses of study. I am thinking, for example, of an analysis of the history of medicine from the sixteenth to the nineteenth century. Not one focused on the discoveries made or the concepts employed, but rather on grasping, not just within the construction of medical discourse, but also within the entirety of the institution that supports, transmits, and reinforces it, the ways in which these principles of author, commentary, and discipline were brought into play. One that would seek out how the principle of the great author was exercised: Hippocrates, Galen, of course, but also Paracelsus, Sydenham, and Boerhaave. And then it would turn to how the practices of aphorism and of commentary were exercised, even up to the nineteenth century, and how little by little these came to be replaced by a practice based on cases, collecting cases, on a concrete model of clinical learning. Finally, it would ask what model medicine looked to as it sought to constitute itself as a discipline, leaning first on natural history, then later on anatomy and biology.

We could also contemplate studying the manner by which literary history and criticism in the eighteenth and nineteenth centuries constructed the character of the author and the figure of the oeuvre: employing, modifying, and displacing the approaches of religious exegesis, biblical interpretation, hagiography, of legendary and historical "lives," of autobiography and memoir. We must also, one day, study the role that Freud played in psychoanalytic knowledge-*savoir*, so different was it from that of Newton in physics (and of all the founders of disciplines), and so different as well from the role that authors play in the field of philosophical discourse (even if the author was, like Kant, the source of a new way of doing philosophy).

Here we have a few projects for the critical side of our endeavor, for our analysis of the bodies of discursive regulation. As for the genealogical side, it is concerned with the actual formation of discourses, either within the limits of regulation or outside of them, or, as is most common, on both sides of this delimitation. The critical approach analyzes the processes for rarifying, but also assembling and unifying, discourses; the genealogical approach studies their formation, which is simultaneously dispersed, discontinuous, and regular. In truth, these two tasks can never be entirely separated from one another; it is not as if we had, on one side, the forms of rejection, exclusion, assembly, and attribution, and then, on the other, at a deeper level, the spontaneous eruption of discourses that, either immediately before or after their appearance, are submitted to triage and regulation. The regularized formation of discourse can integrate, under certain conditions and up to a certain point, the regulatory procedures (this is what happens, for example, when a discipline takes on the form and status of scientific discourse); and conversely, these regulatory structures can take shape within a discursive formation (as is the case with literary criticism as the discourse that constitutes the author). Therefore, any critical project seeking to put into question the regulatory structures must also simultaneously analyze the discursive regularities through which these came to be formed; and any genealogical description must take into account the limits at play during the actual process of formation. Between the critical enterprise and the genealogical one, the difference does not lie so much in the object or the domain, but in points of attack, perspectives, and delimitations.

Earlier, I raised a possible avenue of inquiry: examining the prohibitions stamped upon the discourse of sexuality. It would be difficult and abstract, in any event, to undertake this study without at the same time analyzing the body of discourses—literary, religious, and ethical, biological, medical, as well as legal—that deal with sexuality, and in which it is named, described, made into a metaphor, explicated, and judged. We are far from having constituted a unitary and regular discourse on sexuality. Perhaps we will never be able to do so, and perhaps this is not even the direction in which we are heading. It matters little. Prohibitions do not take the same form and their interplay is different in the literary discourse as it is in the medical one, in the psychiatric discourse as in the discourse of the direction of conscience. And, conversely, these different discursive regularities do not reinforce, circumvent, or displace prohibitions in the same manner. The only way to undertake this study would therefore be to examine a plurality of series in which these prohibitions come into play. In each case, at least in part, the prohibition will be different.

We might also consider the series of discourses from the sixteenth and seventeenth centuries dealing with wealth and poverty, money, production, and commerce. Here we are dealing with a powerfully heterogeneous body of utterances, formulated by rich and poor, educated and uneducated, Protestants and Catholics, royal officers, merchants, and moralists. Each of them with its own form of regularity, and its own systems of constraint as well. And none of them that would prefigure precisely another form of discursive regularity that would adopt the allure of a discipline and would come to be called the "analysis of wealth," and then "political economy." Yet it was out of them that this new regularity formed itself, picking up on or rejecting, justifying or brushing aside, their various statements.

We might also imagine a study focused on discourses concerning heredity, such as they might be found, spread and scattered across disciplines, observations, techniques, and various beliefs, up until the beginning of the twentieth century. Then it would be a question of showing the interplay of connections through which these series ultimately came to be reassembled in the figure, both epistemologically coherent and recognized by the institution, of genetics. This is in fact what François Jacob has just accomplished, with unparalleled brilliance and scientific rigor.

Thus, critical descriptions and genealogical descriptions must alternate back and forth, confer mutual support to each other, and complete one another. The critical portion of the analysis engages the systems that envelop the discourse; it attempts to identify, to pin down, the principles for ordering, rarifying, and excluding from discourse. Let us say, if a play on words will be permitted, that it practices a rigorous indirection *[une désinvolture appliquée]*. The genealogical portion of the analysis, in contrast, attaches itself to the series of the actual formation of discourse: it attempts to grab hold of it in its affirmative power, and by this I do not mean a power opposed to that of negation, but rather the power to constitute domains of objects, on the basis of which true and false propositions could be affirmed or negated. Let us call these domains of objects positivities; and let us say, to play with words a second time, that if the critical style is one of a rigorous indirection, then the genealogical mood will be that of a chance positivism [*positivisme heureux*].

In any case, at least one thing merits emphasizing: discourse analysis as understood here does not seek to unveil the universality of a meaning, it brings to light the play of imposed rarity, with a fundamental power to affirm. Rarity and affirmation; rarity, finally, of affirmation, rather than continuous generosity of meaning, rather than the monarchy of the signifier.

And now let those with limited vocabularies say—if they prefer its sound to its meaning—that this is structuralism.

I am well aware that the research whose outline I have tried to describe here would have been impossible without the assistance of models and reference points. I believe that I owe a great deal to Monsieur Dumézil, since it was he who encouraged me to work at an age when I still believed that writing was a pleasure. But I also owe a great deal to his work itself; I hope he will forgive me if I have led his texts, which dominate us today, astray from the path of their meaning and rigor; it was he who taught me to analyze the internal economy of a discourse in a manner entirely different from the methods of traditional exegesis or linguistic formalism; he is the one who taught me to identify, through the play of comparisons, systems of functional correlations from one discourse to the next; it was he who taught me how to describe the transformations of a discourse and its relationships to an institution. If I sought to apply this method to discourses other than legends or mythological narratives, it was because I was looking at the work of historians of science, especially that of Monsieur Canguilhem. It is to him that I owe my understanding that the history of science was not necessarily restricted to the following alternative: either a chronicle of discoveries or a description of the ideas and opinions bordering science on the side of its faint genesis or the side of its external fallout. But that instead we could, and indeed we should, see

170 *Michel Foucault*

the history of science as simultaneously coherent and changeable body of theoretical models and conceptual instruments.

But I think that a great part of my debt is to Jean Hyppolite. I know that, in the eyes of many, his work falls under the sign of Hegel, and that our whole era, whether it be through logic or epistemology, through Marx or Nietzsche, has attempted to escape from Hegel. And what I attempted to say earlier about the discourse is quite unfaithful to the Hegelian logos.

But truly escaping Hegel would require appreciating exactly what it would cost to detach ourselves from him. This would require knowing just how far Hegel, perhaps insidiously, has moved in our direction. This would require knowing what remains Hegelian about that which allows us to argue against Hegel, and to measure the extent to which our recourses against him are perhaps a lure that he has set for us, at the end of which we will find him waiting, immobile and elsewhere.

Moreover, if more than one of us owes a debt to Hyppolite, it is because he tirelessly went ahead and cleared for us the path away from Hegel, down which we find ourselves brought back to him again, but in a different way, before being obliged to take leave of him anew.

First, Hyppolite took great pains to give substance to the great, somewhat phantomlike, shadow of Hegel that had lurked since the nineteenth century and with whom an obscure combat had been waged. It was through a translation, that of the *Phenomenology of Spirit,* that he gave Hegel this substance; and Hegel himself is quite present in the French text, the proof of this being that Germans have consulted it in order to better understand what, for a moment at least, became the German version.

In addition, Hyppolite searched and explored all of the avenues of this text, as if his fear was: Can we still philosophize where Hegel is no longer possible? Can a philosophy continue to exist that is not Hegelian? Is that which is non-Hegelian in our thought necessarily also nonphilosophical? And is the antiphilosophical also necessarily non-Hegelian? In such a way that he did not simply wish to offer a meticulous description of the Hegel whose presence he brought to us: he wished to make him into a framework for the experience of modernity (is it possible to think in the Hegelian mode of the sciences, history, politics, and of everyday suffering?), and conversely, he wished to make our modernity the testing ground of Hegelianism and, through that, of philosophy. For him the relationship to Hegel was the site of

The Order of Discourse 171

an experience, a confrontation, from which it was never certain that philosophy would emerge victorious. He did not employ the Hegelian system as a reassuring universe, far from it. He saw in it the extreme risk taken by philosophy.

This explains, I believe, the displacements that he carried out, I will not say within Hegelian philosophy, but rather upon it, and upon philosophy as Hegel conceived of it; it also explains a whole inversion of Hegel's themes. Instead of conceiving of philosophy as totality finally able to think of and grasp itself in the movement of the concept, Hyppolite saw it, against the backdrop of an infinite horizon, as an endless task: though always early to rise, his philosophy was never prepared to draw to a close. A project without end, and therefore a project that was always begun anew, dedicated to the form and the paradox of repetition: philosophy, as the inaccessible thought of the totality, was for Hyppolite that which could be repeated in the extreme irregularity of experience; it was that which presented and exposed itself as a question that arose continually in life, in death, in memory: thus he transformed the Hegelian theme of the achievement of self-consciousness into a thematic of repetitive interrogation. But, because it was repetition, philosophy did not come after the concept; it did not need to pursue the edifice of abstraction, instead it would always need to beat a retreat, to break with its acquired generalities, and bring itself back into contact with nonphilosophy; it needed to move toward, as close as it could, not to that which would complete it but to that which preceded it, to that which was not yet awake to its anxiety; it needed to gather up the singularity of history, the regional rationalities of science, the depth of memory in the consciousness, not to reduce them, but to think them again; thus emerge the themes of a philosophy that is present, anxious, and mobile all along the length of its contact line with nonphilosophy, existing only by it and revealing the meaning that this nonphilosophy has for us. Moreover, if philosophy lies in this repeated contact with nonphilosophy, what was the beginning of philosophy? Was it already there, secretly present in what it was not, beginning to whisper its own formulation within the murmur of things? But, if so, then the philosophical discourse will perhaps not have a raison d'être; or perhaps it had to begin on a foundation that was at once both arbitrary and absolute? We can thus see the Hegelian theme of the movement proper to the immediate being replaced by a theme of the foundation of the philosophical discourse and its formal structure.

172 *Michel Foucault*

And finally, there is the final displacement that Hyppolite worked upon Hegelian philosophy: if philosophy must indeed begin as an absolute discourse, what can we make of its history and of this beginning that began with a solitary individual, within a society, a social class, and surrounded by struggles?

These five displacements, leading to the extreme edge of Hegelian philosophy, by taking it undoubtedly beyond its own limits, invoke one after another the major figures of modern philosophy that Hyppolite continually brought into confrontation with Hegel: Marx with his questions of history, Fichte with the problem of the absolute beginning of philosophy, Bergson with the theme of contact with nonphilosophy, Kierkegaard with the problem of repetition and truth, Husserl with the thematic of philosophy as an infinite endeavor, tied to the history of our rationality. And, beyond these philosophical figures, we can observe all of the domains of knowledge-*savoir* that Hyppolite brought to bear upon his own questions: psychoanalysis and the strange logic of desire, mathematics and the formalization of discourse, the theory of information and its application to the analysis of the living, in short all of the domains from which we can ask the question of a logic and an existence that are continually knotting and unknotting their ties to one another.

I think that his oeuvre, articulated in several major books, but even more invested in research, teaching, a perpetual attention, an everyday alertness and generosity, through seemingly administrative and pedagogical responsibilities (which is to say in truth doubly political responsibilities), intersected, formulated the most fundamental problems of our time. In my infinite debt to him, I am but one of many.

It is because I undoubtedly borrowed the meaning and the possibility of my work from him, as he often lit my way where I had been stumbling in the dark, that I would like to dedicate my work to him, and why it was so important for me to conclude this presentation of my projects with an expression of my gratitude to him. It is in his direction, in the direction of this lack—where I feel both his absence and my own shortcomings—that the questions I am now asking cross paths.

Because I owe him so much, I quite understand that the choice you made in inviting me to teach here was, in great part, an homage to him; I am grateful to you, deeply grateful, for this honor, but I am no less grateful for how much this choice is a reflection of him. While I do not consider myself to be up to the task of succeeding him, I know that, on the other hand, if this happiness could have been granted to us, I would have been, this evening, encouraged by his indulgence.

And now I better understand why it was that I felt such difficulty earlier. I know now which voice it was that I had wished to precede me, to carry me, to invite me to speak, and to inhabit my own discourse. I know what was so daunting about beginning to speak, because it is from this floor that I listened to him, and because he is no longer here, now, to hear me.

Translation by Thomas Scott-Railton

NOTES

1. [René Char was one of Foucault's favorite poets and was often quoted by him. The phrase "épave heureuse" comes from a poem by René Char titled "Allegiance" in which Char uses a lover's language to describe the experience of a poet delivering a finished poem to a public that risks misunderstanding it. Translator Mary Ann Caws renders the phrase as "joyous shipwreck"; Nancy Naomi Carlson translates it as "blissful sunken wreck." Another possibility might be "happy wreck," which connotes someone besotted and plays with both Char's and Foucault's invocations of desire. Char may be toying with Shakespeare, who uses the phrase "happy shipwreck" in *Twelfth Night*.—Ed.]

2. [Foucault will later use the term "événements discursifs" in the March 17, 1971, lecture from the same *Lectures on the Will to Know: Lectures at the Collège de France 1970–1971*, English series ed. Arnold Davidson, trans. Graham Burchell (New York: Palgrave Macmillan, 2013), 194. Foucault also used that phrase, along with the phrase "discours comme événement," in his 1968 essays "Réponse à une question" and "Sur l'archéologie des sciences: Réponse au Cercle d'épistémologie," in *Dits et Écrits II* (Paris: Gallimard, 2001), 701–23 and 724–59.—Ed.]

CHAPTER 6

The Public Sphere
and Public Opinion   (1990)

Roger Chartier

In "The Public Sphere and Public Opinion," Roger Chartier draws on historical inquiry to critique the conventional views of "public" associated with Kant, Hegel, and Habermas. Chartier's inquiry focuses on the devolution of authority onto historical publics, their connection to voice and political agency, and the instability of mechanisms of political representation. The essay speaks directly to the symbolic weight of the lettres de cachet *as they reflected the secrecy of judicial procedures of the time, and the dissimulations that left public audiences no more than captive spectators before a* theatrum mundi. *Secrecy prevented audiences from becoming publics. Only through the large-scale circulation of printed texts (including judicial memoirs and popular literature) and the pluralization of the "I" could popular opinion be converted to a legitimate court of judgment. Paradoxically, the move to raise particular plaints to matters for general concern was fueled by the* lettres de cachet—*and led to their demise.* ⬦

A reading (which necessarily will be an interpretation) of Jürgen Habermas's classic work *Strukturwandel der Öffentlichkeit* (in English translation, *The Structural Transformation of the Public Sphere*) offers a first guide to how the notion of public opinion was constructed in the eighteenth century.[1] Habermas stated his thesis clearly: at the heart of the century (in some places sooner, in others later) there appeared a "political public sphere," which he also called "a public sphere in the

176 *Roger Chartier*

political realm" or a "bourgeois public sphere." Politically this sphere defined a space for discussion and exchange removed from the sway of the state (that is, from the "sphere of 'public authority'" or "public power") and critical of the acts or the foundation of state power. Sociologically it was distinct from the court, which belonged within the domain of public power, and from the people, who had no access to critical debate. This is why this sphere could be qualified as "bourgeois."

The Political Public Sphere

Several organizing principles governed the political public sphere, which issued directly from the public literary sphere and was based in the salons and cafés and in periodical literature. Its first definition was as a space in which private persons made public use of their reason: "The bourgeois public sphere may be conceived above all as the sphere of private persons come together as a public."[2] A fundamental link thus existed between the emergence of a new form of "publicness"— which was no longer simply that of the exhibition or celebration of state authority—and the constitution of a domain of the private that included the intimacy of domestic life, the civil society founded upon exchange of merchandise and labor, and the sphere given over to the critical exercise of "public reason."

The process of privatization typical of Western societies between the end of the Middle Ages and the eighteenth century is thus not to be considered merely as a retreat of the individual into the various convivialities (conjugal, domestic, or sociable) that removed him from the demands and surveillance of the state and its administration. Doubtless there was a basic distinction between the private and the public in that the private person did not participate in the exercise of power and took his place in spheres not governed by the monarch's domination. But it was precisely that newly conquered autonomy that made it possible and conceivable to constitute a new "public" founded on the communication established between "private" persons freed of their duties to the ruler.

Such a communication postulates that the various participants are by nature equal. The political public sphere thus ignored distinctions of "orders" and "estates" that imposed hierarchy on society. In the exchange of judgments, in the exercise of critical functions, and in the clash of differing opinions, an a priori equality was established between individuals that differentiated between them only for the self-evidence and coherence of the arguments they advanced. To the fragmentation of an order organized on the basis of a multiplicity of bodies, the new public sphere opposed homogeneity and uniformity; in place of a distribution of authority strictly modeled on an inherited social scale, it offered a society that accepted only its own principles of differentiation.

The exercise of public reason by private individuals was to be subjected to no limit, and no domain was to be forbidden. The critical exercise of reason was no longer reined in by the respect due to religious or political authority, as the exercise of methodical doubt had been. The new political public sphere brought on the disappearance of the division instituted by Descartes between obligatory credences and obediences, on the one hand, and, on the other, opinions that could legitimately be subjected to doubt. The first of the "maxims" in the "provisional code of morality" with which Descartes armed himself was to "obey the laws and the customs of my country, retaining the religion which I judged best, and in which, by God's grace, I have been brought up since childhood."[3] This led Descartes to a fundamental distinction: "After thus assuring myself of these maxims, and having put them aside with the truths of faith, which have always been most certain to me, I judged that I could proceed freely to reject all my other beliefs."[4] In the public sphere constructed a century later, this reservation disappeared, since no domain of thought or action was to be "put aside" and removed from critical judgment.

Such judgment was exercised by the institutions that made the public into a tribunal of aesthetic criticism—the salons, the cafés, the clubs, and the periodicals. The publicity these groups provided, wresting from the traditional authorities in such matters (the court, the official academies, a small circle of connoisseurs) their monopoly on the evaluation of artistic production, involved both an enlargement and an exclusion: an enlargement because the large number of outlets for publicity (periodicals in particular) created a critical community that included "all private people, persons who—insofar as they were readers, listeners, and spectators [supposing they had wealth and culture], could avail themselves via the market of the objects that were subject to discussion";[5] an exclusion because "wealth and culture" were not everyone's lot, and the majority of people were kept out of the political

178   *Roger Chartier*

debate that derived from literary criticism because they lacked the special competence that made possible "the public of private persons making use of reason."[6]

It was the process of exclusion that gave full importance to the debates centering on the concept of representation during the eighteenth century. Eliminated from the political public sphere by their "literary" inadequacy, the people needed to make their presence felt in some manner, "represented" by those whose vocation it was to be their mentors or their spokesmen and who expressed thoughts the people were incapable of formulating. This was all the more true since all the various lines of political discourse that founded the sphere of public power developed, each in its own way, a theory of representation. Following Keith Baker, we can distinguish three such theories: the absolutist theory, which made the person of the king the only possible representative of a kingdom divided into orders, estates, and bodies; the judiciary theory, which instituted the parlements as interpreters of the consent or the remonstrances of the nation; and the administrative, or "social," theory, which attributed the rational representation of social interests to municipal or provincial assemblies founded not on privilege but on property.[7] In light of these contrasting and competing definitions (all of which, however, focus on the effective or desired exercise of governmental and state authority), the new public sphere defined an alternative mode of representation that removed the concept from any institutional setting—monarchical, parlementary, or administrative—and that postulated the self-evidence of a unanimity designated by the category "public opinion" and faithfully represented by enlightened men who could give it voice.

The Public Use of Reason

Reading Habermas opens an entire field of reflection that leads, first, to questioning the articulation between the concepts of public and private, and, from there, to pausing to consider the text that served Habermas as the matrix for his demonstration: Kant's response to the question "What is Enlightenment?" which appeared as an article in the *Berlinische Monatsschrift* in 1784.[8] Kant discussed the conditions necessary to the progress of enlightenment, which he defined as humanity's emergence from its nonage. His answer rested on two observations. First, an emancipation of this kind supposes that individuals will take control of the use of their own understanding and will be capable of freeing themselves from "statutes and formulas, those mechanical tools of the rational employment or rather misemployment of . . . natural gifts" that hinder the exercise of the mind. Enlightenment thus requires a rupture with obligatory thought patterns inherited from the past and the duty of all to think for themselves.

But—and this is Kant's second observation—for the majority of men this is not an easy conquest, thanks to the force of ingrained habit, "which has become almost [their] nature," and to the weight of the accepted authority of mentors to whom humanity has entrusted responsibility for doing its thinking: "Therefore, there are few who have succeeded by their own exercise of mind both in freeing themselves from incompetence and in achieving a steady pace." The progress of enlightenment could not result from a reform of understanding embarked on by separate, isolated individuals left to their own devices. "But that the public should enlighten itself is more possible; indeed, if only freedom is granted, enlightenment is almost sure to follow." Thus, the progress of enlightenment required the constitution of a community to back up each individual's advances and in which the daring moves of the most forward-looking could be shared.

At this point in his argument Kant proposed a distinction between the "public use" and "private use" of reason that, as he formulated it, entails an apparent paradox. Private use of reason is "that which one may make of it in a particular civil post or office which is entrusted to him." Private use of reason is thus associated with the exercise of a charge or an office (Kant offered the examples of the army officer under orders and the pastor teaching his congregation) or with the citizen's duty toward the state (for example, as a taxpayer). The exercise of understanding in such circumstances could legitimately be restrained in the name of "public ends" that guarantee the very existence of the community to which the officer, the pastor, or the taxpayer belong, in what Kant called "the interest of the community." This obligatory obedience, which leaves no room for criticism or personal reasoning, is not prejudicial to enlightenment, because it facilitates avoidance of the disruption of the social body that would necessarily be engendered were discipline refused.

Why, though, should this use of reason, which seems the most "public" sort of reason in terms of the old definitions that identified "public" as partaking in state or religious authority, be designated by Kant as

180 *Roger Chartier*

"private," thus inverting the accepted meanings of these terms? Using the example of the churchman teaching the faithful, Kant sketched his reasons for this paradoxical definition: "The use . . . which an appointed teacher makes of his reason before his congregation is merely private, because this congregation is only a domestic one (even if it be a large gathering)." The category "private" thus refers to the nature of the community in which use is made of understanding. An assembly of the faithful, a particular church, an army, even a state, all constitute single, circumscribed, and localized entities. In that they differ radically from the "society of world citizens," which occupies no determined territory and the composition of which is unlimited. Social "families," whatever their size and their nature, are thus so many segments fragmenting the universal community; they must therefore be considered as belonging to the order of the "private," in contrast to a "public" defined not by participation, as agent and subject, in the exercise of any particular authority but by identification with humanity as a whole.

Placed on a universal scale in this manner, the public use of understanding contrasts term for term with the "private" use exerted within a relation of specific and limited domination. "By the public use of one's reason I understand the use which a person makes of it as a scholar before the reading public"; "as a scholar"—that is, as a member of a society without distinctions of rank or social condition; "before the reading public"—that is, addressing oneself to a community not defined by being part of an institution. The "public" necessary for the advent of enlightenment and whose liberty cannot be limited is thus constituted of individuals who have the same rights, who think for themselves and speak in their own names, and who communicate in writing with their peers. No domain should be out of reach of their critical activity—not the arts and sciences nor "religious matters" nor "lawgiving." The enlightened prince (read Frederick II) is enlightened precisely because he allows this public use of reason to develop without constraint or restriction, thus permitting men to reach full maturity. A tolerance of this sort in no way endangers "civil order," which is guaranteed by the limits imposed on the use made of reason in the duties required by social status or profession. Furthermore, tolerance has the merit of providing a striking example: "This spirit of freedom spreads beyond this land, even to those in which it must struggle with external obstacles erected by a government which misunderstands its own interest" (as was the case in the kingdom of France, which Kant perhaps had in mind without saying so).

Kant broke with two traditions in this text. First, he proposed a new articulation of the relation of the public to the private, not only by equating the public exercise of reason with judgments produced and communicated by private individuals acting as scholars or "in their quality as learned men" (as Habermas held), but also by defining the public as the sphere of the universal and the private as the domain of particular and "domestic" interests (which may even be those of a church or a state). Second, Kant shifted the way in which the legitimate limits put on critical activities should be conceived. Such limits, then, no longer lay in the objects of thought themselves, as in Cartesian reasoning, which starts from the postulate that there are domains forbidden to methodical doubt; they lay in the position of the thinking subject legitimately constrained when he was executing the duties of his charge or of his status, necessarily free when he acted as a member of "a society of world citizens."

That society was unified by the circulation of written works that authorized the communication and discussion of thoughts. Kant insisted on this point, systematically associating the "public use of one's reason" with the production or reading of written matter. As an educated person, every citizen must be allowed to "make his comments freely and publicly, i.e., *through writing,* on the erroneous aspects of the present institution" (emphasis added). Here the "public" was not construed on the basis of new forms of intellectual sociability such as clubs, cafés, societies, or lodges, because those groups doubtless retained something of the "domestic congregation" by gathering together a specific, discrete community. Nor was the "public" constituted in reference to the ideal of the city in classical antiquity, which presupposed being able to listen to the spoken word and deliberate in common, and which involved the physical proximity of all members of the body politic. For Kant, only written communication, which permitted exchange in the absence of the author and created an autonomous area for debating ideas, was admissible as a figure for the universal.

Kant's conception of the domain specific to the public use of reason was drawn from the notion and the functions of the *Respublica litteratorum,* a concept that united the lettered and the learned, through correspondence and through print, even before the Enlightenment.[9] Founded on the free engagement of the will, on equality among its interlocutors, and on the absolutely disinterested exercise of the intellect, the Republic of Letters (invented not by the Philosophes but by men of learning in the preceding century) provided a model and a support for free public examination of questions regarding religion or legislation. At the same time, reference to the notion of freely engaged will marks the distance separating the theoretical universality of the concept of public and the actual composition of that body. In Kant's time, the "reading public" was not the whole of society by any means, and the public capable of written production was even smaller. Kant explained the distance that he implicitly recognized between the public and the people as a whole by saying that "as things now stand, much is lacking which prevents men from being, or easily becoming, capable of correctly using their own reason in religious matters with assurance and free from outside direction" (or, we might add, in matters pertaining to the arts, the sciences, or legislation as well). "The whole community" only potentially constituted "a society of world citizens." When those two entities coincided, one could augur the advent of "an enlightened age."

The Public or the People

Kant held the distinction between the public and the popular to be temporary, transitory, and characteristic of a century that was "an age of enlightenment" but not yet "an enlightened age." For other thinkers of the eighteenth century, however, the two constituted an irreconcilable dichotomy. "The public was not a people," Mona Ozouf stated as she showed how, during the last decades of the old regime, public opinion was defined in precise contrast to the opinion of the greater number. Lexical contrasts show this particularly forcefully: Condorcet contrasted "opinion" with "populace"; Marmontel opposed "the opinion of men of letters" and "the opinion of the multitude"; d'Alembert spoke of "the truly enlightened public" and "the blind and noisy multitude"; Condorcet, again, set "the opinion of enlightened people which precedes public opinion and ends up by dictating to it" against "the popular opinion."[10] Public opinion, set up as a sovereign authority and a final arbiter, was necessarily stable, unified, and founded on reason. The universality of its judgments and the constraining self-evidence of its decrees derived from that unvarying, dispassionate constancy. It was the reverse of popular opinion, which was multiple, versatile, and inhabited by prejudice and passion.

These writers reveal a strong persistence of older representations of "the people"; a negative image of the public to which all opinions must submit. The definition of *peuple,* which varies little in dictionaries of the French language from Richelet to Furetière and from the *Dictionnaire de l'Académie* to the *Dictionnaire de Trévoux,* emphasizes the fundamental instability attributed to popular opinion throughout the eighteenth century.[11] For example, the 1727 edition of Furetière's *Dictionnaire Universel* gives: "The people is people everywhere; that is, foolish, restless, fond of novelties." Two examples follow: "The people has the habit of hating in others the same qualities that it admires in them (Voiture)," and "There is no happy medium in the humor of the people. If it does not fear it is to be feared, but when it trembles it can be scorned with impunity (d'Ablancourt)." Subject to extremes, inconstant, contradictory, blind, the *people* in eighteenth-century dictionaries remained true to its portrayal in classical tragedy: always quick to change course, from one minute to the next docile or furious, but always manipulable. Thus, in the last act of Corneille's *Nicomède,* first performed in the winter of 1650 and published in 1651, popular revolt was simply a weapon disputed by the mighty. Revolt is first fomented by Laodice:

> Par le droit de la guerre, il fut toujours permis
> D'allumer la révolte entre ses ennemis.

> 'Tis by the laws of war permitted always
> To kindle revolt among one's foes.

Next, it is perhaps to be defused by Prusias, if he listens to Arsinoé's advice:

> Montrez-vous à ce peuple, et flattant son courroux,
> Amusez-le du moins à débattre avec vous.

> Show thyself unto the people
> And, bowing to their wrath, at least beguile them
> By arguing with them.

Finally, it is snuffed out by a gesture from Nicomède:

184 *Roger Chartier*

Tout est calme, Seigneur: un moment de ma vue
A soudain apaisé la populace.

All is calm, sire. The people instantly
Have been appeased by the mere sight of me.[12]

Burdened with these deep-rooted representations, the people could not easily be seen as a political agent, even when discourse was not deliberately disparaging. The article "Peuple," compiled by Jaucourt for the *Encyclopédie,* stands as proof of this.[13] The article proposes a strictly sociological definition: the people are exclusively "the workers and the plowmen," excluding men of law and men of letters, businessmen, financiers, and even that "species of artisans, or rather, mannered artists who work on luxury items." Considered as forming "always the most numerous and the most necessary part of the nation," this worker and peasant people, pitied and respected, was considered in no way capable of participating in government by counsel and representation but rather as linked with the sovereign in a relationship of fidelity offered in exchange for safeguard, of attachment in return for the assurance of a "better subsistence." The article continues: "Kings have no more faithful subjects and, dare I say, better friends. There is more public love in that order perhaps than in all the others; not because it is poor but because it knows very well, in spite of its ignorance, that the authority and protection of the prince are the only gage of its security and its well-being."

The *Encyclopédie* does not acknowledge the notion of "public opinion." The term *opinion* can be found in it as a logical category ("a judgment of the dubious and uncertain mind," opposed to the self-evidence of science) or, in the plural, as a technical term in the language of justice.[14] The term *public* is used only as a qualifier, as in "the public good" or "the public interest," the safeguarding of which is entrusted "to the sovereign and to the officials who, under his orders, are charged with this responsibility."[15] We need not force the analysis to the extent of contrasting the *Encyclopédie*'s definition of "the people" with a notion of "the public" that did not yet exist in this philosophic *summa* of the eighteenth century (proof, incidentally, of the late affirmation of the newer notion). Nonetheless, when it reiterates the traditional images of the people as either loving or rebelling, the *Encyclopédie* manifests the continuing validity of a representation that considered the harsh demands of the popular condition incompatible with participation in the reasoned conduct of government.

When the power of public opinion did emerge—defined as the superior authority to which all particular opinions must bow, even those of the king and his administration—the distinction between public opinion and popular opinion became essential. As Keith Baker has indicated, the concept of public opinion arose in discussions that took place around 1750, first in the controversy over the refusal of the sacraments to the Jansenists, then over the liberalization of the grain trade, and finally over the financial administration of the kingdom.[16] Powerless to forbid public debate, the monarchy itself was forced to enter into it to explain, persuade, and seek to win approval and support.

A new political culture thus took shape, recognized as a novelty by contemporaries in that it transferred the seat of authority from the will of the king alone, who decided without appeal and in secret, to the judgment of an entity embodied in no institution, which debated publicly and was more sovereign than the sovereign. This increased the acuity and the urgency of new questions: How could one distinguish this authority that had devolved on the public from the violent differences between rival factions so detestably illustrated in England? Who were the true spokesmen for the opinion that had become public in this manner: the men of letters who fashioned it, the magistrates of the Parlement who formulated it, or the enlightened administrators who carried it out? Finally, how was one to evaluate the self-evidence of its decrees that was the guarantee of consensus? Although everyone recognized the existence of public opinion and postulated its unity, there was no unanimous answer to these questions because public opinion was both a voice that demanded to be heard and a tribunal that had to be persuaded.

The Tribunal of Opinion

In 1775, in his maiden speech before the Académie Française, Chrétien-Guillaume Malesherbes forcefully expressed the idea—by then commonly accepted—that public opinion was to be considered a court of justice more imperious than any other:

> A tribunal has arisen independent of all powers and that all powers
> respect, that appreciates all talents, that pronounces on all people

of merit. And in an enlightened century, in a century in which each citizen can speak to the entire nation by way of print, those who have a talent for instructing men and a gift for moving them—in a word, men of letters—are, amid the public dispersed, what the orators of Rome and Athens were in the middle of the public assembled.[17]

There are several arguments contained in this comparison. First, it invested the new judges—"in a word, men of letters"—with an authority that ordinary judges did not have. Their competence knew no bounds and their jurisdiction no limits; their freedom of judgment was guaranteed because they were in no way dependent upon the power of the ruler; their decrees had the force of self-evident propositions. Setting up men of letters as the magistrates of an ideal and supreme tribunal in this manner was to invest them with the fundamentally judiciary legitimacy of all the traditional powers, beginning with those of the king and the Parlement. Thus the power of "men of letters" was no longer exclusively founded—as in the *Système figuré des connaissances humaines* of the *Encyclopédie*—on the submission of the "science of God, or natural Theology, which it has pleased God to correct and to sanctify by Revelation" to a "science of being in general," the first branch of the "philosophy or the science (for these words are synonyms)" that was "the portion of human knowledge which should be related to reason." This subjection permitted the role of guide for humanity to be transferred from the scholastics to the philosophers.[18] With the invention of public opinion, "the enlightened nation of men of letters and the free and disinterested nation of the philosophers" found itself entrusted with a veritable public office.[19]

Reference to the judiciary had another function, however. It aimed at establishing a connection between the universality of judgments and the dispersal of persons, and at constructing a uniform opinion that, unlike that of the ancients, had no physical location in which it could express or experience its unity. As for Kant later, it was the circulation of printed matter that made it possible for Malesherbes, in the remonstrances that he presented in May 1775 in the name of the Cour des Aides, to envisage the constitution of a unified public in a nation in which people were necessarily separated from each other and formed their ideas individually: "Knowledge is being extended by Printing, the written Laws are today known by everyone, everyone can comprehend his own affairs. The Jurists have lost the empire that other men's ignorance gave to them. The Judges can themselves be judged by an instructed Public, and that censure is much more severe and more equitable when it can be exercised in a cool, reflective reading than when suffrages are constrained in a tumultuous assembly."[20] By associating the public nature of the written word—vastly increased by the presses (an indispensable resource in combating the "clandestinity" of the administration)—with the supreme authority of the judgments pronounced by opinion binding even on the judges, Malesherbes converted the congeries of particular opinions that emerge from solitary reading into a collective and anonymous conceptual entity that is both abstract and homogeneous.

Condorcet developed the same idea in the opening pages of the eighth "epoch" of his *Esquisse d'un tableau historique des progrès de l'esprit humain,* written in 1793. He launched his argument by contrasting the spoken word, which touches only nearby listeners and excites their emotions, with the printed word, the circulation of which creates the conditions for unlimited and dispassionate communication:

> Men found themselves possessed of the means of communicating with people all over the world. A new sort of tribunal had come into existence in which less lively but deeper impressions were communicated; which no longer allowed the same tyrannical empire to be exercised over men's passions but ensured a more certain and more durable power over their minds; a situation in which the advantages are all on the side of truth, since what the art of communication loses in the power to seduce, it gains in the power to enlighten.

Printing thus made possible the constitution of a public realm that was unreliant on proximity—a community with no visible presence: "The public opinion that was formed in this way was powerful by virtue of its size, and effective because the forces that created it operated with equal strength on all men at the same time, no matter what distances separated them. In a word, we now have a tribunal, independent of all human coercion, which favours reason and justice, a tribunal whose scrutiny it is difficult to elude, and whose verdict it is impossible to evade."[21] That tribunal, in which readers were the judges and authors the interested parties, was a manifestation of the universal because "all men who speak the same language can become alive to any questions

188   *Roger Chartier*

discussed anywhere."[22] Even though Condorcet gave the most "democratic" definition of it, public opinion, ideally universal, had to come to terms with obvious cultural rifts, and it was not an easy matter to make the absolute concept coincide with the realities of the social world: "And so, though there remained a great number of people condemned to ignorance either voluntary or enforced, the boundary between the cultivated and the uncultivated had been almost entirely effaced, leaving an insensible gradation between the two extremes of genius and stupidity."[23] The very terms Condorcet used ("though"; "almost entirely") clearly indicate the persistence of a distance that was, however, considered to have been abolished.

Thus, from the seventeenth century to the eighteenth century there had been a radical shift in the manner of conceiving the public. In the age of "baroque" politics the traits that defined the public were the same as those that typified the theater public: heterogeneous, hierarchized, and formed into a public only by the spectacle that they were given to see and to believe. This type of public was potentially composed of men and women from all social levels; it brought together all whose adherence and support were sought—the mighty and the common people, shrewd politicians and the ignorant plebs. It was also a public to be "led by the nose"; to be "seduced and deceived by appearances," according to Naude, the self-appointed theoretician of a politics in which the most spectacular effects always masked the maneuvers that produced them and the goals they sought.[24] Ensnared, held captive, and manipulated in this manner, the spectators of the *theatrum mundi* in no way constituted a "public opinion" (even if the expression can be found before 1750, for example, in Saint-Simon).

When the concept of "public opinion" did emerge, it effected a dual rupture. It countered the art of pretense, dissimulation, and secrecy by appealing to a transparency that was to ensure the visibility of intentions. Before the tribunal of opinion all causes were to be argued without duplicity: causes that evidently had justice and reason on their side would necessarily triumph. But all citizens were not (or not yet) adept at exercising their judgment in this fashion or at joining together to form enlightened opinion. Thus, a second rupture rejected the public that mingled in the theaters, where the inexpensive places in the pit adjoined the boxes and where everyone had his own interpretation—subtle or rough-hewn—of a spectacle destined for all, in favor of the more homogeneous public that served as the tribunal to judge literary or poetic merits and talents. When opinion was thought of as actor rather than as acted upon, it became public and lost its universality, and by that token it excluded many people who lacked the competence to establish the decrees that it proclaimed.

The Constitution of the Public

Constituting the public as an entity whose decrees had more force than those of the established authorities supposed several operations. Two examples should suffice to illustrate them. The first operation, which concerns the memoirs published in great numbers by both lawyers and litigants from 1770 onward, was to take the judicial comparison literally. Malesherbes justified this operation in his remonstrances of 1775, in which he spoke against the criticism of judges who thought that "the public should not be constituted as the judge in the courts": "Basically, the common order of justice in France is that it be rendered publicly. It is to a public hearing that all cases should normally be brought; and when one takes the Public as a witness by means of printed Memoirs, all that does is to augment the public character of the hearing."[25] In all cases, an affair being examined by a normal tribunal should be exposed before opinion. To take a specific case that set private persons against one another and was subjected to the secret procedures of justice and transform it into a public debate charged with letting the truth shine through and, in effect, with shifting the context in which judgment took place necessitated the adoption of several strategies.

The most fundamental strategy consisted in endowing the cause one was defending with general and exemplary value. Lacretelle, a lawyer, said as much: "Any particular affair that leads to general considerations and that is apt to become a major focus of public attention must be considered as a major event in which experience testifies with full authority and public opinion rises up with all its influence." An admiring witness tells us that this was also Lacretelle's practice: "Instead of shutting himself within the narrow circle of an ordinary subject, he soars above the constitutive laws of the various governments; he sees only major outcomes; each particular case becomes in his hands the program of a question of state." The debt that a court noble refused to pay to his commoner creditors thus became an ideal occasion for denouncing unjust privilege, just as the arbitrary imprisonment of a Breton gentleman was an opportunity to denounce the *lettres de cachet*.[26]

Two other things had to be accomplished before specific cases could be endowed with universal significance. First, the secrecy of judicial procedure had to be broken by mobilizing the potential of the circulation of printed texts on the largest possible scale. This accounted for both the large press runs of judicial memoirs (three thousand copies at the least, often six thousand, and occasionally ten thousand or more) and their low price (when they were not distributed free). Second, a different writing style had to replace the customary legal prose, a style that took its models and references from successful genres and gave narration a dramatic form, or else a style based in first-person narrative that lent veracity to the defendant through an exhibition of the "I," as in the literature of the times. Universalizing the particular, making public what had been secret, and "fictionalizing" discourse were the techniques that lawyers used to appeal to opinion and, in doing so, to proclaim themselves the authorized interpreters of that opinion.

The traditional direct, discreet, and exclusive relationship that bound individuals to the king—the guarantor and guardian of domestic secrets—gave way to a totally different mechanism in the public exposition of private differences.[27] From that point of view, judicial memoirs are the exact inverse of the *lettres de cachet* accorded by the sovereign in response to requests from families interested in stifling "disorders" that sullied their honor. The memoirs displayed what the *lettres* concealed; they expected from the judgment of opinion what the *lettres* hoped to gain from the omnipotence of the monarch; they converted into a civil suit the scandals that the *lettres* were charged with burying. The "politicization" of the private sector thus seems to have arisen out of a development that based the very existence of a new public sphere on a process of "privatization" in which individuals gradually conquered autonomy and freedom from state authority.

The second operation, the emergence of the public as a higher court of judgment, is clear in the evolution of artistic criticism. After 1737, when the Salon became a regular and well-frequented institution, its very existence transferred legitimacy in aesthetic appreciation away from the narrow milieus that up to that point had claimed monopoly (the Académie royale de Peinture et Sculpture, aristocratic and ecclesiastical clients, collectors, and the merchants who sold to them) toward the mixed and numerous public who passed judgment on the paintings hung on the walls of the Salon carré of the Louvre. Setting up that throng of visitors as a tribunal of taste was not without its problems. As Thomas Crow wrote, one question was central in the minds of all those who backed the expectations and the tastes of the new spectators against the old authorities:

> What transforms [an] audience into a public, that is, a commonality with a legitimate role to play in justifying artistic practice and setting value on the products of that practice? The audience is the concrete manifestation of the public but never identical with it . . . A public appears, with a shape and a will, via the various claims made to represent it; and when sufficient numbers of an audience come to believe in one or another of these representations, the public can become an important art-historical actor.[28]

Transforming spectators into a "public" encountered strong resistance from the Académie, the connoisseurs, and even the artists themselves. The move was nonetheless achieved, more or less successfully, by independent critics (often anonymous, on occasion clandestine) whose numbers increased after the 1770s and whose writings circulated discernibly more widely than the comments Denis Diderot reserved for the subscribers to Melchior Grimm's *Correspondance littéraire.* Just like the public that was both invoked and represented by the lawyers who wrote judicial memoirs, the public that was thought to regulate taste in the fine arts found its earliest interpreters in the critics who set it up as the aesthetic lawgiver.

Even if, or because, it was defined as a conceptual entity, and not in sociological terms, the notion of public opinion that invaded the discourse of all segments of society—political, administrative, and judicial—in the two or three final decades of the old regime operated as a powerful instrument both for division and for social legitimization. In reality, public opinion founded the authority of all who, by affirming that they recognized its decrees alone, set themselves up as mandated to pronounce its judgments. It was in constructing opinion into a unified, enlightened, and sovereign public that men of letters, as Tocqueville wrote, "took the lead in politics." Universal in its essence, the public capable of making critical use of reason was far from

192 Roger Chartier

universal in its actual composition. The public sphere, emancipated from the domain in which the ruler held sway, thus had nothing in common with the shifting opinions and blind emotions of the multitude. Between the people and the public there was a clear break. From Malesherbes to Kant, the line of demarcation ran between those who could read and produce written matter and those who could not.

Translation by Lydia G. Cochrane

NOTES

1. Jürgen Habermas, *Strukturwandel der Öffentlichkeit: Untersuchungen zu einer Kategorie der bürgerlichen Gesellschaft* (Neuwied: Hermann Luchterhand Verlag, 1962), available in French as *L'Espace public: Archéologie de la publicité comme dimension constitutive de la société bourgeoise,* trans. Marc B. de Launay (Paris: Payot, 1978), and in English as *The Structural Transformation of the Public Sphere: An Inquiry into a Category of Bourgeois Society,* trans. Thomas Burger and Frederick Lawrence (Cambridge: Policy Press, Cambridge: MIT Press, 1989). See also Peter Hohendahl, "Jürgen Habermas: 'The Public Sphere' (1964)," *New German Critique* 1.3 (1974): 45–48, and Jürgen Habermas, "The Public Sphere: An Encyclopedia Article (1964)," *New German Critique* 1.3 (1974): 49–55.

2. Habermas, *L'Espace public,* 38; *The Structural Transformation of the Public Sphere,* 27.

3. René Descartes, *Discours de la Méthode,* in his *Œuvres complètes* (Paris: Gallimard, Bibliothèque de la Pléiade, 1953), part 3, 141; quoted from *Descartes's Discourse on Method,* trans. Laurence J. Lafleur (Indianapolis: Bobbs-Merrill, Liberal Arts Press, 1960), 18.

4. Descartes, *Discours de la Méthode,* 144; *Discourse on Method,* 22.

5. Habermas, *Structural Transformation of the Public Sphere,* 37.

6. Ibid., 51. On the place of women in the public sphere, absolutist or bourgeois, see Joan B. Landes, *Women and the Public Sphere in the Age of the French Revolution* (Ithaca, N.Y.: Cornell University Press, 1988).

7. Keith Michael Baker, "Representation," in *The French Revolution and the Creation of Modern Political Culture,* vol. 1, *The Political Culture of the Old Regime,* ed. Keith Michael Baker (Oxford and New York: Pergamon Press, 1987), 469–92; reprinted as "Representation Redefined," in Keith Michael Baker, *Inventing the French Revolution: Essays on French Political Culture in the Eighteenth Century* (Cambridge: Cambridge University Press, 1990), 224–51.

8. Immanuel Kant, "Beantwortung der Frage: Was ist Aufklärung?" *Berlinische Monatsschrift* (1784), available in English as *Foundations of the Metaphysics of Morals and What Is Enlightenment,* trans. Lewis White Beck (Indianapolis: Bobbs-Merrill, 1975), 85–92. On this text, see the commentaries of Ernst Cassirer, *Kants Leben und Lehre* (Berlin: Cassirer, 1918), available in English as *Kant's Life and Thought,* trans. James Haden (New Haven: Yale University Press, 1981), 227–28, 368; Habermas, *Structural Transformation of the Public Sphere,* 104–7; Michel Foucault, "Afterword: The Subject and the Power," *in Michel Foucault: Be-*

yond Structuralism and Hermeneutics, ed. Hubert L. Dreyfus and Paul Rabinow (Chicago: University of Chicago Press, 1982), 208–26, especially 215–16; and Michel Foucault, "Un cours inédit," *Le Magazine littéraire* 207 (1984): 35–39. All quotations from Kant in this section are from the Beck translation of "What Is Enlightenment?"

9. Reference to the practices of intellectual life in the seventeenth century, founded, since the age of the learned libertines, on the exchange of correspondence, the communication of manuscripts, books lent or offered as gifts, and, after the 1750s, on learned periodicals; see Robert Mandrou, *Des humanistes aux hommes de science (XVIᵉ et XVIIᵉ siècles)* (Paris: Fayard, 1988), 263–80, available in English as *From Humanism to Science: 1480 to 1700,* trans. Brian Pearce (Harmondsworth and New York: Penguin Books, 1978), 151–53. It coexists in Kant's text with an implicit recognition of the situation in Germany, which, even more than in France, where intellectuals were more concentrated in a capital city, depended on the circulation of written matter. In 1827 Goethe noted this national trait with particular force: "All our men of talent are scattered across the country. One is in Vienna, another in Berlin, another in Königsberg, another in Bonn or Düsseldorf, all separated from each other by fifty or a hundred miles, so that personal contact or a personal exchange of ideas is a rarity" (quoted by Norbert Elias, *Über den Prozess der Zivilisation, soziogenetische und psychogenetische Untersuchungen* [1939; Frankfurt-am-Main: Suhrkamp, 1969], 1:33–34, and given here from Norbert Elias, *The History of Manners: The Civilizing Process,* vol. 1, trans. Edmund Jephcott [New York: Pantheon Books, 1978], 28). See also Paul Dibon, "Communication in *Respublica litteraria* of the 17th Century," *Res Publica Litterarum* 1 (1978): 42–55.

10. Mona Ozouf, "L'Opinion publique," in Baker, *The French Revolution and the Creation of Modern Political Culture,* vol. 1, *The Political Culture of the Old Regime,* 419–34. Quotations are given as per note 24, 432–33.

11. Elizabeth Fleury, "Le peuple en dictionnaires (fin XVII–XVIIIᵉ siècle)" (Diplôme d'Études Approfondies, Paris, École des Hautes Études en Sciences Sociales, 1986), typescript.

12. Pierre Corneille, *Nicomède, Œuvres complètes* (Paris: Éditions du Seuil, L'Intégrale, 1963, 1970), verses 1696–97, 1621–22, and 1779–80, 539–41, quoted from *The Chief Plays of Corneille,* trans. Lacy Lockert (Princeton, N.J.: Princeton University Press, 1952), 382, 380, 384.

13. *Encyclopédie, ou Dictionnaire raisonné des sciences, des arts et des métiers,* 36 vols. (Lausanne and Berne: chez les Sociétés typographiques, 1778–81), 25:543–45.

14. Ibid., 23:754–57.

15. Ibid., 27:752–53.

16. Keith Michael Baker, "Politics and Public Opinion under the Old Regime: Some Reflections," in *Press and Politics in Pre-Revolutionary France,* ed. Jack R. Censer and Jeremy D. Popkin (Berkeley: University of California Press, 1987), 204–46; reprinted as "Public Opinion as Political Invention," in Baker, *Inventing the French Revolution,* 167–99.

17. Quoted from Ozouf, "L'Opinion publique," 424.

18. Jean Le Rond d'Alembert, *Discours préliminaire de l'Encyclopédie* (Paris: Éditions Gonthier, Médiations, 1965), "Explication détaillée du système des connaissances humaines," 155–68, quotations 159–60, quoted from "Detailed

Explanation of the System of Human Knowledge," in *Preliminary Discourse to the Encyclopedia of Diderot*, trans. Richard N. Schwab, with Walter E. Rex (Indianapolis: Bobbs-Merrill, Library of Liberal Arts, 1963), 143–57.

19. Ibid., "Dédicace à Monseigneur le comte d'Argenson," 14–15. See also Robert Darnton, "Philosophers Trim the Tree of Knowledge: The Epistemological Strategy of the *Encyclopédie*," in *The Great Cat Massacre and Other Episodes in French Cultural History* (New York: Basic Books, 1984), 190–213.

20. Malesherbes, "Remontrances relatives aux impôts, 6 mai 1775," in *Les "Remontrances" de Malesherbes 1771–1775*, ed. Élisabeth Badinter (Paris: Union Générale d'Éditions, 10/18, 1978), 167–284, quotation 272–73.

21. Condorcet, *Esquisse d'un tableau historique des progrès de l'esprit humain* (Paris: Flammarion, 1988), 188, quoted from *Sketch for a Historical Picture of the Progress of the Human Mind*, trans. June Barraclough (London: Weidenfeld and Nicolson, 1955), p. 100. For a discussion in another context of the connection between the circulation of printed matter and the public sphere, see Michael Warner, *The Letters of the Republic: Publication and the Public Sphere in Eighteenth-Century America* (Cambridge, Mass.: Harvard University Press, 1990).

22. Condorcet, *Esquisse d'un tableau historique des progrès de l'esprit humain*, 189; *Sketch for a Historical Picture of the Progress of the Human Mind*, 101.

23. Condorcet, *Esquisse d'un tableau historique des progrès de l'esprit humain*, 229; *Sketch for a Historical Picture of the Progress of the Human Mind*, 140.

24. Christian Jouhaud, "Propagande et action au temps de la Fronde," in *Culture et idéologie dans la genèse de l'Etat moderne*. Actes de la table ronde organisée par le Centre National de la Recherche Scientifique et l'École française de Rome, Rome, 15–17 October 1984 (Rome: L'École française de Rome, 1985), 337–52; Christian Jouhaud, *Mazarinades. La Fronde des mots* (Paris: Aubier, 1985).

25. Malesherbes, "Remonstrances relatives aux impôts, 6 mai 1775," 269–70.

26. Sarah Maza, "Le tribunal de la nation: Les mémoires judiciaires et l'opinion publique à la fin de l'Ancien Régime," *Annales E.S.C.* (1987): 73–90. I am indebted to this article for both quotations and ideas concerning the judicial memoirs. See also John Renwick, *Voltaire et Morangiès 1772–1773, ou, Les Lumières l'ont échappé belle*, Studies on Voltaire and the Eighteenth Century 202 (Oxford: Voltaire Foundation, 1982); Hans-Jürgen Lüsebrink, "L'affaire Cléreaux (Rouen, 1786–1790): Affrontements idéologiques et tensions institutionnelles autour de la scène judiciaire de la fin du XVIIIe siècle," *Studies on Voltaire and the Eighteenth Century* 191 (1980): 892–900.

27. Arlette Farge, "Familles: L'honneur et le secret," in *Histoire de la vie privée*, ed. Philippe Ariès and Georges Duby (Paris: Éditions du Seuil, 1986), vol. 3, *De la Renaissance aux Lumières*, ed. Roger Chartier, 580–617, available in English as "The Honor and Secrecy of Families," in Ariès and Duby, *A History of Private Life* (Cambridge: Belknap Press of Harvard University Press, 1989), vol. 3, *Passions of the Renaissance*, ed. Roger Chartier, trans. Arthur Goldhammer (1989), 570–607; Arlette Farge and Michel Foucault, *Le Désordre des familles: Lettres de cachet des Archives de la Bastille* (Paris: Gallimard/Julliard, Collection Archives, 1982).

28. Thomas E. Crow, *Painters and Public Life in Eighteenth-Century Paris* (New Haven: Yale University Press, 1985), 5.

CHAPTER 7

The Return of the Event (1972)

Pierre Nora

Pierre Nora uses this intervention to challenge the prevailing attention of the Annales school of history to the effects of deep structures on shaping and continuing the present. Instead, Nora seeks to salvage the revolutionary valence of the event, or that "pebble in the machine." He asks what it would mean to work as a "historian of the present"—and so inaugurates an attention to singularities that Foucault will later develop in his own work as a "diagnostician of the present." This essay gestures toward a post-1968 political moment, yet remains defined by the Cold War and a trust in intellectual expertise. The essay serves as a pivot point between the Annales school and a new historiography; in this sense, it foreshadows the fiery exchange between Jacques Léonard and Foucault on the divisions between history and philosophy published in L'Impossible Prison *(1980).*　　●

What is called "contemporary" history evokes two contradictory images: first, the poor relation of a nobler history—that of Antiquity, the Middle Ages, and the Modern Era—condemned to shamble along in its elder's shadow; and second, the inspiring sovereign of any examination of the past, a repository of the secrets of the present day and as such worthy of general interest. Neither of these two images is entirely false.

It is true that contemporary history is still far from finding either its identity or its autonomy. As the fruit of purely French history, it was born of Victor Duruy's reforms in secondary education, upholding the caesura imposed upon national history by the Revolution.[1] Those subsequent three-quarters of a century were merely a continuation, the span of a single lifetime over which the scientific methods being developed had little hold. Over time, new curricula would also, with reason *[légitimement]*, set the beginning of contemporary history at the outset of the Third Republic, or in the immediate aftermath of either of the two world wars: in none of these cases did the principle of continuity suffer.

However, no prior era experienced, as ours has, its present as already bearing a "historical" meaning. That alone should be enough for it to be endowed with its own identity, for contemporary history to be cured of its infirmity. The total wars and revolutionary upheavals, the increased speed of communication, and the penetration of modern economies into traditional societies, in short everything that we tend to mean by "globalization," have led to a general mobilization of the masses who, on the home front of events, had previously represented the civilians of history. Seemingly overnight, the subsequent movements of colonization and decolonization brought into the Western model of historicity entire societies that had been lost in the deep slumber of a people "without history" or the silence of colonial oppression. This vast democratization of history, which makes the present so particular, possesses its own logics and laws: one of them—the only one that we shall isolate here—is that current events *[l'actualité]*, that generalized circulation of historical perspectives have culminated in a new phenomenon: the event. Its emergence would seem to date to the final third of the nineteenth century, or between the war of 1870 and the Fashoda Incident; in France, between the Commune and the Dreyfus Affair.[2]

We cannot examine the rapid advent of this historical present, born from the sense that the masses participate in the fates of nations, without looking at its relationship to the simultaneous efforts of a generation of positivist historians to construct a properly scientific school of history. Furthermore, the entire project of the positivists consisted partly in planting the foundations of history in the study of the past, carefully delineated from the present, and partly on furnishing this past with a continuous chain of "events." "The history of a period is born only once it has died entirely; the realm of history is the past."[3] Driven by an ambition to introduce the methods of experimental science into the field of social science, this group of historians sought only facts that could be scientifically verified, patiently reconstructing them so as to grasp the past through a series of events, themselves constituted by a body of facts, and to bring the discontinuity of singular events back within a chain a continuous causality. It was as if positivism had bestowed upon the present the majority of the elements that would shape it, but had done so in order to push back validity exclusively into the past; as if they, for whom the historian should belong to no time period or country, bore the effects of the present, but did so in order to unconsciously exorcise its perils by granting the event free range only in an unthreatening past. On the condition that the present, dominated by the tyranny of the event, was denied a travel permit back into history, it was agreed that history would be constructed upon the event.

The modalities of this distribution, the consequences of this clash of civilizations, as important as they may be, do not concern us here. The essential thing, in order to define the status of the event, is to emphasize this reversal. The positivists sanctified their field with the seal of science at the same time that they were inaugurating a tradition in which the historian was made the great organizer of the event, the Pygmalion who would confer upon it the *dignus es intrare* or not, at the very moment when . . .

The Production of the Event

The mass media were beginning to assume the monopoly over history. In our present day, this process is now complete and from now on it belongs to them. In contemporary societies, it is through them and them alone that the event reaches us, and cannot fail to do so.

But it is not enough to say that they follow reality *[le réel]* so closely that they have become an integral part of it, re-creating the immediacy of its presence for us, molding themselves to its twists and turns, making up its inseparable cortege. Print, radio, and images act not only as means of transmission from which the events themselves could be relatively independent, but as the very condition of their existence. Publicity shapes their very production. Decisive events can occur without being discussed. It is the fact of learning of them retrospectively, as with Mao's decline in power following the Great Leap Forward, that constitutes the event. That something took place simply makes it historical; for there to be an event, we must know about it.

198 *Pierre Nora*

This is why the affinities between certain types of event and certain means of communication are so tight that they can seem inseparable. How could we not put the rise of the mass press, the formation of a middle-class readership by mandatory primary schooling and urbanization in the late nineteenth century, in relationship with the scandals of the Third Republic, the Panama Affair,[4] the importance given to political and parliamentary life, the battle over secularism, the rivalries of European nations, in short, the very style that public life came to adopt?

Thus, for France, the Dreyfus Affair might indeed represent the first irruption of the modern event, the prototype of those *images d'Épinal* that emerged, ready and armed, from the belly of industrial societies, and of which contemporary history provides endless examples, on the basis of a comparable matrix.[5] Take the initial rumors, the exploitation of official silence by an opposition right-wing press, a stubborn paralysis of official information ("There is no Dreyfus Affair"), the assumption that circles of power were incriminated, popular racism, the implication of the two most highly regarded government bodies, the army and the judicial system, at a critical moment for the republican regime, a confrontation of grand abstract principles around the head of a single individual, a dichotomization of the world into good guys and bad guys, suspense stoked by forged documents and secret information passed down through the grapevine, appeals to public opinion through open letters, the significant appearance of the neologism "intellectual" that signaled a new social role as a mediator of mass opinion;[6] the Dreyfus Affair owed everything to the press and gave it everything in return.[7] Its role has not been diminished by competition. It seems to exemplify its own archetype for events: when the facts themselves are evasive, it calls for skepticism of the information provided, the confrontation of different eyewitness accounts, the breaking of secrets maintained by official denials, the undermining of principles calling for careful consideration and reflection, and the obligatory appeal to prerequisite knowledge that only the written press could provide. From the local newspapers to the national dailies, from the mass-market press to the editorial weeklies, only the printed word wielded an unrivaled range of potentialities, an exceptionally rich selection of manipulations of reality. Thus, the Algerian War did not belong entirely to the press, but particular episodes, such as the question of torture or the narrative of the negotiations, remained especially attached to it. The entire Watergate scandal, in its initial revelatory stages, took place in print media before embarking, once it had reached the legal stage, onto the screen.

Other historical phenomena, on the other hand, first emerged on the radio. A fair amount of the interwar period, as well as World War II, was perceived auditorily. There is a particular era of contemporary history that begins with Roosevelt's fireside chats, with the thundering speeches at Nuremberg, that the television screen, in other countries, might have subverted through opening them to ridicule or by making their consequences all too clear. For Arabs, Nasser's speeches marked the beginning of a new era. Another era began in the Congo in the 1960s, when all it took was an African statesman announcing over the radio that he had taken power for power to effectively be in his hands. Broadcast speech itself operated at several levels. First of all, it was a guarantor of an event's importance, as a function of the quantity of words it dedicated to it: it was a voice that informed, explained, commentated, criticized, paraphrased, extrapolated, conjectured, it was the public echo of private conversations and, at times, the sole vehicle of modernity. Frantz Fanon has shown the revolutionary role that voices of Arabs played in wartime Algeria,[8] and we are all aware of how the transistor continues to act as an instrument for the penetration of history into the African continent. But it is history itself, through the voices of its actors, that the radio allows to speak, thus reactivating, on a grand scale, the most powerful motor of history since the Greek orators and prophets. Media transform into acts what might have only been words in the breeze, they bestow upon the speech, the declaration, the press conference, the solemn efficiency of the irreversible gesture. May 1968 was, as we know, a festival of speech as action. Different forms of it comingled to create the event itself;[9] the speech of leaders and of the anonymous, speech shouted or scrawled across walls, the speech of students and laborers, inventive or repetitive, political, poetic, pedagogic, or messianic speech, speech without words and speech as noise, from the night of the barricades in the Latin Quarter where transistors instantaneously echoed out to the sleeping countryside the incidents that became an event, up to General de Gaulle's speech on the 30th of May, which was not televised, but whose Olympian voice marked precisely the end of the event.

While events of this kind, such as the invasion of Prague, political press conferences, or the moon landing now seem irreversibly tied to the moving image, and while this will only become increasingly true, we should not therefore conclude that television can be assimilated to "paneventuality." But it has led to a decisive step in the democratization of the event. First, this is because the small number of channels and the current lack of differentiation have assured the narrowest possible range in the way the story is told. There are several ways of commentating on the Olympic Games, there are very few different ways of showing it. And, while we might be aware that what we're seeing is a montage, and therefore reflects a deliberate choice of images, the impression we get is of live experience. Everyone is taken in, whether willingly or not, alone or as a group, always off guard, by the televised news story directed at full bore toward no one in particular. Television is to modern life what the church bell was to the village, the Angelus of industrial civilization, but it is also the bearer of an unexpected message; it as, as McLuhan has said, a cool medium, one that, compared to all the rest, engenders intense participation that is both effortless and domestic. Participation that is, one might say, not participatory, that precise mixture of intimacy and distance that is, for the masses, the most modern form, and more generally the only one available to them, of experiencing contemporary history. In both senses of the word, the event is projected, launched, into private life and offered up as spectacle.

The mass media have thus made history into an assault, and rendered the event monstrous. Not because it is by definition out of the ordinary, but because the redundancy intrinsic to the system is geared toward the production of sensationalism, the perpetual creation of novelty, feeding a hunger for events. Not because it creates them artificially, as those in power would like to believe when it is in their interests to suppress an event, or as one might be led to believe on the basis of a few performances when information became drunk on its new powers, such as Orson Welles's famous War of the Worlds broadcast. Information secretes its own antibodies, and the written and broadcast press, as a whole, generally have the effect of setting limits on wild opinions running amok. The role of information guarantees that the media will have an increased reach over the event. But the detection system that the mass media represent will inevitably have the effect of promoting the birth of massive events, volcanoes of current events such as the recent Six Day War, May '68, the invasion of Prague, the departure and death of de Gaulle, and the American moon landing, monster events that have repeated themselves and that will quite likely continue to repeat themselves with greater and greater frequency.

If, for the historian, the event is monstrous, the modern event is even more so. Because, of all those on the receiving end of it, he is the most powerless. The event had been, in the traditional system, his privilege and his purpose. It had given him his position and his value, and no event could enter into history without his stamp of approval. Yet today the event presents him with its external face, with all the weight of a fact, prior to any elaboration, before being subject to the work of time. And doing so with even greater force because the media immediately proffer experience as history and the present offers up ever more experiences. A staggering promotion of the immediate to the historical, of experience to the legendary, is taking place at the very moment when the historian finds his customary habits derailed, his powers threatened, confronted by the very thing that in other places he seeks to diminish. But is this the same event?

The Metamorphoses of the Event

To the extent that the event has become intimately tied to its own expression, its intellectual significance, a close relative of an initial form of historical elaboration, has withdrawn in favor of its emotional virtualities. Reality proposes, imaginations incline. For the suicide of Marilyn Monroe to become an event, it was necessary, and sufficient, for millions of men and women to see her as embodying the drama of the star system, the unlucky debutante skyrocketed into a superstar, the tragedy of interrupted beauty, the sadness of living one's life behind a mask, the vanity of all success. And the most devastating fires often escape the control of the person who lit the match: the event has moved closer to the *fait divers,* the tawdry human-interest story, itself born in the mid-nineteenth century during the development of industrial society.

The theoretical difference between the two phenomena is quite clear. By nature, the event belongs to a well-defined category of historical reason: whether political or social, literary or scientific, local or national, an event's position is inscribed in newspaper columns. But within its well-defined category, the event signals itself through its significance, the novelty of its message, becoming less chatty the less banal it is. The *fait divers* occupies a symmetrically opposite position:[10] drowned in its own diffusion, beyond categorization, dedicated to the unclassifiable and the insignificant, through its strangeness it reflects back on social conventions, through the logic of a causality that is either twisted (such as: a mother murders her four children) or upside-down (such as: man bites dog). It is this theoretical differentiation that is becoming blurred. Not because there is no longer any difference between the *fait divers* and the event, but because in our day popular imagination wants to graft onto all events, in the modern sense of the word, something of the *fait divers,* its drama, its magic, its mystery, its strangeness, its poetry, its tragicomedy, its powers of compensation and identification, the sentiment of fatality that inhabits it, its luxuriousness, and its gratuitousness. This imagination can therefore grab hold of any *fait divers*—we saw this with the Dreyfus Affair as with May '68—and raise it up, through a sequence of successive investments, past the threshold of the most massive event, at the very moment when history seems to be devolving into the *fait divers.*

The event represents the marvelous *[le merveilleux]* in democratic societies. But the very integration of the masses also had the effect of assimilating the marvelous. Popular and working-class literature from the first half of the twentieth century illustrates how the fantastic traditionally borrowed its elements from the supernatural world. Today these are provided by industrial society itself. Thus, we can observe an overproliferation in which the performances of a technocratic society appear to mirror exactly the themes of the traditional fantastic. This was the case, for example, with the American moon landing.[11] All while obeying contrasts that were legitimately exploited by the organizers of this interplanetary "show": an unimaginable demonstration of technological power realized with dreamlike precision, the superselectiveness of the three heroes, with their comic-book superhero physiques, the futuristic aesthetic of the module from which emerged, on our television screens, those space suits whose movements had finally been liberated from Earth's gravity, the contrast between the immensity of the financial, human, and political stakes, and the fragility of the physical and psychological reflexes of three simple human beings; here, popular imagination founded on the juggernaut of modern science was fed by mankind's oldest dream. The real moment, the informational moment, the consumer moment, all walked in lockstep: the moon landing was the model for the modern event.

Its form resided in its direct transmission by Telstar.[12] The speed of its transmission was undoubtedly not a sufficient cause for the transformation of the event, but it was absolutely a necessary one. We can see a demonstration of this with the Ali–Frazier boxing match, which was an event in all of the countries with a live television broadcast, but not in France, where it could only be watched with a delay. By abolishing all delays, by transmitting events of uncertain outcome as they unfold, live broadcasting rips away the last of the event's historical character in order to project it into the lived experience of the masses.

And did so in order to return the event's historical character to it in the form of spectacle. Do we owe the theatricality characteristic of so many contemporary events to advertising, or has it rather been live broadcasting that endowed them with this dimension? The democratization of the event and the spirit of spectacle have always moved forward in lockstep. Contemporary history might have symbolically begun with Goethe's pronouncement at Valmy: "And you can say: I was there!" . . . The characteristic feature of the modern event is that it takes place on an immediately public stage, never being without the reporter-spectator or the spectator-reporter, being seen as it makes itself. And this "voyeurism" gives current events both their specificity with regard to history and their already historical flavor. From whence the impression of a game truer than reality, of dramatic entertainment, of a festival that society offers to itself through the grand event. Everyone has a role and no one does, because everyone forms the mass to which no one belongs. This event without historian is created out of the affective engagement of the masses, the sole way for them to participate in public life: an alienated and exigent participation, voracious and frustrated, multiple and distant, powerless and yet sovereign, autonomous and remote-controlled like that impalpable reality of contemporary life we call "public opinion."

This history is still waiting for its Clausewitz, someone who could analyze the strategies of the total event that, like wars before it, have now drafted the civilian population into service; there is no such thing anymore as being "behind the lines" of history, no more so than there is a single front on which soldiers fight. The trench that traditionally separated the two worlds, the informationally dominant and dominated, two cultures, educated and common, has been disappearing, or rather, more accurately, a more stable hierarchy is reestablishing itself within the world of information, within the universe of the media. In a

204 *Pierre Nora*

world where no one is completely without knowledge or power, if only through universal suffrage, where no one has a permanent monopoly on the event; media seem to be telling us, to quote John Donne, "Ask not for whom the bell tolls, it tolls for thee."

It was to everyone that de Gaulle addressed his appeal of June 18, even if few heard it; it is for everyone that a champion skier breaks a record at lonesome altitudes, for everyone that an Israeli tank rolls into the desert: publicity is the loftiest rule of the modern event. And with this same stroke, information was condemned to be total; a condemnation so rigorous that in moments when publicity vanishes, the resulting silence becomes event. That the Nigerians denied the media access to occupied Biafra, that Indonesia massacred a million communists to the indifference of the capitalist world, endowed these events with an additional tragic significance. That the Leningrad Trial took place at the same time as the Burgos Trial and behind similarly closed doors influenced their outcome. The newsreader who, the day after de Gaulle's death, did not immediately announce, "General de Gaulle died last night," created the outline of a political event. The fact that the Chinese did not learn of the American moon landing was an event for the non-Chinese universe. The most totalitarian rule in the free world is the rule of spectacle.

Torn between the real and its projection as spectacle, information has lost its neutrality as an organ of simple transmission. By nature, despite higher-level distortions, it had been only a go-between, a necessary conduit. The event was emitted, transmitted, received. Hence the narrative, which brought the event from a milieu where it was already dead to the milieu where it would be absorbed, down the traditional lengthy slope from the most knowledgeable to the least informed. Information referred back to a real fact that was foreign to it, that it signified. Whatever the technical nature of the meaning it is given might be, Information, with a capital I, in principle always serves to reduce uncertainty. It would remain unintelligible if it didn't serve to enrich knowledge that has already been organized, to restructure the preexisting framework into which it would inscribe itself. Yet, considered generally, the media information system produces the unintelligible. It bombards us with knowledge that is interrogatory, enucleated, devoid of meaning, that waits for us to give it meaning, simultaneously frustrating and spoiling us with its cumbersome obviousness: if not for the intervention of the historian's reflex, it would be, at the extreme, nothing more than a sound muddling the intelligibility of its own discourse. We are continually crying out for more events, out of an anxiety about the smooth and uniform time of industrial societies, out of the need to consume time like an object, out of fear of the event itself. For its part, the machinery of information itself, by its very weight, continually demands this endless supply and crafts it on demand daily: each edition of *France-Soir,* for example, constructs events, most of which are stillborn. Therefore these are not, as [Daniel] Boorstin had claimed, pseudoevents, which would require postulating a parasitic relationship of false events to true ones.[13] Artifice—but is it really artifice?—is the truth of the system. It would be better to say that in the past the event required the extraordinary in order to take place and that the event now tends to be, in a present day about which there is nothing absolute, the source of its own sensationalism. There is a Gresham's Law of Information; the bad chases out the good. Contemporary history has witnessed the death of the "natural" event, in which we could ideally swap information for real facts; we have fallen under the reign of the inflation of events and we must, for better or for ill, integrate this inflation into the fabric of our daily existence.

Modernity exudes the event, whereas traditional societies had a tendency to rarefy it. The event as experienced in peasant societies was religious routine, natural disaster, or demographic shifts; a nonstory. But instituted powers and organized religion were geared toward eliminating novelty, reducing its corrosive power, digesting it through ritual. Established societies all sought to perpetuate a system of news whose ultimate goal was to negate the event, because the event could be precisely the rupture that would put into question the equilibrium upon which they were founded. Like the truth, the event is always revolutionary, the pebble in the machine, the accident that catches people unawares, upending everything. There are no fortunate *[heureux]* events; there are only catastrophes. But there are two ways of exorcising the new: warding it off through an information-free information system, or integrating it within the information system. An entire swath of the world in the East lives under a regime of news without novelty. Reading the news in these countries, you will never stumble upon anything unexpected: internal Party news, official anniversaries and commemorations, staged performances, news from the West twisted in a flattering way, the great hum of the propaganda machine, designed to sap the news of any information that could possibly undermine the institution that produced it. Medieval hagiographies thus gave only the month and the day of an event in the life of a saint, never the year, in order to inscribe this event in an eternity without memory, and thus without any temporal efficacy. The second method of guarding against the new consists in turning it into the essence of the narrative message, pushing this to the boundaries of redundancy, at the risk of turning the informational system into the engine of its own destruction. This is the universe in which we live.

The state of being perpetually overinformed and chronically underinformed characterizes our modern societies. The exhibition of the event no longer permits us to recognize the exhibitionism of events; an inevitable confusion, perhaps, but one conducive to uncertainty, anxiety, and social panics. Knowledge is the preeminent form of power in a society of democratic information. The corollary of this is not always false: one who holds power is presumed to have knowledge. From this comes a new dialectic, which in our societies gives rise to a type of event connected to secrecy, the police, conspiracies, rumor, and hearsay. It is simultaneously true and false that so much talk serves to conceals the essential, that this system that promotes the birth of events is also—but not only—a creator of illusions, that so many confessions serve to mask a lie. This is true whether we are looking at the great wave of fear that swept through the French countryside and the paranoid spy hunts of 1793, or the supposed link between Freemasons and the Elders of Zion during the era of the industrial revolution, the Jewish international under Hitler, Trotskyism under Stalin, or anti-imperialism in decolonized countries. The use of these outlets and scapegoats by so many witch doctors wielding charismatic authority has accompanied the historical experience of the new participation of the masses in public life, which is to say, in the sense that Tocqueville used the expression: the rise of democracy. These events clumsily, savagely, reflected [traduisaient] the arrival of the masses onto center stage and the profound frustration of the crowds, who clung to false knowledge in order to compensate for their lack of power.

The proliferation of novelty, the crafting of events, the devaluation of information, all are surefire ways of defending against information. But the ambiguity at the heart of information finds its fullest representation in the paradox of the metamorphoses of the event.

The Paradox of the Event

Herein lies the opportunity of the historian of the present: the displacement of the narrative message through its imaginary, spectacular, parasitic potentialities, has the effect of emphasizing the element of the event that is noneventful *[non-événementiel]*. Or rather, it makes the event nothing more than the neutral and temporal site of the sudden, isolable emergence of a tangle of social phenomena rising up from the depths, which, in the absence of the event, would have remained ensconced in the folds of the collective mind. The event serves as witness less through what it transmits *[traduit]* than for what it reveals, less for what it is than for what it triggers. Its significance is absorbed in its reverberations; it is but an echo, a mirror for society, a void. We might ask ourselves what de Gaulle's death would have represented if he had died ten years later, a diminished, forgotten old man. Yet he died one year after his departure, so soon after the votes of the French people had pushed him from power, yet long enough afterwards for them to feel only regret. And this at the outset of a regime born by his hand, which wished only to render him a funereal homage, but whose father had done it the ultimate insult of leveling against it the same laconic critique of the Fourth Republic. His death, which the fact that his memoirs, his final opportunity, remained unfinished, rendered only more tragic, seemed like the unintentionally perfect final scene of a great actor obsessed with his exit. A sudden, magical death, the kind that everyone wishes for oneself on the inside, but that, in this solemn case, resembled nothing so much as a saint summoned back to Heaven while still alive. His death, to foreign eyes, carried off the final survivor of World War II, the ally of the Soviet Union, the decolonizer, the friend of the Arab countries, a symbol of resistance, the man who had recognized China; in short, a man who had meant something to each of the powers of the world. And for the French people, it brought them back in contact with the most ancient, the most venerable, of royal traditions: the death of the king. But a death that, through the organization of a dual ceremony, by the chance of the moment, gave the monarchy precedence over the legacy of the republic, out of nostalgia for a lost greatness and a fleeting national reconciliation. And, through the cunning of history, the ceremony at Notre-Dame ironically enthroned for the second time the man who turned out to have felled the oak; it was French nationalism as a whole that escorted his

208 *Pierre Nora*

coffin, brought from Colombey.[14] There was more providential meaning in de Gaulle's death than in his life itself.

Immediacy renders the deciphering of an event simultaneously easier and more difficult. Easier because it strikes all at once; more difficult because it unloads everything simultaneously. In a more traditional system of information, the event would define its field of transmission through its content. Its network of influence was, more or less, defined by those it touched. Its course was more linear. If the event had not had the virtue of reducing itself to a single one of its significations, would it not have been much more difficult, even in the nineteenth century, for Marx, Tocqueville, or Lissagaray, but also for so many other more obscure commentators, to draw together recent history and historical analysis?[15] Even the most lucid contemporaries would have been, like today, greatly mistaken about current events. Now that the intermediaries have been short-circuited, a great compression has taken place, and in the dazzle of significations we have been blinded. An important news item such as, for example, the Kennedy assassination, through its immediate transmission, instantly realized its destiny as an event in the universal, but it welled up from the depths of the world's emotions at their source, rather than descending from a circle of initiates down to those that it might eventually interest. And in this rise, it swept up everything along with it. In the intransitive event, without theoretical banks or borders, the levels of meaning overlap and the exploded constellations become entangled. It is easier to pin it down from the outside: what is event and for whom? If there is no event without a critical consciousness, then there is only an event if, while offered to all, it is not the same for everyone. Limits of meaning, limits posed by the groups involved, and also limits of time: when does it end and what does it become? The fallout from events, the collective amnesia like the one that haunted the Algerian War, and all the underground twists and turns, add the final touches to the shape of the event.

This means that a strange reciprocity is created between a type of society and its eventful [*événementielle*] existence. On the one hand, it is the progression of events that constitutes the continuous surface of society, that institutes it and defines it, to the extent that the network of information-transmission represents one of its institutions. The information systems that, in the USSR, in China, or in the United States, produced the Twentieth Congress, the Cultural Revolution, or the Calley affair, offer illustrations of the society as a whole: the system is the form itself of the event's institutionalization. But, inversely, such events also carry with them a whole bundle of emotions, habits, routines, and representations inherited from the past, which suddenly trouble society's surface. As a site of social projections and latent conflicts, an event is like chance was for Cournot, the intersection of several causally independent series, a tear in the social fabric that the system itself is responsible for weaving. And the most important events are ones that lift the most archaic inheritance up to the surface. Here again, the system in the East offers an instructive counterpoint. The absence of *fait divers* is certainly not insignificant. This remnant offers a perfect illustration, in a minor mode, of the depths below. By purging what remains of the *fait divers* in the event, the system in the East eliminated with the same stroke the uncontrollable and scandalous element of social significations contained in the *fait divers*.

From this point on, it is not the event, over whose creation she has no control, that interests the historian, but the intersection of two systems within it, the formal system and the system of meaning, which she is better placed than anyone to grasp.

As independent as it might appear, there is nothing arbitrary about the unfolding of an event. If not its arrival, at the very least its eruption, its volume, its rhythm, its sequence, its relative position, its aftermath, and its unforeseen fallout all obey certain regularities that make the most distant phenomena appear to share a clear kinship and a bland identity. Studies of public opinion, which have now become standard, might find it useful to complement themselves with comparative analyses that would establish the sequences of information, how media were deployed, the relationship of the message and repetition, reactions all along the chain of transmission, in short the formal phenomenology of the event.[16] A quick study was made of the death of John XXIII.[17] What comparisons and conclusions would be reached by similar monographs of the deaths of other national figures, such as those of Stalin, Kennedy, Churchill, Adenauer, Togliatti, Nasser, de Gaulle? What similarities would we find in the scansions of certain scandals or trials, in cases that might not seem to have an immediate connection, such as the Dreyfus Affair and the Algerian War? Formal analysis spontaneously opens into an analysis of meaning, if only, at first, of the signification of the appearance of the formal system, which is itself an event. What transformation was signaled by the decisive intrusion of a new *événementialité*, in the late twentieth century, at the very moment when the triumph of positivism meant that scientific history was claiming the concept of the event solely in order to apply it exclusively to the past? What connections were there between these two contemporaneous phenomena, the birth of a science that had as its object only the events of the past and the emergence of a specifically contemporary history?

Thus, the historian of the present, in order to grasp meanings, employs none other than the serial method of the historian of the past, with the sole difference that the goal of her approach is the culmination of the event rather than its reduction. She consciously draws the past into the present rather than unconsciously drawing the present into the past. We know, today, that the night of August 4 was not solely the hysterical masquerade that Raymond Aron saw in the student assemblies that wished to claim its mantle in May '68. Was this evident on the morning of August 5, 1789? The only thing that decided what would come next were the application decrees [décrets d'application], which execute laws passed by parliament, and their implementation. And today, who could doubt that, reciprocally, the student assemblies expressed something other than what they explicitly proclaimed? The event has the virtue of bundling together dispersed meanings. It is up to the historian to untie them, to pull back from the brightness of the event in order to better illuminate the system. This is because the unity necessary for an event to become intelligible always requires postulating the existence of a series that novelty has brought to the surface. Even the claim "This is the first time that . . ." virtually presupposes the possibility of a second time. As Edgar Morin writes:

> Even if we remain at the level of a cybernetic model of social life, the information-event is precisely the thing that allows us to understand the nature of the structure and how the system operates, which is to say the feedback process of the integration (or rejection) of information, which is also to say the modification carried out either within the system or by the system itself.[18]

In the eruption of the volcano, the historian of the present, let us repeat, plays no role, unlike the historian of the past, whom the passage of time has permitted to artificially transform these volcanic events into so many landmarks for the landscape that he is clearing. But as a geologist, she finds her sovereignty once again. It is up to her to identify the geological strata, the network of internal explosions and secondary detonators, to distinguish between fundamental conflictual realities and mechanisms for integrating and reabsorbing the spilled lava. There is no difference in the nature of a crisis, which is a knot of events, and an event, which signals a crisis somewhere in the social system. A dialectic is established between these two phenomena, a dialectic of change, before which the historian of the past is as powerless as the historian of the present.

The future will belie his interpretation and, playing with his provisory attributions, will erase the series he had established in order to present the event itself within a whole other network, but the elaborations that were forged in the heat of the moment will remain meaningful; they are part of the event itself. The entire history of the French Revolution in the nineteenth century did nothing but proclaim the incompleteness of the revolutionary event. The writings of May 1968 are inseparable from their subject, they escort it through time; they reveal an impossible history of that May. Contemporary history, that exploration of current events, does not consist in applying to the present the time-tested historical methods used for the past. No, it is the final exorcism of the event, the last residual sign of its resolution. Even if history will later contradict it, it cannot be denied that, like the event itself, it will have been.

Through the new status that the event has acquired in industrial societies, our present-day world searches for a consciousness of itself. The problematic of the event—which remains to be formulated—is tightly bound to the specificity of "contemporary" history. Within our so-called consumer society, perhaps the treatment to which we submit the event is just a way, like many others, to reduce time itself into an object of consumption and to affectively invest it in a similar manner.[19] If it is indeed true that history begins only once the historian asks the past, in relation to her own present, questions that contemporaries would not have dreamed of, then who will say—beginning today— what anxiety lurks behind this need for events, what nervousness is implied by this tyranny, what major event for our civilization is expressed in the establishment of this vast system of event making that is current events?

Mastering the contemporary event, whose "consequences" are not yet known, is an impossibility. The positivists were unconsciously aware of its coming to power as they founded their science of history, and as such charged the present with being impoverished. Today,

212 *Pierre Nora*

when historiography as a whole has reached its modernity through the erasure of the event, the negation of its importance and its dissolution, the event returns to us—a different event—and accompanying it, perhaps, is the very possibility of a properly contemporary history.

Translation by Thomas Scott-Railton

NOTES

1. [Victor Duruy was both a historian and a minister of education (1863–69) under Napoleon III, and known for his reform of secondary education. Among other changes, Duruy introduced modern history into the curriculum, a cursus that ended with the study of "contemporary history" so as to equip students with an understanding of their changing world.—Ed.]

2. [Nora here refers to the Franco-Prussian War that ended in 1871 with France's defeat and the German empire's unification. The 1898 Fashoda Incident was the climax of territorial disputes between England and France in West Africa. The Paris Commune (March 18–May 28, 1871) was an insurrection led by socialists and anarchists against the French government that followed France's defeat in the Franco-Prussian War and the collapse of Napoleon III's empire. The Dreyfus Affair was a scandal in which the military framed Jewish Captain Alfred Dreyfus for treason based on falsified documents and then covered up the affair. Both the Fashoda Incident and the Dreyfus Affair provoked intense public outrage.—Ed.]

3. Auguste Geffroy, Jules Zeller, and Jules Thiénot, "Rapport sur les Études historiques," published by the minister of public instruction (Paris, 1867).

4. [The Panama Affair began in 1892 and refers to the corruption scandals surrounding the building of the Panama Canal during the Third Republic. Specifically, it denotes the discovery that a number of French officials had accepted bribes to downplay the financial misfortunes of the Panama Canal Company; as a result, the government fell. The scandal provoked a wave of anti-Semitic sentiment and marked the place for the media, with its newly granted freedom of the press (law of July 1881), in everyday political life.—Ed.]

5. *Images d'Épinal* refers to prints of popular subjects depicted in bright colors; the expression also indicates a naive or traditional depiction of something, one that shows only its good sides.

6. This term was born on January 14, 1898, when *L'Aurore,* demanding a review of the Dreyfus trial after [Ferdinand Walsin] Esterhazy was acquitted, published the "Manifeste des intellectuels."

7. Cf. Patrice Boussel, *L'Affaire Dreyfus et la presse,* collection Kiosque, Colin, 1960.

8. Cf. Frantz Fanon, *L'An V de la Révolution algérienne* (Paris: Maspero, 1959).

9. Cf. Roland Barthes, "L'Écriture de l'événement," special issue, *Mai 1968: La prise de la parole* of *Communications* 12.1 (1968): 108–12.

10. Cf. particularly Georges Auclair, *Le Mana quotidien: Structures et fonctions de la chronique des faits divers* (Paris: Éditions Anthropos, 1970), and Roland Barthes, *Mythologies* (Paris: Éditions du Seuil, 1967).

11. Cf. an in-depth study of the case before the press, carried out by the team

Centre d'études de presse de Bordeaux and published under the direction of André-Jean Tudesq, *La Presse et l'événement* (Paris: Mouton, 1973).

12. [Telstar was the world's first active communications satellite, and relayed the first transatlantic television signal from Andover Earth Station in Maine to the Pleumeur-Bodou Telecom Center in Brittany, France.—Ed.]

13. Cf. Daniel Boorstin, *L'Image,* trans. Janine Claude (Paris: Julliard, 1963); in English, *The Image* (New York : Vintage Books, 1992).

14. [Charles de Gaulle died unexpectedly on November 9, 1970, in Colombey-les-Deux-Églises, one year after resigning office and bringing an end to France's Fourth Republic. Despite his wishes to be buried at his home in Colombey with no officials present, the number of foreign dignitaries wishing to honor him obliged Georges Pompidou, president of the Fifth Republic, to hold a second ceremony for him at the Cathedral of Notre-Dame in Paris. De Gaulle's notoriously tall build necessitated a specially designed oak casket. Because Colombey had come to signal de Gaulle's periods of retreat from politics, that he left Colombey one last time was thought to be portentous.—Ed.]

15. [Hippolyte Prosper Olivier Lissagaray was a French journalist, speaker, and revolutionary socialist. His *History of the Paris Commune of 1871* drew from his participation on the barricades of the Commune and was aided by Karl Marx and translated into English by Marx's daughter Eleanor.—Ed.]

16. Cf. in particular Abraham Moles, *Socio-dynamique de la culture* (Paris: Mouton, 1967).

17. Cf. Jules Gritti, "Un récit de presse: Les derniers jours d'un 'grand homme,'" *Communications* 8.1 (1966): 94–101. As well as the other works of the author in general, notably *L'Événement, technique d'analyse de l'actualité* (Paris: Éditions Fleurus, 1969).

18. Edgar Morin, "Principes d'une sociologie du présent," in *La Rumeur d'Orléans* (Paris: Éditions du Seuil, 1969), 225.

19. Cf. in particular Jean Baudrillard, *Le Système des objets* (Paris: Gallimard, 1967).

CHAPTER 8

Thinking and Defining
the Event in History
(2002)

Arlette Farge

*Arlette Farge describes her project: "In history, an event lasts for
a time that reaches beyond its constituent facts. It is loaded with
perceptions and feelings that have formed before it actually happens. The event then plays out in its own time. But inside this
time frame, those who make or undergo the event experience it
in a temporal and historical setting that comprises its past, its
genealogy, its present form, and the vision of the future held by
those who accept or refuse the event itself. An event plays out
over a rather long span of time through social and political relations with formative effects." Writing twenty years after the initial publication of* Le Désordre des familles, *Farge consolidates
historians' appropriations of Foucault's attention to the composition of the event, the infusion of affect into the event, and the
event's own trailing implications.*   ➤

The practice of history is social, intellectual, and academic, its production geared to the eyes of peers and the transmission of knowledge
to an audience. It is also a "will to know" and a power that obeys
certain laws: those of the intellectual and academic milieu, those of
truthfulness and of the potential for verifiability.

The narrative of the event is its cornerstone; but by this term we
could mean any number of extraordinarily different things. Much
has already been written and said about the link between history and
the event, and it is a question to which the discipline has continually

returned. The nature and essence of the event, the grounds for selecting it in particular as the object of analysis, the location, itself important, at which it enters the historical narrative, all have been the subject of many discussions, varying along with the era and schools of thought. Whatever the case may be, the event was always that which seemed to seize time in an intense contraction, giving the course of history a new tonality. But nothing seems to offer a definitive definition of what exactly is meant by "that which seizes time."

This text will outline several possible approaches to the event, as well as the historical ability to think about situations that individuals experience as events. It will also reflect on the reception and the effects of the event, which are constituent elements of it as well and which create meaningful temporalities and landscapes of memory that, albeit following it chronologically, are an intrinsic part of it.

On the Event

The occurrence of an event is a moment, a perceived fragment of reality with no other unity than the name we have given it. Its arrival in time (this is the sense in which it is a focal point around which a before and an after are determined) is immediately shared by those who receive it, witness it, hear it spoken of, announce it, and then preserve it in memory. Creator and created, constructor and constructed, it is from the outset a slice of time and action that has been split into fragments, through the manner in which it was both shared and discussed. It is through this splintered existence that the historian must work if she wishes to grasp its scope, its meaning, and its mark(s) on temporality.

As a slice of time, the event also creates: it creates the time that follows its completion, it creates relationships and interactions, confrontations or phenomena of consent, it creates language, discourse. We could even say that it creates light because it can instantaneously illuminate mechanisms that had up until then been invisible. Traumatic or ordinary, events can have significant effects that are tough for the historian to detect, or that she might deliberately avoid uncovering. And the event creates when it displaces acquired representations and when it is experienced as a shock so traumatic that it might seem to have stopped time itself (which is of course both an illusion and a perception that the historian must interrogate).

The historian "loves" the event; its allure for her is as great as her anxiety about the "silence of the sources." This does not mean that she always knows how to recognize it; easily identifiable, prominent moments, of course, serve as guiding thread and adhesive for her narrative, allowing her to articulate her hypothesis around their emergence and their consequences. The result of this is an undisturbed current of thought, flowing from one event to the next, from war to new regime, from tax increase to riot. The event becomes the very legitimation itself of her discourse; this is one of the perverse paradoxes of its presence in historical discourse, because from this point on it is no longer seen as a thing in itself, but rather becomes frozen in place as a justification for what comes next. Moreover, the historian has an advantage over many other social scientists in that she always knows what will happen afterwards and how everything will turn out. Severed from its sources, sometimes even from its context and the long term of its temporality, which is the very transformation of its essence, the event becomes a reliable field for a historian blind to those events that have not yet been perceived, and becomes easily absorbed into what Michel Foucault called the "boiling down of history," which renders the history of human beings far too smooth (see Foucault, "Lives of Infamous Men" in this volume).

The architecture of historical narration, built upon the concept of the "advent" of a new object, a change in government, an epidemic, an event, runs a great risk of inadvertently organizing itself around a smoothed-over version of the facts. If it is true that the writing of history requires a passage from disorder to order (the disorder of the sources, of hypotheses, of documents; the reasoned order of narration), then we must accept that there is no history without a recognition of that which creates disorder, enigmas, gaps, irregularities, silence and rumblings, disharmony in the connections between things and the facts, between individuals and the social or political situation. Spotting the event, therein lies history: doing so requires that we accept being surprised, stymied, contradicted. Events are sometimes almost inaudible, sometimes unintelligible; only the movement that comes to constitute their temporality allows us to understand them and integrate them, even in all their roughness, into the narrative.

Low Intensities

First of all, there are, as Paul Veyne (1996) has long studied, events that are not strictly speaking events, or rather that are a series of events created by the "low intensities" of human and social movements.

218   *Arlette Farge*

Historians are not very good at recognizing events that do not take place on a grand scale. Yet it is frail and fragile events, ones with no great breadth, that are in a certain sense the "somewhat" of history. One can be "somewhat" of a rioter, or "somewhat" Catholic but not excessively so (yet this does not necessarily mean being run-of-the-mill). If we become attentive to the infinite range of social and human mechanisms, this "somewhat" becomes one of the touchstones that guides, fixes in place, or, on the contrary, pushes forward the great body of opinions and visions of the world.

Historians have long searched intensively for the deviant and the marginal, for the transgressive and the wayward, before leading them safely back to the norm. But we have not yet reached a point of establishing bodies of thoughts, attitudes, moments, or mental categories that, shrouded in the faintness of their intensities, constitute events that are just as important as others, transforming the very terms of discourse, the concepts and the ideas that are normally integral parts of it. The ordinary social act, through its faintness and through its habitualness, constitutes one of the great motors of events. The thread of existence and eventuality is spun from the imperceptible production of events out of the "somewhat," the banal, the hardly felt.

About his movie *Sans soleil* (1983), Chris Marker has said: "After a few trips around the world, only banality still interests me." Retranscribing banality inside of dramas and the undramatic, understanding and interpreting the expectations and sometimes the silence of public opinion, examining the way in which the apparent banality of sentiments is linked to the manner in which tragedies are constituted, this is indeed a different way of seeing the event.

The Event Harbors a Vision of the Future

In keeping with this theme of the almost imperceptible but nonetheless significant event, we should now turn to an example that is quite significant for our search into the status of the event. An event, as tragic or insignificant as it may be, once it has emerged, which is to say once traces of it have managed to reach us, harbors within it (or at least in the way it is enunciated) the vision of the future of those who just experienced or apprehended it. This vision of the future is constitutive of the "event-moment," as is that of the past: we speak of an event by characterizing it in relation to an expectation of what will happen, an announcement of what will fortunately or unfortunately come to pass. We speak about it in relation to what we know existed in the past. In the eighteenth century, for example, a public gathering, no matter how small, as described by the police or by chroniclers and filed in the archives, would be inflated by what might have happened beforehand and by the terrible consequences that would soon come to pass if . . .

No event can be severed from what it caused people to remember, and from what it threatened to portend—all of which historians will have difficulty perceiving so long as they are chronologically fixated on the rule and the moment, without considering the potential width of an occurrence's temporality.

The Minuscule

If we wish to study the subtlety of the event, we must also learn how to recognize a different dimension of it. When the historian works with the minuscule and the singular (for example, in the archives of police crackdowns and interrogations), the words spoken, the short narratives reported by the scribes, are events. This is because, even in fragments, this language carries with it attempts at coherence by those being questioned. Within it we can find social identities, modes of appropriating the self and others, manners of staging or playing oneself, and a recognition of the public stage, which are all themselves events (Farge 1989). Speech, in certain cases, is an event to the extent that its emergence is submitted to a collective that should in each instance be defined. And it might be interesting to study the manner in which each era directs or induces this connection; this could in fact be an object of historical inquiry.

Similarly, the body is itself a site where the political is inscribed and, if we are willing to follow Pierre Bourdieu in his *Pascalian Meditations* (1997), we could argue that "the most serious social injunctions are addressed not to the intellect but to the body" and that these are important events that transform the being, his speech, and his body. On the other hand (and leaving behind any Bourdieusian assumptions), body and speech, in the close calls of their modes of existence and expression, can, like an event, inflect or surprise the institution or the injunction. An interactive game, in which the winner is nonetheless often the same, comes to create the eventful moments that supply historical timelines. The irruption of the body or speech into the sources

220 *Arlette Farge*

is an opportunity, because it brings, through its intrinsic extraneousness, new interrogations, not only to the interpretation of historical events, but to the very construction itself of the narrative.

On the Construction of the Event

Before any examination of this subject, let us make one thing clear: "the most predictable thing about history is its unpredictability" (Cabanel and Laborie 2002). We could draw an intellectual position from this quote. Why is it that so often "what happened" serves as a boundary on the historian's imagination? Could we not reflect, beyond and below the construction of the event, on everything that did not come to pass but might have? This would allow words to open onto possible elsewheres that could have taken another form, color, or dimension. Once we have arrived at this definition of the occurrence of the non-event, we can ask, "What produces the event?" and "Who produces the event?"

The Field of Emotions

Whatever its nature might be, the event constructs, displaces, and completes itself within the wide field of emotion. It is always difficult to discuss this subject without being immediately misunderstood—being a female author in no way simplifies the problem, even though this assertion is self-evident. In order to break through, to rise to the surface of history, an event must be perceived and characterized. Because its emergence owes much to the dual vision of past and future to come, it takes place within simultaneous and extremely varied perceptions that are also fed by the affective universe. It might be the surprise and indignation that greets its eruption, or the fear that it provokes, that constitute its identity as event. It is indifference that will dissolve it and shame that will destroy it. Its temporality is constructed by the manner in which it strikes imaginations. Emotion is not that rosy coating that we use to cover so many things; it is one of the constituent elements of thought itself, the part that apprehends what emerges from within a rational nebula in which emotions have their place.

An emerging social situation, a rise in prices, a levy of soldiers, the announcement of a food shortage, a diplomatic treaty, a prince's disgrace, or a tawdry human-interest story are all gathered up by the public (in a differentiated or collective manner, depending on social classes) within its own field of vision, itself forever informed by the field of passions.

The poor relations of the historian's domain, passions are appealed to only as explanations for revolutions or large riots. This overlooks the finesse with which our predecessors in the seventeenth and eighteenth centuries debated them, producing a prodigious number of *Treatises on the Passions*. Moreover, the event has its own horizon of expectation. It is composed of a great many elements, too many to list here. Among them, the emotional field is very present: we might almost argue that it is what provides the motive force for the event and establishes it as a historical phenomenon. Because it is this field that stamps the event with one of its fates.

The Event Foretold

There are cases in history of events that were foretold or experienced as such. For some, this was true of France's defeat in 1940, which of course had an effect on the way it was perceived once it had come to pass.

To a great extent—and I said this already a little above—the status of an event exists, in these cases, before it actually takes place. With foretold events, the unfolding present is subordinated to the future in the eyes of those witnessing it. Thus, to stay with the example of the 1940 defeat (Cabanel and Laborie 2002), those who had been expecting it lived it in a way that reflected their representations of the future and the uses they would make of the present in light of them (collaboration, resistance, flight, allegiance to Pétain, hatred of the Germans, desire for revenge, etc.). In this way, expectations constitute a part of people's mental logics and they organize part of the event's future.

There are also foretold events that do not come to pass, and then we must look for reasons why they failed to occur. A quick example from the eighteenth century—1743, to be more precise—can offer a few clues. At a time when, in Paris, the forced levy of soldiers was quite poorly received, a royal decree was announced ordering that two thousand men be levied. The attitude of the monarchy, reinforced by that of the lieutenant general of police (and vice versa), was to prepare for grave problems, popular resistance, and even a few sporadic uprisings. Here we can see power worried about its own announcement,

222　*Arlette Farge*

as it foresaw a "state of war in the capital." As we know, "levying soldiers" meant drawing lots to determine who would be levied, but it applied only to a very specific rung of the social ladder: the lowest one. Many men were exempt from this levy, including some domestic servants from important houses and well-established artisans, etc. It was the poorer classes that were subject to it. Additionally, letters of recommendation facilitated quite a few exemptions. Suffice to say that the system was not fair. The authorities were aware of this, through their own perceptions, so they took enormous precautions, imagining that there was no way a riot would not be triggered by these injustices. The event that was "foretold," which is to say foreseen, was an uprising, yet it did not take place. This is a quite interesting subject for study. It was decided that the drawing of lots would take place very early in the morning in two specific and carefully delineated parts of the city. The police were, naturally, given special assignments and soldiers were summoned to surround the site of the levy and lottery, facing out toward the crowd that would necessarily be oppositional and combative. None of what had been expected occurred; the calm in which the day of recruitment passed astonished everyone from the king to the most famous chroniclers and memorialists. Thus, by organizing the event and its future before it even took place, political elites had banked on an emotional state among the public that did not exist, though such a state could always explode in other unexpected ways.

We do not have the space here to examine the minutiae of this day's events: we can simply remark that, for the first time, the monarchical framework of expectation failed. But it is interesting to see that it belied a perception of the people that was so deeply rooted among the authorities: the people, at each instance, will be uncontrollable, impulsive, and rebellious. This perception of women and men as perpetually unruly could not be replaced by any other perspective: they were mistaken about certain forms of indifference that existed in the poorer neighborhoods. Organized recruitment, which by definition had excluded the better-off, as well as domestic servants from important houses and the apprentices of well-regarded artisans, meant that the individuals most vulnerable to being shipped off were the lowliest and most marginalized. Paris could watch them depart for the borders without problem.

The people as an entity, which had fed into elite thinking and understanding, collapsed; the people, extremely socially stratified and with quite differentiated layers, in fact possessed opinions and positions that were quite complex. The generalized picture of this entity was mistaken; the people would not allow for any prediction of so general a nature. And if, in this example, this was fortunate for public order, it also meant that the event was not something that could be predicted and that, in order for it to occur, certain rather specific alchemies were needed. Alchemies that an entire monarchy, dedicated to the idea that its subject population had neither competency, nor understanding, nor public personality, could absolutely not understand. Thus, it took as support for the war what was in fact only an absence of solidarity between the more fortunate layers of the population and the most marginalized, which is something else altogether, and this offers a fascinating insight into the state of social and popular mechanisms during the mid-eighteenth century.

Giving Meaning to the Event

Once the historian has integrated into the concept of the event its most minuscule elements, such as silences, utterances, emotions, low intensities, and the ordinary course of things, she will have to ask herself the question of meaning with greater acuity than before. In doing so, she will introduce the dimension of the singular, of individual activity, of the single project, inside of that which took place and ultimately constructs the event. We must think about the way in which the link is drawn between individual attitudes and the emergence of a new time span for a specific group of persons.

This is one of the most difficult points that historical research must resolve, because it is not a question of crumbling the historical narrative into clusters of singular anecdotes, nor of organizing a historical discourse that slips into the universe of particularities, eventually drowning its meaning in the multiplicity of individual positions. Instead, we should look to everything that converges toward groupings that we can grasp (psychological attitudes, group actions, discourses that have more or less the same register of enunciation and are supported by similar ethical postures, which can be appropriated from a relatively coherent public stage). To these we can add everything that can be detected from the most visible forms of transgression, but also from exchanges involving gestures, distancing, sidestepping, remembered words, outlines of gestures, and social practices

224 *Arlette Farge*

for which spoken words are not necessary. Distance is the location of a quite particular adjustment to the public stage, though certainly the grouping organized by distance, the norm, the singularity, seems like disorder and chaos. In fact, this order and chaos create meaning, to the extent that they can delineate a unity of time or action, which will contain an event that will only take on its true dimensions in the time to come. It is the duration *[durée]* and the consequences of the event that emerged that will give meaning to these apparently incoherent shards. If we consider the example of public opinion and its state at such and such a historic moment, it is important to take into account what has constructed it, through its major tendencies as much as through its incoherencies, its rumors, and its irrational elements. Even if it can be explained by the events around it, public opinion is never an automatic consequence of them. The event is in fact a permanent construction that spreads out considerably over time. For the historian, it is difficult to say when an event ends, because it operates through a network of relationships whose effects are structuring. Certain externally important events continue to structure our social, perhaps even our economic, behavior. Thus, the short term can be long-lasting, over the course of which its meaning will continue to change, encompassing mobile systems of representation that will inflect the first initial interpretation it might have been given. We can also say (Laborie 2001) that the event takes its entire meaning from the way in which individuals perceive it and internalize it, and ultimately, through quite different experiences, grant it an outline with visible contours. There is no event without a meaning that is bestowed upon it by its reception. There is no a priori meaning to an event.

The Memory of the Event

We will not wade into the current debate here over memory and history (Ricoeur 2004). By memory of the event, we simply mean the way in which it insinuates itself into the collective social body, finding one or several novel positions that will vary with time. A major event that has been repressed for political reasons (the war in Algeria, for example) runs a high risk of taking on a sharp and extremely blameful face forty years after its occurrence. In a similar manner, entire generations can be accompanied by an event that will mark their ethical positions, their ways of approaching the world. Far less important events can also have consequences over a quite long stretch: festivals, rituals, ceremonies, all punctuate our calendars, mixing republican, religious, and heroic repertoires. Society moves to the rhythm of these past events. The event, of course, is endlessly reconstructed, in multiple ways, varying according to the era in which it is being received. Elsewhere and at the same time, the memory of the event among those who lived it, even in the distant past, can assist the historian with her most difficult task: rediscovering the emotional, social, or political manner by which others reconstructed the event, or identified with it, or rejected it inexorably. The memory of the event determines its meaning to the extent that it remembers it.

It would be impossible to conclude this historiographic reflection concerning the nature of the event without highlighting the nearly self-evident way that, if its perception is not a fact in itself, and if we can agree that the reality of the event is constructed, there will be utterly contradictory kinds of interpretations, depending on whether someone belongs to one social stratum or another. And these appropriations can no doubt become intertwined: no event can be defined without taking into account societal situations of dominance and submission, the multiplicity of injunctions arising from social order, the economic and political situations that generated it and those, which are quite different, into which it will suddenly emerge and have a lasting effect. An event in history is a conjunction of alterities; in addition to being a slice of time, it will be called upon to derive its fate and its meaning from its reception and representations of it. Alterities can also be conflicts, and social struggles, either voiced or muted, expressed or not, are also sites for the inscription of the event. This is why the mobility of the event demands an infinite flexibility from the historical gaze that comes to rest upon it.

Translated by Thomas Scott-Railton

REFERENCES

Bourdieu, Pierre. *Pascalian Meditations*. Trans. Richard Nice. Stanford, Calif.: Stanford University Press, 2000 [1997].

Cabanel, Patrick, and Pierre Laborie. *Penser la défaite*. Toulouse: Privat, 2002.

Farge, Arlette. *The Allure of the Archives*. Trans. Thomas Scott-Railton. New Haven: Yale University Press, 2013 [1989].

Laborie, Pierre. *L'opinion française sous Vichy: Les français et la crise d'identité nationale, 1936–1944.* Paris: Éditions du Seuil, 2001.

Ricoeur, Paul. *Memory, History, Forgetting.* Trans. Kathleen Blamey and David Pellauer. Chicago: University of Chicago Press, 2004.

Veyne, Paul. "L'interprétation et l'interprète: À propos des choses de la religion." *Enquête,* no. 3 ("Interpréter, surinterpréter"): 160–80.

CHAPTER 9

Home, Street, City

Farge, Foucault, and the Spaces of the *Lettres de Cachet*

Stuart Elden

Providing a synoptic overview of the Disorderly Families *project, Stuart Elden argues that the letters offer a view of power that adopts the perspective of those "from below." Attentive to the lives of everyday people (rather than elites), the letters chart the spaces of so-called disorder. If Foucault's* Discipline and Punish *offers a sense of the architecture for the spaces of punishment, then these letters attest to the fluidity of conjugal spaces as well as the wider household, as these family disputes spill out raucously into the street. The disorders the characterize these spaces are those of trespass: vagabonds leave their home villages, the debauched trespass into others' conjugal spaces, while libertines frequent clandestine sites removed from the circulations of police. Elden offers insight into how power composes, shapes, and delineates geographic territories.*　　　　　　　　　　➤

In the Introduction to *Le Désordre des familles*, Arlette Farge and Michel Foucault note that the project was a combination of their individual research interests: "One of us studied Parisian street life in the eighteenth century; the other, the procedures for administrative imprisonment from the seventeenth century up to the Revolution."[1] In that research, both were led to the archives of the Bastille, held in the Bibliothèque de l'Arsenal: there the letters they analyze in the book were found.[2]

In terms of research interests, the second reference is of course to

Foucault, and his famous *Surveiller et punir,* a book we know in English translation as *Discipline and Punish.*[3] While the subtitle of that work is *The Birth of the Prison,* this is both the prison in the obvious sense and the figurative sense of the soul as the "prison of the body."[4] Foucault's examples, of course, range far wider than the prison, and encompass the factory, the school, the workshop, and, especially, the army. While wide-ranging, his books, both in this 1975 work and his earlier studies of madness and clinical medicine, had tended to focus on institutions of one kind or another. But in his lectures and collaborative research conducted in and beyond his Collège de France seminars he had widened the lens to look at wider social settings. This can found, for example, in his work with Félix Guattari's Centre d'Études, de Recherche et de Formation Institutionnelle (CERFI) on public utilities and infrastructure; projects developing from that research on public health; his edited report *Politiques de l'habitat* and his famous lectures on governmentality.[5]

The wider setting is a major theme of Farge's work too. The reference in this text is to her study *Vivre dans la rue à Paris au XVIIIe siècle* (Paris street life in the eighteenth century), which appeared in 1979,[6] but Foucault was initially led to her work by her first book, *Délinquance et criminalité: Le vol d'aliments à Paris au XVIIIe siècle* (Delinquency and criminality: Food thefts in eighteenth-century Paris), which he cites in *Discipline and Punish.* This was a rare citation of one of his contemporaries.[7] Farge was also one of a number of historians involved in the 1978 discussion of Foucault's work collected in Michelle Perrot's *L'Impossible prison.*[8] In these early writings, as well as in many of her subsequent works, Farge develops a thoroughgoing analysis of the details of Parisian life: individual, family, and collective. While Farge would, occasionally, focus on what she and André Zysberg called "the everyday theatre of violence,"[9] she is often as interested in the mundane, the prosaic details of daily life rather than the extraordinary. In this she perhaps balanced Foucault's regular interest in the baroque, the macabre, and the grotesque. Indeed, Farge would go on to use some of the letters she and Foucault collected for, but did not include in, *Le Désordre des familles* in her contribution to the multivolume *Histoire de la vie privée* (History of private life), edited by Philippe Ariès and Georges Duby.[10]

Bringing together Foucault's interests and Farge's was productive because in combination they were able to situate the work in relation to wider themes. From Foucault's work, these encompassed the history of European society, and the transition from sovereign regimes of the early-modern period to the disciplinary or punitive societies that emerged, in Foucault's terms, in the eighteenth century. From Farge, the rich detail of everyday life in Paris adds color and detail to the broader sociopolitical transitions. While Foucault's archival work is often underappreciated in assessments of his work, Farge's career has been built on such labors, and her standing in this area is undisputed. In combination, a historically minded philosopher at the end of his tragically shortened career, and an archival historian much earlier in hers, use the letters to open up a range of topics. While the explicit focus of the work is on the family, and especially matrimonial and parental relations, the letters and their analysis provide a valuable insight into workings of power and questions of space.

Sovereignty and Power

As the letters had the king's seal, it is tempting to see them as examples of the autocratic power of the Ancien Régime, and they could certainly be used in that way. But, as Foucault shows in his lectures *The Punitive Society,* we should see the letters less as examples of state or royal power, but rather as the power of those who request them: "individuals, families, religious groups, esteemed citizens [*notables*], legal persons (notaries, etc.), and corporations."[11] This, then, entails a different model of analysis:

> While being part of this pyramid rising up to the king, the *lettre de cachet* operates in an opposite direction to that of royal arbitrariness. The letter, which is the instrument of a sort of capillary and marginal counterinvestment, rises back up the "parajudicial" state apparatus. It should be noted that the points at which these counterinvestments by the *lettre de cachet* take place are, in a way, socially important places in that they become relays and diversions [*dérivations*] of power: we see these letters requested and authenticated at the level of communities like the parish—an administrative, fiscal, and religious unit, and, at the same time, the place of the formation of a sort of consensus that asks power to respect its morality, order, and regularity—the family, the corporation. These places are exchangers [*échangeurs*] between power from above and power from below.[12]

230   *Stuart Elden*

The notion of an "exchanger" is like an electrical junction box, or a switch point between these different modes of powers. Foucault had used similar language to examine the way that medieval ordeals or tests had functioned as a "mechanical operator *[opérateur]* of the law, a switch or commutator *[commutateur]* of force into law, a *shifter* that enabled the transition from force to law."[13] These topics of examination, then, whether the medieval ordeal or the *lettre de cachet,* allow an analysis of wider sociopolitical relations. Examining the relations would therefore look at the "local micro-powers" between people, and the actions of more lowly administrators.[14] This is crucial, because "the *lettre de cachet* was a way of regulating the everyday morality of social life, a way for the group or groups—family, religious, parochial, regional, and local—to provide for their own police control and ensure their own order."[15]

The letters are thus examples of the "codified description of deviance," "the banality of the everyday."[16] The analysis therefore follows the earlier work of Frantz Funck-Brentano, who argues that rather than being "a means of oppression at the hands of a royal power," the king actually "enforced a limitation on their use." The letters should be better understood as a "spontaneous outburst from the underbelly of the people."[17] Nonetheless, Funck-Brentano tends to focus on elites in his work on the letters, and when Farge and Foucault develop his line of analysis, they follow it more to its conclusion. Thus, they suggest that reading of the material highlighted not "the rage of the sovereign . . . but rather the passions of the common people."[18] Central to those passions are "family relationships—husbands and wives, parents and children."[19] Indeed, the book is structured around two main parts, each framed by an introduction, and then an extensive dossier of letters. The first part on marital relations was largely the work of Farge; Foucault took the lead on the part on parent–child relations. Some of Foucault's late-1970s and early-1980s interests can be glimpsed here and there: one of the initially planned volumes of the *History of Sexuality* had been on children; another on women; and the Malthusian couple a projected focus of the volume on races and populations.[20]

Farge and Foucault's project is therefore directed toward understanding "the concrete functioning of a power mechanism," though they underline that this is not "an anonymous 'Power,' oppressive and mysterious," but rather "a complex web of relationships between multiple partners, an institution for control and sanction."[21] The use of *lettres de cachet* enabled people to bypass standard judicial procedures, as well as publicity, so they were used by both for reasons of poverty and privacy. As such, the letters are not so revealing of the political administration of the time as they are of the internal working of families, the relation between men and women, adults and children. These are the ways through which the family institution fits into the "greater administrative apparatus *[appareil]*."[22] While the wider analysis of power that appears in this book is a possible avenue of inquiry, the focus here will be on the spaces at multiple scales that are revealed and analyzed by the letters, themselves a site of power relations. This is what Farge and Foucault call "a fascinating peek into the landscape of everyday life for the lower classes in Paris."[23]

Spaces of Disorder: From the Home to the Street

The spaces of family disorder analyzed in the book come from a close reading of the documentary material, out of which "a landscape begins to take shape."[24] This is a point Farge elaborates in her wonderful study of the working practice of the archival historian: "Beneath the archives lies an organized topography *[le relief s'organise]*. You need only know how to read it, and to recognize that meaning can be found at the very spot *[endroit]* where lives have involuntarily collided with power."[25] The relation between space and power in more general terms had been crucial throughout Foucault's work. It is there in the analysis of the architectural design of the asylum, the clinical hospital and the prison; from the design of factories, boarding-school dormitories, and military camps to public-health campaigns, the policing of urban space, and governmental regimes in "spaces of security" through the wider society. Space, for Foucault, is historically produced and entirely permeated by power relations, while at the same time histories are always also geographies, and power relations are determined by the spaces through which they operate, shape, and are constrained. While Foucault does provide some short pieces that are principally focused on space—his "Of Other Spaces" lecture from 1967, and interviews with the geographers of *Hérodote* review in 1976 and with Paul Rabinow in the *Skyline* architecture journal in 1982—a spatial attunement permeates almost all his historical work.[26] As Foucault said in that 1982 interview, "space is fundamental in any form of communal power, space is fundamental in any exercise of power."[27]

232   *Stuart Elden*

These spatial relations are an important focus of Farge and Foucault's work in this volume, though the spaces examined tend to smaller scale than institutions and the wider society. As such, the volume provides rich insights for geographers and others interested in questions of spatiality, and in a different register than most of Foucault's work. Given the focus on family relations, it is perhaps not surprising that the smallest scale analyzed in the work is the home. After the individual body, this is often seen as the most immediate and intimate type of social space. One example given concerns the importance of beds, looking at the case of a man who had sold those of his family: "An essential, and singular, piece of furniture; even when you had nothing, you still had your bed, whose symbolic function cannot be ignored."[28] As Farge notes elsewhere, even though lodgings opened directly onto each other, and there was "very little intimacy in the modern sense of the word . . . conjugal space *[lieu]* did exist and the man wanted to see it respected just as much as the woman."[29]

One of the things that becomes clear is that the relation between man and wife, parent and child, cannot be easily separated. There were precious few individual spaces available at this time. Farge and Foucault therefore suggest:

> The frequent conjunction of elements related to economic existence alongside others related to personal attitudes demonstrates the manner in which the conjugal bond was also a place *[lieu]*. It was the place of socioeconomic establishment as much as it was the place of sexual and emotional understanding. The place of the body, of the heart, and that of social roles cannot be separated as neatly as one might wish; the couple was the intersection of these spaces *[espaces]*, an expectation of harmony between them and a certainty that they were tightly interdependent on one another.[30]

We shift, here, between spatial terms in an almost metaphorical sense to more concrete ones. It might appear that thinking of marriage as a place or site is just an expression, without a grounding in social, physical location. But, unlike many of the structuralist thinkers who used spatial language to express looser dynamics of thought, Foucault almost always connected his use of terms with analysis of concrete spatial phenomena. This comes through in this work, both in Foucault's parts and in those by Farge, and is a central theme of so much of Farge's independent work. One of the section titles in the first part— the section largely by Farge on the husband–wife relation—is titled "masculine spaces, feminine spaces."[31] But the space of the home is also a major theme in the section led by Foucault on parent–child relations:

> At the other pole of motives for imprisonment was the behavior of children within the internal space of the family. In a number of dossiers, the house appeared as a place of war, of extreme violence, of brutality. Two themes come up time and again, more often than not in conjunction with one another: insults, oaths, threats, blows, on the one hand, and, on the other, theft, robbery, money extorted by cunning or by force. Large sums were rarely involved, as the protagonists were by and large poor. By far the most commonly described situation was theft, under threat, of a little money or a few belongings; the scoundrel has created an atmosphere of terror in the home, he hits and he takes. For boys, drunkenness was very often pointed to as the reason for this behavior; he comes home drunk, he steals so that he can continue to get drunk.[32]

In her book *Fragile Lives,* Farge describes a typical Parisian apartment building as an "anthill" *(termitière),* that is, "a profusion of shops and workshops *[ateliers]* intersected by passages and alley-ways and packed to the roof with lodgings and dormitories, it lays bare its secrets and wounds, it offers scant refuge but nonetheless affords some sleep and rest of a kind, albeit without comfort and with practically no privacy."[33] She elsewhere examines how the workshop was "an intermediary place between the inside and the outside," a traditional work space for artisans, but also their apprentices, who were either members of, or who often lived with, the family. Such workshops were directed toward the outside, for sales and trade, and for the coming and going of other workers; but they were all linked to the family dwelling.[34] Given this collective nature of housing, and the frequent blurring of domestic and work spaces, truly private space remained largely unknown, and elsewhere Farge notes that even reading early eighteenth century police orders did not shed much light on what happened "in houses and hearts while they do give a glimpse into workshops, markets, the street and the river" as wider, public spaces of the city.[35] This is a theme Farge regularly returns to: "the confusion existing between public and private space and the impossibility of distinguishing between 'open' and 'closed' in a situation where each space communicated with the next, opened out onto another, or overlooked and was overlooked by everyone else, offering no protection at all."[36]

234 *Stuart Elden*

This confusion of public and private space is important, and helps to understand some of the challenges of the work Farge and Zysberg had pursued in their analysis of Paris's "theaters of violence."[37] The blurring of spaces means that there were precious few safe environments, little privacy or security. The loss of anything straightforwardly "private" means that so much life is lived in the collective, and as might be expected given Farge's earlier work, there are many revealing insights into life in "the street, the tavern *[le cabaret]*, the workshop" to be found in her work with Foucault.[38] This comes through especially clearly in the geography, both of relations and of spaces, of these letters:

> Distant members of the family, the innkeeper from the street-corner, the merchant grocer from the ground floor, or the tenants from across the hall were the principal signatories. In order to render a petition more convincing, one would do well to convince the parish curé, an influential person in the neighborhood, or the primary leaseholder, that feared, honored and hated guarantor of Parisian buildings.[39]

The examples given provide, as Farge suggests in her work on the street, "a materialization of space more than a detailed urban geography,"[40] a flavor, details, illustrations, rather than a comprehensive, totalizing account. Far from a weakness, this provides both color and nuance, an approach to be followed rather than a theory to be applied. Foucault has, in particular, suffered from this, where the theoretical tools and approaches he developed to analyze specific questions and interrogate discrete questions are now torn from their context and applied indiscriminately. The detailed historical and archival work that underpins Foucault's work is often foregone in an attempt to apply his concepts. Farge, then, both here and in her other independent work, is much closer to Foucault's approach than many Foucauldians.

The Police and the City

At the time of the letters analyzed, Paris was "half urban, half rural,"[41] with countryside poorly integrated into the expanding urban fabric. As Farge notes: "Paris in the eighteenth century was a complex city: the use of its space by its inhabitants, everyday behaviors and urban practices are themes that researchers are trying to identify and model."[42]

This comes through in much of Farge's subsequent work, but also in collaborative research projects that developed out of the CERFI work Foucault had been involved with in the early to mid-1970s. Two reports were published by CORDA (Comité de la Recherche et du Développement en Architecture). One was led by Bruno Fortier: *La politique de l'espace parisien (à la fin de l'Ancien Régime)* (The politics of Parisian space at the end of the Ancien Régime); the other by Foucault: *Politiques de l'habitat (1800–1850)* (Politics of habitat (1800–1850)).[43] Here "habitat" is to be understood as that work not just in what we would now call public space, but also as the general context of living space and especially the intersection of these spaces, in places such as pavements, roads, and crossroads. As such, the work provides some important insights into how police mechanisms expand from the local and small scale to wider and larger social networks, and so extend to the organization of the city.

One of the striking conceptual distinctions in the Farge and Foucault book comes from contrasting understandings of space and time. As they note in the section on parents and children, the unruly poor body could be disruptive of both types of dominant ordering:

> It would be interesting to compare this notion of "disturbance" *[dé-rangement]* with that of "dissipation" *[dissipation]*, which would be so frequently employed in the nineteenth century in the moralizing of the poor. Dissipation fundamentally came down to temporal behavior; a "dissipated" laborer did not know how to prepare for the future, he spent his paycheck as soon as he got it, he did not practice thrift, anticipate the possibility of illness or the threat of unemployment, did not make provisions for old age or the education of his children. To counter dissipation, the poor must be taught the continuity of time, the accumulation of small profits, in short, the economy of life. Disturbance, for its part, involved primarily spatial behaviors. It would seem that these forms of behavior alarmed parents beyond anything else. The future was only invoked in the form of troublesome consequences down the line: crime, death, ruin, and sometimes, albeit rarely, the difficulties that the bad behavior of certain children would cause for the establishment of their siblings. In contrast, the pressure point for the conflict between children and parents was located at the boundaries of the family space.[44]

While today it might be tempting to see "boundaries" here in terms simply of behavior, the point is surely a more concretely geographic one. What goes on in the family home, and what outside, is a recurrent issue for parents, but at a time when the private/public line was blurred, with the permeation of the spaces, this was even more the case. This spatial question, as Farge and Foucault underline, is "not easy to delimit precisely," because it stretched from the home to the neighborhood [voisinage], and to a wider reputational space where behavior might be reported back. Farge and Foucault suggest it is notable that it is often the most proximate who sign requests.[45] For this reason, among others, it makes sense that they concentrate on the family relations exposed by the *lettres de cachet,* though neighborhood relations run as a constant theme throughout. With young people, the spaces they inhabit might be wider still, with some of the letters written owing to behavior nearby, but others apply to their short-term absence such as not returning home for the night, or more continual roaming. Farge and Foucault observe:

> The boy's presence in the home was excessive, but as soon as he left he entered a domain full of risks where the worst could happen and from which the family sought to retrieve him, so that they might reestablish their control over him. As for a girl, although she may have left home and settled elsewhere, either with a married man or in semi-prostitution, she caused trouble for the family through her bad reputation, gossip, and scandal. These were neither fully internal conflicts (as would be opposing one's parents in the matter of marriage, refusing to work, or disputes of personal interest), nor clean breaks (which would perhaps have been more acceptable if they were definitive). These were comings and goings, the back-and-forth of a pendulum, drawing away and then coming back through disappearances and returns, false exits and noisy reentrances.[46]

In the wider social spaces, another key factor is the "police," not to be confused with the current organization of that name, but a much wider public-policy apparatus, the emergence of what we might now call a political administration, or that Foucault elsewhere describes as a "program of government rationality."[47] In this work, they describe its tasks as including "overseeing the provisioning of Paris to regulating the height of signs, from punishing blasphemy to clearing the streets of prostitutes, from banning assemblies to dissecting corpses."[48] While the police is a significant theme in Foucault's work, from *History of Madness* through *Birth of the Clinic* to his 1970s Rio lectures on social medicine, it is also a major focus of Farge's work.[49] Indeed, Colette Pétonnet describes the focus of Farge's early-eighteenth-century work as looking at how "the roads, bridges, and fields of Paris were a perpetual theater of the overflowing of life that the police tried to control."[50] The police are trying to make sense of, to control, and to improve the spaces of the city. Political administration here is a spatial administration, an organization of the city into discrete areas, zones, and individual roads in which the life of the city and the dreams of the bureaucrats are in constant tension. We might think of the famous plague town that introduces the chapter on "Panopticism" in Foucault's *Discipline and Punish,* but the administration of spaces of the city goes far beyond such extraordinary measures. A key concern, just as it is in Foucault's "governmentality" lectures and his work on public health and habitat, is the question of circulation—the flow of goods, capital, people, waste, and resources. This is a key theme in Foucault's 1972–73 lecture course *The Punitive Society,* but is also important in his analysis of the *Nu-pieds* revolt and its repression in seventeenth-century Normandy in the 1971–72 course *Théories et institutions pénales.*[51]

This is a Paris, remember, before Baron Haussmann's massive renovation in the nineteenth century, a Paris of crowded medieval streets, markets, and houses, with filthy sewers and regular cholera epidemics. As one nineteenth-century reformer described it, "Paris is an immense workshop of putrefaction, where poverty, pestilence, and illness work in concert, where neither air nor sunlight penetrate. Paris is an awful place where plants shrivel and die, where, of seven small children, six die a year."[52] Like this eighteenth-century reality, Farge and Foucault continually challenge any straightforward distinction between private and public space, with a blurring that is more akin to a frontier than a boundary, as they move between the home, the workplace, the street, the neighborhood, and the wider city.[53] As a result of family and social situation, what we might now think of as distinct modes of life were intertwined. For example:

> Precarious living conditions *[conditions d'habitat],* socioeconomic instability, lodgings, workshops, and shops were open to the outside, permeable to everything that seeped in from the porous outdoors,

238 *Stuart Elden*

to the point of symbiosis, creating particular spaces opaque to order, but interwoven out of webs of complicity, solidarity, and conflict whose violence was almost equal to their forces of cohesion. No one could claim to be absent from the lives of others, and the experience of this lack of privacy *[promiscuité subie]* provoked behaviors both of integration and of rejection.[54]

The question of "habitat" is crucial here, a collective living that continually overflows any barriers that might be drawn; while at the same time the same happens in reverse, and the outside intrudes into the domestic. The notion of *"promiscuité"* is telling—an abundance of relations, endured or suffered by those who have no choice. So much of the book is to do with matter out of place, disorderly bodies in the family home, outside of it, at the threshold of the city or beyond. Concerns with vagabonds and the itinerant, along with those who do not subordinate themselves to a routine, a rhythm of times and spaces, run through the police concerns, and the letters collected here. Farge and Foucault write:

These are many forms of excess that share as a common trait that they were committed outside of the traditional geography of the spaces of labor and family. In lives already marked by itinerancy *[l'errance],* the search for work and lodging, rhythmed by instability and long journeys on foot across the capital both day and night, bad conduct would be additional roaming on top of what was already required, adding disreputable absences to the habitual ones, further reinforcing these scattered lives, by bursting in a spectacular manner the already tangled map of their habitual trajectories. Bad conduct was necessarily linked to different uses of spaces, shattering their precarious coherencies.[55]

Ultimately, the sanction could be to imprison or detain someone in a hospital or asylum. There is, however, relatively little said about the prison in this collection, perhaps because Foucault had so extensively discussed it elsewhere. He and Farge note:

Most of these cases are what we might call "conflicts at the threshold." At the threshold of adulthood, at the threshold of the house; at the threshold between dependence and independence. Naturally, these provoked two contradictory reactions, definitive expulsion— let us be rid of this child and never hear her spoken of again; or complete reabsorption—we are willing for her to come back to us, but on the condition that she has repented and will behave herself. Of the two, the second solution was often seen as preferable.[56]

Yet imprisonment did happen, as did requests for exile, sending to the Islands—penal colonies, mainly in the West Indies—a place from which few returned and almost no correspondence was possible:

> Being sent to the Islands had a profound resonance in the imagination of the lower orders. Invisible but real, the Islands were a "non-place" where the mark of the wrong done disappeared in silence. It was on the horizon of this whole system of punishment as the ultimate threat, the one that would be invoked when patience had run out, after so many promises of improvement had showed themselves to be empty. Not the least of the paradoxes was that the establishment of moral discipline and the improvement of these exiles, many of whom were never to return, was one of the concerns most frequently invoked—if not one of the most important—by the governor.[57]

Not all exile was so far afield. One example is the case of Gilbert Dolat, who was held at the Bicêtre hospital in the southern suburbs of Paris, and later exiled and told to remain thirty leagues from the city. His family gave him clothes and money so he could go to Orléans, but he sold his belongings, spent the money, and remained in the capital. He was later rearrested and returned to the hospital.[58] The political problem of vagrancy, vagabondage, and itinerancy is central to the historical texts Foucault interrogates in *The Punitive Society,* and *Discipline and Punish* perhaps does not fully reflect the work done in its preparation. Foucault spends some time in *The Punitive Society* examining the Physiocrat Guillaume Le Trosne's 1764 text *Mémoire sur les vagabonds et sur les mendiants.* This text is only briefly mentioned in the subsequent book.[59] Foucault suggests that for Le Trosne, vagabondage is not merely begging, but a matrix or network of crime and delinquency, disruptive to working rhythms and spaces, because bodies may not be fixed in a particular place or available at the right time to provide labor for production. Le Trosne discusses different ways that mobile, undisciplined bodies might be controlled, fixed in a location and forced to conform to a more ordered labor chronology.

As Farge explores in her wider work, imprisonment might fix an

240 *Stuart Elden*

individual in a location in a way that the person's life generally did not allow: "Pickpockets, the common soldiery, beggars, ladies of fortune, accomplished thieves, ringleaders and poor devils, they were all there."[60] Farge and Foucault's independent work here is mutually reinforcing, even though Farge's book *Fragile Lives* was published after Foucault's death, and there is no record that she attended his 1972–73 lecture course. Farge's example here is of the register kept by Inspector Poussot, of arrests in the Les Halles area of Paris between 1738 and 1754.[61] She highlights the way that the register is paradoxical—individual lives are fixed for a brief moment, but also for historical eternity, in this written record, even though it is clear that these are people in a state of "incessant movement." After the arrest, they might escape prison, "be set free or transferred, recaptured or eternally at large, 'roaming the countryside,' according to the expression of the period."[62] We might think of the lives in the *lettres de cachet* in a similar way. We likely know nothing of the individuals who wrote, or who are named in, these letters before or after, but this fleeting moment of their existence is inscribed on a page, filed away, waiting for a reader in the future: first, Farge and Foucault in the archive; then their contemporary French readers; now those of us who pick up the translation.

The spatial concerns, of the police as a political and spatial organization, and the lives of those who petition or who are directed by letters, range from the body to the home to the street, the neighborhood and the wider city. There is little insight in these letters, or their analysis, into the larger-scale territorial organization of France, which was undergoing its own transformations at this time. Farge and Foucault move the emphasis from seeing the letters as a shift from sovereignty to a different kind of power, and instead focus on the microphysics of familial relations. In a similar way, their spatial focus is on the smaller scale, the more everyday geographies of the city, rather than wider territorial organization. Yet we could recall Foucault's claim in the "Space, Knowledge and Power" interview that one of the objects of the science of police was to scale up the organization of the city to the wider scale of the territory as a whole, developed on "the premise that a state is like a large city; the capital is like its main square; the roads are like its streets . . . the police become the very *type* of rationality for the government of the whole territory."[63] As I have argued elsewhere, Foucault can be historically misleading in his understanding of territory, but the insights of his work have nonetheless proved enormously valuable for me as I have pursued a history of the concept and practice.[64] The key has been that the same kinds of technological and calculative rationalities that he sees as crucial to the emergence of the concept and practice of population are, at the same time, transformative of territory.

One thing that comes through clearly from Farge's work, both generally and in this collaborative work with Foucault, is the individual and collective lives of people in Paris. That is a common focus of her labors, removing the accumulated grime of history, the dust of the archive, in order to reveal the biographies beneath. Foucault did not always work that way. *Discipline and Punish,* for example, after the execution of the regicide Damiens in its opening pages, rarely mentions individual criminals or victims of crime. Yet some of Foucault's other writing does focus on individual lives—the cases he examines in *The Abnormals* lectures of 1975, for example, developing themes explored in his early Collège de France seminars, which also provided him with the case of Pierre Rivière; his later work on the story of the hermaphrodite Herculine Barbin; and the planned project on "the lives of infamous men," which is the direct antecedent of the collection with Farge.[65] Foucault said, at various points, that he intended to publish further dossiers of cases from the archives. One mentioned in several places is a dossier of further accounts of hermaphrodites, some of which is preserved at the Bibliothèque Nationale de France. The archivist has become the archived.[66] Unfortunately, the materials there relating to the Farge and Foucault book are not yet available.[67]

The letters, thus, in Farge and Foucault's words, provide us with an insight into a "strange theater in which violence, misery, and tribulation were expressed through the ceremonial obligations owed to authority."[68] Foucault's interest in the *lettres de cachet* dates back to the late 1950s and early 1960s, and they are briefly discussed in *History of Madness* and from time to time in his lectures,[69] but it was to be decades before he finally published on them. Farge recalls that Foucault originally had thought of just publishing the letters, without commentary, and it was her suggestion that they needed explanation that led to their working together.[70] While it is, of course, possible to see this book as a continuation of Foucault's interest in the microphysics of power, his project on the "lives of infamous men," and his own

242 Stuart Elden

analysis of spaces, Farge's role in the work is arguably the more significant. At the time the book appeared, Foucault's own focus, in both his lectures and planned publications, was on pagan and Christian antiquity. He anticipated returning to more modern or contemporary concerns following the completion of that work, but, of course, did not live to undertake this.[71] The book has closer parallels to Farge's own writings, in that it directly related to the historical period she has focused on, and is closer to her model of historical work and documentary presentation.[72] It is not only related to her 1970s publications *Délinquance et criminalité* and *Vivre dans la rue à Paris au XVIIIe siècle*, but also she has continued to explore related issues in her work ever since.[73] It is to be hoped that this long-overdue translation and attention leads more Anglophone readers to her own remarkable work.

NOTES

1. Arlette Farge and Michel Foucault, *Le Désordre des familles: Lettres de cachet des Archives de la Bastille au XVIIIe siècle* (Paris: Julliard/Gallimard, Collection Archives, 1982); reprinted in Folio Histoire (Paris: Gallimard, 2014), 7. Page references are to Arlette Farge and Michel Foucault, *Disorderly Families: Infamous Letters from the Bastille Archives,* ed. Nancy Luxon, trans. Thomas Scott-Railton (Minneapolis: University of Minnesota Press, 2017), 19. All quotes to the original French are to the second Folio edition.

2. For her account of working with Foucault, see Arlette Farge, "Travailler avec Michel Foucault," *Le Débat* 41 (1986): 164-67; Keith Gandal and Paul Simmons, "La vie fragile: An Interview with Arlette Farge," *History of the Present* 2 (1986): 23-24; Laurent Vidal, "Arlette Farge, le parcours d'une historienne," *Genèses,* 48 (2002-3): 115–35; and Arlette Farge, "Souvenir d'un dérangement," *Le Magazine littéraire* 435 (2004): 52–54. Her most extensive discussion of his work can be found in *Des lieux pour l'histoire* (Paris: Éditions du Seuil, 1997). For a discussion of their work together, see David Macey, *The Lives of Michel Foucault* (London: Hutchinson, 1993), 452–56; and Stuart Elden, *Foucault's Last Decade* (Cambridge: Polity, 2016), 192–94.

3. Michel Foucault, *Surveiller et punir: Naissance de la prison* (Paris: Gallimard Tel, 1975); translated by Alan Sheridan as *Discipline and Punish: The Birth of the Prison* (London: Penguin, 1976).

4. Foucault, *Surveiller et punir,* 38; *Discipline and Punish,* 30.

5. See, among other works, François Fourquet and Lion Murard, *Les équipements du pouvoir: Villes, territoires et équipements collectifs* (Paris: Union Générale d'Éditions, 1976 [1973]); *Généalogie des équipements de normalisation: Les équipements sanitaires,* ed. Michel Foucault (Fontenay-sous-Bois: CERFI, 1976); *Politiques de l'habitat (1800–1850),* ed. Michel Foucault (Paris: CORDA, 1977). The wider social issues are also explored in Foucault's lecture courses, notably, *Sécurité, territoire, population: Cours au Collège de France (1977–1978),* ed. Michel Senellart (Paris: Éditions du Seuil/Gallimard, 2004); translated by Graham Burchell as *Security, Territory, Population: Lectures at the Collège de*

France 1977–1978 (London: Palgrave Macmillan, 2008). For a detailed discussion of all this work, drawing on published materials and archival documents, see Stuart Elden, *Foucault's Last Decade,* chapter 4; and Stuart Elden, *Foucault: The Birth of Power* (Cambridge: Polity, 2017), chapter 6.

6. Arlette Farge, *Vivre dans la rue à Paris au XVIIIe siècle* (Paris: Julliard/Gallimard, 1979). See 10 for her debt to Foucault.

7. Arlette Farge, *Délinquance et criminalité: Le vol d'aliments à Paris au XVIIIe siècle* (Paris: Plon, 1974), cited in Foucault, *Surveiller et punir,* 91n4, 92n3; *Discipline and Punish,* 311n2, 77.

8. "Table ronde du 20 mai 1978," in Michelle Perrot, ed., *L'Impossible prison: Recherches sur le système pénitentiare au XIXe siècle: Débat avec Michel Foucault* (Paris: Éditions du Seuil, 1980), 40–63; reprinted in Michel Foucault, *Dits et Écrits: 1954–1988,* vol. 4, ed. Daniel Defert and François Ewald (Paris: Gallimard, 1994), 20–34; translated by Colin Gordon in Graham Burchell, Colin Gordon, and Peter Miller, eds., *The Foucault Effect: Studies in Governmentality* (Chicago: University of Chicago Press, 1991), 73–86.

9. Arlette Farge and André Zysberg, "Les théâtres de la violence à Paris au XVIIIe siècle," *Annales: Économies, sociétés, civilisations* 34.5 (1979): 984–1015, 1012.

10. Arlette Farge, "Familles: L'honneur et le secret," in Philippe Ariès et Georges Duby, eds., *Histoire de la vie privée,* vol. 3: *De la Renaissance aux Lumières* (Paris: Éditions du Seuil, 1986), 581–617.

11. Michel Foucault, *La Société punitive: Cours au Collège de France (1972–1973),* ed. Bernard E. Harcourt (Paris: Gallimard/Seuil, 2013), 130; translated by Graham Burchell as *The Punitive Society: Lectures at the Collège de France 1972–73* (London: Palgrave Macmillan, 2015), 127.

12. Foucault, *La Société punitive,* 133–34; *The Punitive Society,* 131; translation slightly modified.

13. Michel Foucault, "Vérité et formes juridiques," in *Dits et Écrits, vol.* 2, 567; "Truth and Juridical Forms," in *Power: Essential Works of Foucault, 1954–1984,* vol. 3 (New York: New Press, 2000), 39, translation modified. "Shifter" is in English in the French. The medieval ordeal is examined in detail in Michel Foucault, *Théories et institutions pénales: Cours au Collège de France (1971–1972),* ed. Bernard E. Harcourt (Paris: Gallimard/Seuil, 2015). For a fuller discussion, see Elden, *Foucault: The Birth of Power,* chapter 2.

14. Foucault, *La Société punitive,* 131; *The Punitive Society,* 128.

15. Foucault, "Vérité et formes juridiques," 601; "Truth and Juridical Forms," 66; translation slightly modified.

16. Foucault, *La Société punitive,* 134n* and 134; *The Punitive Society,* 131n† and 131). The first phrase comes from the manuscript.

17. Frantz Funck-Brentano, *Les Lettres de cachet* (Paris: Librairie Hachette, 1926), 249.

18. Farge and Foucault, *Le Désordre des familles,* 8; *Disorderly Families,* 20. I have preferred "the rage of the sovereign" to "royal anger."

19. Farge and Foucault, *Le Désordre des familles,* 8; *Disorderly Families,* 20.

20. For a discussion of these planned books, of which the main traces can be found in lectures, see Elden, *Foucault's Last Decade,* especially 62–71.

21. Farge and Foucault, *Le Désordre des familles,* 416; *Disorderly Families,* 253.

22. Farge and Foucault, *Le Désordre des familles,* 415; *Disorderly Families,* 252.

244 Stuart Elden

23. Farge and Foucault, *Le Désordre des familles,* 8; *Disorderly Families,* 19, translation modified.

24. Farge and Foucault, *Le Désordre des familles,* 12; *Disorderly Families,* 21.

25. Arlette Farge, *Le Goût d'archive* (Paris: Éditions du Seuil, 1997), 41; translated by Thomas Scott-Railton as *The Allure of the Archive* (New Haven: Yale University Press, 2013), 30; translation modified. Similar points are made elsewhere in her work.

26. References on power and space in Foucault's work would be too numerous to make. For a wider discussion, see Stuart Elden, *Mapping the Present: Heidegger, Foucault and the Project of a Spatial History* (London: Continuum, 2001), especially chapters 4 and 5; and the essays and references in Jeremy W. Crampton and Stuart Elden, eds., *Space, Knowledge and Power: Foucault and Geography* (Aldershot: Ashgate, 2007).

27. Michel Foucault, "Space, Knowledge and Power," in *The Foucault Reader,* ed. Paul Rabinow (New York: Pantheon, 1991), 252.

28. Farge and Foucault, *Le Désordre des familles,* 33; *Disorderly Families,* 34–35.

29. Arlette Farge, *La Vie fragile: Violence, pouvoirs et solidarités à Paris au XVIIIe siècle* (Paris: Hachette, 1986), 56; translated by Carol Shelton as *Fragile Lives: Violence, Power and Solidarity in Eighteenth-Century Paris* (Cambridge: Polity, 1993), 43.

30. Farge and Foucault, *Le Désordre des familles,* 31–32; *Disorderly Families,* 34; translation modified.

31. Farge and Foucault, *Le Désordre des familles,* 35; *Disorderly Families,* 35; translation modified.

32. Farge and Foucault, *Le Désordre des familles,* 196; *Disorderly Families,* 128.

33. Farge, *La Vie fragile,* 17; *Fragile Lives,* 9; translation modified.

34. Farge, "Familles," 587.

35. Arlette Farge, "L'espace parisien au XVIIIe siècle d'après les ordonnances de police," *Ethnologie française* 12.2 (1982): 119–26, 121.

36. Farge, *La Vie fragile,* 28; *Fragile Lives,* 19–20.

37. See Farge and Zysberg, "Les théâtres de la violence à Paris au XVIIIe siècle"

38. Ibid., 1006.

39. Farge and Foucault, *Le Désordre des familles,* 19; *Disorderly Families,* 25.

40. Farge, *Vivre dans la rue à Paris au XVIIIe siècle,* 12.

41. Farge, "L'espace parisien au XVIIIe siècle d'après les ordonnances de police," 124.

42. Ibid., 119.

43. Bruno Fortier, ed., *La Politique de l'espace parisien (à la fin de l'Ancien Régime)* (Paris: CORDA, 1975); Michel Foucault, ed., *Politiques de l'habitat (1800–1850)* (Paris: CORDA, 1977).

44. Farge and Foucault, *Le Désordre des familles,* 193–94; *Disorderly Families,* 126–27.

45. Farge and Foucault, *Le Désordre des familles,* 194; *Disorderly Families,* 127.

46. Farge and Foucault, *Le Désordre des familles,* 198; *Disorderly Families,* 129–30.

47. Foucault, "Space, Knowledge and Power," 241.

48. Farge and Foucault, *Le Désordre des familles,* 412; *Disorderly Families,* 251.

49. See, for example, Farge, "L'espace parisien au XVIIIe siècle d'après les ordonnances de police."

50. Colette Pétonnet, "L'Espace et les lieux de la ville," *Ethnologie française* 12.2 (1982): 117.

51. See, in particular, Foucault, *La Société punitive*, 107; *The Punitive Society*, 104–5; and *Théories et institutions pénales*, especially 134–35, 185. For readings of these two courses, see chapters 2 and 3 in Elden, *Foucault: The Birth of Power*.

52. Victor Considérant, *Considérations sociales sur l'architectonique* (Paris: Libraires du Palais-Royal, 1834), 12. For a geographic discussion of Haussmann's urban reforms, see David Harvey, *Paris: Capital of Modernity* (New York: Routledge, 2003), especially chapter 4.

53. See Nancy Luxon, "Editor's Introduction," *Disorderly Families*, 13.

54. Farge and Foucault, *Le Désordre des familles*, 424; *Disorderly Families*, 258.

55. Farge and Foucault, *Le Désordre des familles*, 33–34; *Disorderly Families*, 35.

56. Farge and Foucault, *Le Désordre des familles*, 199; *Disorderly Families*, 130.

57. Farge and Foucault, *Le Désordre des familles*, 200–201; *Disorderly Families*, 131.

58. Farge and Foucault, *Le Désordre des familles*, 67–71; *Disorderly Families*, 56–58. He is called Filbert or Philibert in some letters.

59. Foucault, *La Société punitive*, 47–53; *The Punitive Society*, 45–52; *Surveiller et punir*, 92, 104–5; *Discipline and Punish*, 76–77, 88–89.

60. Farge, *La Vie fragile*, 164; *Fragile Lives*, 142.

61. Farge, *La Vie fragile*, 161; *Fragile Lives*, 138.

62. Farge, *La Vie fragile*, 164; *Fragile Lives*, 142; translation modified.

63. Foucault, "Space, Knowledge and Power," 241.

64. I discuss this question in general terms in *The Birth of Territory* (Chicago: University of Chicago Press, 2013); and in relation to Foucault in "Governmentality, Calculation, Territory," *Environment and Planning D: Society and Space* 25.3 (2007): 562–80, and "How Should We Do the History of Territory?" *Territory, Politics, Governance* 1.1 (2013): 5–20.

65. Foucault, "La Vie des hommes infâmes," in *Dits et Écrits*, vol. 3, 237–53; Foucault, "Lives of Infamous Men," in *Archives of Infamy*, 67–84.

66. Foucault's dossier of material on hermaphrodites is discussed in Elden, *Foucault's Last Decade*, 65–66, and is available at the Bibliothèque Nationale de France in Fonds Michel Foucault, NAF28730 (15), Folder 1. See also NAF 28730 (13).

67. The typescript of their book is in NAF 28730 (75), but it is possible more material can be found in as yet inaccessible boxes. The available material is used extensively in Elden, *Foucault: The Birth of Power*. In my work in the archive, I did discover an offprint of Farge's article "Les artisans malades et leur travail," *Annales, Économies Sociétés Civilisations* 32.5 (1977): 993–1006, with the dedication "En cordiale et modeste homage, A. Farge." Foucault had indicated two texts on pauper medicine in the notes to follow up. See NAF 28730 (7), Folder 5, Subfolder 1.

68. Farge and Foucault, *Le Désordre des familles*, 422; *Disorderly Families*, 257.

69. See Michel Foucault, *Histoire de la folie à l'âge classique* (Paris: Gallimard

Collection Tel, 1976 [1961]), especially 142–43, 466–67; *History of Madness,* ed. Jean Khalfa, trans. Jonathan Murphy and Jean Khalfa (London: Routledge, 2006), 125–26, 446–47; as well as the discussion in *La Société punitive,* 129–37; *The Punitive Society,* 126–35; see Michel Foucault, *Les Anormaux: Cours au Collège de France (1974–1975),* ed. Valerio Marchetti and Antonella Salomani (Paris: Éditions du Seuil/Gallimard, 1999), 34–35; translated by Graham Burchell as *Abnormal: Lectures at the Collège de France, 1974–1975* (London: Verso, 2003), 37–38.

70. Farge, "Travailler avec Michel Foucault"; Vidal, "Arlette Farge, le parcours d'une historienne" 117–18.

71. Two examples include, first, his comments in his final Paris lecture course, where he anticipates the end of "this several years long Greco-Latin 'trip'" and then plans to return to some more "contemporary problems." A second example includes the plans at Berkeley to work with students on governmental practices in the early twentieth century. See *Le Courage de la vérité: Le Gouvernement du soi et des autres II, Cours au Collège de France,* ed. Frédéric Gros (Paris: Gallimard/ Seuil, 2009), 3; *The Courage of Truth: The Government of Self and Others II, Lectures at the Collège de France, 1983–1984,* ed. Frédéric Gros, trans. Graham Burchell (London: Palgrave Macmillan, 2011), 2; Keith Gandal and Stephen Kotkin, "Governing Work and Social Life in the USA and the USSR," *History of the Present* 1 (1985): 4–14; Keith Gandal, "New Arts of Government in the Great War and Post-War Period," archived at IMEC as document E.1.29/FCL2.A04-06. For a discussion, see Elden, *Foucault's Last Decade,* 200–201.

72. See, in particular, Arlette Farge, *Le Miroir des femmes: Textes présentés par Arlette Farge* (Paris: Montalba, 1982).

73. As well as works already cited, see especially Arlette Farge, *Dire et mal dire: L'opinion publique au XVIIIᵉ siècle* (Paris: Éditions du Seuil, 1992); translated by Rosemary Morris as *Subversive Words: Public Opinion in Eighteenth-Century France* (Cambridge: Polity Press, 1994); and chapter 3 in *Effusion et tourment, le récit des corps: Histoire du people au XVIIIᵉ siècle* (Paris: Odile Jacob, 2007).

CHAPTER 10

Parisian Homosexuals
Create a Lifestyle, 1700–1750

The Police Archives   (1985)

Michel Rey

*Owing to the paucity of documents and research, little is known
about the practice of sex between men before the eighteenth
century. The documents available, and even the use of the term
"sodomy," seem to suggest that for a long time, sodomy implied
neither a particular lifestyle nor a self-recognized identity. Michel
Rey's essay proceeds by examining the reports dictated by agents
provocateurs paid by a specialized office, and the reports and registers of officers charged with investigating claims to homosexual
acts. These reports shed unusual light on intimate matters, as they
are written by those spies* (mouches) *who insinuated themselves
into others' confidences so as to gain as much information as
possible about their desires and acquaintances. A student of the
historian of sexuality Jean-Louis Flandrin (whose work is cited
by Foucault), Rey died of AIDS before completing an envisioned
book-length project on the subject.* ➤

Because of a lack of documents and studies, the actual practice of
a homosexual lifestyle before the eighteenth century is little known.
Those insights that are available, and even the definition of sodomy
(including homo- as well as heterosexual acts), seem to suggest that for
a long time, sodomy implied neither a particular lifestyle nor inclusion
in a clearly designated minority. Most often, moreover, an attraction

248 *Michel Rey*

to boys did not preclude other tastes. In respect to this matter, however, the police archives of the eighteenth century indicate, at the heart of the Parisian population, a transformation that had perhaps begun earlier at court: male homosexuality becomes a taste that sets one apart from other men, being seen both as a refinement and a source of particular identity.

Police sources consist, for the most part, of reports dictated by agents provocateurs paid by a specialized office, and by officers charged with overseeing those royal gardens open to the public. These reports contain abundant and valuable details about the daily lives of those arrested, because the agents, appropriately called *mouches* (flies), encouraged those who approached them to give as much information as possible about their desires and acquaintances.[1]

The Geography of "la Bonnaventure"

For hours on end, police observers were on the lookout for those cruising for a sex partner. It is actually possible, from these reports, to reconstruct cruising routes in Paris. Most of the sites frequented are mentioned from the beginning of the century, and it is difficult to discern precisely the evolution of popular rendezvous sites just from the fragmentary evidence of police interest in the sites. The boulevards laid out along the lines of the former fortifications that girdled Paris are mentioned with regularity only beginning in the 1730s, but they are cited as early as 1714 in a log recording those booked by the police at the prison hospital at Bicêtre.[2] Were there more homosexuals on those boulevards, or did the police simply send more staff to report them?

The use of meeting places was socially diversified. In principle, the archers allowed into the royal gardens only persons of quality, or at least those who dressed as such. The people arrested in the Tuileries, Luxembourg, or Palais-Royal gardens, or the Champs-Élysées, were thus mostly of the nobility or middle class, but included some master craftsmen, schoolboys, students, and household servants. These same groups frequented the streets, public squares, and river embankments; but there they could lose themselves in the mass of small shopkeepers, workers, and young tradesmen.

Like numerous heterosexual couples, or like prostitutes, homosexuals did not hesitate to engage in sexual relations in any places that were somewhat sheltered from view—and scarcely that at times—

behind ramparts, in thickets or ditches, in alleys. In any case, dwellings offered little more privacy: walls were thin and doors could be opened quickly.[3] Few people had the means or inclination to obtain real privacy. In fact, all busy places (such as the Pont-Neuf or the fair of St. Germain) attracted those in pursuit of *la bonnaventure.*

Those who found public places too exposed had recourse to a tavern:

> Scouring the pathways, when he finds someone alone, he accosts him and asks him to go have a drink. He is always very careful to ask for a private room, anticipating the fulfillment of his infamous passion.

Caution had to be exercised with the proprietor and the waiters: "Since half of Paris was so inclined [homosexual], none of the innkeepers was unaware of the practice, and all were on their guard concerning such activities."[4] However, one who knew his way around could find complicitous owners; so in 1749, when homosexual encounters were multiplying, the police arrested twelve "sellers of wine" for *pédérastie.*

Rendezvous sites were kept under surveillance almost daily, with, so far as surviving archives can substantiate, increased intensity in spring and summer, on Sundays and holidays, and at certain times of day: a certain Renard "did not fail to come to the Luxembourg gardens looking for a pickup *[pour y raccrocher]* from around ten in the morning until noon, and the same in the evening from seven to nine."[5] Most people seemed to circulate between 10 a.m. and 2 p.m., and from 8 to 10 p.m.

All these people had a singular perception of the city, directly related to the satisfaction of homosexual desires; but the majority of the places we have pointed out were equally well known for female prostitution, which the police readily equated with the homosexual solicitation (the term *raccrochage* was used for both cases), even when there was no payment for sex: in short, all types of errant sexuality were pursued alike by the police, who had scorn for men who offered their bodies to other men, or whom they saw as satisfying a law of supply and demand. To complicate the situation further, certain nobles did systematically offer money, thus reproducing in their homosexual lives the master–servant model on which the society was founded.[6] Some of those propositioned had the courage or self-esteem to decline: "He refused to take . . . [the hundred halfpennies *(sols)*] because he was not doing it out of interest, but only for his pleasure."[7]

Cruising: A Brief Discussion of Methods

Making a pickup was a trade *(métier)* whose techniques had to be mastered if one was to escape being considered a novice. In the eyes of certain practitioners, cruising distinguished homosexuals as a group similar to an important social configuration of the period: *la corporation.*

Methods of operation differed depending on sites, time of day, and conditions. During the day, at the Tuileries or the Luxembourg and in public walkways, the pickup was carried out mostly by dialogue: "He asked what time it was"; he walked up "while asking me for a pinch of tobacco."[8] The conversation might continue for some time, touching first on mere pleasantries, then slipping into the topic of pleasures in general, before broaching any more specific pleasurable possibility. On the river embankments, on the streets or walkways at nightfall, or in pissoirs, the approach could be more direct. Certain people called attention to themselves by protracted circulating "in places where the infamous ordinarily hung out." The police were familiar with the codes governing these encounters: "having come up to me, making all the signals to me which these infamous types are accustomed to, in order to speak to me," or "having approached me, staring me in the face several times," or staring "with affectation," or "having pissed . . . in front of me several times—being one of the signals that all these sordid types have at their disposal." One might indicate his interest and attempt to create excitement by showing his penis: "I'm sure you prefer that to a pinch of tobacco." The *mouche* himself sometimes elicited a conversation: "As I was about to let flow, [he] asked me what time it was according to my cock *[vit]* and said that according to his it was high noon."[9] On the quais, one could relieve oneself *[faire ses nécessités]* and "expose oneself from the front and rear." These gestures in themselves were not unusual: only the ostentation that accompanied them identified homosexuals, and they were quickly followed by a question—"Do you have an erection?"—and a rapid reach to find out.

Without exception, each time violence occurred during solicitation or sex, nobles, particularly those in military office, were the aggressors. In 1725, the Count de la Tournelle was arrested in the Tuileries gardens "while he was leaning against a tree with said individual, forcibly coercing him and tearing his breeches in order to fondle him in a shameful manner." In 1724, in the same location, three gentlemen were arrested under similar circumstances. One of them, a brigadier general, "met an individual before whom he showed his penis outside his breeches, saying: "Let me fuck you" [Attends que je te foute]. The three now seized the person encountered around the waist, more or less gently, but without his being allowed to refuse the offer. This sort of force also reappears in the noblemen's parties to which Deschauffours, a pimp [proxénète] and murderer burned in 1726, brought young boys who were given drinks before being molested.[10] Moreover, such sexual force rounds out the endless list of violent acts committed by the old, or military, nobility [la noblesse d'épée] against those whom they considered inferior.[11]

The police were not satisfied merely to observe pickup techniques with a scientific eye; officials claimed to have caused adaptations in them. In 1748, two homosexuals known to him by sight followed a police agent along a quai and "stepped into a recessed area, a sort of gateway, where they showed themselves without speaking, a practice that certain of these infamous types have adopted recently, especially those who have been summoned before the lieutenant general of the police."[12] It was a wise precaution to find out whether one was or was not dealing with a police agent; one exposed oneself in the ordinary way (as though urinating, etc.) without ostentation. Then the *mouche* had to become involved in order to catch his victim "in the act." The only other possibility was to make a report merely on suspicion. Thus, the police, just as much as their quarry, influenced the "disorderly conduct" they were after.

Reactions and Hostility

Police sources provide some idea of opinion among ordinary citizens regarding homosexuals, for they present the reactions of those who had been approached unsuccessfully. In 1736, a man named P. Champ tried to "handle" a bather on the Pont-Neuf: "The young man pushed him away, trying to slap him, and saying, 'You dog, have you washed your hands,' and 'Are your hands clean?'" In 1738, a young man went to urinate behind the palings of the Tuileries. A man (L. Chaumont) joined him, fondling himself in front of him. The young man "began to shout at him, calling him: 'scoundrel.'" In a cabaret in 1748 a man named Tranchant had placed his hands inside the breeches of another. The man would not let him do it; he told people about the attempt, and Tranchant was publicly reproached in the neighborhood.[13] "Dog," "scoundrel"—these mild insults could as easily have been addressed to an unsavory drunkard. The texts show the importance of the neighborhood; with the possible exception of some districts at the center of the city, Paris was still arranged like a series of villages where everyone knew everyone, and where the community oversaw the conduct of each of its members: communication between sexual deviants and their neighbors had not yet been severed. The neighborhood rebuked them as men who had gone too far, who had done something "dirty." They did not incur general hostility, but simply a silent reproach or a physical action such as might have repelled an intruder. In addition, such a deviant was perhaps viewed as not totally devoted to his passion, and therefore not "different," unlike the mason who, in 1723, was turned in to the police by a neighbor. He had a "bad reputation, having always in his company young men of the neighborhood whom he would lure to his home."[14] He had made the mistake of not considering the neighborhood. Not having hidden his activities discreetly enough, he was resented as a menace to public order who continued to seek his partners inside the delineated and watchful community.

It should be noted that in most such instances the police were not summoned. Faced with what it considered unacceptable behavior (and the same held for physical aggression or theft), to enforce good conduct the community used traditional instruments: neighborhood, parish, family, and professional scorn. Thus, in 1723, a man named F. Solle recounted how, in a tavern, he "had been caught by a waiter, who found them with their pants off and told his mistress, who in turn created an outcry."[15] Calling public attention to an act, singling out a black sheep, tarnishing a man's honor, branding him with infamy was apparently sufficient to preserve order in the community.

In 1737, four young men crossing the Pont-Neuf discussed in loud voices their previous evening and their past adventures: "They talked so loudly among themselves about their infamies that other people in the street admonished them for it."[16] Street life, at that period, allowed for such exchanges. Passersby, not content with silent disapproval, willingly intervened in order to preserve respect for dignity and order. The later evolution of refined social decorum, the spread of the notion of private life, and the formation of a milieu reserved exclusively for sodomites all gradually established boundaries between homosexuals and the public's jurisdiction; and in the second half of the century systematic recourse to the district police commissioner appears to have become pervasive.[17]

Manifestations of Sexual Desire and Love

Trying to arouse a potential partner and determine whether he would be suitable, those who cruised among the *mouches* often expressed their desires; but their words present analytical problems as we attempt to discover how the eighteenth century made love. If sexual practices seem finite in number, the fantasies and taboos connected with them may seem infinite. But even now we have very few studies that allow for comparisons: how did people make love in the eighteenth century?

For certain years where files are numerous, it is possible to calculate the number and kind of homosexual propositions. For example:

ACTIVITY	1723	1724
active sodomy	11	24
passive sodomy	0	5
active or passive sodomy	9	20
fellatio	2	8
kissing	2	7

This limited list authorizes several observations. Two major categories stand out: active sodomy and sodomy that is active or passive without preference; by contrast, exclusively passive sodomy appears infrequently. What accounts for this imbalance of preference? If it was particularly degrading to be sodomized, one would seldom have expressed this desire; or else one would have done so while simultaneously expressing interest in sodomizing. The shame of passivity might have been founded on a rigid notion of the male and female sexual roles. Is a man who screws another really "infamous"? Those who declared themselves exclusively active might have thought not. The marked effeminacy of the *assemblées* of homosexuals seems to confirm this, as do remarks made in 1738 by a male servant who wished to leave his master because the latter wanted to sleep with him although he had no money to pay for it. The servant, who fears being regarded as an *infâme,* speaks continually of his master in feminine terms, as "she," and speaks of him as a lewd woman.[18] At this time,

254 *Michel Rey*

those in whose interest it was to be seen as quite distinct from a sodomite depicted him as a man with an effeminate nature. In 1723, a servant out of work and married for three months, conversed as follows with a police agent in the Tuileries: "I asked him if he would allow me to screw him. He answered that he hadn't done that yet, but that he had screwed someone else occasionally, and that usually he only masturbated."[19] Other remarks indicate that though masturbation between men did not seem to present significant moral problems, nor did the fact of sodomizing someone, it was much more difficult to accept being sodomized.

This list of activities leads us to another observation: the infrequent mention of oral practices, which today appear common, even predominant. The kiss is perhaps mentioned only infrequently because it was so commonplace, though this is not at all certain. Kissing is a very old act in the West; however, it is even now not a universal erotic act, not being so in much of Asia, for instance. If we compare male sexuality of the eighteenth century with that of other societies, for example, those of North Africa, we realize that there also sexual relations between men are rather frequent, with a clear distinction being made between active and passive roles, which hinders expressions of tenderness.

If the principal taboos in contemporary Western societies seem to concern anal eroticism (as in *Last Tango in Paris*), this has not always been the case. In his study of Roman sexuality, Paul Veyne indicates that the ultimate abasement for Romans was fellatio; and in a study on homosexuality in court circles in the eighteenth century, Benoît Lapouge is also amazed at the apparent absence of the mouth as an erogenous zone.[20] For the eighteenth century, oral homosexual acts appear to have been seen as depraved or very wanton—in any case, extreme. In 1738, a hustler, S. Fontaine, "says that he did it in all ways, *even that* if I wanted, I could consummate the act in his mouth." In 1748, J. Favé, a baker, was in love with an unresponsive water carrier, "which angered the witness all the more, since he desperately loved the said Vendreville, many times having kissed his genitals and even his anus."[21] In 1735, a hustler discriminated among the locations of homosexual acts: "I perform the act with my mouth, in the same way as with my ass when I see that a man is clean and doesn't smell of women." Similar expressions of disgust for stinking *[puant]* female genitals, which were thought to cause venereal diseases more difficult to cure than those transmitted by men, are numerous: "He said that he hated women so strongly that he thought he saw the Devil whenever he saw them, and that if a married man touched him, he would just as soon have the plague."

In both 1723 and 1737–38, married men constituted one-third of those arrested. They often hid their status while soliciting, however, either from fear of blackmail or of putting off their partner. Married couples did not, perhaps, lead such a self-contained emotional life as today, though marriage assured respectability. Gallimard, a lawyer in the Parlement de Paris, separated from his wife, declared in 1724 "that he had a wife but hardly ever made use of her, that his marriage was a strategem, cover-up, and that he had no taste for women, that he preferred an ass to a cunt."[22] As the research by Jean-Louis Flandrin and Philippe Ariès, among others, shows, marriage and love were not commonly associated at that time.[23] All the passions, including love in various forms, were indulged in outside of the marriage bonds. Gallimard encountered a *mouche* on the Crescent in front of the Bastille and later testified "that he wanted very much to get to know me, and that we would live together, that he would pay for half of the room, that we would live together like two brothers, that we would drink and eat together."

The lifestyle proposed here is very standard: it is that of a companion, almost a brother, with whom one shares bread and daily life. It is an old, typically male arrangement. In 1725, a lackey related to a priest "that he had always encountered much difficulty in finding a friend with a good disposition, with whom he could have established a pleasurable relationship which might last."[24] The image of the couple is twofold here: a pair of friends whose temperaments agree, with all the communication and sharing that this traditionally includes, and a "pleasurable relationship." The expression is ambiguous; it evokes rather more a relationship with a lover. At any rate, the emphasis on *duration, always present in friendship, but associated here with the "liaison de plaisir,"* suggests what we today call "conjugal love"; and we know that until the end of the eighteenth century the relationship between spouses was commonly called "friendship."

A last example (1724)—but they are not very numerous in these reports, which, by their nature, record for the most part relationships of an ephemeral sort—documents the end of a relationship more lasting than a *"liaison de plaisir"*:

> he had lived for six months with Abbé Candor, at that time the parish priest of Faverolles, in the diocese of Soissons . . . he passed

himself off in the area as the man's cousin . . . they had amused themselves in every respect, and . . . he had only left this priest because he was too jealous, and because he loved a man as a lover loves his mistress.[25]

It would be unfortunate to conclude this section without pointing out the single gesture of tenderness that these police documents report. In 1748, a man spoke in the following manner about two lackeys whom he knew: "Duquesnel and Dumaine had been sleeping together for two years. They were unable to fall asleep without having mutually touched each other and without having performed infamous acts. It was even almost always necessary for Duquesnel to have his arm extended along the headboard, under Dumaine's head. Without that Dumaine could not rest."[26]

Congregations of Homosexuals

In 1706, the police officer who regularly inspected the general hospital of Bicêtre noted the presence of inmates who had congregated "in taverns in the St. Antoine district, where they committed the most foul abominations. In these groups Langlois was nicknamed the Grand Master; and Bertauld, the Mother in charge of novices."[27] The same essential characteristics of these meetings reappeared in the middle of the century: they most often took place in a tavern in a populous district, and the participants altered their identity by adopting surnames. These associations show a closing in of the group by imitating the court, a convent, or a secret society, and consequently affirm the necessity of an initiation in order to be admitted.

According to the reports, which are incomplete, this type of gathering appeared to increase beginning in the 1730s. In 1748, one can count no fewer than eight taverns where groups of fifteen to thirty people gathered. The gatherings took place in the evening, with the shutters closed. The participants ate, danced, sang, seduced; they exchanged information, smutty stories, and obscene suggestions; but in several cases it is mentioned that they "did not commit the act on the premises," but on the road home after having paired up. Thus, in 1748, a man who tried to fondle a violin player was reproached by the assembly for his boldness.[28] The group established rules of civility. Other assemblies, more private and more sexual, are at times difficult to distinguish from—in the language of police ambiguity—"houses of disorder full of reprobates" *[des bordels d'infâmes]*, though most often the meeting place had two rooms, one for socializing and one for sexual activities.

In the same year, 1748, several witnesses gave an account of a gathering held in a Parisian suburb, La Courtille, in the Fer à Cheval, a tavern, where a group was called "the locksmith's marriage" because they forcibly seduced initiates to perform infamous acts *[faire des infamies]* for the first time. Again in 1748, another witness described a similar ceremony: "This past summer, he found himself in several gatherings of people from La Manchette, either in La Courtille or at the sign of the *Six Sparrows* in the rue aux Juifs (in the central Marais district). In these assemblies, the conversation is almost always in the same vein. Some members with napkins on their heads imitate women and mince about like them. Any new young man in their midst is called the bride *[mariée]*, and they all try for him. People pair off in order to touch and to perform infamous acts. Sometimes that also takes place after leaving the tavern."[29] In the marriage described here, the initiate *[novice]* is admitted into a family circle; however, he is not joined to one man but to a group who caress him in order to include him in it.

In 1735, J. Baron, a brewer, organized a dinner at his tavern: "The others approached us, embracing us and saying: Hello *Mesdames*. Baron arranged his hair with a woman's headdress that was black, like the hairdo of women at court. He placed pompoms in everyone's hair."[30] The word *Mesdames*, reserved at this time for women of status *[femmes de condition]*, like the allusion to court styles, shows that within this group femininity, refinement, and aristocracy were closely linked to the drama of homosexual intrigue. This intermingling of terms reappears in the use of certain nicknames: *Madame de Nemours, Duchesse Duras, Baronne aux Épingles*.[31]

Here follows the social-class distribution of those arrested, during four years when documents are numerous:

	1723	1737–38	1749
nobility and gentry	8	17	28
craftsmen and merchants	20	63	129
servants	12	59	58
unknown	4	7	19
totals	44	146	234

258 *Michel Rey*

There is a proportional consistency in the distribution: and on the average, 14 percent were people of status; 48 percent were minor craftsmen and merchants; 26 percent were servants. When arrested, many people of uncertain social position declared themselves servants in order to avoid being classified with the lowly poor. However, these figures are only suggestive, as they are not complete.

According to testimony, the craftsmen/merchant group predominated in the assemblies, but it is not surprising that few nobles and important members of the middle class *[grands bourgeois]* were present, as they were moving in other social orbits. More surprising is the near absence of servants and persons of no social status, wretched immigrants from the provinces, beggars, and occasional prostitutes. The organized prostitution networks did not include the assemblies and catered more to the nobility or specific groups like the military. The assembly thus seems to have been a rather coherent social group of small merchants and tradesmen, which fantasized about the freedom of manners and the festivities of the court—as if, in order to fashion a transgressing identity and to become organized, some social demarcation was necessary.

The effeminacy and the politeness associated with these assemblies appear to extend into the streets in the course of the century. Certain members wore rouge and powder, colored ribbons, curtsied in a feminine manner, and greeted one another as "Madame." Thus, in 1737 a *mouche* was asked "whether there were any good-lookers in the Luxembourg gardens." The obvious consciousness of belonging to a group is also attested to by the use of certain expressions: "There's somebody who looks like one. Let's split up and see what this sister is all about. That is an infamous term." When a boy did not seem to respond to advances, "they said to each other: Let's let him go, he doesn't understand Latin." In 1749, a master sculptor attended a gathering where he was asked if he would like to be a freemason. The characteristics of these assemblies caused certain people to shy away: though willing "to perform the act," they would not talk about it, and they rejected effeminacy. In 1748, a painter stated that "he withdrew from these gatherings because they were too scandalous. Several members imitated women and made gestures that showed what they were." He said he often replied to them, saying: "Can't you adopt men's mannerisms rather than women's?" The same year, a hardware merchant, J. B. Thomas, stated that he was angry at having gone to these assemblies at La Courtille "because he didn't enjoy the company at all and because among those present were some who made propositions that were too licentious." In 1749, during a party of seven, where his acquaintances called him their aunt and assigned each other female first names, a secondhand clothing dealer exclaimed: "What! You are men and yet give each other women's names!"[32] These indignant participants seem to have been attracted momentarily by the warmth, relative security, and opportunities for enjoying themselves that these small groups offered; but they were unable to assume a public female role, which seems to have been the characteristic identity defined by these homosexual assemblies. They preferred to retreat to men who were more secretive and those who, from need, occasionally sold themselves in the shadowy anonymity of the usual pickup spots.

Distinctions

During the same years, several educated people (such as a medical student and a priest) distinguished between "those who think along those lines" and "those who think differently" on the basis of tolerated and tolerant attitudes. Seen as a tolerated difference, homosexual desire was no longer merely a forbidden "passion," a sin whose very mention constituted a crime: it was felt to be a mode of thought. In the 1730s, police texts reflect these changes, by replacing the word *"sodomite"* by *"pédéraste."* The first term is biblical and refers to divine prohibition of a sin, whereas the second more neutral term, which dates from the sixteenth century (and is not used here in its etymological sense signifying love of boys), refers to the ancient Greek ethos and designates here a man whose sexual desire is oriented exclusively toward other men. Does the change of wording in the police language indicate a greater acceptance of homosexuals and their subculture; or is the linguistic change insignificant? Similarly, what interpretation, if any, is to be made of the fact that beginning in the 1740s the police reports used another expression, which was to remain in use at least until the French Revolution: *"les gens de la Manchette"* or *"les chevaliers de la Manchette,"* a reference to the aristocracy parallel, say, to the Knights of the Garter in England?

An answer to this question is suggested by the reports of the pederasty patrols *[patrouilles de pédérastie]* that circulated around suspected places during the second half of the century. On October 1,

1781, the inspector "charged with dealing with the pederasts" arrested on the streets "a peculiar individual whom the mob was chasing because of his indecent and characteristic dress *[costume]* . . . If ever an outfit, in every respect, was cause for suspecting an individual of pederasty, said Prainquet had assembled it all and the public judged him by it." Arrested again in the same outfit on October 15 at La Grève and "jeered at and hounded by the people," and arrested a third time on October 20, he was finally locked up in the Petit-Châtelet for "obstinacy in dressing in an indecent manner, which is used only by the most dissolute pederasts." Although only seventeen and merely a cook's helper in the service of an army commissariat officer, he wore a dressing gown or frock coat, a cravat, a knot of hair at the back of his head, and a hat. What was indecent? What made the crowd recognize a pederast? Later, on December 1, the inspector arrested an unemployed nineteen-year-old on the street, "dressed in the most suspicious manner," that is, "dressed in a very long brown coat, with rosettes on his shoes, round hat, knotted hair, wide tie, and short hair around his ears . . . Asked why he was dressed that way . . . [he] answered that his attire was nothing extraordinary, since all people of distinction dressed similarly in the morning."[33] These two young men sported sartorial refinement above their station, whereas for society in general and the police in particular the class hierarchy that delineated an entire social hierarchy had to be clearly visible, and was most obvious in clothing. But that is not sufficient to explain why they were immediately recognizable as homosexual. Two hypotheses, one linked to the other, are possible. First, to people of the lower class, a noble—powdered, pomaded, refined—was both elegant and effeminate; but that bothered no one so long as the mode of attire remained faithful to the specific superior social condition that its wearer represented. If someone lower on the social scale assumed this costume (and it should be asked whether the young age of the two men were not a factor), not only did he betray his social condition, but in addition, his effeminacy, by losing its accepted association with elegance and the upper class, became an indication of the wearer's real effeminacy. The crowd, the police, and the homosexuals themselves all linked aristocratic refinement with effeminacy; and the wish to stand out by imitating the aristocracy must have been very powerful, judging from the perseverance of these young men despite the risks they ran.

During the entire eighteenth century, homosexual men tried to group on the basis of an exclusive and minority sexual desire—a phenomenon not exclusively French. Studies concerning England and Holland during this period arrive at similar conclusions.[34] Parallel with the image of the libertine lord who enjoyed sensual excesses, members of the lower classes created an identity involving a double deception: in gender (and thus in virility) and in social status. The adoption of an effeminate aristocratic mode of refinement was a social sin viewed more and more as the century wore on as an unnatural "passion" or "taste" that immutably characterized certain people. The report of 1765 (the only one in the archives consulted) speaks of the "crime against nature" *[crime anti-physique]*. At the end of the century, Sade's third dialogue of *La Philosophie dans le boudoir* links homosexuals' desires to their physical makeup and to a congenital *caractère* that caused typically feminine traits: "Is it not clear that this is a class of men different from the other, but also created by nature . . . ?" Sade is very close to the forensic pathologists of the nineteenth century who would look for distinguishing stigmata of homosexuality (and all criminal types) on individuals' bodies. He is not very far, in his defense by natural cause, from the idea of a "third sex" and from the psychologists' creation of a category of genetic abnormality, which at the end of the nineteenth century would lead to the mutually exclusive categories of homosexuality and heterosexuality.

Translated by Robert A. Day and Robert Welch

NOTES

1. Paris, Bibliothèque de l'Arsenal, Archives de la Bastille, MSS 10.254 to 10.260.

2. Paris, Bibliothèque Nationale, MS Clairambault 985.

3. See Arlette Farge, *Vivre dans la rue à Paris au XVIIIe siècle* (Paris: Gallimard, 1979), and Daniel Roche, *Le Peuple de Paris* (Paris: Aubier, 1981).

4. MS 10.254, P. Deu, October 31, 1723, and F. Solle, July 15, 1723. MS 10.255, abbé de Boisrenard, February 10, 1724.

5. MS 10.254, T. Ranard, August 23, 1723.

6. See Alan Bray, *Homosexuality in Renaissance England* (London: Gay Men's Press, 1982), chapter 2, "The Social Setting."

7. MS 10.255, S. Guillard, April 26, 1724.

8. MS 10.254, J. Fourty, August 30, 1723, and C. Delamotte, July 11, 1723.

9. MS 10.254, L. Gouffier, May 3, 1723, and marquis de Bressy, April 15, 1723.

10. Paris, Bib. Nat., MS Fond Français 10970.

262 *Michel Rey*

11. See, in particular, Nicole Castan and Yves Castan, *Vivre Ensemble: Ordre et désordre en Languedoc (XVIIe et XVIIIe siècles* (Paris: Gallimard, 1981).

12. MS 10.259, Veglay, June 25, 1748.

13. MS 10.258, P. Champ, May 10, 1736, and L. Chaumont, 1738; MS 10.259, Tranchant, October 1748.

14. MS 10.254, L. Gobert, October 21, 1723.

15. MS 10.254, F. Solle, July 15, 1723.

16. MS 10.258, Brunet, Bourbonnais, Dijon, and Courtois, September 22, 1737.

17. See, in particular, Alexandre Mericskay, "Le Châtelet et la répression de la crimilalité à Paris en 1750," typed thesis, Paris IV—Sorbonne (1984).

18. MS 10.258, Leveillé, May 26, 1738.

19. MS 10.254, J. Berlet, April 10, 1723.

20. Paul Veyne, "La Famille et l'amour sous le Haut-Empire Romain," *Annales E.S.C.* 1 (1978): 35–63, and "L'Homosexualité à Rome," *L'Histoire* 30 (1981): 76–78; and Benoît Lapouge, "Les comportements sexuels déviants à Paris au XVIIe siècle," Mémoire de Maîtrise, typed, Paris-Sorbonne.

21. MS 10.258, S. Fontaine, 1738; MS 10.259, J. Favé, November 1748.

22. MS 10.257, P. Lemoine, October 26, 1735; MS 10.256, C. Galard, July 22, 1725; MS 10.255, F. Gallimard, October 3, 1724.

23. Jean-Louis Flandrin, *Familles, parenté, maison, sexualité dans l'ancienne société* (Paris: Hachette, 1976, and Éditions du Seuil, 1984), and "Amour et mariage an XVIIIe siècle," in *Le Sexe et l'Occident: Évolution des attitudes et des comportements* (Paris: Éditions du Seuil, 1981), 83–96; Philippe Ariès, "L'amour dans le mariage," in *Sexualités occidentales,* Communications, no. 35 (Paris: Éditions du Seuil, 1982), 116–22.

24. MS 10.256, J. Damien, January 3, 1725.

25. MS 10.255, F. N. Gromat, June 11, 1724.

26. MS 10.259, Charpentier, November 1748.

27. Bib. Nat., "Extraits d'interrogatoires faits par la police de Paris de gens vivants dans le désordre, et de mauvaises mœurs, renfermés au château de Bicêtre": no. 81, S. Langlois.

28. MS 10.259, Caron, January 23, 1748.

29. MS 10.259, Pinson, January 1748.

30. MS 10.257, J. Baron, October 25, 1735.

31. MS 10.258, A. Guy, February 12, 1737; MS 10.258, M. Lalonde, June 7, 1736; MS 10.259, Ferret, May 1748, and Feuillon, April 1749, MS 10.260.

32. MS 10.259, Marandel, February 1748, and J. B. Thomas, March 1748; MS 10.260, J. Boudin, January 1749.

33. Paris, Archives Nationales, Y 13408. J. Prainguet, October 11 and 20, 1781, and L. Dufresnoy, December 1, 1781.

34. Bray, *Homosexuality in Renaissance England*; Randolph Trumbach, "London's Sodomites: Homosexual Behavior and Western Culture in the Eighteenth Century," *Journal of Social History* 11 (1977): 1–33; L. J. Boon, "Those Damned Sodomites: Public Images of Sodomy in the Eighteenth Century Netherlands," in *Among Men, Among Women: Sociological and Historical Recognition of Homosexual Arrangements,* text for the international conference of this title, University of Amsterdam, June 22–26, 1983.

CHAPTER II

Sovereign Address (2012)

Elizabeth Wingrove

Elizabeth Wingrove turns to preoccupations with the staging of political speech from the other side of the Atlantic. She explores letter writing late in Ancien Régime France as a means of political contestation. Using Jacques Rancière's notion of "illegitimate speakers," she retraces the story of an obscure Bastille prisoner, Geneviève Gravelle, whose letters to the king and the French public reveal the simultaneously political, literary, and aesthetic barriers impeding such illegitimate speech and the strategies that attempt to overcome them. Attending to the historical-poetic context in which Gravelle's letters were composed and circulated, Wingrove elaborates, first, a politics of voice that highlights the uncertain and multiply mediated processes on which political speech depends and, second, a politics of reading and writing in which sovereignty is both challenged and impersonated through the epistolary form. Although Gravelle's case is not among the letters included by Farge and Foucault, Wingrove's essay situates the epistolary practices of the lettres de cachet *within a fluid, dynamic set of political forces.* ~

The scene of the dead or silent king allows another scene to appear, this one equally crucial for the status of the discourse of historical study: that of a living person who speaks too much, who speaks incorrectly, out of place, and outside the truth. The seriousness of the speech of historical study is challenged by this blind and blinding speech.

—*Jacques Rancière,* The Names of History

264 *Elizabeth Wingrove*

> My writings are catechisms of call and response; I feel it and feel
> also that I don't know anything more about it.
> —*Geneviève Gravelle, Archives de la Bastille*

An Excess of Words

In March 1748, a fiftyish unmarried woman named Geneviève Gravelle
was confined to the Paris monastery of Madeleine-de-la-Flèche by a
lettre de cachet, a sealed letter signed by the king (and cosigned by a
minister of state) that conveyed orders directly to its addressee.[1] The
royal command was issued at the request of Pâris de Monmartel, financier to the court of Louis XV. Gravelle had played a role in nego-
tiating Monmartel's 1746 marriage to the impoverished noblewoman
Mlle de Bethune, and Gravelle's ongoing demands for recompense for
her matchmaking services had become an embarrassment, if not a li-
ability, to the couple. Perhaps the Monmartels' intention in requesting the *lettre de cachet* was to chasten Gravelle's behavior through a
temporary detention that would serve as a warning against pursuing
future claims. Or perhaps they intended to make her disappear per-
manently, confined in relative comfort to a religious community not so
very different from the convents where she had lived most of her adult
life and where she had originally met and befriended fellow pensioner
Mlle de Bethune. Whatever the case, the Monmartels' intentions were
frustrated: both Gravelle's disciplining and her disappearance proved
difficult.

Almost immediately after being detained, Gravelle began writing
letters decrying the injustice of her situation. Passed by hand and deposited at the post by sympathetic or bribed residents of the monastery, her narratives of aristocratic abuse and the disregard for her
"good right" began circulating in Paris. The monastery officials in
charge of Gravelle's care requested and received an order prohibiting her from all writing. But the missives continued to appear. An
exasperated Monmartel sent police chief Berryer letters of complaint,
which resulted in a second *lettre de cachet* ordering her transfer to
the more closely policed Hôpital des Pénitentes outside the capital in
Angers. That move proved ineffective. Letters and memoirs addressed
to the king, members of the nobility, and presidents of various *parlements* continued to surface over the next two years; a third *lettre de
cachet* was requested and issued, this time ordering her transfer to
the Bastille. Gravelle's confinement in the château reserved for politi-

cal prisoners seems to have brought an end to her epistolary output; records indicate that a fourth *lettre de cachet* ordering her transfer to Vincennes two years later was prompted by overcrowding at the Bastille. Her death at Vincennes in 1760 was reported to Monmartel, whose response has a hint of the self-defensive: "I assure you," he wrote to the new police chief Sartine, "that she was at the least a very bad subject *[un très mauvais sujet]*."[2]

Geneviève Gravelle was, to borrow from Rancière, a living person who spoke too much, who spoke incorrectly, out of place, and outside the truth. The Bastille archives conserve this "excess of words" in a prisoner dossier that contains Monmartel's grievances and requests, increasingly desperate pleas from the religious authorities charged with her care, administrative missives recounting behaviors observed and actions taken, and, of course, Gravelle's own reckless prose: a large pile of rag paper overrun with scrawled and scratched-out words, the "blind and blinding speech" of *un très mauvais sujet* who would not, perhaps could not, shut up. How do we read Gravelle's writings today, if indeed we read them at all? The inattention to "illegitimate speakers" that preoccupies Rancière in *The Names of History* underscores the challenges they pose to the writing of history, where orderly explanations of the past cannot accord world-remaking power to such unruly and difficult-to-document speech. Instead, the historian turns to aggregation (through Marxist categories of social class, for example, or through demographic data painstakingly collected and regressed by Annales-style analysts) to fashion an event now shorn, Rancière insists, of the person and the practice of a meaning-making agent. As a result, history is "sacrifice[d]" to historiography, which in its scientific and managerial aspirations becomes "a division of political science."[3]

While cultural-historical analyses seem at odds with Rancière's (1992) characterization, his central concern is how historians craft explanatory stories—the book's subtitle, *On the Poetics of Knowledge*, evokes the linguistic making *(poeisis)* of meaning—and so how the imperatives of an orderly if not omniscient narration dictate interpretive practices, whatever the objects of interpretation (birthrates, crop yields, diaries) might be. But even if, in pursuing this concern, Rancière flattens actual disciplinary practices (historians have by and large not recognized themselves in his account), his charge remains intriguing for its insistence on the simultaneously methodological, political, and aesthetic stakes in literary interpretation. Only such an approach, he

266 *Elizabeth Wingrove*

argues, enables us to attend satisfactorily to the proper subject of history, namely, "the poor"—those whose social and political powerlessness serves (always imperfectly) to keep them silent;[4] thus, the literarily inattentive collude in the process of denying a "part to those who have no part."[5] In refusing the art of retrieval and re-creation that is "the poetics of knowledge," such tone-deaf analyses ignore the attunement to sensory and sensible registers required to hear "the poor." In other words, audibility, visibility, and touchability—what Rancière calls the "partition of the sensible"—affect who gets to count.[6]

And the sensory challenges faced by properly *literary* analysts are multiple. The "blind and blinding speech" that confounds historiographers, for example, suggests words that lack and impair vision. Certainly, the phrase captures an aspect of the experience of reading Gravelle: the hundreds of pages of her letters weave in and out of legibility and grammaticality, while their materiality—smudged ink, torn pages, new prose written beside, around, and over old prose on the letters she sometimes used as stationery—strains and occasionally bewilders the reader.[7] As striking is how the notion of visually incapacitated and incapacitating speech captures her predicament as a criminal correspondent: she could not see where her words were going and her readers could not see them coming. Both Gravelle's historical situation and my desire to retrieve it illustrate the interdependence of Rancière's methodological, political, and aesthetic critiques: to read and so recount her hinges on a repartitioning of audible and visual orders, in her own time and perhaps in ours.

In what follows, I take Rancière's critiques as provocations to think about how the writings of obscure individuals like Gravelle might matter to political theory. Among these provocations is a reconsideration of the place of literary interpretation in the field. On the one hand, close attention to prose content and form, if not the particular practice of something called "close reading," is regularly reputed to political theorists as a whole. Likewise, our canonical texts are generally recognized as literary creations, even as issues of genre can trouble the general recognition (e.g., in what way is the treatise "literary" when compared to an essay or play?). On the other hand, the field's multiple appropriations of language theory—in the form of discourse ethics and speech-act theory more generally—tend to privilege the epistemological and ontological implications of language systems; rarely dwelling long at the sites of an utterance's production, this work typically presupposes the existence of "voice" that literary analysis renders problematic.[8] In reading letters by and about Gravelle with an eye and an ear turned toward Rancière's poetics of knowledge, I reconfigure by bringing together both interpretive impulses: the one focused on the written page, the other focused on how language articulates human relations and claims to knowledge. From this perspective, a literary approach helpfully turns us away from ahistorical linguistic structures to see, perhaps to hear, a discursive world giving shape to political possibilities. It likewise turns us away from the transhistorical expressive subject to consider instead the simultaneously rhetorical, material, and institutional resources through which "voice" is both crafted and denied.

A second, related provocation I draw from Rancière pertains to writing as a political act, or more pointedly, how authorial practice stakes a claim to political standing. At issue is not only the political relevance of the stuff—texts, informed citizens, public spheres—that writing and reading generate. I mean first to ask how reading and writing give form and force to contestations over rule, membership, and power; in other words, how literary practices comprise a politics. Gravelle's writings to the king were surely inspired by her belief, consistent with absolutist ideology, that any subject could by customary right make supplication for his protection,[9] while her appeals to members of the nobility regularly presume or confect the customary relation of protection that bound liege to lord. But these beliefs assumed material and rhetorical form through letter writing: Gravelle staked her claim to political standing in the porousness of postal circulation, a network of literary transmission that, while enabled and surveilled by the monarchical state, always exceeded its reach.[10]

How, I mean to ask, did the letter "work" as an expressive and communicative form in the rhetorical-political context of eighteenth-century epistolary culture, and how might it have "worked" for illegitimate speakers? The rich literary resources provided by dead, delayed, and purloined letters should caution us against any easy assumption that the letter worked only insofar as it arrived at its destination. On the contrary, in addition to fueling the plots of epistolary novels, the uncertainty of the letter's circulation through space shaped events unfolding in the "real time" of court, countryside, and town. Letters suggest an exemplary case of what Patchen Markell calls "the impropriety of action," a phrase evoking both the improper and the uncontainable dimensions of speech acts.[11] I argue that Gravelle's claims to political standing exploited, even as they remained vulnerable to, the impropriety of the epistolary form: ambiguously private and public, expressive and strategic, material and rhetorical, the letter engendered new opportunities for political contestation on the part of illegitimate speakers. Although not quite in the form of Jürgen Habermas's critical, rational public: Gravelle's untimely and ungrammatical excess of words challenged sovereignty just by existing. She certainly makes sense, I will argue, and there is ample evidence (consider the constant pleas from Monmartel to Berryer) that she could be understood at the time. But her challenge to sovereignty comes as much in her excesses as in the good arguments she marshals against it.

I begin Gravelle's story of illicit epistolarity by exploring the barriers she faced in writing and being read (next section), as well as her varied efforts to overcome those barriers (third section). Sometimes her letters reveal a strategic or self-reflexive awareness of their own rhetorical tactics. But I also examine writing practices that cannot be read through the lens of authorial intention. This is, of course, a vexed issue, whether the text and author in question are canonical or obscure. While it's tempting to suggest that a "part-less" person—a disappeared whose recognition as a prisoner would itself count as success—is as invested in compositional choices as was a Hobbes or a Rousseau, my intention is to steer clear of such debates. Whether one reads her letters as a bid for narrative coherence—a well-ordered account in which each word plays a critical part—or as an assemblage of bits and pieces that reflect what just came into her head, in either case they reveal the rhetorical repertoire available to her.[12]

That repertoire both facilitated and frustrated the claiming of a political "part." I pursue this twofold articulation of voice and voicelessness by situating Gravelle's letter writing in its institutional and literary context (fourth section). "Going postal" in eighteenth-century France, I argue, was a path toward new forms of both sociability and political critique. In this context, Gravelle can be seen as exemplary rather than exceptional: a writer in extremis whose performative speech acts probably remained, in J. L. Austin's terms, "unhappy," but that are nonetheless felicitous for laying bare a politics of voice and thus of claims making as it took shape in the waning years of monarchical rule. Central to that politics is a bid for sovereign address: the capacity to direct one's words to another, and in so doing, to presume or perform power over their meaning and effects. I elaborate these claims in the final section, where I suggest that Ancien Régime sovereignty had a genre—epistolarity—and in adopting, adapting, and subverting those generic practices, speakers illegitimate and otherwise made sovereign claims of their own.

Can You Hear Me Now?

The impediments to Gravelle gaining publicity and redress were multiple: from paper "as dear as gold" to the diligence of the police, the transmission of her speech was sorely tested by its impropriety.[13] Finding accomplices who could convey her letters was less of a problem, at least within the two religious institutions where she was detained. Why these women agreed to serve as Gravelle's relays must remain a matter of speculation, as it was to the *supérieure* of Madeleine-de-la-Flèche, Mother Monsallier, who reported to police chief Berryer that this "creature who respects nothing, who neither fears nor dreads anything," was capable of "making our pensioners' heads spin."[14] The collection of Gravelle's old correspondence (taken into custody when she was detained)[15] provides glimpses into her strategies of persuasion: letters to former clients (she appears to have been a professional go-between, arranging furniture sales and employment connections, in addition to spousal introductions) reveal alternatively litigious and flattering styles. Perhaps she threatened her accomplices; perhaps she promised them payment.[16] Or perhaps her fearless, dreadless attitude was itself a draw.

In any case, persuading potential couriers was only the final challenge. The first was composition, an enactment of authorial power through which Gravelle asserted the right to insert herself into a written dialogue with those who were decidedly not her social or political equals. Indeed, Mother Monsallier expressed confidence shortly after Gravelle's detention that an order from the king prohibiting her from all writing and speaking would bring an end to her disordering discourse—both outside the monastery and inside it, where her outbursts disrupted "even our divine exercises and offices"—because his direct command would "calm her and would perhaps be a certain thing for us to obtain her peace."[17] Yet, as Monsallier's equivocation suggests, the order proved not at all certain. Surely, feelings of desperation and righteousness spurred her on: a "well-born maiden," as she often described herself, should expect the care of the king and the protection of *parlement,* in addition to the public's sympathy and indignation. Seeing her persistent self-assertions as the obvious reaction to suffering injustice, however, fails not only to grapple with how suffering becomes intelligible *as* injustice, but also to understand "voice" as a multiply mediated event whose audibility might be precarious. Cries of pain become articulations of injustice only insofar as one can claim a place in political dialogue.

Gravelle's writings evince an acute awareness of the challenge. Consider her characterization of them as "a catechism of call and response." The phrase comes at the end of two doubled-sided pages filled with alternatively cramped and sprawling sentences, addressed to members of a *parlement* and repeating—sometimes verbatim, sometimes with slight variation—the claims of wrongdoing that appear in most of her letters. Imposing a highly choreographed form on her often-digressive account, Gravelle likens her writings to the iterative redaction of religious doctrine intended to inscribe known answers to known questions in readers' ears (the Greek roots of *catechism* give us "to sound down"). But, for the same reason, its capacity to move new readers in new ways remains suspect. The paradox of improvising with a form whose authority rests in its conventionality was perhaps not lost on her, given the postscriptural placement of her description and qualification ("I feel it and I also feel I don't know anything more").[18] Trapped in the language game she has invoked, Gravelle's voice emerges as a scripted inevitability, as authoritative and nonetheless contentious as the declaration of doctrinal truths.

But are Gravelle's words the call, awaiting the certain response about which she nonetheless remains uncertain? Or are they the certain response, affirming the call that would certainly have come but for the Monmartels' interruptions? Inasmuch as the catechismic call always presupposes its response, the significance of the distinction blurs, leaving in its stead either, as Jean-Louis Chrétien frames the options, the vicious circularity or the productive paradox that "every first utterance is really a response—that originary speech, such as poetic speech, responds and originates only by responding."[19] Whether Gravelle's exercises in self-authorship are best understood as viciously circular or productively paradoxical remains to be seen. While her appeal to the always already anticipated voice of call–response exchange suggests a ready opening for her words, it also conjures perpetual self-address, the letter as an echo chamber from which her words might never escape.

But address—the (successful) directing of words or things to another—depends also on comprehension, which Gravelle knew to be uncertain. "I write by the light of the moon," one letter reads, "with all the tranquillity of a woman who sees fire and robbers in the four corners of her house."[20] Her depiction of the scene of writing infuses some helpful suspense into the letter's otherwise numbing (three double-sided pages) repetition of her ordeal. But the description also contextualizes her repetition: urgency produces excess. She would have written a shorter letter, but she didn't have the time; or, in her own words, "Perhaps you'll have trouble reading these [text indecipherable] details . . . as I've hardly the leisure to finish or think my words; in such a situation, one must write voluminously."[21] Gravelle worried about the excess. "As my writings are in the genre [?] of the prophecies of the prophet Ezekiel, the obscure," she writes to the Grand Chamber of the Paris *parlement* in 1750, "if one has too much difficulty reading and divining them, I supplicate the court to order that I be permitted to write them, to clean them up, and to have them printed; the court will be satisfied; there will be nothing useless in them."[22] Again drawing rhetorical resources if not inspiration from religious speech, Gravelle refigures her blinding words as visionary: maybe not immediately accessible to worldly eyes, yet rich with the promises of divinely inspired insight and writerly efficiency if properly revised and typeset.

Here Gravelle's desire to capitalize on the visual ease and temporal horizon of print isn't signaled as a desire to "go public": couched in terms of making her prose legible and her account perceptible to particular addressees, her request signals conformity to the limited circulation of private letters. Likewise, she framed attempts to publish her story in the *gazettes de Hollande* as a necessary if unfortunate supplement to postal communication. Published in Amsterdam, Leiden, and other Dutch cities, the *gazettes* were minimally censored newssheets targeted largely at a French readership that sometimes included interesting "anecdotes" sent in by readers.[23] One of Gravelle's intended submissions, composed in the journalistic third person, explains that she "found no other means for instructing the king and his *parlement* about her unhappinesses, in order to request justice, than to insert them in this *gazette*."[24] Direct address to the state wasn't possible because the Monmartels, having uncovered the many "paths" her letters took, could always intercept them;[25] for this reason, she was obliged to take a detour onto the (transnational) paths of print circulation.

Apparently, the king and his *parlement*'s "instruction" would be assisted not only by the indirect sounding of Gravelle's journalistic voice, but also by the general noise that her published story would generate. One especially ambitious plan took shape during the fall of 1750 when Gravelle successfully passed large stacks of letters out of the Hôpital at Angers. Included with these narratives was a letter instructing their recipient[26] how to disburse them: to whom they should be forwarded (Gravelle's list included Mother Monsallier, in addition to royals, nobles, and judicial officials), how they should be delivered (she indicated which to send by post and which by messenger), and when they should be delivered (she listed the different post offices to use and the different days on which to mail them).[27] At the same time, she sent copies of her writings to the president of a judicial tribunal in Alençon, M. des Orgeries, with the request that he have thirty copies printed and delivered to St Clare, one of Gravelle's predetention residences, where they would find a distributor. Appearing simultaneously in cafés and bookstores in Paris and in the homes of nobles and state officials in the capital, Versailles, and major provincial cities, her writings would expose the corruption infecting the government. Gravelle didn't doubt the effects of such a barrage: it would, her letter of instruction declares, "by print and by post, strike like a thunder bolt."[28]

Gravelle's effort to captivate readers suggests the notion of a public created, in Michael Warner's words, "only in relation to texts and their circulation."[29] Addressing herself to people who, called forth by the force of words that call them to attention, become a public, she might stake a claim to voice in and through the ready-made role of author. But her sudden "strike" conjures less an authorial entrée into the republic of letters than a blinding appearance from out of the blue. Such disruption of the sensibilities—visual, aural, tactile, punctual—of a reading public calls to mind the distinction between making noise and making sense that Rancière, in his reading of Aristotle, presents as the ground on which political standing is determined.[30] In this instance, the *phonê* of every sentient creature—the sounds that register bodily states—and *logos,* arising from that capacity to craft meaning in language that (Aristotle tells us) only humans possess, are coincident forms.[31] Gravelle would make her absence present by making it felt, through a genre-bending combination of penned and printed words that shock, perhaps awe, as they speak, and that call the state to attention as well.

Such a bid for public address falls prey to but also exploits the different rhetorics, materialities, and technologies through which speech acts are performed. On the one hand, Gravelle's dependence on the epistolary form fits poorly with Warner's model of textually constituted publics: she addresses herself to particular persons (rather than anyone or everyone), in the different voices crafted in her differently destined letters (her "public text" requires serial compilation), and calling readers to attention depends on postal punctuality. Perhaps such a precarious and untimely public is the best an "illegitimate speaker" can hope to summon. On the other hand, her epistolary dependency also reveals a (fraught) means of making her presence felt by disrupting the sensible order of public texts. While print signals an author whose bodily presence precedes and exceeds the typeset page, the body of the eighteenth-century letter writer retained a presumptively intimate connection with the body of the letter: in the contiguity of hand and paper; in the letter as a receptacle for tears or locks of hair; and in the study of handwriting (on the rise at the time) as a sign of person and personality, a way to read character and tell copies from originals.

These corporal ties between writer and word enabled romantic, erotic, and other affective fantasies of copresence (in addition to scientistic fantasies of direct correspondence between words and things). The presumptive connections also conjured visions of exposure, degradation, and theft of the original. In a 1783 tract decrying the unauthorized publication of privately received letters, *avocat-général* of the Grenoble *parlement* and future revolutionary actor Michel de Servan shores up his argument that the letter is its author's inviolable property: "the author's pen is the weakest part of an invalid, where the abscessed humors come to a head: letters received, letters written, diaries, intimate reflections: so many papers where a solitary man, often tired of himself, puts himself, as if making a deposit!"[32] The bodily tropes multiply as Servan, somewhat inconsistently, likens the public's inevitable disappointment in reading such letters to a voyeur spying on a woman as she undresses: "but an author no more abandons his wit than a woman her face; the letter is his reflection, just as the *négligée* is her toilette."[33] In a second (epistolary) tract from 1785 challenging state surveillance of private correspondence, Servan returns to the theme of letter-as-(female)-body:

> Deign to reflect on it, Sirs: the comparison between the prostitution of a young girl and the violation and prostitution of a well-sealed letter is not absurd, and I believe that it adds to the case against you. Because, in the end, to sell a girl is not really to rob her; sometimes it enriches her; but to lift, for money, a citizen's thoughts, after they have been put in a letter, like pinching his snuff box in his pocket, that is properly called theft, a burglary, Sirs. And what a burglary! that of a *cachet,* of a veritable seal, as sacred as it is fragile; a *cachet* more inviolable than the lock on a treasure box.[34]

The cachet-cum-hymen announces a precious inside it both protects and invites one to enter. But who enters and so bares the body of the letter determines its reception: as the possession of stolen goods, a degrading and shameful exposure, or a sanctified, generative exchange.

So, what might it mean for Gravelle to invite an "in principle" unlimited audience entrée to her letters? Such promiscuous circulation of words in and of itself seems inconceivable coming from a "well-born maiden." But there is also the matter of how her writing would "reflect" her person, how a maidenly persona might be maintained in an appeal for justice and political recognition. She clearly lacked the time and self-restraint necessary to master one celebrated feminine pose, the *négligée* style associated with Mme de Sévigné's "bold *négligence*" (carelessness, nonchalance) that many found "preferable to the academicians' precision."[35] Although rarely plagued by too much precision, Gravelle's writing is also too ungrammatical and excessive; and while she periodically composes nonchalance ("your orders are a song to me," she tosses off in a letter to Berryer),[36] she more typically writes in a ferocious tone not found in the letters of Mme de Sévigné (who was, of course, no maiden). In the end, the virtue necessary for Gravelle's violation to be intelligible was at risk of being compromised by any move to spread herself before the public.

"The Idea of My Judge"

The voice of the unworldly innocent can express states of pain, shock, and need, but can it be heard articulating *political* demands? The packet of letters Gravelle sent to the judicial official in Alençon provides an opportunity to pursue the question. Responding to a letter advising him that the king had "expressly prohibited" Gravelle from writing and warning that publication of her "defamatory libels" threatened "the citizens' tranquillity," M. des Orgeries promptly forwarded them to Berryer.[37] The many pages from that packet in her archival dossier include letters addressed to the Paris *parlement* and the court, while the intended recipient(s) of others cannot be determined. The contents of these letters are similar, often identical. She typically begins with references to previous efforts to communicate before launching—often with great flourish—into a recitation of her ordeal. Here's a representative sample:

> Seven different times I addressed myself to the Great Court and likewise to the town . . . I recounted so that my just complaints would make themselves heard. But more cruelly treated than a criminal destined for last rites, I have been closed up in prisons for four years without knowing of what crime I am accused. History has perhaps never heard speak of such a scandal, a well-born maiden, reduced to chains for a little known misfortune: to have lavished Mlle de Bethune currently Mme de Monmartel with tenderness at every turn, to have served her like a veritable mother for years, to have miraculously gotten her married, to have sacrificed my goods and my health and everything in me, to have requested from her what I am due, just as I have said in the memoir included here, not being able to explain myself *vive voix*.[38]

The memoir provides a lengthy recitation of Gravelle's role in arranging the Monmartels' marriage, which on her telling took some doing: the bride's pedigreed but financially destitute family objected to the lowly origins of Monmartel's family and his fortune, while Monmartel himself was reluctant to enter what would be his third marriage. Her account includes a redaction of her initial letter to the Monmartel family extolling Mlle de Bethune's religious devotion and lovely figure ("[it] contained few words, but enough to make them curious"), her detailed negotiations in securing both families' agreement, the reaction of the Duchesse de Luynes at Versailles, "who listened with pleasure to the account I gave her of my efforts in bringing about this alliance and [Monmartel's] repugnance at the process," and the newlyweds' shocking refusal to compensate Gravelle for her labors.

Behind-the-scenes revelations of high-society matrimony were sure to appeal to the public. But in this instance Gravelle had a ready-made audience: the Monmartels' February 1746 wedding was widely discussed at the time (according to a report on Paris gossip submitted by then police chief Marville) because no one could fathom why the fabulously wealthy financier "would make a marriage so void of good sense."[39] Gravelle made her case to a primed, credulous public, detailing the maneuvers that produced the match while exploiting the opportunity to show her adversaries to be far less than noble characters. The self-sacrificing mother and loyal liege who appears in her letters to the *parlements* is supplemented by the knowing insider and skilled negotiator writing for the voyeuristic readership of *libelles* and other ephemeral genres.[40]

Shining a bright light on Mlle de Bethune's precarious journey out of maidenhood might distract readers from attending too closely to Gravelle's particular perils on this front. But letters in the packet written to "Mlle de Bethune, presently Mme de Monmartel" also suggest a readiness to forgo such redirection. In these letters, Gravelle again recounts her victimization at the Monmartels' hands, now couched (mostly) in an accusatory second person that opens a new range of interpellative possibilities:

> Let us enter, Mme, into the details of your ingratitude, of your injustice, from the fatal moment that I saw you for the first time, when your name alone gave you merit, bored to death in a convent without any hope of leaving it, here are the insurmountable obstacles that I overcame.

After a looping narrative that covers events up to her detention, Gravelle squares off with her adversary in the present. The tropes of rascally aristocrats and innocents betrayed give way to claims of justice, as the story of her suffering becomes an argument for what should be done about it. Or rather, her prose joins the gothic aesthetic of an epistolary novel with a juridical sensibility in which judges, torts, oaths, and redress figure prominently. Here Gravelle persistently asserts equality with Mme de Monmartel, both as a religious subject ("you are not acquitted before God of the vows we made to Him for the success of your marriage")[41] and as a subject of the king:

> We have changed places, Mme; you have put me where you would be, were it not for my efforts. Here is enough for me to address

our dear monarch with confidence, the [text indecipherable] of the unhappy, the protector of innocent, the just avenger of crime and injustice. I will not forget to tell him of the duplicity of your soul . . . your injustice must be punished or there will no longer be any justice in France. God still has laws.[42]

Despite Gravelle's invocations of divine justice, the judge to be reckoned on in her letters to Mme de Monmartel is the king. This might be owing to his role as Mme de Monmartel's benefactor: having both provided her a pension prior to her marriage and supplemented her meager dowry, Louis XV would be especially interested in her skullduggery, or so Gravelle inferred. But her letters also (predictably, and with predictable excess) hail him as the pater familias to whom all good subjects can address their just complaints. Impartial yet personal, the king will see things clearly:

> It is crazy, they tell me, to think that it will act against the Pâris family. I respond that it's crazy to believe the Court would refuse its *[sa]* protection to a victim of good heart, an oppressed innocent who comes before him *[lui]*. The caesars, the alexanders have used their armies to conquer all the earth, while the Court, for the glory of upholding the good rights of the widow and the orphan and the unknown in chains. The Court has only justice for its guide. Good right is received there naked and wholly exposed *[dépourvu de tout]*. Without this thought I would be dead ten thousand times since my detention.[43]

Self-exposure before the king requires no *négligée* but, on the contrary, a willingness to be seen through. Gravelle confirms both her zeal for such scrutiny and confidence in her purity ("everything is permitted to purely spiritual creatures")[44] precisely by throwing herself before as many readers as possible. Threats to justice come from what remains unseen, unheard, untouched. Her battle, ultimately, is with those who would make justice unthinkable:

> My adversaries look to keep me from every means of reaching the Court, likewise, to pull the wool over the king's eyes *[lui donner le change]* and to confuse the idea of the judge. If I do not follow my path, it will be easy for them to succeed. They alone confuse *[embrouyer]* the idea of the Court, of the judge, and of the public. I oppose them. I want a good judgment in order to succeed. I reject

> and I will continue to reject all obscurity and all that that can confuse the idea of my judge and so cause perplexity.[45]

The coupling of present and future tenses ("I reject and will continue to reject," or elsewhere, "[They] do not and will not intimidate me") is common throughout her letters, suggesting an implacable determination, but also a vision of what is to be. Hers is a battle for the future, one that depends on keeping clear about "ideas" of justice that enable everyone to lay claim to and play an adversarial part. The Monmartels' weapons—money, obscurity, and the Paris police—all work to promote confusion about what justice is.

But clearing up the confusion required a change in how the concept of justice took worldly form. Because the "idea of my judge" was only that: detained by a *lettre de cachet,* Gravelle was subject to an act of "extraordinary" justice that bypassed altogether the elaborate juridical apparatuses of the Ancien Régime. Thus her "thunderbolt" letters include multiple accounts of how "the idea of the judge" might be brought to bear on her case, including this one to the Grand Chamber:

> I will succeed. No one has rights over me and my goods except my king. The brother would sell the sister, the sister her brother, and moreover the innocent would find himself drowned in the most refined waters of roguery if there were no justice. Never will my enemies succeed in veiling their infamous actions. I supplicate the Court to appoint me a commissioner. I would like [text missing] In case the Court, for its part, for reasons known to it, accepts my request, I supplicate the Court to appoint me whomever it judges appropriate and to note that my contrary party has the key of gold. A commissioner of integrity and disinterest, good judgment, good wit, level-headed.[46]

In other letters, Gravelle offers up possible candidates (a former councilor of state, a lawyer), but more often she emphasizes the requisite disposition: a man of integrity, wisdom, and above all, disinterest, someone who is not party to the case. Her litigious imaginary was no doubt rooted in predetention experiences arranging contracts and what appears to be familiarity with civil court procedure. And perhaps members of *parlement* wouldn't have trouble recognizing the logic, if not the propriety, of her appeal for a neutral arbiter. (The only document in the dossier reflecting a successful "strike" is a letter sent by parliamentary president Joly de Fleury to Berryer asking whether he had any knowledge of "an order from the king, conveyed in December of last year, as a result of which Mlle Geneviève Gravelle was taken to the house of Penitent girls in the town of Angers, where she remains. In that case, please be so kind as to instruct me of the motives that prompted this order.")[47] But the king was another matter. Beneficiary of Monmartel's financial resources in running the state, past benefactor of his wife, and signatory of Gravelle's order of detention, he was surely party to the case. Indeed, how could she communicate "the idea of my judge" to one whose exercise of "extraordinary" power made the idea unthinkable?

Going Postal, *Ancien Régime* Style

That a commoner might write to the king was not entirely unthinkable. Consider the content of eighteenth-century letter-writing manuals, or *secrétaires*. Available in both expensive, leather-bound editions and cheap, mass-produced copies, the *secrétaires* offered instruction and entertainment to letter writers and the merely curious. In addition to general advice on how to compose oneself in the "epistolary style," they also included sample letters, lists of proper titles of address, and advice on the finer points of accepted pagination and sealing techniques, including (from the 1744 *Nouveau Secrétaire*) "only members of religious orders may use bread as a *cachet*, as a sign of their poverty and simplicity" and "All letters to the King must be in *folio*."[48] The king's inclusion in these manuals is undoubtedly a holdover from an earlier period: as Janet Altman has shown, eighteenth-century *secrétaires* were typically reissues of seventeenth-century courtly manuals in which the centerpiece of epistolary training was mastery in "the art of pleasing rulers."[49] And indeed, the eighteenth-century editions of the *Nouveau Secrétaire* emphasize the restricted propriety of addressing the king (as well as the general inadvisability of writing letters to queens and princes of the blood). Still, the monarch's regular appearance in the manuals—as both addressee and addresser (e.g., "only the King signs his letters with his proper name")—reiterated his presence in the network.[50] The *secrétaires* might have presented hierarchies of address reflecting a strict social order, but they also showed how to master, and thus manipulate, epistolary codes.[51]

Likewise, by midcentury the modal letter writer was no longer a noble. Increases in roads, relay stations, and literacy over the course of the century suggest the increasing importance of the mail to French subjects of every class.[52] (Although illiteracy was no obstacle: public writers did a brisk business at their stalls in Paris's Saints-Innocents cemetery.)[53] The establishment of a local delivery service in Paris, the *petite poste,* had been a failure when first introduced in 1653 (nobles had their own messengers, while the common folk amused themselves by filling the newly installed mailboxes with mice);[54] it became an instant hit when reintroduced in 1759. Delivery and pickup occurred four times a day ("the *petite poste* rolls from morning 'til night," Mercier remarks), enabling something akin to conversation ("letters are replacing visits," he continues, "which means one doesn't have to move about for nothing").[55] Firmly institutionalized in the commercial and social lives of French subjects, *la poste* was understood to be part of good *police,* those policies and practices of governance that maintained "the convenience and tranquillity of life."[56]

But the postal system also remained central to the conduct of sovereignty, the initial spur to its establishment in the 1480s by Louis XI when a means for (relatively) swiftly conveying his orders across the newly united kingdom became vital.[57] The royal power and needs underwriting the system continued to frame how it was debated, organized, and funded long after Louis XII opened the service to the public in 1506. Not only was government business conducted through the same network used by a corresponding public, but the standard history of *la poste* at the time underscored the state's prerogative to ensure that nothing "injurious to the King" passed through the system.[58] Created by his need and open to the people by his pleasure, the post was both a structure of sovereign rule that gave form to royal commands and an instrument of police that nurtured the citizens' "tranquillity."

Citizens who converse through letters can also plot and conspire there, and the historian's nod to the possibility of letters "injurious to the King" indexed the open secret that was surveillance of the mail.[59] Being read by the state was a real or imagined experience for many letter writers. Some, like Mme de Sévigné, spoke directly to postal snoops in her correspondence, admonishing them to reseal and send her letter on to its proper destination when they were through.[60] Others, like the famously conniving Mme de Tencin, used surveillance to plant false information about state ministers she wanted replaced.[61] And while Surintendant des Postes Grimod-Dufort insisted that there was a line between letters he would open and those of "the public" that he would not, the fact remained that anyone posting a letter ran some risk in addressing the king.[62] The recurrent demands for inviolability of the mail that appear in the 1789 *cahiers de doléances* indicate the strength of citizen feeling on the matter.

But the transmission system worked both ways: at the same time that private correspondents were voicing an expectation if not right to secrecy, police records and private memoirs record a growing concern over letters, typically unsigned, being sent to the king. Anonymous letters caused consternation in general: pamphlets urging support for the 1759 reintroduction of Paris's *petite poste* took pains to deny or deride the risk such letters might pose.[63] But they were especially disturbing when sent to the king, and especially around midcentury when Louis XV's unpopular wars and mistress (Mme de Pompadour) were the talk of Paris and the provinces. His steady retreat from ritual public appearances intensified interest and apprehension. As he refused the "thaumaturgic touch" to his scrofulous subjects and so denied the spectacle of royal contact to his people, worries grew that he could be touched by them: by their complaints, their ridicule, by poison spread across the letter's page.[64] Fear about the epistolary reach of these *mauvais sujets* peaked in 1757 when Damiens touched but failed to kill the king.

Gravelle wrote to Louis XV seven years prior to that event, and we don't know if she was aware of concerns about his epistolary vulnerability. But her address to him is never apologetic or unsure. Sometimes she assumes a supplicating posture that might legitimize her speech; for example, "it is at the feet of your majesty that a miserable in chains dares to speak *[s'adresser]*."[65] She calls upon his parental protection: "I respond to [Berryer's] threats like a child who fears a blow: he cries out to his father with all his force and throws himself into his arms. Sanction, Sire, this gentle name of father."[66] But even as she would throw herself at his feet and into his arms, Gravelle's request for the king's intervention imagines the dire consequences should he refuse:

> God does not prohibit the paths of justice as a means of upholding one's honor and reputation when it is attacked. It is man's only good. He has given this present only to conserve it. I request your majesty with all respect that the creed be carried out *[l'exécution de la foi]*.

282 *Elizabeth Wingrove*

> It orders that all accused will be interrogated on the facts and charges, that the accused be able to respond to their accusers, either to trip them up *[les confondre]* or to be tripped up themselves, that no man will be condemned without first being heard. If your majesty does not uphold his law, if you permit status to annul it, if crime is unpunished, if justice is refused to good right, if vice locks up virtue, will the crown remain safe? Who will uphold the state and religion? What will become of your *parlement,* that well of science, of justice, the protector of the widow and the orphan, the support of good right that puts my own before your eyes?[67]

The return of the prophetic voice, now pitched in ominous tones, suggests that Gravelle is still enunciating a divine vision. But unlike the prophecies of "Ezekiel, the obscure," her predictions of disaster seem clear: because God sanctions the law protecting the accused's right to be heard, the king disobeys it at his own peril. In fact, a "confrontation" between the accused and his accusers was mandated by Title XV of the Ordinance of 1670, which detailed criminal court procedures.[68] But, as already noted, detentions occasioned by a *lettre de cachet* were beyond the purview of law: less an accusation than a direct exercise of sovereign power, the king's private orders (cacheted with his personal seal) required no corroboration and certainly no "confrontation."[69]

Insisting that the king's power remained subject to God's was conventional in absolutist doctrine. But subjecting his authorial power to the dictates of criminal law—denying, in short, the "exceptionality" of *lettres de cachet*—was outside absolutism's truths. Which is not to say that Gravelle's challenge was out of place: on the contrary, outrage over *lettres de cachet* had long circulated. While Arlette Farge and Michel Foucault have shown that noble and bourgeois families made extensive use of them as a supplement to parental power right up to the Revolution, they had by midcentury become a potent symbol of absolutism's excesses.[70] Unlike the *lettre patente,* which was typically addressed to a *parlement,* always sent uncacheted, and once registered was published for general dissemination as the law of the land, the secrecy of the *lettre de cachet* underwrote concerns about its political propriety: Who knew what the letter's contents might be? Who knew whether the information initiating it was accurate? Who even knew whether the king himself had signed it?

Gravelle's letter to the king points to such possibilities. She indicates both that he received false testimony ("[Monmartel] obtained a *lettre de cachet* from your majesty under false representations") and that his power has been usurped ("I cite Berryer as a contrary party [f]or having given me a *lettre de cachet* without instructing your majesty").[71] And she appeals to what she imagines are conventions of the genre: "I supplicate your majesty to lift my *lettre de cachet* under safeguard, like a prisoner of the state, on his word, on the condition that he represents himself; I request SIRE the same grace."[72] But even as she attempts the difficult task of attacking the *lettre de cachet* without directly undermining the sovereignty it enacts, Gravelle persistently pushes the latter to its limits. Biblical allusion makes the case indirectly. Likening Mme de Monmartel to Jezebel and herself to Naboth, she evokes the story of an innocent landowner lured to his death by false letters from the king, Ahab, who received a dooming judgment from the prophet Elijah as a consequence.[73] It was, of course, all Jezebel's doing (she wrote the letters and sent them out under the king's seal), but ignorance on Ahab's part didn't save him.

Gravelle's request to be treated as a prisoner of state is another indirect challenge. *Lettres de cachet* were used to detain, sometimes exile, royal subjects of every rank, and, as noted, were requested by bourgeois as well as noble subjects. Likewise, defenders of *lettres de cachet* underscored the protection their secrecy afforded: circumventing a public process safeguarded individuals and families from "shame, public scandal, and dishonor."[74] So, as an instrument of police, the *lettre de cachet* served a social order rooted in codes of honor regulating what should be (un)seen and (un)said. The prisoner of state, by contrast, was differently addressed. In his (rarely, her) case, at issue was not citizens' honor but state security; hailed as a threat, the prisoner of state was called into the political order. I have not found any instances of release on personal recognizance that might confirm Gravelle's sense of the matter, but there is ample evidence that political prisoners were accorded special privileges, including permission to write the king. Recognition as a state prisoner would lift Gravelle out of the obscurity guaranteed by sovereignty "privately" exercised and put her "just complaints" where they belonged: in direct dialogue with the king.

And that dialogue could not remain epistolary. The extended excerpt from Gravelle's letter to Louis XV quoted earlier turns from ill-omened questions about the stability of the state to the following:

> There is, Sire, an easy way: if your majesty would agree to order
> M and Mme de Monmartel, Marquis and Marquise de Bethune,
> M d'Argenson, and Berryer, all together with myself at the feet on
> your throne, on the day indicated by your majesty, to there state
> and verify the facts that authorized them to lead me over the past
> three years from prison to prison, galley to galley, from strong
> house to strong house. And I, Sire, will prove the truth of what I
> write below.[75]

Whether she was confident of her powers of verbal persuasion or had documents supporting her claims (perhaps an IOU signed by Mlle de Bethune?),[76] Gravelle's demand for habeas corpus would take her, her "contrary parties," and the king out the postal circuit into a confrontation *à vive voix*. Which is not, of course, to say that she rejected epistolary mediation altogether: copies of this letter were being sent to other destinations with what she anticipated, let's recall, would be striking effects.

State Power and/as Epistolary Practice

In refusing the "verdict" of his *lettre de cachet* and demanding a properly litigious process in its stead, Gravelle contested the king's epistolary exercise of sovereign power. His *lettre patente* moved through the circuit but arrived at its final destination—the people—in the material form of universality, that is, print. The *lettre de cachet*'s direct, private, and particular address, by contrast, represented sovereign power arbitrarily wielded. To be sure, among Gravelle's multiple improprieties was the pretended reception of "her" *lettre de cachet*: while she was shown the order when initially detained, it was addressed to Berryer. The misinterpellation—a *mauvais sujet* as a figure of royal address, rather than a woman of no account being erased—prompted her to "respond" with political claims of her own: for recognition of her rights, the application of law, and procedural transparency. In so doing, Gravelle refused to recognize the king as an "exceptional" letter writer.

Perhaps Gravelle was hoping to leverage the rhetorical force of the republic of letters where, constrained only by "the empire of truth and reason," Pierre Bayle writes, "one makes war innocently with anyone."[77] But, as I've suggested, the Ancien Régime of letters was as much about enacting sovereignty as it was about truth or reason. In its absolutist guise, the presumption of control over the meaning and effect of one's words ("I write to inform you that it is my will that . . ." was a conventional opening of *lettres de cachet*) affected political rule. Appropriated by epistolary subjects, such prerogative of address became a means of challenging monarchical sovereignty. At least one artful citizen composed a *lettre de cachet* addressed to the king on behalf of "the public": "We are very unhappy, SIRE, with your conduct toward your *parlement,* which is why we order you to present yourself at the Trappist Abbey, where you will stay until it pleases God to touch you with his grace."[78] More plentiful are private letters written in the first person that attempt to establish corresponding relations, like Gravelle's. Here sovereign impersonation comes not with the reversal of the terms suggested by "the public's" *lettre de cachet*—those who were formerly addressed by the king would now do the talking—but with the assumption of the power of the author to pursue dialogue with whomever one might choose.

Michel Foucault links the author's history to the exercise of sovereignty, but he places letter writers outside that history: the authoritative imprimatur of the state and public that sustains "the author-function" is unavailable to mere correspondents.[79] I'm suggesting that there are other ways that the state and public generate authorial "modes of existence."[80] While always entwined with print, censorship, and property relations, the epistolary mode had its own materialities: namely, the post, which provided infrastructure for literary transmission, cultivated imagined communities, and introduced new ways of watching and touching others. And even though it is regularly figured in opposition to the state, an eighteenth-century corresponding public remained within the reach of the king. As he remained within theirs.

So, in addition to print and its legal, citational, and other apparatuses of transmission, the institutional mechanisms facilitating enactments of authorial power included the reversal of postal privilege: by midcentury, the public was openly desirous of what it would deny the king, namely, a secrecy that enabled letter writers to presume control over their privately composed words. The completed, which is to say revolutionary form of the reversal is evident in the National Assembly's abolition of *lettres de cachet* and institutionalization of the inviolability of mail. That this apogee of antimonarchical epistolarity was followed by a century-long intensification of postal surveillance

("Never was the king such a ruthless prober into secrets as liberty is," insisted the Marquis de Sade, himself the recipient of multiple *lettres de cachet,* in 1790)[81] speaks to the continuities between absolutist and republican regimes: the conceit of self-authorization ("it is my will that . . .") characteristic of monarchical rule is less attacked and dismantled than it is appropriated and redeployed over the course of the century, culminating in its revolutionary reconfiguration as the essential quality of "the people," citizen-readers/writers whose collective will *was* sovereign power.

Sovereignty has always been a roomy signifier, encompassing—from Jean Bodin on—a property of divinities, territories, rulers, and persons more generally. In this sense, to claim or perform sovereign power is nothing more (or less) than the power to assert self-initiating action: agency, we might say, whose ends and effects can never be predetermined but whose existence as self-willed—as inaugural—is the crux of the matter. At the same time, sovereignty as a juridical and political concept risks losing historical and institutional specificity, thus analytic utility, when denotatively decoupled from state capacity: the supreme power of the governmental body to demand allegiance, exercise will, monopolize violence, decide upon the exception, command recognition in the international arena, etc.

The referential capaciousness apropos sovereignty is in my account a reflection of institutional and literary processes that spanned the "long" eighteenth century in France. These dialogic processes—how *logos* came to move across or through *(dia-)* space in ways both old and new—suggest that the epistolary politics of eighteenth-century France provides an occasion to see, perhaps to hear, a rearticulation of sovereignty's terms: from the person of the king and so the body of the state to a capacity presumed of and by every citizen. As his subjects adopted and adapted the epistolary form, they assumed a sovereign position. My claim is not that these were considered attempts to put state power into "the people's" hands, even or especially when the king was their addressee. Rather, my claim is that in the age of epistolary absolutism, the poetic practices of letter writers inculcated a sovereign disposition, an appropriation of the power of address through which their speech acts might become political events.

Likewise, the decidedly less than absolute quality of French absolutism—the in actuality fragmented and multiply mediated processes of kingly rule—is reproduced at the core of republican sovereignty, as it must be whenever claims to power rest on self-authorizing practices. The conundrums of representation characteristic of republicanism might provide a point of entrée into the long afterlife of absolutist sovereignty and its impossibilities. So might the demands for recognition that Markell diagnoses as the ontologically misguided and politically perilous aspiration of would-be sovereign selves.[82] My own approach suggests that such conundrums and demands wend through a politics of voice inseparable from reading and writing practices. But my story has tracked the fantastical aspiration to sovereign address rather than its ultimate impossibility, in order to parse a practice through which real and imagined political rule and contestation took historical and rhetorical shape.[83]

Gravelle's demands for recognition and representation were first and foremost a bid to become visible, audible, and untouchable as an author of moving and just complaints; thus, paradoxically, sovereign recognition of her person hinged on the recognition of a sovereign wrong. For Rancière, the paradox is constitutive of politics: when "illegitimate speakers" disrupt the "partition of the sensible" to claim their part, they expose as they enact a principle of equality that any claim to sovereignty must both leverage and disavow. In Rancière's account as in Gravelle's life, an "excess of words" becomes the means to such ephemeral ends, an excess that could no more be prohibited by a king's command than by Plato's banishment of poets or his abjection of the written tongue.[84]

And in the end, such excess will always elude interpretive order. The agonizingly indecipherable writing, the unknown number of uncaptured letters that circulated "freely," her failure to submit to the grammatical partitions of language: Gravelle's cries must to some extent remain "blind and blinding." But this lack of mastery does not leave her dumb, nor does our incomplete reception leave us deaf. Indeed, the felicity in Gravelle's unhappy performatives lies not in how they reveal historical impediments to political speech, but in how they bespeak a politics that is simultaneously material and literary, expressive and strategic, excessive and never quite enough "just as I have said in the memoir included here, not being able to explain myself *vive voix*."[85]

NOTES

Heartfelt thanks to Pam Brandwein, Sam Chambers, Lisa Disch, Doug Dow, Don Herzog, Artemis Leontis, Peggy MacCracken, Maureen Shanahan, Davide

288 *Elizabeth Wingrove*

Panagia, Andy Parker, Yopie Prins, and Arlene Saxonhouse for discussions and comments on various incarnations of this essay. I thank Mary Dietz and two anonymous reviewers for *Political Theory*, as well as generous audiences at the University of North Carolina, University of Minnesota, Reed College, University of Michigan, and the Western Political Science Association Annual Meeting, where I presented earlier versions of this work.

Research for this project was enabled by a generous NEH/Mellon Fellowship at the Newberry Library and by a grant from the Institute for Research on Women and Gender at the University of Michigan.

1. In addition to Gravelle's prisoner dossier in the Bastille Archives (A.B. 11,769), sources used to reconstruct her story include A.B. 11,785 (prisoners "G": miscellaneous documents); A.B. 12,498 and 12,493 (letters of Nicolas René Berryer [lieutenant general of police], 1753, and 1757), and *Archives de la Bastille: Documents inédits recueillis et publiés par François Ravaisson,* ed. François Ravaisson-Mollien (Paris: A. Durand et Pedone-Lauriel, 1884–1904), vol. 16. Gravelle's imprisonment is discussed briefly in Robert Dubois-Corneau, *Paris de Monmartel, Banquier de la Cour* (Paris: Librairie Fontaine, 1917), 184–90. All translations from the French are my own unless otherwise noted.

2. Ravaisson-Mollien, *Archives de la Bastille,* vol. 16, 207.

3. Jacques Rancière, *The Names of History: On the Poetics of Knowledge,* trans. Hassan Melehy (Minneapolis: University of Minnesota Press, 1994 [1992]), 35, 41. That the subjects figured by political-scientific inquiry—including statistical aggregates and players of games—might also be meaning-making agents is a topic well beyond the scope of this essay. Here my engagement with Rancière's arguably *sui generis* critical framework is mostly limited to its productive insistence on the vital role of literary and aesthetic sensibilities in both politics and political analysis.

4. While Rancière's introduction of "the poor" inevitably (and properly) conjures class distinctions, in his usage the term cannot be reduced to a socioeconomic category. See Samuel A. Chambers, *The Lessons of Rancière* (New York: Oxford University Press 2013), chapter. 3. The term's multiple significations are more legible in the original French *(les pauvres).*

5. Jacques Rancière, *Dis-agreement: Politics and Philosophy* (Minneapolis: University of Minnesota Press, 1998), 11.

6. Jacques Rancière, *The Politics of Aesthetics,* trans. Gabriel Rockhill (London: Continuum, 2006), 12–19. I've changed Rockhill's translation of *partage* ("distribution") to "partition." See also Jacques Rancière, *The Nights of Labor: The Workers' Dream in Nineteenth-Century France,* trans. John Drury (Philadelphia: Temple University Press, 1989); Rancière, *Dis-agreement*; Jacques Rancière and Davide Panagia, "Dissenting Words: A Conversation with Jacques Rancière," *Diacritics* 30.2 (2000): 113–26.

7. Although always orthographically challenged, Gravelle's writings show progressive syntactic and semantic disarray over the course of her imprisonment. On women's "bad" spelling, see Dena Goodman, "L'ortografe des Dames: Gender and Language in the Old Regime," *French Historical Studies* 25.2 (2002): 191–223.

8. While especially attentive to historical-linguistic context (and so to works by lesser-known writers), political analysts associated with the "Cambridge school" tend to embrace a notion of authorship that fixes identity, intentionality, and ideology as touchstones of textual interpretation. So, while they dwell longer than most at the site of the utterance's production, they continue to presume the

stability of authorial "voice." For a critique of Quentin Skinner's seminal account that draws on Rancière's notion of "excessive speech," see Davide Panagia, "The Piazza, the *Edicola,* and the Noise of the Utterance," in *The Political Life of Sensation* (Durham, N.C.: Duke University Press, 2009), 45–73.

9. In a letter to Minister of State the Comte d'Argenson she writes: "you ignore the fact that there has never been a prohibition on writing to one's prince or in justifying one's innocence to him; highway robbers have this privilege and you pretend to annul mine;" A.B. 11.769, f. 142 [v].

10. A place to begin on this vast subject is Eugène Vaillé, *Histoire des Postes Françaises jusqu'à la Révolution* (Paris: Presses universitaires de France, 1948). The truly smitten might move on to Vaillé's seven-volume *Histoire générale des Postes françaises* (Paris: Presses universitaires de France, 1947–55).

11. Patchen Markell, *Bound by Recognition* (Princeton, N.J.: Princeton University Press, 2003), 63–64. Markell draws from Hannah Arendt's notion of "nonsovereign" action. See Hannah Arendt, *The Human Condition* (Chicago: University of Chicago Press, 1958).

12. Panagia discusses the limitations of what he calls a "narratocratic" reading procedure in *The Political Life of Sensation* (Durham, N.C.: Duke University Press, 2009), 56–57.

13. A.B. 11,769, f. 101 [v].

14. Ibid., f. 50. Those identified as conduits for Gravelle's writings include Mlle de Franche-Comté, a pensioner at Madeleine-de-la-Flèche, and an unnamed teacher who worked at the Hôpital des Pénitentes d'Angers; see Ravaisson-Mollien, *Archives de la Bastille,* vol. 16, 202.

15. Seizing one's personal papers along with one's person was standard practice in the case of criminal and political detentions. Impounded writings were bundled and closed with the detainee's cachet, or, more commonly, when they didn't have one, sealed with a paper that included both his or her signature and the detaining officer's; the papers were returned to the prisoner upon his or her release. Although this procedure was followed when Gravelle was taken into custody, there is every indication that she recorded copies of her illicit letters on older letters from the sealed bundle.

16. The promise of a "large sum" is suggested by Mother Monsallier; see Ravaisson-Mollien, *Archives de la Bastille,* vol. 16, 199.

17. A.B. 11,769, f. 61.

18. Her qualification (presented also in my epigram) poses translation challenges. The original reads: *mes ecrits sont des catechisms de dit et de reponce je le sent et sans aussi que je n'en say pas davantage.*

19. Jean-Louis Chrétien, *The Call and the Response,* trans. Anne Davenport (New York: Fordham University Press, 2004 [1992]), 6.

20. A.B. 11,769, f. 131 [v].

21. Ibid., f. 118 [v]. I use several formulations to signal challenges as well as impasses in translating (reading) Gravelle's writing. "Text indecipherable" refers to my inability to make sense of the words as a result of how they appear on the page (e.g., smudged text; illegible handwriting). "Text missing" refers to the absence of words (e.g., ripped, torn, or missing pages; incomplete sentences that run off the paper's edge). I likewise include more of the original French than is customary in order to expose especially problematic translation choices.

22. Ibid., f. 89 [v]. The original begins: "comme mes ecrits sont en legont des professis du profeet etzchiel obscure si on a trop de difficulte a les lire . . . etc."

290 *Elizabeth Wingrove*

23. Eugen Hatin, *Les Gazettes de Hollande et la presse clandestine* (Paris: Chez René Pincebourde, Librairie Richelieu, 1865), 45–46. At least one state ministry was among their regular subscribers; see Anne-Marie Enaux and Pierre Rétat, "La *Gazette d'Amsterdam*, Journal de Référence: La Collection du Ministère des Affaires Etrangères," *Revue d'histoire moderne et contemporaine* 40 (1993): 152–69. Likewise, state discussions about the *gazettes* at midcentury cited concerns that, in an effort to make them "curious and interesting," their Paris distributer was accepting increasingly "eccentric" inserts from "anyone *[tous mains]*"; see Gilles Feyel, "La diffusion des gazettes d'étrangères en France et la Révolution postale de 1750," in *Les Gazettes Européennes de langue française (XVII–XVIIIᵉ siecles)*, ed. Henri Duanton, Claude Labrosee, and Pierre Rétat (St.-Étienne: Publications de l'Université de Saint-Étienne, 1992), 83.

24. A.B. 11,769, f. 137 [v].

25. Ibid., f. 39 [v].

26. This letter's addressee is unknown. A likely candidate is Mlle Bay, a pensioner at one of Gravelle's predetention religious residences.

27. A.B. 11,769, ff. 98–99.

28. Ibid., f. 99 [v].

29. Michael Warner, *Publics and Counterpublics* (New York: Zone Books, 2002): 66; see also 87–89.

30. While Aristotle takes the distinction to be (ontologically and epistemologically) foundational, Rancière insists that how the distinction gets made is itself the sine qua non of politics: "[Any] simple opposition between logical and phonic animals is in no way the given on which politics is then based. It is, on the contrary, one of the stakes of the very dispute that institutes politics" (*Dis-agreement*, 22).

31. I am finessing an arguably critical distinction between *logos* as speech and as reason (Heraclites' specification), which in turn calls into question the distance between *logos* and *poeisis*. Elaborating these issues would go well beyond the scope of this essay and into, among other places, crucial dimensions of Rancière's larger argument concerning philosophy (whose imperative remains order), politics (as the ceaselessly disordering), and aesthetics (as both the means and ends of sustaining such [dis]order).

32. Joseph-Michel-Antoine Servan, *Réflexions sur la publication des lettres de Rousseau et des lettres en général*, in *Œuvres choisies* (Paris: Imprimerie de P. Didot, 1822 [1783]), 417. The original of the final clause—*se met comme en dépôt*—evokes notions of entrustment and safekeeping that my translation doesn't capture.

33. Ibid., 408.

34. Joseph-Michel-Antoine Servan, *Commentaire sur un passage du dernier livre de M. Nekre* (n.d. [1785]), 20–21.

35. Mme de Sévigné's correspondent Roger de Bussy makes these observations about her writing in 1679; quoted in Roger Duchêne, "Le Mythe de l'épistolière: Mme de Sévigné," in *Epistolarité à travers les siècles: Geste de communication et/ou de l'écriture*, ed. Mireille Bossis and Charles A. Porter (Stuttgart: F. Steiner-Verlag, 1990), 15.

36. A.B. 11, 769, f. 142 [v].

37. Ibid., f. 107.

38. Ibid., f. 48. The original reads: *je contais que mes juste plaintes . . . etc.*

39. *Lettres de M. de Marville au Ministre Maurepas*, ed. A. de Boislisle (Paris: H. Champion, 1903), vol. 2, 244–45.

Sovereign Address 291

40. See Robert Darnton, *The Literary Underground of the Old Regime* (Cambridge: Harvard University Press, 1982). Gravelle's memoir also shares a resemblance with *mémoires judiciaires*; see Sarah Maza, *Private Lives and Public Affairs* (Berkeley: University of California Press, 1983).

41. A.B. 11,769, f. 120.

42. Ibid., f. 83 [r+v].

43. Ibid., f. 87.

44. Ibid., f. 88.

45. Ibid., f. 87 [r+v].

46. Ibid., f. 86 [r+v]. "Key of gold": "Certain officers of the Court of the Emperor or of the king of Spain and other princes have the right to enter these princes' private room, and they carry a gold key at their belts to mark this right"; *Dictionnaire de l'Académie Française*, 4th ed. (1762), accessed through The ARTFL Project (http://artfl-project.uchicago.edu.proxy.lib.umich.edu/).

47. A.B. 11,769, f. 18.

48. *Le Nouveau Secrétaire de la Cour ou lettres familières sur toute sortes de sujets . . . etc.* (Amsterdam: chez l'Honoré et Chatelain, 1744), 417, 444.

49. See Janet Altman, "Women's Letters in the Public Sphere," in *Going Public: Women and Publishing in Early Modern France*, ed. Dena Goodman and Elisabeth Goldsmith (Ithaca, N.Y.: Cornell University Press, 1995), 110; see also Janet Altman, "Teaching the 'People' to Write: The Formation of Popular Civic Identity in the French Letter Manual," *Studies in 18th-Century Culture* 11 (1992): 147–80.

50. *Le Nouveau Secrétaire de la Cour,* 491. Other examples: *Le Nouveau Secrétaire du cabinet* (1739) offers detailed instructions on proper spacing in letters sent to the king, while *Le Secrétaire de ce temps* (1709) provides a list of appropriate epistolary titles for addressing European rulers.

51. For an in-depth discussion of epistolary codes and social order, see Thomas Beebee, *Epistolary Fiction in Europe 1500–1850* (Cambridge: Cambridge University Press, 1999).

52. As does the exponential increase—from 2,500,000 livres in 1700 to 10,000,00 livres in 1777—in what the state charged *fermiers* for a monopoly on the national courier system; see Maxime du Camp, "L'Administration et l'Hôtel des Postes," *Revue des Deux Mondes* (January 1867): 171.

53. See Christine Métayer, *Au Tombeau des Secrets: Les Écrivains Publics du Paris populaire et Cimitière des Saints-Innocents, XVIᵉ–XVIIIᵉ siècles* (Paris: Albin Michel, 2000). François Furet and Jacques Ozouf calculate an increase in men's literacy rates over the course of the eighteenth century, from 29 to 47 percent, and in women's from 14 to 27 percent; see Furet and Ozouf, *Reading and Writing: Literacy in France from Calvin to Jule Ferry* (Cambridge: Cambridge University Press, 1982 [1977]), 26. There is, of course, much debate about how best to determine these rates.

54. Du Camp, "L'Administration et l'Hôtel des Postes," 172.

55. Louis-Sébastien Mercier, *Tableau de Paris* (Amsterdam, 1782), 1 :340.

56. Entry for "Police" in *Encylopédie ou Dictionnarie raisonnée des sciences, des arts, et des métiers* (1752–72), 12:911. For a detailed account of *la poste* as *police,* see Nicholas de la Mare, *Traité de la Police* (Paris: Chez Brunet, 1719–38), vol. 4, section 14, chapter 1 ("les postes et messageries"), 522–627.

57. The uncertain date reflects a murky history, including an edict forged two hundred years after the fact; see Vaillé, *Histoire des Postes Françaises jusqu'à la Révolution,* 27–29.

58. Lequien de la Neufville, *Origine des Postes chez les anciens et chez les modernes* (Paris: Pierre Giffart, 1708), 73. Eugène Vaillé identifies Neufville's history as the period's definitive account in *Histoire générale des Postes francaises*, 2:9–10.

59. Although never officially acknowledged, postal surveillance—what would come to be known in the nineteenth century as *le cabinet noir*—was indirectly publicized by Finance Minister Jacques Necker in his *Compte rendu au Roi* (1781).

60. Eugène Vaillé, *Cabinet Noir* (Paris: Presses universitaires de France, 1950), 76.

61. *Correspondance du Cardinal de Tencin et de Mme de Tencin avec le Duc de Richelieu* (Paris, 1790), 16.

62. Archives Nationales, series F (90 20235), 6. Both Vaillé's historical survey and contemporaneous accounts record the king's pleasure in perusing intercepted mail, which, when he was in residence at Versailles, was a weekly event; see Vaillé, *Cabinet Noir*, and Edmond Jean François Barbier, *Chronique de la Régence et du Règne de Louis XV* (Paris: Charpentier, 1857), vol. 8.

63. *Lettre de M*** à un de ses amis de province sur l'établissement de la poste intérieure de Paris* (April 20, 1760).

64. See Marc Bloch, *Les Rois thaumaturges* (Paris: Gallimard, 1983 [1924]), and Dale Van Kley, *The Damiens Affair and the Unraveling of the Ancient Regime* (Princeton, N.J.: Princeton University Press, 1984).

65. A.B. 11,769, f. 36.

66. Ibid., f. 38.

67. Ibid., f. 37 [v].

68. Andre Laingui and Arlette Lebigre, *Histoire du droit penal* (Paris: Presses universitaires de France, 1979), vol. 2: la procédure criminelle (§2: "la confrontation"), 98.

69. For a detailed (and sympathetic) account of the history of *lettres de cachet*, see Brian Strayer, *Lettres de Cachet and Social Control in the Ancien Régime, 1659–1789* (New York: Peter Lang, 1992).

70. Arlette Farge and Michel Foucault, *Disorderly Families* (Minneapolis: University of Minnesota Press, 2016).

71. A.B. 11,769, f. 36, 38.

72. Ibid., f. 40 [v].

73. King James Bible, 1 Kings 21:1-21, 2 Kings 9:25-26.

74. Strayer, *Lettres de Cachet and Social Control in the Ancien Régime, 1659–1789*, 23.

75. A.B. 11,769, f. 37 [v].

76. While I have not located any such document in her archival dossier, there are various intimations in her letters that such an evidentiary text did exist.

77. Pierre Bayle, *Analyse raisonnée de Bayle . . .* (London, 1755), 1:122 (accessed through Eighteenth-Century Collections Online, http://gdc.gale.com/products/eighteenth-century-collections-online/).

78. *Œuvres Diaboliques pour servir à l'histoire du tem sur le Governement de France* (À Pantin, Chez Jean Satyre rue des mauvaises pensées à la Sotise [n.d.]), 234–35. The conduct referred to was the king's 1753 banishment by *lettres de cachet* of large numbers of parliamentarians who refused to register *lettres patentes* concerning a Jansenist "crisis"; see John Rogister, *Louis XV and the Parlement of Paris, 1737–55* (Cambridge: Cambridge University Press, 2002).

79. Michel Foucault, "What Is an Author?" in *Language, Counter-Memory, Practice* (Ithaca, N.Y.: Cornell University Press, 1977), 113–38.

80. For a discussion of the "multiple modes of authorship" amenable to Foucault's account, see Roger Chartier, "Figures de l'auteur," in *L'Ordre des livres* (Aix-en-Provence: Alinea, 1992), 35–67.

81. Cited by Gilbert Lély, *The Marquis de Sade, a Biography* (New York: Grove Press, 1961), 317.

82. Markell, *Bound by Recognition,* 10–14.

83. The story of an "absolutism-that-is-not-one" would find rich resources in a closer examination of monarchical epistolarity: the convention that a minister of state cosign *lettres de cachet,* for example, or the abundant archival evidence that by midcentury they were printed *en blanc* (leaving only the names of the addressee, the detainee, and the detention facility to be filled in), or the king's own vulnerability to epistolary exposure, especially at court, where on more than one occasion his intercepted missives to lovers and other intimates led to his embarrassment and a hasty change of plans.

84. See Jacques Rancière, *The Philosopher and His Poor,* trans. John Drury, Corinne Oster, and Andrew Parker (Durham, N.C.: Duke University Press, 2003 [1983]), 30–56. See also Samuel A. Chambers, "The Politics of Literarity, *Theory and Event* 8.31 (2005), and Chambers, *The Lessons of Rancière,* chapter 3.

85. A.B. 11, 769, f. 48.

CHAPTER 12

Gender, Agency, and the Circulations of Power

Nancy Luxon

Nancy Luxon revisits the stakes of Disorderly Families: *what role does gender play in a politics where justice and public order do not yet coincide? She examines how refiguring the household as "the family" becomes central to establishing this new political order. First, Luxon presents household context of* mesnagement *and analyzes its normative instability so as to make visible the challenges posed to patriarchy by unruly female miscreants. Second, she analyzes the trespasses and connections undertaken by women and their variant effect on cultural representation. The essay concludes by considering the family as a "field of exchange" between power from above and power from below. With this space, women both trespass and connect. They serve as intermediaries between state and society, between literate and oral cultures, and between a commercializing economy of producers and consumers. The result is an account of the not-yet, in-between spaces of insurrection and women's efforts to distend these spaces beyond the encompassing structures of patriarchy.* ➥

In "Lives of Infamous Men," Foucault attests to the sublime spectacle of the violence that beset *les petits fous*, as he called them—the unruly vagabonds, petty thieves, gamblers, and libertines whose cries rose up from the stained letters held in the archives of the Bastille. These *lettres de cachet* and the quotidian dramas that they stage recount the violence central to the everyday life of a France not yet convulsed by

296   *Nancy Luxon*

the Revolution. With these letters, Foucault establishes the violence central to the consolidation of political order through the expanding prerogative of the police. The passage through this violence—the contest waged through the "traps, weapons, cries"[1] authorized by the familial *lettres de cachet*—serves as the inaugural moment for both infamous and ideal subjects, as well as for modern political order. As argued in my Introduction to this volume, these letters did something other than reflect the dynamics of an already-existing public. Obligated to formulate their demands in the name of a not-yet-existing "public order," letter writers sought to conjure an imaginary whose affective force would elevate it to the level of the social and symbolic. In this sense, these letters needed to elevate the particulars of their petty dramas to something with the force of a primal scene; that is, the imaginary aroused by these letters needed to gather together a heterogeneous group of social actors, organize the particularities of circumstance into broader social meaning, and affectively invest author and readers alike in the drama recounted. On more narrowly Freudian terms, these scenes thus indirectly evoke the organizing force of sexuality and sexual difference. Read from a feminist perspective, then, these letters dramatize the emergence and retrospection of a "sexual contract" that comes to organize civil society and undergird political order.[2]

The scenes of violence emerging from these letters fascinate in part because of the stark contrast between their baroque salutations and the vividly concrete events they recount. Initially, the letters perform an unholy mix of sovereign authority and violence beyond measure. In "Lives of Infamous Men," Foucault describes his initial response upon reading them as one of "near-physical vibration" provoked by the "fear and stupefaction" dramatized on their pages.[3] The force of the letters seems rooted in the aesthetic response of shock that they produce. To capture that effect, Foucault reaches for the distancing language of the theater—he calls their "mise-en-scène" a "dramaturgy of the real"—to characterize the scenes of suffering that they enact, a language that rests on a distance between reader and actor and whose politics thus relies on the reader's weak identification with the writer.[4] What would it mean to differently read the violence of this archive and to probe the wounds left behind? Are readers called upon as voyeurs, to participate in the frisson of these domestic dramas even as this titillation is cloaked by moral indignation? Does this violence attest to the corporeality and vulnerability of political bodies? Or should we read as social historians, concerned to recover a sociality populated by ordinary people somehow more "real" than the stereotypes of revolutionary heroes, aristocratic effetes, and furiously knitting spectators often associated with the eighteenth century? Does the presence of female as well as male letter writers establish a more egalitarian practice or does it attest to the bagginess found in some relations of domination? And most intractably: in what sense do these ninety-six letters, curated from the roughly sixty thousand written, serve as "evidence," and for what political histories?

I raise these issues as questions precisely because the claims made when answering them implicate the reader in the consequences of stabilizing fragmentary archival material. Even as these letters push us toward the politics and aesthetics of reading wounds, might not these wounds be subterfuges of their own sort, scarred over through the passage of time, and so designed to truncate the rediscovery of these same practices in the contemporary world?[5] At issue here are the symbolic and social practices involved in moving from uncertain moments of insurrection to the gendered abstractions of political and social order.[6] What interests me in these letters is the play between individual contestation of household norms and the drive toward the family's naturalization. The letters written by these disorderly families do not so much reveal a *prior* fantasy of domestic order as they inadvertently contribute to its formulation. Women play a paradoxical role in this process. On the one hand, they are agents with a unique ability to trespass across the threshold of the home, in and out of the politics of the street, in and out of legal contracts, and in and out of developing market economies. These trespasses offer conduits of activity that lead beyond the more structured spaces of patriarchal domination. On the other hand, the letters cumulatively chart the household's drift toward a moral economy of correction whose symbolic force becomes legally entrenched through the 1806 Napoleonic Code. What, then, do these letters reveal about gender, authorship, and authority?

Rather than concentrating on the aesthetic *jouissance* of reading, I have chosen instead to concentrate on the gendered dynamics barely discernible in the letters and left to the margins of Foucault's own research (but central to Arlette Farge's marvelous historical work). Such a reading makes it possible to discern those resistant practices *unable* to rewrite the terms of social order. Two central points emerge. First, these infamous lives were lived out as much by women as by men. Fully half of the letters were penned by female authors, and raised plaints against husbands and children; the king responded just as much to these letters as those written by men. The letters' plaints, however, do not sort easily along conventionally gendered lines; for example, women take men to task for being poor parents, while men lament the loss of income caused by an imprisoned wife. Second, reading these letters contrapuntally against their political and social context redirects attention to the structuring norms and practices of household administration, or *mesnagement*. As argued in my Introduction, these letters achieve their psychological resonance and social abstraction by actively involving letter writers, public scriveners, neighbors and other witnesses, and police in the circulation of these accounts through a nascent civil society. These circulations relied on social and economic practices not neatly contained to so-called public and private spheres. The practices of *mesnagement* regulate a very different set of gender roles than those legally codified, and reflect the variation of patriarchy as lived across different socioeconomic classes. Much more than weapons of the weak, these struggles against domination germinated in the relatively overlooked and underregulated domain of the household. The sense of operating within but against patriarchal practices made daily life more bearable. Yet, these capacities were decidedly ambivalent. As long as women didn't stray too far, they could act, negotiate, and resolve disputes on terms of their own design. This discretionary space—to press an advantage or retreat—permitted women to negotiate legal, economic, and social roles that often sought conflicting ends. Women could thus hew a rough "intimate justice" from the welter of conflicting circumstances that made daily life precarious, and that were not obviously or immediately subsumable to a single set of ends.[7]

Divided between letters from 1728 and those from 1758, *Disorderly Families* thus tracks the slow trend toward refashioning the family as a natural unit—one that uses the language of correction and public order to reassign the terms and conditions of agency. The 1804 Napoleonic Code consolidates these changes. Taken as a whole, the letters in *Disorderly Families* illustrate the trends converging toward the production of the family as a specifically *political* unit, and the overt, retrospective naturalization of family relationships to cover over the gendering of political order. I argue that eighteenth-century families thus serve as the pivot through which social energies become divided and redirected. If initially the marital and household threshold traced only a hazy boundary between ordinary households and the Maison du Roi (literally, the King's Household), the eighteenth century witnesses a series of changes that activate civil society and households as political actors deeply penetrated by politics. Far from standing in opposition to a public realm, these households alternately contest and contribute to its terms. Although Foucault failed to see it, gender norms lay at the heart of challenges to eighteenth-century power and authority.

To approach these issues, I work on two registers. First, at the level of individual women, I examine the role that women played in this contested and contestatory politics. Both their historical role and the specific form of epistolary correspondence demonstrate their part in seeking to move seemingly particular, personal issues to the level of general interest as a concern for a nascent public order. However, my inquiry into gender and politics is more than a question of adding women back in by recovering a lost historical presence. Instead, and second, I move to think the household as a *switch point of power.* Through this schema, I conceive of women as intermediaries between state and society, between literate and oral cultures, and between a commercializing economy of producers and consumers. Just as my Introduction to this volume drew attention to the importance of circulation and movement in newly emerging domains of public order, or civil society, here I analyze women's role in networks of sociability and labor. My goal is to understand the substance and meaning that these daily interactions gave to an early-modern practice of patriarchy. Specifically, I examine how refiguring the household as "the family" becomes central to establishing this new political order. My argument proceeds as follows: I first present the household context of *mesnagement* and analyze its normative instability so as to make visible the challenges posed to patriarchy by unruly miscreants; second, I analyze the trespasses and connections undertaken by women and their effect on social space; and finally, I read these networks of sociability and labor against these switch points at the core of eighteenth-century political unrest. The result is an account of the not-yet, in-between spaces of insurrection, and women's efforts to distend these spaces beyond the encompassing structures of patriarchy.

Structures of Domination, Practices of *Mesnagement*

For all that the circulations of the police and countercirculations of ordinary people affect the nature and reach of power, these same circulations also redefine the roles played by so-called disorderly families in the construction of a gendered political order. Although these letters could never fully be outright practices of revolt—after all, their authors seek the approbation of order—they *were* enactments of a social struggle to think the political on new terms. In this sense, these letters were part of a broader array of tactics to manipulate established order and differently inhabit spaces of domination. It has become commonplace to describe eighteenth-century France, if not politics writ large, as patriarchal.[8] *Patriarchy* is often generically used to describe any society where men monopolize authority and where women's access to it is restricted. However, it is less common to think of patriarchy as something that varies across history, or to interrogate what political work, specifically, it performs. As letter writers scrabble for apt words, I argue that their actions belie shifts in these practices of patriarchy. Early on, the letters reflect what historian Julie Hardwick defines as a household domain of *mesnagement* loosely organized around thrift, sociability, and the administration of property.[9] The emphasis on *mesnagement* meant that the *administration* of property or household was just as important as *holding* property—an important distinction for thinking about women as economic actors. By the late eighteenth century, *mesnagement* comes to be supplanted with a sexual division of labor that shrinks the space of the household to the family, and uses sexual difference to define political difference. I turn to the letters with an eye toward the activities that men and women took up jointly, and to analyze where differentiation emerged and how it was justified. The historical roles of women as capable of owning property, entering into guilds, and signing contracts are significant for the tension they evince between these activities and the production of femininity in the letters themselves.

"The conjugal bond was also a site," write Farge and Foucault in "Marital Discord," the essay that precedes plaints about husbands and wives in *Disorderly Families*.[10] Farge and Foucault's spatial language calls attention to the sprawling relations organized by marriage and downplays the psychology of affection. Their primary quality is "a decent level of economic survival" captured by the norms and practices of household administration, or *mesnagement*.[11] This economic survival depended not on abstract respect for property but on tangibles. What matters is the administration of objects such as dowries, debts, income, and household furniture (the only goods with durable value in most households).[12] So, when Madame Raymond Lafond requests release from prison because her husband has since "sold and eaten up all the furniture," she underscores the extent of her financial depletion and betrayal.[13] To the extent that women and men both contributed to the resources of the household, they were financially on equal terms. Of course, differences in magnitude of contribution led to resentments in some cases. Nonetheless, eighteenth-century cultural critic Louis-Sébastien Mercier described that women "work in partnership with their men and do very well as a result. They are used to handling small amounts of money and there is a perfectly equal sharing of responsibility for which the household is all the better."[14] Thus, in place of familial affections, "family" carries with it a sense of household rule or regime. This sensibility is borne out by common usage. More than members of immediate relation, "family" extends to distant relations, includes servants, and has a clear economic dimension.[15] It is defined against, on the one hand, the Maison du Roi (the royal court, but literally, the King's Household) and, on the other, the unruly, undifferentiated "dregs of the populace" often kept in *maisons de détention* (houses of detention). By contrast, *mesnagement* best describes the "middling" households of persons with some social status. Its economy is characterized by thrift, good management, and wise kinship alliances.[16] Its norms are expressed through a sociability premised on hard work and temperance, one that established constancy and so credibility (and credit) in the neighborhood.[17] So Margueritte Le Maire requests that her husband be imprisoned so as "to purge the public of a man who seeks only to make an affront to his family by coming to a shameful end."[18] Good *mesnagement* ensured an economic survival rooted not in abstract respect for property but in household administration.

Written in the eighteenth century, the *lettres de cachet* circulate on the cusp of the emergence of market economies that will profoundly reorganize these households. The households assembled in *Disorderly Families* reflect the lives of a range of occupations—from servants, to shopkeepers, to lawyers, notaries, master stonemasons, and seamstresses—that reflect the social and economic order of the eighteenth century. Disputes—sometimes referred to as relations of "bad commerce"—threatened a highly stratified social order premised more on personal relations of reciprocity than on economic property or accumulation.[19] Women's access to guild membership varies according to occupation and region; Paris had all-female merchant-mistress dressmakers and linen drapers, while these same guilds in Brittany were male-dominated.[20] Even in the mixed trades, gender roles shared a certain fluidity. Historian Cynthia Truant comments: "One remarks, in such [mixed] trades, a licensed or tolerated 'disorderliness' for masters' wives or widows who could aggressively defend their shops, husbands, and workers."[21] Although the exercise of guild privileges varied by region and occupation, guild mistresses often had extensive legal rights. For example, the women in the all-female dressmakers' guild in Paris were able to negotiate contracts in their own name and on their own authority; to hold offices within all-female guilds regardless of marital status; and so, in a limited sense, exercised greater legal rights than their male counterparts (who usually were expected to be a settled resident, with rented accommodations, and married).[22]

Beyond the guilds, women had a formal representation in other trades: in Nantes, they were one-third of all innkeepers, and dry-goods merchants, fully half of the whole-cloth merchants and fishmongers but not a single clockmaker, carpenter, or mason.[23] They registered with the police, submitted to inspections, and paid their taxes, and so were integrated into the broader economic landscape. Both as guild mistresses and as shopkeepers managing accounts while their husband was away, women interacted frequently with police and appear numerous times in police registers.[24] Women also participated in social networks that ranged from guild connections (although participation in guild confraternities was usually limited), to religious communities (including the clandestine Jansenist sects that opposed wealth, hierarchy, and the absolutist monarchy), to political networks (often connected to these same Jansenist activities). These networks redefine the topography of social and economic order on a timeline out of joint with the slow, fitful changes to the administration of political order. For a short period, then, not only were these social and economic cartographies noncoincident with political order, they were in advance of it; that is, adaptation to market economies, critiques of royal authority, and shifting social mores left these networks more agile than the police that had yet to develop themselves into administrators of order.[25] Considerable room for maneuver existed between formal status and its informal practice—to a point. After all, even the attainment of guild mistress status was never expected to bring with it political entitlements. Also, the guild logic that regulated social status was often at odds with the economic ideologies, from the mercantilist to the physiocratic, that undergirded visions of political order. Nonetheless, such differences allowed a range of figures and classes to presume a gendered authority as the basis for political and social order, without needing consensus on precisely the terms or implications of such an order. While the desire for "civic order" was widespread, it was not a stable concept, and different interests maintained different ideas about how it should be realized.

Women's ability to work and administer property bears not only on the practices of *mesnagement* within the household, but also on women's legal subjectivity. The practices of *mesnagement* come to encase women's legal subjectivity by shading the terms of the not-yet-public sphere in which informal practices and formal rights jostle for organizational power. Women in France were not consistently excluded from legal standing and protections, nor were they defined entirely in terms of their husband; indeed, married women did not take their husband's names until the revolutionary period.[26] Recent work by social and economic historians reveals the extent to which women could sign and negotiate contracts in their own name, pursue legal contests, and, in some areas like Brittany, inherit property through partible inheritance.[27] Although their gender roles conditioned how and when they intervened, women's economic and informational roles were often quite powerful; class and social status were more determinate on their ability to act.[28] In the seventeenth and eighteenth centuries, both men and women wrote or dictated memoirs that detailed their encounters with the law. These memoirs and legal briefs became one way to acquire information about legal contests as well as a rhetorical device for vetting arguments in the court of opinion as in the court of law. All sorts of news circulated in a variety of formats—rumors, maxims, cartoons, doggerel, legal briefs, bulletins, and so on—and women used this variety to inflect popular opinion. As historian Sarah Hanley has documented, women wrote in a variety of voices and on a variety of topics, ranging from philosophical tracts on marriage to judicial indictments of property, contract, and their role in trapping women in unbreakable marriage contracts. These writings shuttled between streets and law courts, and so created a curiously personal form of legal knowledge. Practically, the *lettres de cachet* offered an appealing alternative solution for circumventing a legal system disinclined to grant requests for divorce.[29] However, the dissonance between women's authorial roles and their legal figuration is substantial. It points to a significant tension between the historical and legal personas available to women. The letters, then, were but one way that women sought to restore standing among the bustle of the not-yet-public spaces emerging alternately through police patrols and legal right.

The potential redress offered by the *lettres de cachet* thus entailed operating within the enlarged scope of policing, staging shattered relationships as disorderly, and all in the hope of establishing a more bearable household order. As historian Judith Coffin notes, "Once one leaves behind the familiar gender certainties of the nineteenth century, it is nearly impossible to find any single set of convictions, whether elite or popular, about men's and women's respective economic domains."[30] The capaciousness of this eighteenth-century category enabled the irregularities of gender practices. The very language of disorder opened up the social world to evaluation and intervention in the name of an as-yet-undefined normative horizon, be it one of natural domesticity, honor and social status, moral correction, or something else entirely. The letters stage a desperate wish for the repair of household obligations in a period when the abandonment, violence, or debauchery of one household member threatened all. The dossier for journeyman clockmaker Germain Varillon, for example, is voluminous. His wife accuses him of permitting his friends to insult her "at every turn giving her pinches and saying insults to her."[31] The beatings that she enumerates read almost as "proof" of this social humiliation. Varillon's business partner, master clockmaker Michel Balthazar, "remonstrated with him that his debauches, games, absences, and poor management interrupted their work."[32] Even his mother writes against him "to avoid shame and affront" as well as the legal fees they cannot afford.[33] For all that gender played a part in assuring the constancy of order, it was one dimension among many and keyed to thrift, property administration, and above all the sociability that together were the necessary conditions for economic survival, not to mention prosperity. Threats to this stability came just as much from the disruptions of emerging market economies as from those persons whose restlessness chafed against these normative fixities. Much as ordinary neighborhoods were largely "unseen" to a seventeenth-century sovereign authority focused on territory and byways, the practices of ordinary households were largely ignored; that is, until they became tied to a popular opinion and not-yet-public order that the monarchy wanted desperately to deny—and to control.

Recovering this range of socioeconomic practices that shade legal subjectivity reveals the interpretive and political complexities in evaluating agency. At first blush, the project of historical recovery offers an opportunity to rebalance previous accounts and seems consonant with Christine Delphy's feminist project of "making the social emerge," if not with her Marxist politics.[34] However, "making the social emerge" is a project that depends on the position of both historical subject and spectator. Simply adding women and labor back in does not shift how present-day readers think about agency; such a project allows agency to remain thought on categorical terms; that is, it encourages questions such as *whether or not* women participated in economic activities outside the household, or whether women had *more or less* capacity to act than previously thought. These categorical questions quickly succumb to a series of claims and counterclaims about the historical veracity of accounts, their generalizability across geographic regions and history, or the relative strength of countervailing structures of domination. Such categorical questions also risk importing criteria to define and evaluate agency that make sense only from a later historical perspective.[35] As Joan Scott has argued, to see women as "agents" only when they have the ability to vote, hold property, and control their reproduction is to limit women's roles to a narrow historical period in the west and to render other kinds of activity obscure.[36] Beyond these questions of accuracy, there is a risk of seeing women only as objects of patriarchal domination, and so defining them entirely by the terms of patriarchy. My efforts to trace the diversity of women's economic activities, their informal participation in politics, and their role in neighborhood networks of sociability are less the work of recovery than a means to think more broadly about the interactions that characterize eighteenth-century popular culture and women's role within it.[37] Thinking of practices this way makes them into more than the unfolding of a structure of domination.

The language of "practices of patriarchy" thus seeks to be more than descriptive. Instead, practices attest to the pliability of rule, and suggest that patriarchy is capable of being distorted and subverted. Usually, efforts to think about political agency and domination stall on this question of pliability; the account given is one of the "gap" between structures and agents, between ideal theories and material interests, or between legal code and cultural custom. Instead, the unruly writers and denizens of these letters demand attention on different terms. The juxtaposition of legal status and socioeconomic practices recalls Foucault's complicated claim that subjects are always formed through violence. It further opens the possibility of conceiving this subjectivity not in terms of a "gap" but as the "encasement" of legal subjectivity by socioeconomic practices.[38] To think through both challenges, it's important to remember that *arche,* one of the etymological roots of "patriarchy," connotes both rule and beginnings; it reminds us that rule rarely is rigid and unchanging. That is not to say that these practices were somehow outside or free of domination. Subjects, for Foucault, find their beginnings through confrontation, struggle, and violence. Foucault argues that organizing oppositions, such as those of "men over women, of parents over children" are struggles that "attack everything which separates the individual, breaks his links with others, splits up community life, forces the individual back on himself, and ties him to his own identity in a constraining way."[39] Such a passage through violence is not lived once and for all. Violence touches here on all subjects and marks the straining reach of categories and concepts either to capture these personages or to determine which interpretive framework should encase them.[40] The socioeconomic practices that encase juridical status, expand that status, and give it form also contain the potential to undo the relations that affix that status within a given order. These practices, on Foucauldian terms, seek not to abolish power but to reactivate its older forms, reverse its ends, and then work with symbolic imagery to create their own myth of power.[41] The relationship of agency and domination, then, rests on a complicated effort to subvert and redirect the quotidian practices that maintain patriarchy as something enduring and resistant to direct challenge. Women are at once subjects and objects within these struggles; they are both historical actors within these relations of power and constrained by the patriarchal structures that seek to produce them as passive. Any consideration of women's agency, then, must confront this paradox. Women's agency cannot transcend this historical condition, but instead indexes the modes of being it permits.

The language of encasement thus enables a story of the adaptability of patriarchy, and of the regulatory work that happens in other registers so as to police access to legal subjectivity specifically. Encasement works through the confrontation of these modes of being with legal code. With such an approach, there is no longer a gap to be narrowed or bridged, as a way of marking some kind of progress even as more far-reaching structures are left unexamined and untouched. The language of encasement instead puts pressure on the doubling of subject-position across cultural practices and juridical code.[42] It captures both the institutional pliability in deviating from its prerogative and the creativity in finding conduits of action even in conditions of inequality. The effort to achieve some measure of control over daily life by acting out unsanctioned roles and challenging a disinterested royal authority unites this incongruous set of everyday practices. Challenging the authority of husbands and family members was a way to alleviate the injuries caused by failed social obligations and their physical, economic, and reputational strain on households. These were deeply felt. However, these actions concede that the general structural conditions of women across all ranks will likely remain the same, even though the surrounding popular context increasingly challenged the terms of order and the authority of the word. Women, and others perched on the frontier between formal and informal socioeconomic practices, sensed the amorphous relation between daily life and legal order, and seized the pliable language of "public order" as an occasion for redress. Redressing the everyday injuries of drunken husbands or wayward children was a means to seek security at the cost of inviting the police into the household and potentially losing income. Yet such redress was neither instrumental nor wholly intentional. Once again, privileging the practices that structure the domestic *scenes* found in the *lettres de cachet* makes it possible to back away from the intent of actors involved.

Turning to the letters with these questions about agency and domination does not suggest that they participate in the uncovering of any "real" that somehow offers "more transparent access to social reality."[43] The significance of the letters lies less in their restoration of women to historical accounts than in the household's undeveloped potential as a site for a collective enunciation of public order beyond the Three Estates. This site was not obviously or immediately that of the French Revolution. Women played a central role in defining this struggle, as the terms of household power, economic labor, and their accompanying political entitlements all became open to contestation. However, the impact of the letters, or of women's activities more broadly speaking, is not to be determined by their political effect. To say that the letters or other practices that manipulated practices of *mesnagement* resulted in witting or unwitting collective organization, or something as coherent as a "politics," would be to overstate and misunderstand their effects. Practices of *mesnagement*—like the practices of manipulating political rumor, or staging quotidian dramas, or writing legal *mémoires*—could become subversive precisely because they sought a terrain that was not immediately political. Such choices allowed women to fade into the crowd as the police showed up to bread riots, to rid themselves of abusive husbands when divorce was all but impossible, and to create a legal knowledge that gave women standing despite their exclusion from formal politics. The emphasis on gender, household practices, and subordination not only denaturalizes the moral authority of the family, it also forces a confrontation with the figuration of woman on moral terms.

Representations of Disorderly Families

What happens in the move from the historical persona of social history to cultural figure? The preceding section ended by noting the tension between the women as historical subjects and their figuration in correspondence and other texts. Contemporary readers can easily lose sight of this tension. The letters themselves are composed by a mixture of stock phrases and oral vernacular, with words that tumble over one another and so create the impression of direct speech. Reading across the multiple letters contained in a dossier, the reader immediately confronts the challenge of *how* to read. Like their original eighteenth-century audience, the reader is begged to heed one set of imprecations and not another. How should spectators respond to being hailed—and what does it mean to be hailed when the terms of order are in flux? Eighteenth-century paintings and engravings were all too ready to answer that question and seized on these household scenes as an opportunity for moral instruction. A number of these pieces are included in the French publication of *Disorderly Families* that includes twenty-four plates at the center of the volume. The series of plates opens with an engraving of a woman recounting her woes to a male scrivener set up in a market stall; it concludes with an engraving of a male servant's arrest, a plate that illustrated the entry for *lettres de cachet* for Louis-Sebastien Mercier's *Tableaux de Paris*.[44] In between are reproductions of eighteenth-century domestic scenes, including genre paintings by Jean-Baptiste Greuze and Jean-Baptiste-Siméon Chardin, popular etchings and engravings by Nicolas de Launay, Pierre Alexandre Wille, and Levasseur; and drawings by Étienne Jeaurat, Carle Vernet, and Hubert Robert.[45] Most of these artists are known for popular street scenes, domestic tableaux, and heavy-handed sentiment. Women play a central role here: they are largely confined to domestic settings, and figured as physically weaker than men, emotionally overwrought by conflict, and defined by their caretaking role. Curiously, the reproductions are presented with absolutely no commentary from Farge and Foucault.

The effect of these pictorial representations, juxtaposed against the events composed by the letters, is to call attention to the *production* of these scenes. The contrast of medium used in each case makes this production more visible. More than journalistic reporting or theatrical performance, the letters composed scenes of disorder through the collaboration of a number of people: scrivener, neighbors, priest, police, and king. Examining the circuits of this production is one way to explore the persistence of patriarchy: Why, despite the pliability of the practices of patriarchy, are its structures so recurrent—and what psychosocial investments on the part of the spectator hold these in place relatively unchanged? If the preceding section outlined the *fact* of encasement, turning to the *dynamics* of encasement offers insight into the processes that hold patriarchal structures in place. Debates over the veracity of women's virtuosity or viciousness would leave intact a natural moral order and divert attention away from debates about the limitations of this ordering of persons. Encasement instead relies on the encounter between women's *status* and their *mode of inscription*. The variation of women's modes of inscription, or lived experience, shows up the contradiction between their socioeconomic activities and their legal status. Such contradictions, when they become intolerable, produce charges of disorderliness to mark and regulate the anxiety provoked. And so I argue that the contradictions between practices of patriarchy and emergent public order become vivified in the contrast between the epistolary circulations of the *lettres de cachet* and the representations of domestic life found in the artwork originally included in *Disorderly Families*. If the letters bring into contact an array of persons and domains, and mobilize them to define public order, then the representational logic of the accompanying artwork shuts down this mobility. These representations quietly call upon viewers to endorse a vision of domestic order that stabilizes women's roles and thus stills the disruptive potential of the letters. In this way, it becomes possible to examine the play between women as historical

310   *Nancy Luxon*

actors and the figurative practices of gender, as well as the anxieties that these figurative practices seek to obscure. Controlling the "secret" of gender embeds gender at the heart of public order, renders its effects on at least partially affective terms, and makes its control central to modern politics.

References to gender and disorder in eighteenth-century France are rife: from Rousseau's claim that "never has a people perished from an excess of wine; all perish from the disorder of women," to letter writer and parliamentary clerk Duchesne's plaint about "the most frightful and universal disorder" of his wife, to a mother's distress that her son's "disorder increases every day and he has such an excess of it."[46] Farge and Foucault muse on the distinction between those eighteenth-century "disturbances" that located conflict "at the boundaries of the family space" and the later nineteenth-century "dissipation" where failed, future-oriented behavior becomes tied to "the economy of life."[47] Disorder is almost always characterized by excess and by movement across a threshold. Reflecting on these proliferating uses of disorder, political theorist Carole Pateman divides them into two basic senses: first, "the socio-political sense of a 'civil disorder'" such as a riot or protest; and second, "an internal malfunction of an individual as when we speak of a disordered imagination or a disorder of the stomach or intestines."[48] Indeed, the initial title for *Disorderly Families* was *Le Dérangement des familles*—a title discarded because *dérangement* also evokes roiling intestines. The confusion of inside and outside is reflected in the figurative language of the letters. Letter writers routinely complain that others "vomit out against me a thousand maledictions and imprecations."[49] The letters from the early eighteenth century demonstrate constant preoccupations about honor, mobility across social strata, and the differing and reversible perspectives rooted in status. One wood seller who found himself in court complained that when he seized control of their finances, it "threw [his wife] into a fury so strange that it is not possible to live tranquilly in his home, and that his wife distances all the other businesses from him, and vomits against him insults and damnations."[50] The status of these internal disorders, so easily expelled, differs from the psychological interiority that deepens as the century wanes. By contrast, the accompanying artwork seeks to displace such tumultuous movements back into the family (and so outside of public order), or deep within human nature (and so beyond civic personas). As we will see, the pedagogical impulse of these representations seeks to manage and contain these threats of disorder.

The original artworks were displayed publicly and so created a visual space for debates about the nature of marriage—as in the engraving *La Dispute de la culotte* in which husband and wife literally fight over possession of a pair of breeches. Behind these figures floats a banner that reads "Is it woman's ambition to wear the breeches?" The engraving's formal composition sends the spectator moving between the different figures—beleaguered husband, angry wife, frightened child, barking dog—so as to compose the domestic scene of things falling apart. If the banner were not instructive enough, the engraving is captioned with the exchange: "You want to be master and to make me pass for a fool;—You can go to the devil, I'll be mistress despite you and your teeth." Effectively enframed by the inaugural question and the pedagogical response, the dispute between husband and wife remains contained to a question of "woman's ambition." The need to contain disorder to the family is clear, and underscored by the child's frightened gaze that reaches directly outwards beyond the engraving and presses the viewer into service.

While the *lettres de cachet de famille* circulated primarily among popular classes, several of these artworks were shown publicly at the Paris Salon Exhibitions; other engravings found their way into middle-class homes through popular memoirs and weeklies. The paintings of both Greuze and Chardin from the 1750s concentrated initially on depictions of a romanticized rural life that indirectly critiqued the worldliness of aristocratic society. They were followed by idealized scenes of father and mothers, frequently associated with children so as to emphasize themes of natural virtue and paternal education. Such scenes could be considered as aspirational for those in the middle class and a subtle critique of moral decadence. By 1769, the sentimentality remained but became indexed toward the "lurid sensationalism" of scenes of domestic conflict, prostitutes, and impoverishment; the engraving of Greuze's *The Stepmother,* who scandalously distributes stale bread to her curly-haired moppets, is a case in point. Many of these paintings sought to recover paternal tendresse so as to rehabilitate the figure of paternal authority. These representations were bluntly pedagogical and addressed to the spectator. Indeed, one commentator on the initial showing of *The Death of an Unnatural Father* (1769), noting that many visitors drew back from the painting,

Anonymous, *La Dispute de la culotte,* early-eighteenth-century print, Île-de-France. Musée de la coopération franco-américaine. Copyright RMN-Grand Palais/Art Resource, NY.

After Jean-Baptiste Greuze, *La Belle-Mère* (The Stepmother). Etching by Jean-Charles Levasseur. Musée de la coopération franco-américaine. Copyright RMN-Grand Palais/Art Resource, NY.

commented: "Must the weakness of the Spectator be the measure of the merits of the Composer?"[51] With these juxtaposed images emerges a tightly controlled educational experience for spectators. Greuze's work, argues art historian Emma Barker, serves as a "technology for the formation of new models of subjectivity . . . not . . . reflecting some pre-existing middle-class identity so much as itself constituting such an identity in terms of new concepts of 'family,' 'nation,' and so on."[52] Indeed, these paintings have recently been read less as illustrations of moral sensibility (where sensibility is taken to be a private virtue) and more in terms of the surrounding civic discourse that sought to bind public to private.

In other group scenes, the drama of looking is more complicated and tugs at the viewer in different ways. In Étienne Aubry's pious *Fatherly Love* (1775), a series of recursive regards avoid direct contact between the grouped figures; instead, children and wife focus loving attention

Étienne Aubry, *L'Amour paternel* (Fatherly Love). Copyright The Trustees of the British Museum. Reprinted with permission.

on the father, himself with eyes lowered in modest benevolence. The viewer can adopt the view of either the adoring children gazing upwards or the elderly figure at the edge of the painting who looks on with pride at the family he has built. By contrast, vicious looks jaggedly intersect the all-female composition of Greuze's *The Stepmother*. These gazes break apart the family as the figures largely fail to look at one another and instead look beyond the frame of the drawing. In both cases, these sight lines interpellate the viewer. Art historian Janie Vanpée describes that, "In many of the dramatic family scenes, a figure who is not part of the main group's activity is placed strategically at the periphery of the group and painting, bridging that no-man's-land between the inside, private space and the outside, public space."[53] Peripheral to the contact at hand, these figures look on like the viewer, with a range of emotions playing across their faces. Through their own posture, they call attention to the act of looking, and thus mediate between viewer and family drama. Often these mediating figures are children, whose beseeching looks leave the viewer aware of their presence as witnesses to the scene. Regardless of whether the viewer succumbs to the overt pathos of the scene, their didactic content, or an ironic self-reflection on both, the viewer must confront her participation in this composition. The overriding impulse, however, is to stabilize both these primal scenes and the viewer's response.

By contrast, the spectator's participation in the letter-writing process intensifies that interpellation into something more than a hail. It belies a more collaborative participation of bystanders, either to family conflicts themselves or through more distant encounters with these letters as they circulated. With the *lettres de cachet,* readers enjoy the pleasure of being invisible spies on what they are not meant to see—on the letters secretly sent, and orders kept hidden by the king's seal. Readers are trapped between their curiosity to see and their reluctance to judge because of their position as intruders onto these scenes. But in what sense are readers also *intruders*? If the letters here disorient—the cries and countercries appeal to different visions of order, indeed to multiple social, moral, and public orders with competing jurisdictions—then they're intruders in the sense of trespassing where one shouldn't be and where one's own status is uncertain. Foucault describes the upset to readerly rules of signification: "The rules of this stilted discourse were thus upset by a vibration, by wild intensities muscling in with their own ways of saying things."[54] Rather than reality chasing representational form, the obverse happens; these are "fragments of a discourse trailing the fragments of a reality they are part of. One won't see a collection of verbal portraits here."[55] Historically displaced from the networks of sociability and commerce that traverse the neighborhood, the position of reader-spectator is unclear. That so many letters are passionately written only to request a reversal a few months later further upsets the reader's interpretive position as witness or judge. Much as the circulations of the letters from author, to scrivener, to king and police involved all parties in the construction of norms for "public order," the reader must actively participate in such orderings. She must scaffold up an interpretive framework to receive the letters, accommodate the multiple and competing frames that refuse resolution, and acknowledge the exclusionary logics prowling at the letters' margins. As curators of these letters, Farge and

Foucault declined to do so precisely to oblige the reader to take up this discomfiting work.

Rather differently, the drawings, engravings, and paintings use the position of intruder to suggest that viewers are *invested* in the exclusionary logic visible in *The Punished Son* (1778) and *The Confused Girl* (1773). Through the manipulation of social regard, these paintings suggest that the reciprocal sociability of the early eighteenth century has already been broken. The paintings stabilize the oppositions that organize family drama while acknowledging the viewer's ambivalence about these—and about her own family position that she would perhaps prefer to repress. By conceding to the desire to peep, desire invests a new politics: "A whole political network became interwoven with the fabric of everyday life . . . if one meant to take advantage of it, it was necessary to 'seduce' it. It became both an object of covetousness and an object of seduction; it was desirable, then, precisely insofar as it was dreadful."[56] These genre scenes offer a symbolic order in which to understand ambivalence about one's place within the family; they also seek (perhaps too arduously) to defuse the capacity for judgment that the viewer might exercise as bystander. Put bluntly, they give the voyeuristic viewer the alibi of moral instruction. In both genre paintings described above, these scenes remove the household from public life and instead invite the viewer to pivot on this desire and turn more deeply inward. Political conflicts become internal, family affairs, with bystanders invested in this displacement. As desire saturates looking and promises the power to investigate and judge, it disarms spectators' initial ambivalence. Secure in their position of moral judge and seduced by its voyeuristic distance, spectators refuse the ambivalences that might have allowed *mesnagement* to subvert patriarchy.

By the end of the eighteenth century and with a growing tide of letters, brimming with secrets and potential disorders, gender became a site and a strategy of population control, and a means to contain popular energies. The simultaneous visibility of the family and the secrecy of its dynamics are central to obscuring the political asymmetries embedded in the core of a modern politics premised on equality. Biddy Martin observes, "If *women* have been marginal in the constitution of meaning and power in western culture, the question of *woman* has been central, crucial to the discourse of man, situated as she is within the literary text, the critical text, the psychoanalytic situation and social texts of all kinds as the riddle, the problem to be solved, the question to be answered. Foucault has not acknowledged the specificity of women's situation with respect to secrecy and truth."[57] Merely recognizing that women contributed letters of arrest does not alter the rhetorical work done in producing either figures of femininity or of political order. More than historical subjects, women are caught up in the discursive production of the female figure. The tension between the social histories of the eighteenth century and women's figuration allows women to be coded as the secret: they are at once the secret bearers of disorder to be controlled and the secret to establishing a stable moral order. The figure of the disorderly woman, then, is not tied to a historical referent but regulates a wider range of social anxieties.[58] Thus the family comes to have a stubborn recursivity, one whose material and symbolic power is less easily disturbed than the fluid sociality of the street.

The attention to *scenes* of subjection thus alters the framework for considering the work of domination itself. Even as it is simplest to conceive of domination as the imposition of one person's will on another, domination rests on the indirect support of others to execute and support the will of the powerful. Think of the letter from Jean Legris as he sought to disentangle himself from a wife beside herself with grief after the birth of a stillborn child. Unable to determine what happened, readers must confront their inclination to side with either person—and then weigh that inclination against the paternalist compassion of the police officer who found Legris's wife, Jeanne Lemoine, too pained to arrest.[59] By thinking about the scenes that enframe women's lived experiences and that compose the dramas staged in the letters, it becomes possible to pull into sharper focus the role of spectators from both the eighteenth century and the present day. The emphasis on the practices that organize these scenes, or in this case the circulation of the letters, throws into relief the *mechanisms* that regulate the distribution of power and that cannot be reduced to individual subjects—the dominating and the dominated. It becomes possible to interrogate how the support of bystanders functions quietly and behind the scenes while stepping outside of the narrow, legal language of agency and accountability. Instead of a narrow investigation of the act, scrutiny falls on the processes of *forming* actors who are then subsequently accountable to the moral framework that encases their action. Looking ahead to the next section, women's double-edged role

318   *Nancy Luxon*

as both actor and signifying woman is premised on her role as "the excessively said" about gender and household practices.[60]

Thinking the Household as Field of Exchange

Encasing practices, forged in the tension between women's agency and its mode of inscription, do not automatically engender a politics. If the preceding section argued *against* positioning women in terms of conscious interests, social reality, and "true" representation, then how should this politics be understood? Within his own work, Foucault's emphasis on the political struggles that long precede the French Revolution becomes a way to analyze the social, economic, and political shifts that play out over decades without reading those shifts through the lens of the Revolution itself. Sidestepping ideology, Foucault instead identifies what I term *switch points of power*—sites defined by those "fragments" of power, or "exchanger elements" between different forms of power—that serve as matrices for political transformation.[61] Foucault's brilliance was to suggest that these material (in the sense of structural and political) and symbolic changes *span* two politically divergent regimes. His arrogance is to pass over the regulating role played by gender. Differently from Foucault, I argue that the discretionary scope for agentic practices (outlined in the section titled "Structures of Domination, Practices of *Mesnagement*") and their ability to differently invest local communities (outlined in the preceding section) come together to make the household a switch point of power. Within this switch point, women take on the role of "exchangers" who crisscross public and private, household and street, personal and political. On this reading, households are not a microcosm or domestic stage for a broader conflict between either proletariat and bourgeoisie or Third Estate and absolutist order. Rather, the exchangers highlight a feature of any system of signification—namely, the play between subject and figurative referent that enables the system (here, politics) to be characterized by entrenchment and adaptation both. Where the preceding section argued that the play between representations of households and their social context obscured the political bases of gendered politics, here I offer a new way to conceive this politics. Returning to the household as a switch point recovers the bases of political struggle. Specifically, it recovers the site and dynamics for the confluence of material and discursive conditions capable of producing the family as a social form.

Foucault comes to the language of exchange and social form in his work to define political struggle on material rather than ideological terms. Crucial to this struggle are the institutions that facilitate new articulations of power. Invoking Hobbes, Foucault defines disciplinary society against what he alternately calls a "civil" or "social war": the uprisings of the eighteenth century that contour the disciplinary power exercised in the nineteenth.[62] To characterize these uprisings, Foucault refuses to locate them outside of power and instead insists on the interpenetration of state power and social elements. These social contexts offer "a matrix within which elements of power come to function, are reactivated, break up, but in the sense of parts breaking away from each other without thereby losing their activity, in which power is re-elaborated, taken up again in a mythical form of ancient forms."[63] At the heart of this story lies those "switch points of power" that facilitate the transfer of power between political regimes through a conjoinment of sovereign and institutional registers.[64] Foucault will go on to highlight the different modes in which state officials (such as tax agents) and "criminal-social enemies" (such as vagabonds) occupy these exchanger roles, along with their ability to subtly shift the terrain of confrontation. Exchangers govern the very nature of change itself. For Foucault, the exchanger element evokes alternately Marx, whose "bearers" *(Trägern)* ease the move from use-value to exchange-value; and Hegel, whose account of the State rests on transformative conflicts with the family, then civil society, and then between civil society and the state.[65] However, these exchangers are neither the playthings of alien powers nor rent by the conflicts of world-historical *Geist*; their structural position enables them to act and facilitate shifts in political order but with unwitting consequences.

What happens when families are sited as a switch point of power? To think through this possibility, we might turn to other switch points to think analogously. Much as Marx neglects to theorize the place for reproductive or household labor, and Hegel leaves women the "everlasting irony in [the life of] the community," Foucault passes over domestic and reproductive labor in his discussion of household economies. The social site of the family and its role in the transmutation of economic hierarchies into social domination never are interrogated as such.[66] In Foucault's *The Punitive Society,* he examines a different site: the emergence of the prison as a social institution in which punishment rests on the extraction of time from people's lives, and accounts for it in proportion to the severity of an offense. Foucault calls this the

320   *Nancy Luxon*

"prison-form" and argues that it is functionally analogous to Marx's "wage-form."[67] As social forms, these embody a set of practices that extend beyond the specific site of factory and prison—these practices comprise a surrounding ecosystem, if you will, of economic relations, social organization, and values that enable these institutions to function. Both the wage-form and the prison-form exchange time against power, and both fundamentally alter the way that *power circulates through society and is valorized.* More than an account of new economies, these switch points also signal transformations of value. Curiously, Foucault never considers the specifically reproductive dimension of these forms, let alone the role for sexual reproduction within them.

Could the household be considered alongside the factory and the prison as a site that has similar effects: to exchange time against power, to alter its circulation through society, and to transmute value? After all, as Christine Delphy has masterfully argued, the initial restriction of women's economic activities to the domestic sphere and the devaluation of their labor is a way of exchanging time against patriarchal power.[68] As the household constricts, second, the sexual division of labor also encourages the reformulation of networks of sociability into relations of competition. Thus, activities previously regulated through practices of *mesnagement* become reorganized through the social form of the family that sets households against one another. These two changes necessitated, third, an emergent norm of domesticity that defined and defended a sharp distinction between public and private— one that defers to public authority in matters of intimate justice. Thus, the transformation of household to family capitalizes on the redirection of affective energies that pushed outwards—previously seen circulating through legal memoir, epistolary correspondence, and popular opinion—into the closed circuits of the household's moral economy. Consequently, as households become redefined in terms of moral education, the family becomes a powerful site for the redirection of affective and labor energies.[69] Taken together, the new terms of this exchange against patriarchal power constrain how eighteenth-century women circulate through society as economic agents and participate in republican politics.

Notably, by reading the household as a switch point of power, women can be seen to have a bivalent role. Much like other exchanger figures, they both trespass and connect different domains, and then come to be defined by these movements. Broadly speaking, "exchangers" can take the form of lawyers, notaries, tax agents, police, or vagabonds, among others. Foucault later defines them as the "social entourage" who define individuals through their relation to institutions that traverse society such as hospitals, courts, social agencies, the police, and so forth.[70] They mark potential threats to order. On Foucault's reading, these figures result from the conjunction of a tradition of sovereignty rooted in the social contract, and an institutional tradition that renders the criminal as an enemy of the sovereign of society. The first telescopes civil war onto a single criminal act; the second renders the criminal unresponsive to formal laws and informal norms, and so an "enemy of society." Exchangers function either as those who are "criminal-social enemies" or as the figures who would regulate them. Such bifurcated origins enable these figures to use their mediating positions to bind different domains of lived experience; through them, power and normative conventions circulate. Foucault concludes, "This element functions as exchanger between the two [traditions] and is behind a whole series of theoretical, practical, and epistemological effects throughout the nineteenth century"—namely, the use of law, medicine, and psychiatry to define both criminals and those who would counter them.[71] Drawing on the "lateral interests" of those not obviously aligned with rulers, the "class in power" uses these "epistemic relays" to manage unruly subjects.[72] Yet exchangers can also take the form of those who trespass against the order of things and disrupt its half-submerged classificatory schema.[73] The social and collaborative dimensions of *mesnagement* used these same epistemic relays to put pressure on power from above. The circulations of exchangers offer the possibility of disrupting and transforming the political practices and values that organize collectivities. Within the household switch point of power, women can be seen both to *mediate* increasingly incommensurable domains and also to use these same circulations to *trespass*—that is, to move unsanctioned from one domain to another. The early-eighteenth-century household thus becomes an in-between space, one that is framed by the events that alternately might redirect resistant practices into full-throated uprisings or banish those practices to the fine print of the fraternal social compact.

Remarkably, the status of this switch point of power initially resists co-optation. On the one hand, the proliferation of categories used to patrol "morality, order, and regularity"[74]—debauchery, dissipation, libertinage, vagabondage, waywardness, drunkenness, infamy, gambling, violence, delusion, and on and on—suggests an intolerance for those whose peregrinations upset the household equilibrium. On the other hand, this switch point also knew a lively debate around the central tenets of order and on whose authority they could be established. The capriciousness of some requests—Jeanne Catry's request to imprison her seventy-four-year-old husband for his habit of drinking and disrobing—counterbalances the sobriety of others, the chorus of voices pleading for Duplessis's imprisonment after he beat his wife violently with a fire shovel.[75] Because families paid the room and board of the person imprisoned, they also decided when that person could be released. In the absence of a universal law to be applied equally across all acts, those proximate to the situation decided its particulars. Gradually, these judgments become replaced by those rendered by the police (as their patrols and registers begin to define street life) and the burgeoning connection between *maisons de détention* and *hôpitaux* (one that permits psychiatry to emerge as a new body of knowledge). Following the 1784 circular that ended the *lettres de cachet*, a more centralized system of confinement emerged: *maisons d'arrêt* for those charged with an arrest, the *maisons de justice* found in the provinces, juvenile detention centers *(maisons de détention)*, and reformatories *(maisons de correction)*. These *maisons* (literally, houses) consolidate the new correctional role of the family and allow what previously had been a duality—the domains of public order and of justice—to be incorporated into a single coherent state apparatus. If the early-eighteenth-century household had served as a switch point of power that used the norms of *mesnagement* to regulate disputes, by the end of the century those capacities become transferred to the state and the family operates on different terms. On Foucault's reading, the family becomes a moral technology subsumed by the coercive demands of the state.

Once again, Foucault here misses an opportunity for political critique. By suggesting that the family is but one moral technology among others—no different from the factory, the school, or the military—he suggests that the mechanisms of internalization are the same in the family as in these other social institutions.[76] However, the household as switch point differs from others (such as prison) in several ways. The disciplinary society of the nineteenth century relies on discipline and normalization to isolate within a mass: individuals ceaselessly monitor and adjust themselves to a norm, thereby reproducing and entrenching its power. Differently from such self-surveillance, families sit at the intersection of multiple and imperfectly compatible domains—those affective, social, economic, and moral. Families are organized around multiple and conflicting relations of inequality, authority, and reciprocity that define parents, children, and siblings.[77] Family roles are profoundly relational; the family's role-based organization becomes a means to nurture self-cultivation through the push-pull of attachment and detachment.[78] These relations have tremendous affective range; from infancy, through sexual latency, and then into maturity, individuals work to confront and imperfectly integrate feelings of love and hate. The psychological work of the family is, ideally, to learn to balance those countervailing relationships and come to terms with the moral dilemmas they raise; that work may equally be accomplished by leaving and disavowing the family. At its core, the family is the site where individuals first experience claims to power, justice, and truth. Thus, Foucault misses a crucial insight: both structurally and functionally, households serve as the nodal point for the reproduction of political order and contain the possibilities of deviating from it. To the extent that the household reduces to the family, the scope of that moral work itself constricts and no longer draws upon the sprawling relationships of *mesnagement*.[79] From the perspective of the sovereign, such a constriction serves a clear political purpose: to siphon energies that might be directed towards politics, and instead to redirect those to the educative project of the family. Families would seem to reduce the threat of insurrectionary households to the newly independent public authority of the state.

And indeed, women were a threat; as household "servants" they found natural allies with those in other economic classes, while in the street they made skillful use of rumor to disrupt. They contain the possibility of disrupting political order by reproducing it on deviant terms. Differently from Foucault, I argue that mapping roles of "mother" and "wife" onto women has political-economic, rather than primarily moral, consequences. It becomes, first, a means to divide men and women within families, and thus, second, to constrain the economic reach of sprawling middle-class households.[80] This constraint develops in two ways. First, the norms of *mesnagement* that allowed women to serve as exchangers gradually become replaced with commercial activity—and just as that activity becomes focused around commercial exchange.[81] Women's particular reproductive labor excludes them from participation in commercial exchange because this domestic labor does not hold exchange-value.[82] On the one hand, aspects of "care work"—through financial income, parenting, household management, sociability—are central to the reproduction of family relations. However, its nonmarket value confines women to the family and serves as the basis for their exclusion from politics and commercial activity. The family thus reproduces the exclusions—of women, children, and propertyless servants—at the heart of the modern social contract as well as the social war that fuels Foucault's account. It also consistently marks the contradictions and cover-ups of the contractual story. For example, by the mid-eighteenth century when marriage was no longer organized around dowries, lower-class women found themselves pushed into poorly paid industrial labor around weaving. They also found themselves in competition with convented women who engaged in the same work; their basic needs met by the church, they considered teaching and weaving to be welfare work of sorts. By 1849, working women had attacked several convents and burned their looms in response.[83] Efforts to convert the social existence of women into economic labor transformed existing networks of sociability into relations of competition stratified by class. Second, by rendering domestic labor as feminine, the possibility of an economic alliance between women and servants becomes precluded. Households come to cover over a number of major political fault lines.

However, the household's potency as a switch point of power remains latent. After all, household plays a pivotal role in managing the relations of attachment and detachment that characterize not just family members but the relations of the marginalized to community. Households, much like wage labor and incarceration, come to straddle the conjoinment of emerging states and markets. Their ostensible exclusion from politics, not unlike prisons, belies their centrality to modern political order. Their intermediary position—now they organize power from below, now they convey power from above—locates them both inside and outside politics and markets, and thus makes the precise nature of the family impossible to stabilize. As switch points of power, households become sites that refuse to resolve into any single framework. Much like the Creature in Mary Shelley's *Frankenstein,* they can be conclusively viewed neither as natural nor as conventional; neither as individualizing nor as communal; neither counter to the state nor fully integrated into it. As a result, households, and their female members especially, often find their activities both central to politics and market economies, and theorized as outside of them. This exclusion has been more systematically and thoroughly argued by Carole Pateman in *The Sexual Contract*.[84] My point here is simply to call attention to the *oscillation* between different frameworks of interpretation—one defined by a strategy of inclusion, the other by the need to resignify order—that distracts and divides those who would agitate for change. In particular, it allows the politics around moral education as well as changing definitions of property and inheritance to proceed relatively unscrutinized.[85] Materially, power rearticulates itself on political and economic terms that exclude women. Discursively, the retrospective naturalization of the family obscures its latent insurrectionary power. These comprise the political context for the play between women's figurative roles alternately as moralizing mothers *(mères-éducatrices)* or monstrous stepmothers *(marâtres)*. By contextualizing the household as a switch point of power, and women as exchanger figures, a different politics comes into focus. The debate no longer centers on women's agency and their inclusions or exclusions; it also moves beyond analysis of the modes of inscription that contour women's presence as either moralizing or monstrous. Instead, the political struggle lies in the mechanisms that manage the *oscillation* between these two.

Feminists have long called attention to both failures of universalist inclusion and the naturalization of woman and the family. They have not, however, considered the oscillation between the two to be a political challenge in its own right. In the eighteenth century, the problem was not that society was unaware of women's actions; society was all *too* aware of the labor, and surrounding ambivalence, of those who embodied "the excessively said."[86] Duchesne, clerk to the procurator general of the Parlement de Paris uses "excess" no less than eight times to describe his wife, Marguerite Gobet.[87] The criminality used to exclude female subjects is that of an *excès de la bouche* (gluttony; literally, excess of the mouth).[88] To reprise Foucault's terms, women conjoined political order and institutions not as "criminal-social enemies" but as "stepmotherly-social enemies." That is, women were those whose unnatural ways drew attention to the ultimately conventional inequalities—between husbands and wives, parents and children, or masters and servants—taken to be natural when founding sovereign order. These references to excess index trouble spots within conceptions of sovereign order and its reliance on claims to nature so as to define and exclude women. Their exclusion establishes women as a threat to sovereign order while obscuring their labor, care for the household, and reproductive activities—as well as the politics of the household. These excesses, like the practices of *mesnagement,* threaten to flood the embankments of customary practices that left some authority to popular judgment and community, if only in those areas where the sovereign looked away.[89] Women's labor and political presence rendered visible the inconsistencies of public order and justice.

Returning to the *lettres de cachet,* their usage can be seen to knit together power from above and power from below on precisely these material and symbolic dimensions. The public nature of their circulation makes the letters more than private reflections of interest; indeed, the very process of their writing—oral dictation, transcription and shaping according to epistolary convention by the scrivener, their corroboration through supporting letters, their delivery to officials—is a public, collaborative activity. They both outline a conception of "public order" and determine its order of signification—that is, whether "order" is one of security, economic sustenance, or something else. For example, when women write a letter against their husbands, they unwittingly determine how their husbands will be seen as acting against public order and exposed to its criminalizing logic. Or, in remaining silent, dismissing the police upon arrival, or asking to have the imprisonment reversed, women invoke the domain of the household and the primacy of its relations of economic care and reproduction. Simply put, encasing this letter writing are two visions of order: one that privileges the protection and physical security later associated with public authority, and the other that privileges economic survival of the household, later associated with the market. In this sense, households conceived as switch points of power determine which organizing logic and value domain will organize any particular event. For better or worse, those involved in this process wrestle to control the framing of these events and to settle claims to intimate justice (that is, matters of household care, reproduction, and economic survival).

The process also suggests that an alternate moral authority, located in popular judgment, might be sought to regulate claims to justice.[90] After all, the *lettres de cachet* functioned precisely in those areas where justice and public order did not coincide.[91] The letters offered families a way to regulate two areas of dispute—violence and disorderliness—that either did not rise to the level of criminal conduct or were not yet criminalized. They invoked "the site of the formation of a sort of consensus that asks power to respect its morality, order and regularity—the family, the corporation. These sites are exchangers between power from above and power from below."[92] By situating these sites as "fragments of social power" that *interpenetrate* the state, Foucault acknowledges both the effect of their structuring inequalities on political order and their potential for insurrection. Only later, and through the late-eighteenth-century consolidation of the household in the family, does the family become defined *against* public authority and in terms of a property that secures public order. Both redefinitions have powerfully limiting claims on the reach of justice and make it difficult to access and rework the ambivalent role of the household.

Within Foucault's own work, the political presence of the household is exactly what becomes analytically elided and historically covered over. This effect is partially the by-product of other choices Foucault makes as he seeks to upend other, often conservative, historical narratives. When writing *Discipline and Punish,* volume 1 of *History of Sexuality,* and *Disorderly Families,* Foucault notoriously skirts the French Revolution. It hovers at the margins of those texts but never is explicitly analyzed. Foucault's omission is deliberate. By framing *his* analysis around the political processes that precede, succeed, and exceed the Revolution, he both highlights their importance and sidesteps the framing effects of the Revolution. Instead, the shaping effects of various political processes—discipline, governmentality, confession, and avowal—come into view. These bridge institutions house the "exchangers" who mediate the material and symbolic registers of politics. Yet these processes themselves rest on the a priori exclusion of women from politics—an exclusion that becomes imported into Foucault's own analysis even as he remains attentive to the exclusions of others. Presuming that the family serves only to ease this transition from prison to couch is to ignore completely the dynamics of *mesnagement,* the threat women pose to political order, and a critique of the foreclosures that result.

Thus, I argue both with and against Foucault that these *lettres de cachet* offer new insight into the conditions that structure political agency. The legacy of these letters is to trace the process of social abstraction, whereby we move from the particularities of persons to the patterns taken to characterize a population, that currently *inhibit* political challenge by making it appear too distant and remote. Any contemporary challenge to political order would need to contest or supplant the symbolic and material power of the family form so as to politically charge the practices within patriarchal structures of domination.[93]

From the letters: "I believed that the public interest demanded that a man of this character be separated from civil society."—"[He] lives with a woman of ill repute who is dangerous in her talk."—"He is a bad subject who fears neither God, nor law."—"After such excesses, what is there the supplicant would not have reason to expect?"[94] Informants recorded other observations, to the incredulity of the police: "Paris is flooded with words, people are speaking loudly and openly; leaflets are scattered in the shops, people are stubborn in their opinions."[95] Paris was indeed awash in an excess of words and a tide of uncategorizable deeds. People were thinking, speaking, and acting, something that "was veritably against Nature."[96] Both in the eighteenth century and now, the *lettres de cachet* elevated everyday claims of injustice by challenging public authorities to respond. In some ways, the claim was a basic one for political subjects: to demand protection in the face of vulnerabilities too great to survive. With these challenges, however, came another: the challenge of redressing what are to become the alternately intrusive and dismissive incursions of public authorities into the lives of political subjects. At the heart of these conflicts lies the material and symbolic role played by women in navigating the threshold of household and politics. In bringing power from below into contact with power from above, women and the household served as "switch points of power" between different conceptions of public order as much as different economic domains. They are part of a political moment that reconsiders the authority of public opinion, the nature of property, and the relations between parents and children. At stake are no less than the values that will bear on "public" life.

These questions of value recenter how theorists have come to think of the family as a kind of symbolic form. If this symbolic form will later be predicated on repression of desire—male repression of the desire to sleep with the mother and kill the father—then the deliberate staging of primal scenes in these letters suggest that they, initially, played a different role in conjuring social imaginaries. Organized around relationships of attachment and detachment (where attachments are primarily economic and social), these family letters were caught in a conjuncture between two different models of public life. Ordinary people saw households as their affair to regulate and of no interest to sovereign authority. There was an enormous difference, in their eyes, between using the *lettres de cachet* to have wayward children arrested and the king's decision to use the police to round up young "vagrants." The mechanisms in both cases were the same—the police intervened in the name of public order—but the detainers of power and authority in the two cases, let alone the visions for public order, were quite different. The first model was defensive (and risked paternalism, if also oriented toward corporate interests), while the second was expansive (if premised on an exclusionary liberty). The letters invite us, then, to consider the conditions embedded in the creation of any new social imaginary that enable its elements to be more or less resistant. It matters less whether some group of social actors are taken to have agency; the more salient feature is the structural context of domination against which this agency struggles, and the capacity for people to tug, stretch, and distend these spaces so as to open them to new modes of governance. The mere existence and plurality of these imaginaries, however, does not automatically contribute to a conversation about power and its operations. The value of these imaginaries comes from narrating them back to politics. In the instance of the letters and their primal scenes, then, attention must return over and again to the confluence of material conditions and symbolic force as the mechanisms that shape these imagined spaces and anchor them in political order.

Stepping away from these letters, what do they tell contemporary readers? First, they remind readers of the perils of the representational trap—of reading the letters and trying either to attach them to a "more real" depiction of women or to read them as somehow representative of all approximately sixty thousand letters written in the Paris region or the one hundred thousand letters written across France. For all that Farge and Foucault's criteria of selection may seem arbitrary or unduly aesthetic, these criteria are also a refusal to universalize from an unavoidably fragmentary historical record and emphatically particular points of view. Writing in the same period, Monique Wittig likewise admonishes those who would universalize from the particular, and take a heterosexual social contract to be relevant and binding to all.[97] The challenge is not to "bring women back in" to this history;

it is instead to analyze the mechanisms of formal exclusion and the encasing practices that resist within and against these larger structures.

Second, and building on the work of Wittig and others, the letters demand attention less to protagonists with a presumably stable set of interests and instead speak to the regulatory mechanisms that unite, divide, and group these people. Rather than reading the letters as attesting to a clash between proto-proletariat and bourgeoisie, or between men and women, they should be read for the strategies they promote: namely, the use of policing, sexuality, and sex difference to modulate how power touches ordinary people to constrain, traumatize, and diminish. For all that sexuality, policing, and sex difference have become stable domains of inquiry, these domains are in a constant state of production and adaptation, and so rely on specifically positioned individuals—those "exchangers"—for that maintenance. Rather than turning to individuals—in this case, to women—with the expectation of finding a coherent set of ideologies, material interests, or social beliefs, these exchangers gain prominence for the role they play in knitting together material and symbolic. Their position is fundamentally ambivalent: as argued in the Introduction, they can trespass like guild mistresses into forbidden domains, or they can more tightly connect power and ordinary life like police and their informants.[98] Calling attention to such circulatory power means stepping away from claims about political consciousness; women writing to arrest their husbands in the name of public order were not wittingly trying to define a "public." Instead, the *act* of first composing and then sending a letter traced the emerging conduits of power that allowed for new conceptions of "public order" to circulate. This activity—seizing an old epistolary form to create new legal procedures of arrest—became a way to universalize a particular point of view, to paraphrase Monique Wittig. When considered against a resurgent, unstable popular opinion, these letters and other writings become more clearly seen as an appeal to an alternate source of authority and expertise on daily life. After all, the police came to *them* for information. The exchangers' power derives from their connection to different manifestations—legal, moral, natural, and so forth—of symbolic form that allows them to revise existing genres or improvise new ones. They were limited, however, in their ability to reflect collectively on how this unsteady, new authority might be brought back to politics.

As a result, and third, these letters attest to paradox that led popular efforts to demand "intimate justice" and state protection only to have those demands become the excuse for state violence. This paradox is doubly cruel. Initially, letter writers turned to police and monarchy for some reprieve and protection against family members who strained the bonds of the tolerable. The letters served as an invitation to think about the relations that obliged, protected, enabled, and shared—at their best, these relations organized communal life in a way that went beyond redistribution. Rather than seeking stability by expanding the purview of popular opinion—that is, by facilitating the authorization of popular subjects—the police instead sought to expand their own purview. Just as the wage-form and the prison-form became a means to siphon popular energies and to exchange time against power, so the family-form became a different kind of container. Women become confined to the home, and middle- and lower-class women become differentiated by whether they aid or live in "troubled homes" as defined by state institutions. The police as an administrative apparatus have the prerogative of regulating untoward intimacies—the intimate relations between those raced, sexualized, and gendered bodies who exceed the reproductive value of the heterosexual family. With the rendering of women's exchanger role as a stepmotherly-social enemy, women become seen as perpetrators, rather than victims, of violence.[99] Looking ahead to contemporary America, this burden will fall especially on African American women who are more exposed to the effects of poverty, incarceration, and state violence. In reporting domestic violence, charging sexual harassment, advocating for sexual freedom, or acting as feminist killjoys, women become responsible for failing to overcome "their circumstances." Failures of state institutions become naturalized as background circumstances, while women are rendered as unnatural subjects. Concurrently, these same actions—reporting domestic violence, charging sexual harassment, advocating for sexual freedom, or acting as feminist killjoys—effect an institutional labor no longer visible as such.[100] The interpenetration of the family, prison, and factory as three paradigmatic social forms is such that even as one comes into view, the others recede. Women are perched across all three; their work outside the home makes them absentee mothers, their motherhood makes them itinerant workers, while their impoverished families make them criminal.

Reading these letters thus recovers fragments—fragments of discourse not quite authorized, fragments of public life not yet legitimated, and fragments of spaces found in between public and household domains. The work of this essay has been to resist the temptations of integration and inclusion, and instead to examine how these philosophic shards work in their historical context. Such work illuminates the mechanisms—political, economic, and social—that take on the work of integration, administration, regulation, and exclusion central to political order. It also resists the impulse to see these mechanisms as determinate and seeks to recover the practices, counterclaims, and solidarities that push back against these mechanisms. Eighteenth-century households were hardly domains of pure resistance; they had their contradictions, complicities, and incoherences. Within these sites, however, they also sought to create some kind of redress from felt injuries and injustices. The primal scenes staged in the letters proved to engender fantasies that at once excited and excluded—they excited ordinary people to invite power and justice to bear on their daily lives, and then incited those in power to regulate this access and authority more intently. Conduits of mobility and circulation become rerouted and policed such that these activities become the containments of politics, and household concerns for poverty, violence, food insecurity, and household care disappear. So too disappears the participation of those witnesses to these scenes—those parish priests, upstairs neighbors, concierges, innkeepers, and notaries—whose desire to see and anxiety to judge requires its own regulation. More simply, the letters suggest that our first experiences of power and justice are those most proximate and ordinary; and that these same experiences of inequality, domination, and care for others should be the touchstone for claims to political redress and justice.

NOTES

1. Michel Foucault, "Lives of Infamous Men" (first chapter of this volume).

2. Carole Pateman, *The Sexual Contract* (Stanford, Calif.: Stanford University Press, 1988).

3. Arlette Farge, "L'Archive et l'histoire du social," presentation at the colloquium "L'Effetto Foucault," Milan, Italy, May–June 1985, document held at IMEC FCL 5.11. See also Michel Foucault, "Lives of Infamous Men," 158; Arlette Farge, "Souvenir d'un dérangement," *Le Magazine littéraire*, no. 435 (October 2004): 54; Arlette Farge, "On the Perception of the Intolerable," *Foucault against Himself*, interviews with François Caillat, trans. David Homel (Vancouver: Arsenal Pulp Press, 2015), 44.

4. Foucault, "Lives of Infamous Men," 76, 70. For a longer discussion of the language of dramaturgy and its implications, see the Introduction for this volume.

Gender, Agency, and Circulations of Power 333

5. Lynne Huffer offers a brilliant analysis of the art of "reading wounds" in her essay "Foucault's Rhythmic Hand" that also appears in this volume.

6. My approach in this essay directly speaks to the encounter between philosophers staged through the essays in this volume and by Foucault in his lifetime. By working with this concept of practices, I draw on philosophers Michel de Certeau and Foucault's later attention to relational practices of the self. This relationality has been further developed in the work of feminist theorists Jennifer Nedelsky and Joan Tronto. Likewise, the language of practices and representation has been developed by Roger Chartier and Arlette Farge, and further developed in recent works such as *Practicing New Historicism,* ed. Catherine Gallagher and Stephen Greenblatt (Chicago: University of Chicago Press, 2000). Political and representational practices have been admirably drawn together in works such as Jean Comaroff, *Body of Power, Spirit of Resistance* (Chicago: University of Chicago Press, 1985), and Saidiya Hartman, *Scenes of Subjection* (Oxford: Oxford University Press, 1997).

7. This conception of "intimate justice" draws on the work of Shatema Threadcraft and Beth Richie. Richie and Threadcraft are concerned to theorize the "arrested justice" or "intimate justice" that speaks to the daily experiences (of women and African Americans in particular) where public authority is, at best, in abeyance. Both thinkers challenge others to rethink justice from the perspective of the marginalized, and to hear the cry for justice as emanating from conditions not captured by right. See Shatema Threadcraft, *Intimate Justice* (Oxford: Oxford University Press, 2016); Beth Richie, *Arrested Justice: Black Women, Violence, and America's Prison Nation* (New York: New York University Press, 2012).

8. A number of French feminist theorists contemporary to Foucault theorized the nature and persistence of patriarchy, and have called varying attention to its materialist, gendered, and sexual dimensions. One of these studies, by Christine Delphy, originated in a dissertation on family property *(le patrimoine)* because her thesis director thought it impossible to study patriarchy. See Christine Delphy, *Close to Home,* trans. Diana Leonard (New York: Verso, 2016). For a critique of the heterosexual social contract, see Monique Wittig, *The Straight Mind and Other Essays* (Boston: Beacon Press, 1992).

9. Julie Hardwick, *The Practice of Patriarchy: Gender and the Politics of Household Authority in Early Modern France* (University Park: Pennsylvania State University Press, 1998). See also Suzanne Desan, "Making and Breaking Marriage," in *Family, Gender, and Law in Early Modern France,* ed. Suzanne Desan (University Park: Pennsylvania State University Press, 2009), 1–25.

10. Arlette Farge and Michel Foucault, *Disorderly Families: Infamous Letters from the Bastille Archive,* ed. Nancy Luxon, trans. Thomas Scott-Railton (Minneapolis: University of Minnesota Press, 2016), 34.

11. Arlette Farge, *Fragile Lives,* trans. Carol Shelton (Cambridge: Harvard University Press, 1995), 42.

12. Hardwick, *The Practice of Patriarchy,* 78–84, 97–98.

13. Farge and Foucault, *Disorderly Families,* 75.

14. Louis-Sebastien Mercier, cited in Farge, *Fragile Lives,* 23.

15. A longer discussion of *famille* can be found in the Introduction to this volume. The definition for *famille* is retrieved from the ARTFL database, cooperatively produced by the Centre National de la Recherche Scientifique (CNRS) and the University of Chicago. The entry can be retrieved at http://artflsrv02.uchicago .edu.ezp1.lib.umn.edu/cgi-bin/dicos/quickdict.pl?strippedhw=famille.

16. The classic text on family economies is Louis A. Tilly and Joan Wallach Scott, *Women, Work, and Family* (New York: Routledge, 1989 [1978]). Since then, more detailed studies have followed in its wake to chart regional and occupational variations, along with differences that result from marital status. See Hardwick, *The Practice of Patriarchy*; Karen Offen, *The Woman Question in France, 1400–1870* (Cambridge: Cambridge University Press, 2017); Daryl M. Hafter and Nina Kushner, eds., *Women and Work in the Eighteenth Century* (Baton Rouge: Louisiana State University Press, 2013); Julie Hardwick, *Family Business: Litigation and the Political Economies of Daily Life in Early Modern France* (Oxford: Oxford University Press, 2009).

17. Farge and Foucault discuss the space and sociability of the household at length in *Disorderly Families*, 126–29.

18. Ibid., 100.

19. Ibid., 103, 120.

20. Social and economic historians have written extensively on women's work (especially in the garment trade), guild membership, and identity. Notable texts include Hafter and Kushner, *Women and Work in the Eighteenth Century*; Nancy Locklin, *Women's Work and Identity in Eighteenth-Century Brittany* (Burlington, Vt.: Ashgate Publishing, 2007); Judith Coffin, *The Politics of Women's Work: The Paris Garment Trades, 1750–1915* (Princeton, N.J.: Princeton University Press, 1996); Christine Roulston, *Narrating Marriage in Eighteenth-Century England and France* (Burlington, Vt.: Ashgate Publishing, 2010); Sarah Maza, *Servants and Masters in Eighteenth-Century France: The Uses of Loyalty* (Princeton, N.J.: Princeton University Press, 1983). For an account that privileges patriarchal structures, see Clare Crowston, *Fabricating Women: The Seamstresses of Old Regime France, 1675–1791* (Durham, N.C.: Duke University Press, 2001).

21. Cynthia Truant, "Guildswomen of Paris: Gender, Power, and Sociability in the Old Regime," *Proceedings of the Annual Meeting of the Western Society for French History* 15 (1988): 130–38, 131.

22. Ibid., 133.

23. Locklin, *Women's Work and Identity in Eighteenth-Century Brittany*, 51.

24. Jacob D. Melish, "The Power of Wives: Managing Money and Men in the Family Businesses of Old Regime Paris," in Hafter and Kushner, *Women and Work in Eighteenth-Century France*; Clare Crowston, "Family Affairs," in Desan, *Family, Gender, and Law in Early Modern France*.

25. For an example of these resistances within asymmetrical power relations, see Cynthia Bouton, *The Flour War: Gender, Class, and Community in Late Ancien Régime French Society* (College Park: Pennsylvania State University Press, 1993), especially chapter 5.

26. Locklin, *Women's Work and Identity in Eighteenth-Century Brittany*, 15.

27. Ibid.

28. Carla Hesse, "Reading Signatures: Female Authorship and Revolutionary Law in France, 1750–1850," *Eighteenth-Century Studies* 22.3, The French Revolution in Culture (spring 1989): 469–87; Bouton, *The Flour War*; Arlette Farge, *Subversive Words: Public Opinion in Eighteenth-Century France*, trans. Rosemary Morris (University Park: Pennsylvania State University Press, 1995).

29. On divorce practices, see Giacomo Francini, "Divorce and Separations in Eighteenth-Century France: An Outline for a Social History of Law," *The History of the Family* 2.1 (1997): 99–113; and Julie Hardwick, "Seeking Separations: Gen-

Gender, Agency, and Circulations of Power   335

der, Marriages, and the Household Economies in Early Modern France," *French Historical Studies* 21 (1998): 157–80; Desan, "Making and Breaking Marriage."

30. Coffin, *The Politics of Women's Work*, 21.

31. Farge and Foucault, *Disorderly Families*, 87.

32. Ibid., 89.

33. Ibid.

34. Christine Delphy, "Rethinking Sex and Gender," *Women's Studies International Forum* 16.1 (1993): 1–9. For a contemporary reconsideration of Delphy's theoretical innovations, see Lisa Disch, "Christine Delphy's Constructivist Materialism: An Overlooked 'French Feminism,'" *South Atlantic Quarterly* 114.4 (October 2015): 827–49; Stevi Jackson, "Why a Materialist Feminism Is Still Possible—and Necessary," *Women's Studies International* 24.3/4 (2001): 283–93; and Clare Hemmings, "Telling Feminist Stories," *Feminist Theory* 6.2 (2005): 115–39.

35. Locklin, *Women's Work and Identity in Eighteenth-Century Brittany*, 3.

36. Joan Scott, "Gender: A Useful Category of Historical Analysis," *American Historical Review* 91.5 (December 1986): 1053–75.

37. Bound up in these conceptual questions about agency and gender are questions about how historians should proceed. French historians and their American counterparts have proceeded on parallel tracks but without much cross-pollination. Suzanne Desan examines French historiography and the transition from the structural *Annales* school, to lived experience, to "political culture." My work (and this volume) echo the French turn to social history, however, through the work of Jacques Revel, Roger Chartier, and Pierre Nora (and more recently Jean Boutier, Simona Cerutti, and Bernard Lepetit), which sidesteps these debates about agency and structure to examine instead networks of sociability that are irreducible to agents, economic interests, or ideological position. See Suzanne Desan, "What's after Political Culture? Recent French Revolutionary Historiography," *French Historical Studies* 23.1 (2000): 163–96. For the perspective of French historians, see Cécile Dauphin, Arlette Farge, Geneviève Fraisse, et al., "Women's Culture and Women's Power: An Attempt at Historiography," *Journal of Women's History* 1.1 (spring 1989): 63–88. To read more broadly on these interpretive issues, see Bernard Lepetit, "Histoire des pratiques, pratique de l'histoire," in *Les Formes de l'expérience: Une autre histoire sociale*, ed. Bernard Lepetit (Paris: Albin Michel, 2013 [1995]), 9–22; Simona Cerutti, "La Construction des catégories sociales," in Jean Boutier and Dominique Julia, *Passés recomposés: Champs et chantiers de l'Histoire* (Paris: Autrement, 1995), 224–34; and Simona Cerutti, "Normes et pratiques, ou de la légitimité de leur opposition," in Lepetit, *Les Formes de l'expérience*, 127–49; Jacques Revel, ed., *Jeux d'échelles: La Micro-analyse à l'expérience* (Paris: Gallimard-Le Seuil, collection Hautes Études, 1996). See also Gareth Stedman-Jones, "Historiographie française, historiographie anglaise: Une autre histoire sociale? (note critique)," *Annales: Histoire, sciences sociales* 53 (1998): 383–94. Jean Boutier, "Les Courtiers locaux du politique," *Annales historiques de la Révolution française* 66 (1994): 401–11.

38. The turn to practices here takes direct inspiration from Saidiya Hartman's discussion of those practices that encompass the legal subjectivity of slaves, in *Scenes of Subjection*, 51 and 61.

39. Michel Foucault, "The Subject and Power," in *Power: Essential Works of Michel Foucault, 1954–1984*, vol. 3, trans. Robert Hurley et al., ed. James Faubion

(New York: New Press, 2000), 330. See also Michel Foucault, "Nietzsche, Genealogy, History," in *Aesthetics, Method, and Epistomology, 1954–1984,* vol. 2, trans. Robert Hurley et al., ed. James Faubion (New York: New Press, 1998).

40. As Arlette Farge puts it in her reflections on the *Disorderly Families* project: "By putting conflict at the heart of social existence, and considering beginnings as a site of the disparate and disorderly, in defining a beginning by what is base and derisory, man is thus the subject who invents and constructs based on this disparate and disorderly" (Arlette Farge, *Des lieux pour l'histoire* [Paris: Éditions du Seuil, 1997], 39).

41. These possibilities are most clearly seen in the eighteenth-century grain riots that appealed to earlier communal privileges, as Foucault argues in *The Punitive Society: Lectures at the Collège de France, 1972–1973,* ed. Bernard Harcourt, trans. Graham Burchell (New York: Palgrave Macmillan, 2015). The four practices outlined derive from his analysis of these uprisings (28–31). As historian David Andress notes, those eighteenth-century appeals to community authority risked being "defensive and paternalist"; they are less appeals in the name of some as-yet-undefined freedom than a refusal of state intervention. See David Andress, "Neighborhood Policing in Paris from Old Regime to Revolution," *French Historical Studies* 29.2 (spring 2006): 231–60, 256–57. For other accounts that trace the push–pull of agency under conditions of domination, see Maza, *Servants and Masters in Eighteenth-Century France*; Comaroff, *Body of Power, Spirit of Resistance*; and Hartman, *Scenes of Subjection.*

42. Foucault, "The Subject and Power."

43. Although I'm sympathetic to a return to materialist politics, one of the aims of this essay is to resist distinctions between materialist, symbolic, and representational dimensions of politics—and to demonstrate their entanglements. Here I diverge from Clare Hemmings in her "Telling Feminist Stories."

44. Plate 1: engraving attributed to Pierre Alexandre Wille, *La Dénonciation chez l'écrivain public: Le décompte des griefs,* around 1780, Collection Viollet, Paris; Plate 24: engraving by Balthasar Anton Dunker, "La Lettre de cachet" for Louis-Sébastien Mercier, *Les Tableaux de Paris,* around 1783, Bibliothèque nationale de France.

45. The plates are organized by themes that correspond to those that group the letters: The Happiness of Couples, The Unhappiness of Families, Parents and Children, The Morality of Families, and Recourse to the King.

46. Jean-Jacques Rousseau, "Lettre to d'Alembert," in *The Collected Writings of Rousseau: Letter to d'Alembert and Writings for the Theater,* trans. and ed. Allan Bloom, Charles Butterworth, and Christopher Kelly (Lebanon, N.H.: UPNE, 2004), 332; Farge and Foucault, *Disorderly Families,* 69, 88–89.

47. Farge and Foucault, *Disorderly Families,* 126–27; *Punitive Society,* 192.

48. Carole Pateman, *The Disorder of Women: Democracy, Feminism, and Political Theory* (Stanford, Calif.: Stanford University Press, 1989), 18.

49. Farge and Foucault, *Disorderly Families,* 70.

50. Melish, "The Power of Wives," 81.

51. Louis Petit de Bachaumont writes these words in the context of an essay on various paintings shown at the Salon du Louvre on August 25, 1769. He goes on to describe this painting in particular as one that captures "the disorder of his [a father's] abandonment." See Louis Petit de Bachaumont, *Mémoires secrets pour server à l'histoire de la République des Lettres en France depuis 1762,* vol. 13 (London: John Adamson, 1780), 70.

Gender, Agency, and Circulations of Power 337

52. Emma Barker, *Greuze and the Painting of Sentiment* (Cambridge: Cambridge University Press, 2005), 12–13.

53. Janie Vanpée, "Jean-Baptiste Greuze: The Drama of Looking," *L'Esprit Créateur* 28.4 (winter 1988): 56.

54. Foucault, "Lives of Infamous Men," 80.

55. Ibid., 70.

56. Ibid., 78.

57. Biddy Martin, "Feminism, Criticism, and Foucault," *New German Critique* 27 (autumn 1982): 3–30, 13; emphasis added.

58. See Linda Zerilli, *Signifying Woman: Culture and Chaos in Rousseau, Burke, and Mill* (Ithaca, N.Y.: Cornell University Press, 1994); and Elizabeth Wingrove, *Rousseau's Republican Romance* (Princeton, N.J.: Princeton University Press, 2000).

59. Farge and Foucault, *Disorderly Families,* 65–66.

60. Foucault identifies those figures that move between "power from above" and "power from below" as exchangers, and describes this field of exchange as "the excessively said." Foucault, *The Punitive Society,* 37nβ.

61. Ibid., 31.

62. Ibid., 28–29.

63. Ibid., 31. As seen in the passage just quoted, these exchanger elements have five features: (1) the appropriation of power; (2) along with the reactivation of its earlier forms; (3) to effect a reversal of power relations; (4) followed by the reactivation of symbols into (5) a myth of power (29–30).

64. Ibid., 34. Foucault uses the same language in the next year of lectures, on *Psychiatric Power,* when he writes that the family "is the switch point, the junction ensuring passage from one disciplinary system to another, from one apparatus *[dispositive]* to another." See Michel Foucault, *Psychiatric Power: Lectures at the Collège de France, 1973–1974,* ed. Jacques Lagrange, trans. Graham Burchell (New York: Palgrave Macmillan, 2006), 81. These lectures contributed to material in vol. 1 of *The History of Sexuality* but the family was only ever discussed in terms of sexuality.

65. For a longer defense of this relationship of Foucault to Hegel, see the Introduction to this volume. Foucault's research for *Disorderly Families* contains notes on Hegel's *Philosophy of Right* and *Encyclopedia,* Marx's *Grundrisse,* as well as Jean Hyppolite's "La Conception hégélienne de l'État et sa critique par Karl Marx," *Cahiers Internationaux de Sociologie,* vol. 2 (January 1947): 142–61, 146; Bernard Quelquejeu's *La Volonté dans la philosophie de Hegel*; and Karl Mannheim's *Freedom, Power, and Democratic Planning,* among others (BNF-Richelieu, Fonds Michel Foucault, NAF 28730, Boîte 67).

66. Foucault discusses families only as subordinate moral technologies that facilitate the move toward disciplinary regimes of power. See *The Punitive Society,* 133–35, 230–31. His subsequent series of lectures, *Psychiatric Power,* indicates greater ambivalence. In the same lecture, Foucault claims both that within the family power "is not, as one usually says, disciplinary, but rather of the same type as the power of sovereignty" (79) and later that the family "is the hinge, the interlocking point, which is absolutely indispensable to the very functioning of all the disciplinary systems (81). More precisely, the family is the "entanglement of what could be called heterotopic relationships: an entanglement of local, contractual bonds, bonds of property, and of personal and collective commitments" (80).

67. Ibid., 71–72, 225–41.

338   *Nancy Luxon*

68. Christine Delphy makes these arguments first in *L'Ennemi principal,* vol. 1, *Économie Politique du Patriarcat,* 3d ed. (Paris: Éditions Syllepse, 2013 [1976]), and then in *Close to Home.*

69. Foucault's student Jacques Donzelot describes his own inquiry into the policing of families as "addressed to three main interlocutors, three forms of discourse whose contents, to say nothing of their implications, leave too many questions hanging, or reply with certainties too repetitious to be credible. I am referring to Marxists, feminists, and psychoanalysts." See Jacques Donzelot, *The Policing of Families,* trans. Robert Hurley (Baltimore: Johns Hopkins University Press, 1997 [1977]), 19. Feminists at the time engaged precisely these questions; see Juliet Mitchell, *Psychoanalysis and Feminism* (New York: Basic Books, 2000 [1974]). And doing so would further speak to Biddy Martin's argument that feminist materialists often neglect the material effects of psychosocial elements in "Feminism, Criticism, and Foucault."

70. Foucault defines this group in terms of their "lateral utility" to the ruling class. They are those "who do not necessarily belong to the ruling class or have the same interests, [and who] can [divert] a fraction of power and use it on their own account." Examples include "lawyers, village residents, tradespeople, craftsmen" as well as "families, religious groups, notables, legal people (notaries, and so on)" more broadly (*The Punitive Society,* 126, 127). Foucault uses the phrase "social entourage" *(l'entourage immédiat)* a few years later in *Society Must Be Defended: Lectures at the Collège de France, 1975–1976,* English series ed. Arnold Davidson, trans. David Macey (New York: Picador, 2003), 32.

71. Foucault, *The Punitive Society,* 34.

72. Ibid., 36.

73. Foucault notes that in addition to punishment, the letters "sometimes also [produce] movement, or prohibition to go to a place" (*The Punitive Society,* 129 n*).

74. Ibid., 131.

75. Farge and Foucault, *Disorderly Families,* 80–85.

76. Foucault's lectures for *Abnormal* focus on desire and family surveillance. At one point he notes that families from 1760 onwards become oriented toward marriage as a way to "get rid of all those servants and usual intermediaries who get in the way of, disturb, and upset your relationship with your children" (269). However, he doesn't pursue how these relationships specifically characterize women and the household. See Michel Foucault, *Abnormal: Lectures at the Collège de France, 1974–1975,* ed. Valerio Marchetti and Antonella Salomoni, trans. Graham Burchell (New York: Picador, 2003), 263–87.

77. Of course, these mechanisms are further complicated by the gender roles associated with family members and its regulations of sexuality.

78. Such attention to family attachments characterizes the object relations and relational schools of psychoanalysis. See Nancy Luxon, *Crisis of Authority: Politics, Trust, and Truth-telling in Freud and Foucault* (Cambridge: Cambridge University Press, 2013).

79. Joan Tronto makes a similar claim in *Moral Boundaries: A Political Argument for an Ethic of Care* (New York: Routledge, 1993).

80. Again, Foucault misses an opportunity to argue such points in his lectures for *Abnormal.* He notes that few poor families eschew marriage, likely because "marriage was linked to a system of property exchange. In any case it was linked to the maintenance or transformation of social status" (269). However, Foucault does not analyze the specific effects of property exchange on women.

Gender, Agency, and Circulations of Power 339

81. As noted earlier, women did own property; however, William Sewell has argued that they were often perceived to own property in feudal privilege. Thus, their demands to expand this ownership were understood as efforts to move up within social stratification. As definitions of property changed over the eighteenth century and became attached to labor on products with exchange-value, women's labor and property ownership failed to be recognized as such. See William Sewell, *Work and Revolution in France: The Language of Labor from the Old Regime to 1848* (Cambridge: Cambridge University Press, 1980), especially 114–42.

82. Contemporaneous to Foucault, Christine Delphy argues this point in chapters 4 and 5 of *Close to Home.*

83. Donzelot, *The Policing of Families,* 36–39. Foucault writes about similar "factory-convents" in *The Punitive Society,* 201–10.

84. Pateman, *The Sexual Contract,* especially 72–77; Pateman, *The Disorder of Women.*

85. Sewell, *Work and Revolution in France,* especially 114–42.

86. Foucault writes that the exchanger element "is not the unsaid; it is the more-than-said. The excessively said" (*The Punitive Society,* 37nβ).

87. Duchesne further uses "disorder" three times, and versions of "debauchery" five times, to describe his wife's action when consorting with the wigmaker Donis. See Don Herzog, "The Trouble with Hairdressers," *Representations* 53 (winter 1996): 21–43.

88. The charge of *excès de la bouche* indicates gluttony of food and drink; similar metaphors of intestinal disorder are used to characterize those women who "vomit up insults" and other calumnies. See Farge and Foucault, *Disorderly Families,* 70, 110.

89. In his preparatory notes, Foucault writes: "Thus appears a process which was important: the movement by which families acquired the habit of resolving certain of their most intense conflicts, there where the authority proper to their internal hierarchy was powerless, and when recourse to ordinary justice was neither possible nor desirable. A demand chasing a form" (BNF-Richelieu, Fonds Michel Foucault, NAF 28730, Boîte 67, poche 7, 10).

90. In his preparatory notes for *Disorderly Families,* Foucault notes that families and officials came to the letters from two different perspectives: "Both shared the desire to short-circuit judicial intervention, thought to be excessive for matters of honor and ineffective for matters of order. And these perspectives came into agreement insofar as, from the administrative point of view as much as the public one, family honor increasingly defined itself by the respect one shows for good order in general. Thus elaborated, across these practices of coercion and others, a sort of conception of 'civic' honor" (BNF-Richelieu, Fonds Michel Foucault, NAF 28730, Boîte 68, poche 6, 11–12).

91. Consonant with this argument, the letters in *Disorderly Families* touch on the same relations of inequality between husbands and wives, parents and children, as well as masters and servants. These are the same relationships addressed by Locke in the *Second Treatise* as he attempts to square the equality of a hypothetical state of nature with the inequalities found in "the beginnings of political society" (John Locke, *Two Treatises of Government,* ed. Peter Laslett [Cambridge: Cambridge University Press, 1988], §77).

92. Foucault, *The Punitive Society,* 131.

93. Indeed, feminists contemporary to Foucault—notably Christine Delphy, Monique Wittig, and Juliet Mitchell—argued just that. Delphy argues that more

340   *Nancy Luxon*

attention needs to be devoted to "the material basis for the articulation of the antipatriarchy struggle and the anticapitalist struggle." In citing relations between husbands and wives as the antagonistic basis for struggle, she suggests that these relationships serve as an important hinge, much like the ligaments that at once bind and enable the articulation of a joint. Wittig argues that not only is the social contract exclusionary, it is deeply heterosexual; grappling with its gendered and sexualized relations is unavoidable for political change. Finally, Mitchell argues that theorists ought tend to the psychosocial dimension of kinship and marriage relations. See Christine Delphy, "The Main Enemy," *Feminist Issues* 1 (1980): 23–40, 832; Wittig, *The Straight Mind and Other Essays*; and Mitchell, *Psychoanalysis and Feminism.*

94. From Farge and Foucault, *Disorderly Families*, 93, 63, 195, 62.

95. From an informant report to the police; quoted in Farge, *Subversive Words,* 24.

96. Ibid., 25.

97. Wittig, "On the Social Contract," and "The Point of View: Universal or Particular?" in *The Straight Mind and Other Essays,* 33–45 and 59–67.

98. Something of this duality remains today. In his work on poverty governance, Joe Soss has analyzed the extent to which social-services workers have internalized their institutional perspective; by contrast, Jamila Michener has noted how the circulations of African American female caregivers alter access to services such as Medicaid. See Joe Soss, *Disciplining the Poor: Neoliberal Paternalism and the Persistent Power of Race* (Chicago: University of Chicago Press, 2011); Jamila Michener, *Fragmented Democracy: Medicaid, Federalism, and Unequal Politics* (Cambridge: Cambridge University Press, 2018).

99. Beth Richie makes this argument in *Arrested Justice* (see page 7 for the specific language of perpetrators). By reading women as "exchangers," the historical account for this moral rhetoric of black women as "the ultimate other" becomes more clear (7); my reading also sketches the basis for a theoretical account of the interpenetration of prison-, factory-, and family-forms.

100. For more on the institutional labor of "diversity issues," see Sara Ahmed, *Living a Feminist Life* (Durham, N.C.: Duke University Press, 2017).

CHAPTER 13

Foucault's Rhythmic Hand

Lynne Huffer

*Lynne Huffer pushes concerns for gender, sexuality, and episto-
lary practice forward into the domain of queer theories and histories. Drawing on Eve Kosofsky Sedgwick, Huffer takes seriously
Foucault's claim that these letters are "poem-lives." Huffer reads
these letters as poems and as scars to uncover their oblique violence
that escapes beyond the limits of representation. As scars, these
letters are points of contact and redirection: contact between sovereign and intimate violences, contact between the celebrated and
the infamous, and contact between past and present. As poems,
the truncation and startlement that the letters provoke invite and
demand a redirection of interpretive energies. Huffer finds that
Foucault, like Sedgwick, engages in poetic practice to interrupt the
coherence of history and subjectivity. For Huffer, these letters thus
bear witness to the "queer affinities" that enable a rearrangement
of the archive at the very basis for queer thought.* ➤

In *Discipline and Punish,* Foucault situates the "birth" of the human
sciences in relation to what he calls the "ignoble archives":[1] the result of
"procedures of writing that made it possible to integrate individual data
into cumulative systems" (190). "For a long time," Foucault writes,
"ordinary individuality—the everyday individuality of everybody—
remained below the threshold of description" (191). But with the advent of disciplinary methods, the practice of "turning real lives into
writing" moved away from the heroization of nobles and kings to
procedures that objectified and subjected ordinary people, many of
whom were poor and illiterate (192). Over the course of the eighteenth

342 *Lynne Huffer*

century, the written *fama* of the privileged was reversed into an apparatus for tracking the *infamous* by writing down "the carefully collated life of mental patients or delinquents" (ibid.). The infamy of lives pinned down in their particularity characterizes a new modality of power bound up with the invention of the human sciences.

As a "genealogy of the modern 'soul,'" *Discipline and Punish* tracks the emergence of that new modality of power through the production of new knowledges that draw on "the root 'psycho'" "to invent, study, and objectify human interiority (29, 193). With the "formation of disciplinary society," Foucault writes, comes the invention of the psychological sciences and the production of the mental patient as "a 'case'" (192), Thus the shift from *fama* to infamy also marks "the passage from the epic to the novel, from the noble deed to the secret singularity, from long exiles to the internal search for childhood, from combats to phantasies," from *"Le bon petit Henri"* to "little Hans," from "Lancelot" to "Judge Schreber" (193, 194).

I begin with this shift from the "'ascending' individualization" of sovereign power to the "'descending' individualization" of Freudian cases as a way to frame this essay's exploration of the archives of infamy through the lens of Foucault's much-debated relation to psychoanalysis (193). In my reading, the disorderly families we find in the archival *lettres de cachet de famille* function as a hinge where, as Foucault writes in *Discipline and Punish,* "the normal [takes] over from the ancestral" (ibid.). The disorderly family of the *lettres de cachet* signals a historical unraveling, a shift from one modality of power to another. Indeed, the queer disorderly family of the *lettres de cachet* anticipates the moment of reversal from aristocratic blood into the "reversed and somber escutcheon" *(blason inversé)*[2] of the nineteenth-century family threatened by degeneration in *History of Sexuality,* volume 1, where the family functions as the "switch point" *(échangeur)* between ancestral alliance and the proliferating perversions of our incestuous modern Freudianism.[3]

What are we to make of this archival moment? In bringing out the queerness of the eighteenth-century *lettres de cachet de famille,* I bring into view an archival relation between Freud and Foucault that allows us to discern strange affinities between them. Or, more precisely, the archives of infamy where we encounter these queer, incongruous, tragicomic letters bear witness to affinities between Freudian psychoanalysis and the Foucauldian genealogies that make us, and our Freudian archive, strange. I explore affinity, then, as a poetic invitation to rethink Freud and Foucault together, beyond queer theory's amalgamating "scavenger methodology."[4]

In doing so, I argue that the poetic shift from queer Freudo-Foucauldianism's logic of blending to an alternative logic of psychoanalytic-genealogical affinity can open queer thought to a rearrangement of the archive that allows us to think at all. If, as Foucault argues, the archive names the limits of our thinking, what better way to think those limits than through the lens of affinity? Affinity's etymology brings the limit into focus. From the Latin *finis*—border or boundary—affinity literally means bordering on. As a thinker of limits, Foucault was obsessed with borders and boundaries. Following Bataille, he describes the limit not as a preexisting line whose bounds one either obeys or violates (like an imaginary border dividing Freud from Foucault).[5] Rather, for Foucault the limit *is* the relation. Crucially, that limit is unstable. Foucault sometimes calls that instability transgression: the limit's transgression is not the crossing of a line that was already there but a confrontation or contestation that suspends the line and thereby rearranges the relation. (Thus a Freud–Foucault affinity would rearrange the relation rather than violating a no-Freud-with-Foucault rule already in place.) From this perspective, affinity is a quintessentially Foucauldian term. Despite its nonetymological associations with sympathy or resemblance, affinity's etymology charges it with the diffusive tension of borders. Those borders determine what we are able to think.

How, then, might we track the strange affinities between Freud and Foucault? In *Mad for Foucault* I examined Foucault's story in *History of Madness* about the rise of the sciences of the psyche (a story that, in many ways, anticipates *Discipline and Punish* in its genealogy of the soul as psyche). In his history of reason's "merciless language" about a madness it both excludes and captures, Foucault includes Freudian psychoanalysis within a rationalist tradition, but with a difference.[6] Specifically, Foucault tells a story about Freudian rationalism as a return to Descartes. Like Descartes, Freud excludes the mad from the cogito, not directly, but through what Foucault calls "the sovereign violence of a *return*": "*la violence souveraine d'un* retour" (339, emphasis in the original; 360). But what does this mean exactly?

In *History of Madness,* the doctor-analyst becomes a despot who transforms the moral negativity of those excluded as mad into the

344 *Lynne Huffer*

objectified positivity of a scientific content. Foucault's genealogy of madness shows that in the place of a psychoanalytic dialogue that would free the mad at the end of the nineteenth century, there is only the meaningless blank of a split that continues to divide doctor from patient: "in the between-two, nothing, a void" (205). The supposedly liberated language of the analysand is, in fact, a "caged freedom"; it draws its speech from the void of a mid-seventeenth-century Great Confinement that reduced the mad to silence and elaborated, in their place, a thaumaturgical language of magician-doctors (436). When the mad finally speak as Freud's patients at the end of the nineteenth century, the madness they speak is a ventriloquism of reason's speech. Thus, Foucault writes: "psychoanalysis cannot and will never be able to hear the voices of unreason nor decipher on their own terms the signs of the insane" (511). This has profound implications for queer theory as an incitement to speak about sex: queer theorists sometimes call on psychoanalytic discourse to claim queer speech as what Foucault calls a "'reverse' discourse"[7]—speech about sex—as a mode of resistance to the medical pathologization of sexual deviance. But in highlighting a dialectical logic that links Freud to Descartes, Foucault shows how the deviant sexuality released from the unconscious by the talking cure—that queer "'reverse' discourse" *("discours 'en retour'")*[8]—is a manifestation of a violent return *(retour)* to a sovereign rationalist power: the advent of a cogito that excludes the mad.

Given this story about Freudian speech as a violent ventriloquism of reason's madness, why pursue a poetics of affinity here? Foucault's worries in *History of Madness* about the sovereign violence of a Freudian return to the classical age contrasts, sharply, with his more well-known claims in *Discipline and Punish* about the soul—psyche as the Greek *psuche*—as the primary target not of sovereign violence but of disciplinary power—soul as prison of the body, soul as the target of a supposedly more humane, less violent modern power. This is why he opens with the spectacular scene of Damiens's torture and corporeal annihilation: modern power is not that. Might the strange affinities between Freud and Foucault open new perspectives on how to think about the sovereign violence of return—of the sovereign-subject/dominated-object, empirico-transcendental doublet he calls the analytic of finitude in *The Order of Things*?[9] Might those perspectives challenge a mode of repetition that gives us "man" by doubling the past in the present, what Foucault calls in "Madness, the Absence of an Oeuvre" the violence of a sovereign dialectic where "man" is alienated only to return: to become familiar to himself once more?[10] Might the strange archival affinities between Freud and Foucault help us to think the violence of the past through a *"dedialectizing"* mode of self-doubling that hollows out the present, refusing the consolations of the familiar?[11] Crucially, might queer poetics have something to offer to help us work through these questions?

As we can see, Foucault's term—return/*retour*—opens difficult questions about history. More specifically: does history as a question signal a crucial distinction between psychoanalytic and genealogical methods? Or does a dedialectizing return of the past in the present offer a way to think Freud and Foucault together? Finally, might a queer perspective on these returns of violence and return itself as violent open up larger ethical questions about violence in the present? To answer these questions about archival affinities between Freud and Foucault I begin with an explication of history in Foucault through the lens of what he calls the historical a priori. Drawing on Foucault's *Archeology of Knowledge* and his 1977 essay "Lives of Infamous Men," I offer a literary-philosophical perspective on the historical a priori, the archive, and Foucault's poetic thinking: what I call his rhythmic hand to capture the stylistic qualities of his work in the archives of infamy. Next, I revisit the question of strange affinities between Freud and Foucault by exploring temporality through the queer-poetic lens Eve Kosofsky Sedgwick gives us in "A Poem Is Being Written," her 1986 rewriting of Freud's 1919 essay "A Child Is Being Beaten." Taken together, Freud, Foucault, and Sedgwick expose the obliquity of violence as a queer ethical problem in the present. Like our perception of the relay between the unfamiliar violence of the classical sovereign and the all-too-familiar, intimate violences of modern families exposed in the *lettres de cachet,* something is transmitted through that obliquity even as that something cannot be captured. What we find in the archives are the remains of violence—letters, ashes, dried flowers, bits of cloth. "I feel cloth under my fingers," Arlette Farge writes: these "scraps of lives dredged up from the depths wash up on shore before your eyes."[12] On that shore—the archives of infamy—we touch the chance events that brought the lives to us, but only obliquely, as scars.

346 *Lynne Huffer*

A History That Startles

In a 2016 exchange with Nancy Luxon in *Contemporary Political Theory,* I returned to the question of Foucault's relation to psychoanalysis I had first examined in *Mad for Foucault.*[13] In that exchange, I asked about what we might see as a contrast between Foucault's genealogical attention to historical contingency and the seemingly ahistorical structures of psychoanalysis. And while that distinction certainly deserves our attention, I also want to suggest that there is something too neat and dualistic about the historical/ahistorical opposition undergirding the simple claim that psychoanalysis suffers from a lack of history. Indeed, in using a term—"historical a priori"—that itself articulates, impossibly and contradictorily, exactly the historical/ahistorical opposition, Foucault might be asking us to pay attention to our own unthinking reliance on such dualisms.[14] The subtle exposure of the dualism comes in the form of a paradox: historical a priori. If the a priori is transcendental, a template of order that is not contingent, how can that a priori be historical and therefore contingent?[15] Foucault himself calls the juxtaposition of historical with a priori "startling."[16]

Crucially, the startling effect of "historical" with "a priori" as a conceptual term is inextricably linked to Foucault's genealogical method: an explicitly archival practice of thinking-feeling. Indeed, the startle response is one of the affects Foucault mentions when he describes his experience in the archive. This language of affect is especially palpable in "Lives of Infamous Men." Our archive of infamy is both the epistemic ground and the material site of a historical a priori that startles. The startle response is an affective experience of knowing—an affective form of experience inhabited by thought—in the archival encounter with the alterity of a time that is not our own.[17] Jostled by the startle of thinking-feeling in the archive, we can return to the question that drives this essay: might there be strange affinities between Freudian psychoanalysis and the Foucauldian genealogy that touches the archive of our Freudianism? Many have argued that what distinguishes Foucault from other philosophers is his archival, historical method. But we move too fast if we leave it there. As Foucault himself puts it: "I am not a professional historian: nobody is perfect."[18]

Foucault's paradoxical status as a nonhistorical or ahistorical or antihistorical historian informs his conception of the stuff of history:

the archive. In *The Archeology of Knowledge,* Foucault writes, startlingly: "it is not possible for us to describe our own archive, since it is from within these rules that we speak . . . The archive cannot be described in its totality."[19] And yet, he continues, the archive, "in its actual existence *[actualité]* . . . is unavoidable *[incontournable]*."[20] If excavation of our own archive is the condition of history writing, what kind of a history is this, one where we cannot describe our own archive whose actual existence is unavoidable?

In "Lives of Infamous Men" Foucault returns to the archives of madness that he encountered in writing his *History of Madness* fifteen years earlier. But we already know, after reading *History of Madness,* that the language of madness—what we find in the archive—is a ventriloquism of reason. It is helpful to recall what Foucault wrote about Freud in *History of Madness*: "psychoanalysis cannot and will never be able to hear the voices of unreason nor decipher on their own terms the signs of the insane."[21] Here we can rethink that admittedly provocative claim as it relates to the archive: *the historian cannot and will never be able to hear the voices of unreason nor decipher on their own terms the signs of the insane.* As the thinker of a past alterity redeployed to tell a story about the present, Foucault is Freud in his return to the archive: in this sense, in "Lives of Infamous Men" and throughout his work, Foucault risks repeating what he called the sovereign violence of a Freudian return. The historian encounters strangeness in the form of archival fragments only to make those fragments familiar to us.

But, as an ahistorical historian, Foucault wants to resist this movement of refamiliarization. Thus Foucault's experience of the archive is not historical in that dialectical sense. Indeed, the language of "Lives of Infamous Men" is hyperbolically affective and experiential. "This is not a book of history," Foucault writes in the first line of the essay. "The selection found here was guided by nothing more substantial than my taste, my pleasure, an emotion, laughter, surprise, a certain dread, or some other feeling whose intensity I might have trouble justifying, now that the first moment of discovery has passed."[22] Foucault enters the archive as a poet. As a poet, he comes to "know" the present through contact with the past in an experience of strangeness that renders the familiar unintelligible: the archive makes him feel the startlingly unfamiliar edges of our own time.

This is why Foucault writes in *The Archeology of Knowledge* that "the threshold of [the archive's] existence is installed by the cut that separates us from what we can no longer say."[23] We can only describe our own time from the perspective of "the border of time that surrounds our present, which overhangs it, and which indicates it in its alterity."[24] This is what it means, in Foucauldian terms, to write a history of the present: to write not in order to stabilize the present as knowable, as the past finding its "victory" in us, but to write toward the present's dispersion into "that which, outside ourselves, delimits us."[25] That limit is the edge of the poet's cut into the archive.[26] The archive deploys its possibilities "on the basis of the very discourses that have just ceased to be ours"; it "releases us from our continuities [elle nous déprend de nos continuités]"[27]; it dissipates that temporal identity in which we are pleased to look at ourselves [as a way to] to exorcise [conjurer] the ruptures of history.[28] The archive establishes the break, cut, or limit between us and what we are not; at the same time, it makes us coextensive with that limit as other, what Foucault calls "the Other in the time of our own thought."[29] In poetry, the relation between that cut and that coextension is called *enjambment*: "the poetic gesture of straddling lines together syntactically, but also a pushing apart of lines" that Sedgwick will associate with the beat(ing) of a poem.[30]

If we freeze the psyche and the unconscious as timeless structures—the a priori—we deny the dissolving effect of time passing and the sheer alterity of the past—the historical. To the extent we understand ourselves (as Freudian), it is because of a borrowing of the language and modes of intelligibility of another time. But that self-understanding is built on a dialectical logic that renders the strange familiar. Precisely because we cannot describe our own archive, we cannot know ourselves, except in our coextension with what we are not, living as enjambment: straddling a strange space we cannot comprehend but whose limits define us. This is how history and the archive can surprise us, make us tremble or laugh or fill us with dread: as poets of the present, we can live into the startle of the archive.

The Child's Behind

"'A Child Is Being Beaten'" (1919) is Freud's attempt to comprehend beating fantasies reported by some of his neurotic patients. In the essay he uses psychoanalysis to explain how the adult fantasy of a child being beaten "has feelings of pleasure attached to it" that eventually produce "auto-erotic satisfaction" and masochistic perversion.[31] At the heart of the essay lies the mechanism of repression and the production of the unconscious; in his three-phase explanation of the beating fantasies recounted by his patients, it is the second or unconscious phase—one only accessed as a construction of analysis—that is the "most important" (185). The first phase, which is neither masochistic nor sadistic, describes the patient's conscious memory of another child—a brother or a sister—being beaten by the father: it can be summarized, Freud says, by the sentence "'My father is beating the child *whom I hate*'" (ibid.; emphasis in the original). With the entry into the Oedipus complex, that phase gives way under the force of repression to a regressive and guilt-driven debasement of genital organization to the earlier, sadistic-anal phase. The beating fantasy associated with this second, unconscious phase is masochistic and highly pleasurable; here, the one being beaten is no longer another child but the one who is the author of the fantasy. The sentence Freud offers to describe this phase is "'*I am being beaten by my father*'" (ibid.; emphasis in the original). Finally, the third phase, consciously remembered like the first, is marked by a series of substitutions: the child being beaten becomes other children, the father becomes a teacher or other authority figures, and the one phantasizing looks on "almost as a spectator" (190). The pleasures associated with this phase are sadistic in their form and masochistic in their satisfaction.

Freud uses the beating fantasy to explain how neuroses emerge out of infantile sexuality and the Oedipus complex. As Freud puts it: "the Oedipus complex is the actual nucleus of neuroses, and the infantile sexuality which culminates in this complex is the true determinant of neuroses" (193). Freud describes the beating fantasy and "other analogous perverse fixations" as "scars" left behind in the unconscious "after the process has ended" (ibid.).

Two points are relevant to my reading of Freudo-Foucauldian affinities here. First, Freud shows how spectacles of violence are mediated through fantasy. Indeed, most of the patients who fantasized the beatings were not beaten themselves; further, while some had witnessed the beating of others with a mixture of pleasure and revulsion, many found the act of witnessing a real beating to be "intolerable" (180). This perspective on violence mediated through fantasy undergirds Foucault's conception of historical violence as well: the violence

350 *Lynne Huffer*

of the dialectic is, in part, the violence of historical return as a mediating or masking mechanism. Second, Freud's description of those fantasies as "scars" suggests that the beatings have left traces to be read or interpreted (193). But how might we read them? If Foucault is a poet, that means he reads in ways that differ dramatically not only from the empirical methods of positivists, be they psychologists or historians, but also from the conceptual generalizations of philosophers.

How *do* we read scars? Here queer theorist Eve Kosofsky Sedgwick offers a method of poetic reading to open ways of thinking-feeling the archival startle of our violent Freudo-Foucauldian present. Specifically, in "A Poem Is Being Written" (1985), Sedgwick narrates her own queer poetic practices within the frame of her childhood memories of another child—a sibling less obedient than she—being spanked. At age thirty-six, within "the theatre of this family" that are her childhood memories, Sedgwick returns to poems she wrote as a child, with a special focus on a long narrative poem called "The Warm Decembers" she began at the age of nine and which, twenty-seven years later ("twenty-seven years late," she says) in 1985, she is still in the process of writing.[32] She calls the poem her "sulky problem child," a child to be punished who conjures images of ritualized family violence: a torso folded over a lap that, in Sedgwick's mind, transmogrifies into a trunk, truncated, "over a table" (178, 183). This "imaginative contraction" of the child body being punished is an image of the genre of the lyric poem—the poetic form that exults the "I"—as a spanked, framed, headless body over a table (183). Sedgwick insists on "the importance of French in this story": not table as table but as *tableau* (ibid.). In Sedgwick's imagination, the tableau is scaled precisely to the trunk of the child: that "small, bounded, and violence-inscribed torso" (196) comes to define, for her, the words *tableau* and *truncate* (from the Latin *truncates,* to cut off):

> While I know we were always spanked, in a careful orchestration of spontaneity and pageantry, "simply" over the parental lap, the spanking in my imagination (I can only barely stop myself from saying, the spanking that *is* my imagination) has always occurred over a table, a table scaled precisely to the trunk of the child, framing it with a closeness and immobilizing exactitude that defined, for me, both the English word *truncate* and the French, of course, *tableau.* (183; emphasis in the original)

This contracted, cut-off, theatrical, poetic space is a beat and a beating, a rhythmic "tableau of the beaten child" (197). In Sedgwick's hands, the beat of the lyric is both subject and object of the beating: both the spanked body and the spanking rhythm of the hand writing. Focusing specifically on the child's behind—as Freud puts it, "a small child is being beaten on its naked bottom"—Sedgwick links the behind to a leakage of meaning inextricably linked to the behind as past (181). "One has, . . . behind one, by this time," she writes, "something significant: the place that is signally not under one's ocular control" (199). In signaling our literal inability to see our own backside in her invocation of "the two-sidedness of the insulted body," Sedgwick offers us "a more than latent image of [that body's] necessary temporality" (ibid.).

Might Sedgwick's headless, bare-bottomed lyric give us some insight into what Foucault calls, so strangely, the "poem-lives" he finds in the archives of madness?[33] Might we find in Foucault, in his affinity with that Freudian beat, what Sedgwick finds in her own rhythmic writing-as-spanking: an encounter with poem-lives as the lyric, dedialectizing contraction of violence? When Foucault returns to the archives of infamy he used to write *History of Madness,* what he finds there are "ashes" and dried plants in an "herbarium": the "scars" of history's *petits fous*[34] "marked" by the "claw" of sovereign power.[35] Foucault's sodomite monks and feebleminded usurers are lyric contractions—cuts in the archive that pierce "the dilated space" of the massive narrative *histoires* that surround them.[36] Foucault, like Sedgwick, is engaged in a rhythmic poetic practice that interrupts the seeming coherence of the self and the present. Like "A Poem Is Being Written," which I now want to call Sedgwick's "poem life," Foucault's poem-lives are both subject and object of a beating, both spanked body and spanking hand. As in Freud's essay, the meaning we might attach to these scars of violence is unstable: in Freud it shifts from rival sibling to the authorial "I" to anonymous "whipping boys" or even fictional characters from Madame de Ségur to *Uncle Tom's Cabin.*[37] As Freud puts it: "the child began to compete with these works of fiction by producing his own phantasies."[38]

Importantly, all three essays—Freud's, Foucault's, and Sedgwick's—insist that the spanking rhythm of violence can hardly lead us to the source of that violence in order to heal it. Rather, the rhythm itself—a kind of violence—inscribes a self-doubling play of misrecognitions that

352 *Lynne Huffer*

hollow out their meaning. Sedgwick's 1974 poem "The Palimpsest," embedded within her essay "A Poem Is Being Written," tells "how puckered, long-healed, horizontal scars/were found in that place by the impassive coroner—/ . . . In fact the scars don't answer to the wounds."[39] So too with Foucault and the startle of the archive as a site of violence. "It would be hard to say exactly what I felt when I read these fragments," Foucault writes in "Lives of Infamous Men."[40] Lives "destined to pass away without a trace," they return to us in their "infamy," Foucault writes:

> Lives that are as though they hadn't been, that survive only from the clash with a power that wished only to annihilate them or at least to obliterate them, lives that come back to us only through the effect of multiple accidents—these are the infamies that I wanted to assemble here in the form of a few remains . . . The apostate friar, the feeble minds lost on unknown paths, those are infamous in the strict sense: they no longer exist except through the terrible words that were destined to render them forever unworthy of the memory of men. And chance determined that these words, these words alone, would subsist. The return of these lives to reality occurs in the very form in which they were driven out of the world.[41]

Foucault's poem-lives return in the form of words: not as evidence for the elaborations of a story or as cases to support a generalizable diagnosis or as particular examples that would serve to illustrate larger philosophical claims. They are "flash existences" that come to us only because they were struck down by power.[42] Their return in the real—as fragments in an archive—happens in the same *truncated* form in which they were expunged from the world: as rarity, as flash, as contracted bodies over tables *(tableaux),* as what Foucault calls "the frugal lyricism of citation."[43]

Sedgwick's idiosyncratic reading of the Freudian beating fantasy brings out the repeated ruptures of history's violences, but refuses to sublate them as a present meaning for us. Rather, she brings out the rhythm of a Freudian archive that shakes us up: that startles. Sidestepping Freud, the affect theorist Silvan Tomkins might characterize that queer experience of our own Freudian archive as an intensification of the affect of surprise: Tomkins calls "the startle response" the "interrupter," the "circuit breaker," an "involuntary massive contraction of the body—eyebrows up, eye blink."[44] Too often confused with the affect that follows it—fear following the sound of a gunshot, for example—startle shakes up our present by interrupting it and refusing the consolations of narrative connections that would make us recognizable to ourselves. Startle is, rather, the affect we might associate with the poetic cut: the cut into the archive, the cut at the end of the line. The "high point" of a knowledge made for cutting, poetry becomes narrative's circuit breaker, a counterviolence that dedialectizes history.[45]

Foucault's rhythmic hand is the hand of a poet at work in the archives of that history, breaking the circuits of our own time, resituating us in a present rendered strange through enjambment. This fragmented *poiesis* of archival lives offers reading pleasures that might, indeed, be masochistic. They undo us. Those pleasures flow from the leakage of meaning located in the behind, in a past we cannot know but that defines our present as other to itself: the past as the naked backside of the insulted body is, startlingly and perhaps terrifyingly, the latent image of a necessary temporality that reframes the psychic subject of our Freudian present. Modernity's sovereign subject becomes what Sedgwick calls a "decontextualized, legless, and often headless figure," a "free switchpoint," nothing more or less than "the inbreathing theatrical space of the spanking."[46]

Foucault's work is strewn with verbal lives brought to the king in the form of the "petitions coming from below" that were the *lettres de cachet*.[47] Gathered together in the archives of infamy, the lives struck down as a result of those petitions come to us in the same form in which they departed the world, incinerated by sovereign power: sodomites and hermaphrodites burned at the stake, Damiens tortured, drawn and quartered, turned to ashes and thrown to the winds. The petitions "from below" that led to their demise—from husbands, brothers, sisters, uncles—offer a strange verbal family portrait in which we might discern our present complicity in "a whole political network . . . interwoven with the fabric of everyday life."[48] Through the *lettres de cachet*, our own familial investments ricochet back to us as tragicomic, declamatory speeches addressed to the king of another time. In this way, we Freudians become the enjambment—the straddling of epistemes, the family switch point—between the Classical *lettre de cachet* and the "fine, differentiated, continuous network" that defines postsovereign power.[49]

In "Lives of Infamous Men," Foucault leaves us gawking, like

354 Lynne Huffer

Freud's fantasizing patients, "almost as . . . spectator[s]"[50] of the "strange stage" that is ourselves.[51] If we read the rhythms of those archival words as scars from a past that will help us, in the present, to heal ourselves through the reparative coherence of the familiar, we are missing the incongruous beat of that rhythm. As readers, we too are both spanked and spanking: we follow the beat of the poet-genealogist's rhythmic hand as it cuts into the archive of violence. But even as we take up that poetic beat(ing), our relation to the violent realities genealogy names can only ever be oblique. Poetic genealogy can only signal queerly, through its own fragmenting cuts, without pretending to redeem the violences of history or even to directly expose the masking of violence that is history writing. As Sedgwick reminds us, "the scars don't answer to the wounds."[52] Or, as she writes in another poetic spanking whose beat outlives its author: "Nothing's without/obliquity, pain itself is not, language/about pain least of all."[53]

NOTES

1. Michel Foucault, *Discipline and Punish: The Birth of the Prison,* trans. Alan Sheridan (New York: Random House, 1977), 191. Subsequent references are given in the text.

2. Michel Foucault, *The History of Sexuality,* vol. 1, *An Introduction,* trans. Robert Hurley (New York: Vintage Books, 1978), 124. For the French original, see Michel Foucault, *Histoire de la sexualité,* vol. 1, *La Volonté de savoir* (Paris: Gallimard, 1976), 165. [In most cases, citations are to the English translation; when the translation is ambivalent or significant, citations to both editions will be given.—Ed.]

3. "The family is the interchange *[échangeur]* of sexuality and alliance . . . This interpenetration *[épinglage]* of the deployment *[dispositif]* of alliance and that of sexuality in the form of the family allows us to understand . . . that since the eighteenth century the family has become an obligatory locus of affects, feelings, love; that sexuality has its privileged point of development in the family; that for this reason sexuality is 'incestuous' from the start" (Foucault, *The History of Sexuality,* vol. 1, 108–9; *Histoire de la sexualité,* vol. 1, 143).

4. This "queer methodology," Judith Halberstam writes, "attempts to combine methods that are often cast as being at odds with each other, and it refuses the academic compulsion toward disciplinary coherence" (*Queer Masculinity* [Durham, N.C.: Duke University Press, 1998], 13). In *Mad for Foucault: Rethinking the Foundations of Queer Theory* (New York: Columbia University Press, 2010), a book-length critique of queer Freudo-Foucauldianism, I argued that Anglo-American queer theory is often philosophically incoherent because of its propensity to produce odd amalgamations of Freud and Foucault. But the amalgamations of queer theory's "scavenger methodology" are not the same as affinities.

5. See Michel Foucault, "A Preface to Transgression," trans. Donald F. Bouchard and Sherry Simon, in *Essential Works of Foucault, 1954–1984,* vol. 2, *Aesthetics,*

Method, and Epistemology, ed. James Faubion (New York: New Press, 1998), 69–87.

6. Michel Foucault, *Histoire de la folie à l'âge classique* (Paris: Gallimard, 1972), xxvii. Subsequent references are given in the text.

7. Foucault, *The History of Sexuality*, vol. 1, 101.

8. Foucault, *Histoire de la sexualité*, vol. 1, 134.

9. Michel Foucault, *The Order of Things: An Archeology of the Human Sciences*, trans. Alan Sheridan (New York: Random House, 1970), 318, 312.

10. Michel Foucault, "Madness, the Absence of an Oeuvre," Appendix 1, in *History of Madness*, ed. Jean Khalfa, trans. Jonathan Murphy (New York: Routledge, 2006), 543.

11. See Foucault, "A Preface to Transgression," for a conception of "language stripped of dialectics *[dédialectisé]*" (78); for the French original, see Michel Foucault, "Préface à la transgression," in *Dits et Écrits I* (Paris: Quarto Gallimard, 2001), 265. It is important to note here the difference between a *non*dialectical approach (where the negation of the dialectic as "*non*" plays into the Hegelian trap of a dialectic that subsumes its own negation into itself) and a *de*dialectizing one, where the prefix "*de*" names a logic of taking away or hollowing out rather than a logic of negation. Importantly, "A Preface to Transgression's" term, "*dédialectisé*," draws on the same hollowing out logic that we find in the "*dé*" of "*déraison*" ("unreason") throughout *History of Madness*.

12. Arlette Farge, *The Allure of the Archives*, trans. Thomas Scott-Railton (New Haven: Yale University Press, 2013), 8.

13. Nancy Luxon and Lynne Huffer, "Critical Exchange: Psychoanalysis and Politics," *Contemporary Political Theory* 15 (2016): 119–38.

14. On the historical a priori, see especially Part III, chapter 5, "The Historical A Priori and the Archive," in Michel Foucault, *The Archeology of Knowledge* (New York: Pantheon Books, 1972), 126–34. For an article-length explication of Foucault's historical a priori, also see Lynne Huffer, "Strange Eros: Foucault, Ethics, and the Historical A Priori," Special Issue on the Historical A Priori, ed. Amy Allen and Smaranda Aldea, *Continental Philosophy Review* 49 (2016): 103–14.

15. For a clear articulation of this question, see especially Amy Allen, *The Politics of Our Selves: Power, Autonomy, and Gender in Contemporary Critical Theory* (New York: Columbia University Press, 2008), 32–35.

16. Foucault, *The Archeology of Knowledge*, 127. For the French original *("criant")*, see Michel Foucault, *L'Archéologie du savoir* (Paris: Gallimard, 1969), 167.

17. As Foucault puts it in *The Archeology of Knowledge*: the "analysis of the archive" engages "the border of time that surrounds our presence, which overhangs it, and which indicates it in its otherness" (130).

18. In Allan Megill, "The Reception of Foucault by Historians," *Journal of History of Ideas* 48.1 (1987): 117.

19. Foucault, The *Archeology of Knowledge*, 130.

20. Ibid.; Foucault, *L'Archéologie du savoir*, 172.

21. Foucault, *History of Madness*, 511.

22. Michel Foucault, "Lives of Infamous Men," 67.

23. Foucault, *The Archeology of Knowledge*, 130.

24. Ibid.

25. Ibid. In the 1961 preface to *History of Madness* Foucault challenges a conception of history that would suppose a "victory" or even "the right to victory" in

356 *Lynne Huffer*

us: we must leave "in suspense anything that might take on the appearance of an ending, or of rest in truth" (xxviii).

26. In an interview about Foucault, Georges Didi-Huberman elaborates on the cut: "Foucault also said something essential in his article about Nietzsche and genealogy: 'Knowledge is made for cutting.' I could work with that command (epistemic, but also literary, ethical, and political) for years. Making a documentary film means cutting. You'll have to cut the shot—and my words with it—at some point. Knowledge is knowing how to cut. Writing is knowing how to cut. And the high point is poetry, since we cut at the end of every line" (Georges Didi-Huberman, "Knowing When to Cut," in *Foucault against Himself,* ed. François Caillat, trans. David Homel [Vancouver: Arsenal Pulp Press, 2015], 84–85).

27. Foucault, *The Archeology of Knowledge,* 130; Foucault, *L'Archéologie du savoir,* 172. Importantly, Foucault ses the same verb here—*se déprendre de*—to release oneself from—that he uses in the oft-quoted line from the "Introduction" to *The History of Sexuality,* vol. 2, translated as "to get free of oneself" *[se déprendre de soi-même].* See *The History of Sexuality,* vol. 2, *The Use of Pleasure,* trans. Robert Hurley (New York: Random House, 1985), 8; for the French original, see *Histoire de la sexualité,* vol. 2, *L'Usage des plaisirs* (Paris: Gallimard, 1984), 15.

28. Foucault, *The Archeology of Knowledge,* 131; Foucault, *L'Archéologie du savoir,* 172.

29. Foucault, *The Archeology of Knowledge,* 12. As David Webb points out, that Other is less an allusion to a Levinasian ethical alterity than "a warning against treating time as a unity and, through memory, as the privileged form of interiority." Although this Other is not Levinasian, Webb finds in Foucault's historical a priori resources for "a renewal of ethical practice." See David Webb, *Foucault's Archeology: Science and Transformation* (Edinburgh: Edinburgh University Press, 2013), 46. 165.

30. Eve Kosofsky Sedgwick, "A Poem Is Being Written," in *Tendencies* (Durham, N.C.: Duke University Press, 1993), 185.

31. Sigmund Freud, "'A Child Is Being Beaten': A Contribution to the Study of the Origin of Sexual Perversions," in *The Standard Edition of the Complete Psychological Works of Sigmund Freud,* vol. 17, ed. and trans. James Strachey (London: Hogarth Press, 1955), 179, 180. Subsequent references are given in the text.

32. Sedgwick, "A Poem Is Being Written," 178, 177. Subsequent references are given in the text.

33. Foucault, "Lives of Infamous Men," 69.

34. As Foucault puts it in a 1975 interview with Roger Pol Droit: "for twenty years now I've been worrying about my little mad ones, my little excluded ones, my little abnormals": *"mes petits fous, mes petits exclus, mes petits anormaux"* (quoted in Lynne Huffer, *Mad for Foucault: Rethinking the Foundations of Queer Theory* [New York: Columbia University Press, 2010], 23, translation mine).

35. Foucault, "Lives of Infamous Men," 71.

36. Sedgwick, "A Poem Is Being Written," 184.

37. Freud, "A Child Is Being Beaten," 191, 180.

38. Ibid., 180.

39. Sedgwick, "A Poem Is Being Written," 197.

40. Foucault, "Lives of Infamous Men," 68.

41. Ibid., 73–74.

Foucault's Rhythmic Hand 357

42. Ibid., 69.

43. Translation mine. The phrase appears in the original French version of "Lives of Infamous Men" but does not appear in the published English translation. See Michel Foucault, "La Vie des hommes infâmes," *Dits et Écrits II* (Paris: Quarto Gallimard, 2001): "Mon insuffisance m'a voué au lyrisme frugal de la citation" (239) ("My inadequacy committed me to the frugal lyricism of citation").

44. Eve Kosofsky Sedgwick and Adam Frank, eds., *Shame and Its Sisters: A Silvan Tomkins Reader* (Durham, N.C.: Duke University Press, 1995), 107.

45. Didi-Huberman, "Knowing When to Cut," 85.

46. Sedgwick, "A Poem Is Being Written," 183, 181.

47. Foucault, "Lives of Infamous Men," 77.

48. Ibid., 78.

49. Ibid., 81.

50. Freud, "A Child Is Being Beaten," 190.

51. Foucault, "Lives of Infamous Men," 81.

52. Sedgwick, "A Poem Is Being Written," 197.

53. Ibid., 194.

Contributors

André Béjin is a sociologist, historian of social sciences, and researcher at the Centre National de la Recherche Scientifique (CNRS) in Paris and a member of the Roland Mousnier Center at Paris IV–Sorbonne.

Roger Chartier is a French historian and author or editor of a dozen books, many of which have been translated into English. He is a director of studies at l'École des Hautes Études en Sciences Sociales (EHESS) and the Collège de France, and also produced and hosted the France Culture radio program *Les Lundis de l'histoire.*

Stuart Elden is professor of political theory and geography at Warwick University and Monash Warwick professor, faculty of arts, Monash University. His books include *Foucault: The Birth of Power, Foucault's Last Decade, The Birth of Territory,* and *Terror and Territory: The Spatial Extent of Sovereignty* (Minnesota, 2009).

Arlette Farge is director of research in modern history at the Centre National de la Recherche Scientifique (CNRS), Paris, and the author of more than a dozen books in French, several of which have been translated into English.

Michel Foucault (1926–1984) was a French philosopher who held the chair in the History of Systems of Thought at the Collège de France. One of the most influential political thinkers of the twentieth century, he left an indelible mark on philosophy, the humanities, and the social sciences. Among his notable books are *History of Madness, Discipline and Punish,* and *The History of Sexuality.* The University of Minnesota Press published *Speech Begins after Death* (2013) and *Language, Madness, and Desire: On Literature* (2015).

Jean-Philippe Guinle teaches at the Jean Monnet Faculty of Law, Economics, and Management, Sceaux, and at the Faculty of Canon Law of the Catholic Institute of Paris.

Michel Heurteaux is a French journalist and author.

Lynne Huffer is Samuel Candler Dobbs Professor in the Department of Women's, Gender, and Sexuality Studies at Emory University. She is author of *Are the Lips a Grave? A Queer Feminist on the Ethics of Sex, Mad for Foucault: Rethinking the Foundations of Queer Theory,* and *Another Colette: The Question of Gendered Writing.*

Nancy Luxon is associate professor of political science at the University of Minnesota. She is editor of *Disorderly Families: Infamous Letters from the Bastille Archives* (Minnesota, 2016) and *Discourse and Truth,* as well as author of *Crisis of Authority: Politics, Trust, and Truth-Telling in Freud and Foucault.*

Pierre Nora is a French historian and was director of studies at l'École des Hautes Études en Sciences Sociales (EHESS). His books include the four-volume *Rethinking France: Les Lieux de mémoire.* He has an important publishing career, notably at Éditions Gallimard.

Michelle Perrot is a French historian and author or editor of seven books. Her work forged a path for women's studies in France, notably with the five-volume *History of Women in the West,* edited with Georges Duby. She taught at Paris Diderot–Paris VII, as well as producing and hosting the France Culture radio program *Les Lundis de l'histoire.*

Michel Rey (1953–1993) was a researcher in the Department of History and Civilization at the European University Institute of Florence. He was one of the first professionally trained French historians to work on the histories of homosexuality and friendship.

Elizabeth Wingrove is associate professor of political science and women's studies at the University of Michigan, where she is also affiliated faculty in the departments of Romance languages and comparative literature. She is author of *Rousseau's Republican Romance.*

Publication History

Chapter 1 was published in *Power: Essential Works of Foucault, 1954–1984*, copyright 1994 by Éditions Gallimard. Compilation, Introduction, and new translations copyright 2000 by The New Press; reprinted by permission of The New Press. www.thenewpress.com. Originally published in *Les Cahiers du chemin* 29 (January 15, 1977): 12–29.

Chapter 2 is a translation of the radio program *Les Lundis de l'histoire* hosted by Roger Chartier that was recorded on November 27, 1982, and broadcast on France Culture on January 10, 1983, with participants Michel Foucault, Arlette Farge, Michelle Perrot, and André Béjin. Copyright 1983 INA.

Chapter 3 was originally published in French as Jean-Philippe-Guinle, "Note sur *Le Désordre des familles*," *La Nouvelle Revue Française*, no. 364 (May 1983): 137–39. Reprinted with permission of Jean-Philippe Guinle.

Chapter 4 was originally published in French as Michel Heurteaux, "La Délation, poison latent," *Le Monde* 15.3 (May 15, 1983). Reprinted with permission of Michel Heurteaux.

Chapter 5 was originally published in French in Michel Foucault, *L'Ordre du discours* (Paris: Éditions Gallimard, 1971); reprinted by permission of Éditions Gallimard.

Chapter 6 was published as "The Public Sphere and Public Opinion," in Roger Chartier, *The Cultural Origins of the French Revolution*, trans. Lydia G. Cochrane (Durham, N.C.: Duke University Press, 1991), 20–37, plus endnotes, 201–4. Copyright 1991 Duke University Press. All rights reserved. Reprinted with permission of Duke University Press. www.dukeupress.edu. The essay was first published in French in Chartier's *Les Origines culturelles de la Révolution française* (Paris: Éditions du Seuil, 1990).

Chapter 7 was published in French in Pierre Nora, *Faire de l'histoire: Nouveaux problèmes, nouvelles approches, nouveaux objets* 1, ed. Jacques Le Goff and Pierre Nora (Paris: Éditions Gallimard, 1974); reprinted by permission of Éditions Gallimard. Originally published as "L'événement monstre," *Communications* 18 (1972): 162–72.

Chapter 8 was published as Arlette Farge, "Penser et définir l'événement en histoire: Approche des situations et des acteurs sociaux," *Terrains: Anthropologie et sciences humaines* 38 (2002): 67–78. Courtesy of Les Éditions de la Maison des sciences de l'homme, Paris.

Chapter 10 was published as Michel Rey, "Parisian Homosexuals Create a Lifestyle, 1700–1750: The Police Archives," in *'Tis Nature's Fault: Unauthorized*

362 *Publication History*

Sexuality during the Enlightenment, ed. Robert Purks Maccubbins (Cambridge: Cambridge University Press, 1987), 179–91. Copyright 1985 Cambridge University Press. Reprinted with the permission of Cambridge University Press.

Chapter 11 was published as Elizabeth Wingrove, "Sovereign Address," *Political Theory* 40.2 (2012): 135–64. Copyright 2012 Sage Publications. Reprinted by permission of Sage Publications, Inc.

Index

Abnormals, The (Foucault lecture
  series), 2, 241, 338n76, 338n80
Affordable Care Act, 49
African American women, domestic
  violence and, 47–48
Algerian War, 198–200, 209
Ali–Frazier boxing match, 203
Allis, Jean, 22
Altman, Janet, 279
anal eroticism, 254–56
Annales school, 36, 61n111, 61n113
application decrees *(décrets
  d'application),* 210
Archeology of Knowledge, The
  (Foucault), 345, 347–48
archival history, 231–32
Archives of the Bastille (AB), 1, 51n6,
  56n65, 67, 127, 132, 227, 265,
  288n1, 295
Ariès, Philippe, 88, 255
Aristotle, 290n30
Aron, Raymond, 210
Arrested Justice (Richie), 47
Artières, Philippe, 45
artistic criticism, 190–92
Association for Employment in
  Industry and Trade (ASSEDIC),
  136–37
Aubry, Étienne, 313–14
Aufklärung (Kant), 39, 46
Austin, J. L., 268
authority: families' relationships to,
  56n64; in *lettres de cachet,* 43–47;
  public sphere and, 176
authorship: Foucault on, 150–52;

identity, intentionality, and
  ideology and, 288n8

Barbin, Herculine, viii, 3, 5, 17, 241
Barker, Emma, 313
Bayle, Pierre, 284–85
beating fantasy, Freud on, 349–54
Béjin, André, 85–125
Berryer, Nicolas, 20, 23–24, 57n72,
  263–64, 278–79, 284
Bienfait, Nicolas, 80
Bloch, Marc, 36
Blot, Pierre, 27
Bodin, Jean, 286
Boorstin, Daniel, 205
Bourdieu, Pierre, 219–20
Braudel, Fernand, 36
Breteuil, Baron de, 49

cahiers de doléances, 281
Cahiers du chemin, Les, 67
Cailly, Jean-Jacques, 86
Cambridge school, 288n8
care work, exchanges of power and,
  324
Cartouche (Louis Dominique
  Bourguignon), 73, 84n2
Castan, Nicole, 92
Catholic Church, Jansenism and,
  125n1
Centre d'Études, de Recherche et de
  Formation Institutionnelle (CERFI),
  228, 235
Char, René, 173n1, 311
Chardin, Jean-Baptiste-Siméon, 308

364 *Index*

Chartier, Roger, 41, 85–125, 175–92, 333n6
Chaulieu, Duke de, 78, 84n3
"Child Is Being Beaten, A" (Freud), 345, 348–54
children and parents, *lettres de cachet* and, 105–8
Chrétien, Jean-Louis, 270
class politics, homosexuality and, 257–58
Code of Police (Duchesne), 20–21
Coffin, Judith, 304
colonization, democratization of history and, 196–97
commentary, Foucault on, 151–52
Communication (journal), 88
Condorcet, Marie Jean Antoine de Caritat, Marquis de, 182, 187–88
Confused Girl, The (engraving), 316
congregations of homosexuals, 256–59
contemporary history, Duruy's concept of, 195–97, 212n1
convulsionnaires de Saint-Médard, 90, 125n1
CORDA (Comité de la Recherche et du Développement en Architecture), 235
corporation, 250–51
correction, imprisonment as, 113–15
Correspondance littéraire (Grimm), 191
criminal denunciations, 137–38
Crow, Thomas, 191
cruising: history in Paris of, 248–49; methods for control of, 250–51

d'Alembert, Jean Le Rond, 182, 193n18
d'Argenson, René (Lt. General), 40–41
Death of an Unnatural Father, The (engraving), 311
debauchery, Foucault on, 55n62, 104
de Certeau, Michel, 333n6
de Gaulle, Charles, 200, 204, 207–8, 213n4
Delamare, Nicolas (Lt. Gen.), 9–10, 52n21
Délinquance et criminalité (Farge), 228, 242

Delphy, Christine, 305, 320, 339n93
denunciation, twentieth-century letters of, 131–38
Des Essarts, Nicolas Toussaint Le Moyne, 19–20
Dictionnaire de Trévoux, 24–25, 183
Dictionnaire Universel, 25, 55n62, 183
Diderot, Denis, 191
Didi-Huberman, Georges, 356n26
Diot, Jean, 57n67
Discipline and Punish (Foucault), 2, 5, 8, 13, 16–17, 46; Damien's execution in, 241; families discussed in, 227–28; genealogy in, 40; government authority in, 237–38; history and power discussed in, 341–45; household exchange in, 327; science discussed in, 341; soul discussed in, 344–45; vagrancy and vagabondage in, 239–40
disciplines, Foucault on, 152–54
discourses, Foucault on regulation of, 155–73
disorder: in eighteenth-century politics, 4–5; *lettres de cachet* perspective on, 18–33. *See also* public order
Disorderly Families (Farge and Foucault): disorder discussed in, 310–11; Elden's commentary on, 227–42; Foucault's notes on, 339n90; gender and power in, 295–99, 327–28; Guinle's review of, 127–29; *mesnagement* principles in, 300–308; milieu in, 58n75; Napoleonic Code and, 31–34; pictorial representations in, 308–18; private space in, 24–29; public order in, 1–6, 8, 12–17, 23–24; roundtable discussion about, 85–86, 105–25; social hierarchies in, 34–47; theme of circulation in, 49–50
Dispute de la culotte, La (engraving), 311–12
doctrines, Foucault on, 157–58
Dolat, Gilbert, 239
domestic violence, in *lettres de cachet,* 98–99

domination: *mesnagement* and structures of, 297–308; women in framework of, 317–18
Donzelot, Jacques, 59n80, 338n69
Dreyfus, Alfred, 212n2
Dreyfus Affair, 196, 198–203, 209, 212n2
Duruy, Victor, 195–96, 212n1

economic activity, women's participation in, 303–8, 323–32
Elden, Stuart, 25, 227–42
Eli, Edme Joseph, 22
Emmanuelli, François-Xavier, 92
emotions, history and, 220–21
encasement: pictorial representations of, 309; women's agency and logic of, 306–8
Encyclopédie, 26, 184–86
enjambment, 348, 353
enlightenment, Kant on, 178–82
Eribon, Didier, 56n65
Esquisse d'un tableau historique des progrès de l'esprit humain (Condorcet), 187–88
events: construction of, 220; emotions and, 220–21; Farge on, 215–25; foretelling of, 221–23; history and production of, 196–201; meaning of, 223–24; memory of, 224–25; metamorphoses of, 201–6; paradox of, 207–12; as vision of future, 218–19
exchange: household as field of, 318–32; power and role of, 53n27
exchanger figures: defined, 27; features of, 337n63; Foucault on, 6, 31, 53nn27–28, 230, 319, 327; *lettres de cachet* and, 30, 34; political agency and, 12–13, 38, 229; women as, 318, 320–21, 325, 330–31, 340n99
exclusion, Foucault on, 143–48, 165–73
exteriority, Foucault on, 162

fait divers, 200–206, 209–10
families: cultural representations of, 308–18; in Farge's and Foucault's research, 231–42, 319–24,

337n60, 337nn63–64, 338n76; *lettres de cachet* and dynamics of, 24–29, 90–125, 282–84, 296–99, 328–32; *mesnagement* practices in, 297–308; Napoleonic Code and, 31–34, 96–98; parent–child relationships in, 105–8, 232–33; private space and, 24–29; switch points of power in, 322–32
Fanon, Frantz, 200
Farge, Arlette, 1–6, 333n6; Elden's discusion of, 227–42; on events in history, 215–25; on *lettres de cachet*, 85–125; on marriage, 300–301; on petitions (placets), 132; on police authority, 234–42; on political agency, 6–17; on public exchange, 30; on social hierarchies, 34–47
Fashoda Incident, 196, 212n2
Fatherly Love (L'Amour paternel) (Aubry), 313–14
feminist scholarship: on woman and family, 325–26, 333n8, 339n93
Fieffé, Nicolas, 23
Flandrin, Jean-Louis, 247, 255
Fleury, Joly de, 278–79
Fortier, Bruno, 235
Foucault, Michel, 1–6; Elden's discussion of, 227–42; "eventfulness" of, 38–39; on exchange, 319–24, 337n60, 337nn63–64; on families, 231–42, 319–24, 337n60, 337nn63–64, 338n76, 339n90; feminist interpretations of, 341; on history, 217, 285; on *infâmes*, 56n65; *lettres de cachet* discussed by, 50n2, 51n6, 85–125; on literature and constraint, 33; "Lives of Infamous Men," 2, 39, 44, 67–84; on marriage, 25, 300–301; "Order of Discourse" lecture by, 141–73; on petitions (placets), 132; on police authority, 234–42; on political agency, 7–11; on power, 6–7, 318, 326–27; relativism of, 51n11; on rules of signification, 315; on social hierarchies, 34–47; on sodomy, 57n73; on violence and subject formation, 306

366 *Index*

founding subject, Foucault on, 159–60
Fragile Lives (Farge), 5, 10, 233, 240
Franco-Prussian War, 196, 212n2
Frankenstein (Shelley), 324–25
French Revolution: Foucault's
omission of, 327–28; impact on
families of, 97–101; justice after,
119–24; women's role in, 307–8
Freud, Sigmund, 342–45, 348–54
Funck-Brentano, Frantz, 12, 230
Furetière, 183

gazettes de Hollande, 271, 290n23
gender: historiography on, 335n37;
household as field of exchange
and, 318–32; imprisonment and,
103–4; in *lettres de cachet,* 99–101;
politics and power and, 295–332;
postrevolutionary influences on,
97–98; private space and, 26–29;
public order and, 23–24
Gil Blas (Lesage), 33
Ginzburg, Carlos, 36
Gouges, Olympe de, 25–26, 28
Gravelle, Geneviève, 28, 263–87
Greuze, Jean-Baptiste, 308, 311–14
Grimm, Melchior, 191
Groupe d'information sur les prisons
(GIP), 2, 7
Guattari, Félix, 228
guilds, women's membership in, 301–3
Guinle, Jean-Philippe, 125–27

Habermas, Jürgen, 175–76, 268
habitat, boundaries of, 235–36,
238–42
Halimi, André, 132
Hanley, Sarah, 28, 303
Hardwick, Julie, 300
Hegel, G. W. F., 32, 170–73, 319
Herculine Barbin, 5, 17
heredity, Foucault on, 168–73
Heurteaux, Michel, 131–38
Histoire de la vie privée (History of
private life), 228
history: agency and gender scholarship
and, 335n37; Farge on, 215–25;
Foucault on, 162–63, 355n25;
of homosexuality, 247–61; mass
media monopolization of, 197–201;

meaning of events in, 223–24; Nora
on, 195–206; paradox of events
in, 207–12; psychoanalysis and,
346–48; social hierarchies and,
36–47
History of Madness (Foucault), 2, 10,
67, 88–89, 241, 343–44, 347, 351
History of Sexuality, The (Foucault),
13, 25, 327, 342
Hobbes, Thomas, 319
homosexuality: congregations for,
256–59; desire and love and,
253–56; *lettres de cachet* and,
104–5; reactions and hostility to,
251–53; terminology for, 259–61
honor rhetoric, *lettres de cachet* and,
102–4
hôpitaux, prisons as, 322
households: as field of exchange,
318–32; private space and, 24–29
Huffer, Lynne, 41, 50, 54n45, 341–54
Hyppolite, Jean, 141, 170–73

ideas, Foucault on history of, 164–65
Images d'Épinal, 198, 212n5
immigration: denunciation of, 131–38;
families and, 103
Impossible Prison, The (Perrot),
87–88, 113, 228
imprisonment: as correction, 113–15;
Farge on, 239–40; Foucault on,
319–20; gender and, 103–4;
homosexuality and, 256–59;
prerevolutionary decline of,
119–24; royal penal policy and,
108–10, 115–25
infâmes: archives relating to, 56n65;
arrest and punishment of, 57n67,
253; police references to, 23, 37;
social meanings of, 13
infâmes, les, 23, 56n63, 57n67
infamy: Foucault on, 55n62, 73–84,
341–45, 351; history and archive
of, 346–48; homosexuality and,
253–56
informants, power of, 131–38
information: devaluation of, 205;
society and role of, 208–12
interpretive authority, power and
police and, 17–33

intimate justice, 63n145, 298, 320, 326, 331, 333n7

Jansenism, 54n55, 125n1, 302; public exchange and, 30–31
Jaucourt, Louis de, 26, 184
Jeaurat, Étienne, 309
John XXIII (Pope), 209–10
jurisdiction, political agency and, 11–17
justice: family dynamics and, 330–32, 339n90; *lettres de cachet* and, 277–78; prerevolutionary monarchy and, 108–10

Kant, Immanuel, 18, 39, 46, 178–82, 186–87, 193n9; on public vs. popular, 182–85
Kennedy, John F., assassination of, 208
knowledge-*connaissance*: Foucault on, 147–57; information and, 206

labor: denunciations involving, 136–37; women's participation in, 323–32
Lacenaire, Pierre-François, 73, 84n2
La Courtille, 257–59
Lacretelle, Pierre Louis de, 20–21, 189–90
Ladurie, Emmanuel Leroy, 3
Lapouge, Benoît, 254–55
Launay, Nicolas de, 308
Lecocq, Marie, 27
legal subjectivity of women, 303–8, 316–18
Légende dorée, La: in Foucault's "Lives of Infamous Men," 72–73, 84n1
legends, Foucault on, 72–74
Le Goff, Jacques, 36
Le Maire, Margueritte, 86–87
Lenoir, Bruno, 57n67
Lenoir, Jean Charles Pierre (Lt. Gen.), 9–11, 31–34, 91
Léonard, Jacques, 1
Lesquoy, Françoise, 22
Le Trosne, Guillaume, 239–40
lettre de patente, 282
lettres de cachet (letters of arrest), 1–6; dossiers linked to, 56n65;

examples of, 86–87, 123–25; family dynamics and, 24–29, 90–125, 282–84, 296–99; Foucault on, 67–84, 241–42, 295–96; Guinle on, 125–27; Heurteaux on, 131–38; historical context of, 7–11, 87–90; interpretive authority and, 18–33; jurisdiction and, 11–17; *mesnagement* practices and, 300–308; monarchy and, 89–91, 109–13, 190–92, 277–84, 293n83; origins of, 50n2; pictorial representations of, 308; policing and, 10–11; political agency and, 6–17; as political speech, 263–87; power and sovereignty and, 230–31, 326–32; proposed abolition of, 32–34; psychoanalytic discourse and, 342–45; as public exchange, 29–31; readers' interpretations of, 315; roundtable discussion of, 85–125; social hierarchies and, 19–24; socioeconomic status of writers of, 34–47; state power and, 284–87; women's use of, 99–101, 303–4
Levasseur, Jean-Charles, 308, 313
Lives of Infamous Men (Nora), 37
"Lives of Infamous Men" (Foucault), 2, 39, 44, 67–84, 295–96, 346, 352–54
Locke, John, 47, 58n77, 339n91
logos, 286–87, 290n31
Lundis de l'histoire, Les (radio program), 85
Luxon, Nancy, 1–50, 295–332, 346

Mad for Foucault (Huffer), 343, 346
madness, Foucault on, 144–46, 342–45
maisons d'arrêt, 322
maisons de correction, 322
maisons de détention, 301, 322
maisons de justice, 322
Malesherbes, Chrétien-Guillaume, 185–87, 189
Mandrou, Robert, 36
Manon Lescaut, 33, 126n7
"Marital Discord" (Farge and Foucault), 300–301

368 *Index*

Markell, Patchen, 267–68, 287
Marker, Chris, 218
market economy: impact on families, 301–2
marriage: Farge's research on, 229; homosexuality and, 255–56; *mesnagement* practices and, 300–301; pictorial representations of, 311–12; private space and, 24–29
Martin, Biddy, 316
Martin, Christiane, 61n117
Martin, Trayvon, 48
Marx, Karl, 13, 319–20
mass media, monopolization of history by, 197–201
materialist feminism, 305–8, 329–30, 333n8, 336n43
mathematics, Foucault on, 155–56
May '68 uprising, 200–206, 210–12
McLuhan, Marshall, 200–201
Mémoires de deux jeunes mariées (Chaulieu), 78, 84n3
Mémoire sur les vagabonds et sur les mendiants (Le Trosne), 239
memory: of events, 224–25; history and, 37–38
Mendel, Gregor, 154
Mercier, Louis-Sébastien, 301, 308
Merrick, Jeffrey, 56n65
mesnagement: exchange and, 321–32; structures of domination and, 297–308, 325–26
microstoria, Ginzburg's concept of, 36, 61n114
milieu, Foucault on, 58n75
Mitchell, Juliet, 339n93
mixité, 27, 59n87
modernity, events and, 205–6
monarchy: justice under, 108–11; *lettres de cachet* and role of, 89–91, 109–13, 190–92, 277–84, 293n83; *mesnagement* in Maison du Roi and, 301; prerevolutionary decline of, 120–25; public sphere and, 189–92
Monmartel, Pâris de, 263, 272, 277
Monsallier (Mother), 269
Moretti, Franco, 36
Morin, Edgar, 210

Names of History, The (Rancière), 264–65
Napoleonic Code, 31–34, 96–97, 297
narrative, events in history and, 215–25
National Agency of Labor, 136–37
National Employment Agency, 136–37
National Tax Investigation Agency (DNEF), 135–36
Nedelsky, Jennifer, 333n6
Nietzsche, Friedrich, 39–40
Nora, Pierre, 37–38, 67, 195–212
Nouveau Secrétaire, 279–80
Nu-pieds revolt, 237

Obama, Barack, 48–49
Oedipus complex, 349–54
"Of Other Spaces" (Foucault lecture), 231–32
One Dark Night (film), 48
oral sex, taboos concerning, 254–55
"Order of Discourse, The" (Foucault), 141–73
Order of Things, The (Foucault), 344–45
Ozouf, Mona, 182

"Palimpsest, The" (Sedgwick), 352
Panama Affair, 198, 212n4
Parallel Lives anthology, 67
parent–child relationships: Foucault and Farge on, 232–33; *lettres de cachet* and, 105–8
Pascalian Meditations (Bourdieu), 219–20
passions, history and, 221
Pateman, Carole, 310, 325
patriarchal family: *lettres de cachet* and status of, 90–96; *mesnagement* as challenge to, 297–308; postrevolutionary changes in, 97–101; social order and, 27–29
pederasty, 259–61
Peña, Nonny de la, 48
penal colonies, 239
"people, the," philosophical representations of, 182–85
Perrin, Marianne, 27
Perrot, Michelle, 85–125, 228
Petit, Henry, 27

petite poste, establishment of, 280–84
Pétonnet, Colette, 237
"Peuple" (Jaucourt), 184
Philosophie dans le boudoir, La
(Sade), 261
philosophy: discourse in, 158–73;
Foucault's work and, 333n6
placets (plaints), 1–6, 48–49; origins
of, 50n2
poeisis, 290n31, 353
"Poem Is Being Written, A"
(Sedgwick), 345, 350–54
police: denunciations of, 137–38; in
eighteenth century, 8–11, 113–14;
Farge on, 234–42; Foucault on,
234–42; homosexuality and
archives of, 247–61; interpretive
authority and, 17–33; *lettres
de cachet* and role of, 91–93,
111; monarchy and, 120–21;
postrevolution changes for, 97–98
police judiciaire, 9
political agency: Foucault on,
318–19; gender and, 295–97,
305–8; historiography on, 335n37;
jurisdiction and, 11–17; *lettres
de cachet* (letters of arrest) and,
6–17; public sphere and, 176–79;
Rancière's definition of, 290n30;
Wingrove on, 263–87; writing as,
267–74
*politique de l'espace parisien, La (à la
fin de l'Ancien Régime)* (Fortier),
235
Politiques de l'habitat (Foucault), 235
Politiques de l'habitat (Guattari), 228
Port-Royal affair, 90, 125n1
postal system, establishment of,
280–84
power: gender and, 295–332;
households as switch point of,
319–32; individualization of,
342–45; interpretive authority
and, 17–33; society's valorization
of, 320; sovereignty and, 229–30;
state power and epistolary practice,
284–87; switch points of, 318–22,
342–45
press: history and role of, 198–201,
205–6

private space: Farge on, 233–34;
households and, 24–29
prohibition, Foucault on, 143–44
property rights: for women, 303,
339n81
Psychiatric Power (Foucault), 57n73,
337n64, 337n66
psychoanalysis, Foucault on, 342–45
public exchange, *lettres de cachet* as,
29–31
public opinion: Chartier on, 175–92;
construction of, 30–31; tribunal of,
185–89
public order: gendered authority and,
302–5, 310, 316–17; *lettres de
cachet* and, 16–17, 296–97; social
hierarchies and, 19–24; switch
points of power and, 321–24. *See
also* disorder
public space: boundaries of, 235–36;
Chartier on, 175–92; constitution
of, 189–92; Farge on, 234; politics
and, 176–79; power and police and,
17–33; sexuality and, 248–49
"Public Sphere and Public Opinion,
The" (Chartier), 175–92
Punished Son, The (engraving), 316
Punitive Society, The (Foucault), 2–6,
11, 13, 53n27, 229–31, 237, 239,
319–20

queer theory, 349–54, 354n3

race and racism, justice and, 47–48
radio, history and role of, 199–201
Rais, Gilles de, 73, 84n2
Rancière, Jacques, 263–87, 288n3,
290n30
reason: Foucault on madness and,
144–46; public and private use of,
178–82
representation, politics of, 39–47
Republica literatorum, 181–82
Revel, Jacques, 3
reversal, Foucault on, 161–62, 164–65
Rey, Michel, 23, 247–61
Reynie, Nicolas de la, 21–22
Richie, Beth, 47, 333n7
ritual, Foucault on, 156
Rivière, Pierre, 3, 44–45, 241

370 *Index*

Robert, Hubert, 309
Rousseau, Jean-Jacques, 310

Sade, Marquis de, 73, 84n2, 261
Saint-Médard affair, 90, 125n1
Sans soleil (film), 218
Sartine, Antoine Gabriel, 11
Schnapper, Bernard, 98
Scott, Joan, 305
Second Treatise (Locke), 47, 58n77
secrecy, justice and, 109–12
secrétaires (letter-writing manuals), 279–84
Security, Territory, Population (Foucault), 8–9, 10, 58n75
Sedgwick, Eve Kosofsky, 341, 345, 350–54
Servan, Michel de, 273–74
Sévigné, Madame de, 280–81
Sewell, William, 339n81
Sexual Contract, The (Pateman), 325
Sexualités occidentales: Contributions à l'histoire et à la sociologie de la sexualité, 88
sexuality: Foucault on, 167–73; public order and, 23–24
Shelley, Mary, 324–25
social hierarchies: homosexuality and, 257–58; *lettres de cachet* writers and, 34–47; *mesnagement* principles and, 300–308; Napoleonic Code and, 31–34; private space and, 24–29; public order and, 19–24; women's role in, 301–8
societies of discourse, Foucault on, 156–57
society, information and, 208–12
Society Must Be Defended (Foucault), 8
sodomy: arrest and punishment for, 57n67; definitions of, 259–61; police classifications of, 253–56
sovereignty, 58n75; *lettres de cachet* as challenge to, 268–69, 286–87; power and, 229–30
space: Farge on marital relations and, 232; Foucault on, 231–32
"Space, Knowledge and Power" (Foucault interview), 240–41

specificity, Foucault on, 162
Spierenburg, Pieter, 98
state: epistolary practice and power of, 284–87; *lettres de cachet* and role of, 93–96
Stepmother, The (La Belle-Mère) (Greuze), 311, 313–14
strategic analysis, social hierarchy and, 39–47
Structural Transformation of the Public Sphere, The (Habermas), 175–76
subjection, Foucault on violence and, 306, 316–17
Subversive Words (Farge), 5, 28
surveillance, public order and, 21–24
switch point of power, 9, 12–13, 17, 45, 53n27, 230, 299, 318–32, 342–45

Tableaux de Paris (Mercier), 308
tax fraud, denunciations involving, 135–36
Taylor, Charles, 4, 51n11
television, democratization of history and, 199–201
Telstar, 203
Théories et institutions pénales (Foucault lecture series), 237–38
"thèse d'État," 3
Threadcraft, Shatema, 63n145, 333n7
Three Musketeers, The (Dumas), 33
Tomkins, Silvan, 352
trades, women's representation in, 301–2
Trägern (Marx), 13, 53n30, 319
Traité de la police (Delamare), 9
Tronto, Joan, 333n6
Trouillot, Michel-Rolph, 17
Truant, Cynthia, 302
truth, Foucault on will to, 145–50, 165–73

Union for the Collection of Social Security and Family Benefit Contributions (URSSAF), 136–37
universal mediation, Foucault on, 160

vagrancy and vagabondage, Foucault on, 239–40

Valancier, Toinette, 22
Vanpée, Janie, 314
Vernet, Carle, 309
Veyne, Paul, 217–18, 254
Vichy, letters of, 48, 133–35
violence: Freud on, 349–54;
    homosexuality and, 250–51; in
    lettres de cachet, 98–99; rhythm of,
    351–54
Vivre dans la rue à Paris au XVIII
    siècle (Farge), 3, 228–29, 242
Vol d'aliments, Le (Farge), 3

"Warm December, The" (Sedgwick),
    350
Warner, Michael, 272
War of the Worlds radio broadcast,
    200
Watergate scandal, 199
Webb, David, 356n29
Welles, Orson, 200
"What is Critique?" (Foucault),
    38–39, 45

"What is Enlightenment?" (Kant), 18,
    178–82
Wille, Pierre Alexandre, 308
Will to Know (Foucault), 2
Wingrove, Elizabeth, 28, 263–87
Wittig, Monique, 330–32, 339n93
women: disruption of political
    order by, 323–24; as exchangers,
    320–21; family and private space
    and, 26–29; guild membership
    for, 301–3; household as field
    of exchange for, 318–32;
    imprisonment of, 103–4,
    116–17; legal subjectivity of,
    303–8, 316–18; *lettres de cachet*
    of, 99–101, 303–4; *mesnagement*
    principles and, 301–2; pictorial
    representations of, 308–18; power
    and role of, 316–17; public order
    and, 23–24; writing by, 303–4

Zimmerman, George, 48
Zysberg, André, 228